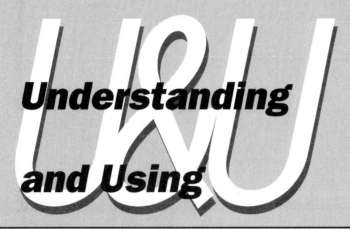

Understanding and Using

MS-DOS® 6.x

Jonathan P. Bacon
Academic Computing Technologies Group
Johnson County Community College

WEST PUBLISHING COMPANY
Minneapolis/St. Paul • New York
Los Angeles • San Francisco

Production, Prepress, Printing and Binding by West Publishing Company.
Project Management by Labrecque Publishing Services

Copyright ©1994 by   WEST PUBLISHING COMPANY
                       610 Opperman Drive
                       P.O. Box 64526
                       St. Paul, MN 55164-0526

Library of Congress Cataloging-in-Publication Data

Bacon, Jonathan.
    Understanding and using MS-DOS 6.x / Jonathan P. Bacon.
        p.   cm.
    Includes index.
    ISBN 0-314-02863-3
    1. MS-DOS (Computer file) I. Title.
QA76.76.06383328   1994
005.4'469 — dc20   93-41645
                                                            CIP

Contents

Overview of MS-DOS

Preface

Who Should Use This Book?

Welcome to *Understanding and Using MS-DOS 6.x*. This book is designed to meet the needs of both students and instructors, novice and experienced users, who seek to learn more about DOS. Whether you are a student, instructor, corporate manager, secretary, or home user, this book is intended to familiarize you with the mysteries of the most popular desktop/personal computer operating system, MS-DOS.

Our aim is to introduce you to new concepts regarding DOS, one at a time. After some explanatory text, we'll follow up with step-by-step Guided Activities to make the new concepts and skills clear. We believe in hands-on learning—with computers there is no other way.

Content Highlights

Understanding and Using MS-DOS 6.x is divided into four parts. Part I introduces you to operating systems and explains what they are. Part II explores the fundamental DOS commands, including those necessary to format disks, manage files, and organize files on a hard disk. Part III includes an exploration of intermediate DOS commands used to unformat disks, edit files, and safely back up and restore your data; it also covers the new DOS 6 utility commands that provide antivirus protection, system diagnostics, and defragmenting of a disk drive. Part IV introduces you to several additional DOS commands and concepts such as using batch files, pipes, filters, and redirection; additionally, RAM drives and the revised DOS 6.x DOSSHELL command are introduced.

You may be tempted to overlook Part I because it is composed strictly of text and no Guided Activities. Please resist that temptation unless you have had previous exposure to the basics of DOS. Keep in mind that the terms defined and the concepts explained in that part of the book are essential to understanding subsequent Guided Activities.

With the exception of Part I, this book is meant to be read while seated in front of your computer, so that you can complete the step-by-step Guided Activities. Each unit includes several important segments:

LEARNING OBJECTIVES the knowledge and skills addressed in the unit.

IMPORTANT COMMANDS the commands to be covered, which will later serve as a quick reference to the contents of the unit.

COMPUTER SCREENS figures depicting the steps and illustrating the results of most commands.

GUIDED ACTIVITIES step-by-step, hands-on exercises guiding the reader through operations discussed in the unit.

COMMAND REVIEW a recapitulation of commands that produce certain actions or effects. The most common forms of the command are listed in this section.

REVIEW QUESTIONS questions designed to test your understanding of the material presented. The answers to even-numbered Review Questions are contained in Appendix A.

EXERCISES additional computer work designed to challenge your knowledge of the material presented in the unit. Some of these have specific instructions, while others provide less guidance.

KEY TERMS a list of the important terms and concepts discussed in the unit. This list is designed for review and self-test.

DOCUMENTATION RESEARCH exercises that require you to use the on-line Help reference to learn more about the commands and features discussed in the unit.

All units, except Unit 1, include one or more Guided Activities, preceded by explanatory text. Unit 1 discusses the hardware and software needed to complete the Guided Activities in the text. In summary, the student or reader should have DOS 6.*x* installed on an IBM PC, XT, AT, PS/2, or compatible with at least a single floppy drive and a hard disk system. Approximately 10 blank disks appropriate for the system you are using are required.

If you will be using this text in a classroom setting, your instructor will indicate which Guided Activities, Review Questions, Exercises, and Documentation Research will be assigned for the units covered.

Approach to the Text

This text has been constructed to allow the instructor and student to select the units and assignments most appropriate for their needs. Each unit includes numerous assignments, Review Questions, and Documentation Research. The text is written to offer instruction by increments, with each subsequent unit building on concepts presented in previous units. However, a pick-and-choose approach may be just as appropriate for students with previous computing experience.

Versions of DOS

Screens and examples used throughout this text are based on MS-DOS version 6.0, though the screens for subsequent releases (6.2 or 6.*x*) are very similar. Software designers, developers, and users typically use the "*x*" to designate any version in the series. For instance, "6.*x*" refers to any version of DOS that composes the sixth major revision. Many of the Guided Activities within the units can be accomplished using earlier versions of DOS between 3.1 and DOS 5.0, though versions 6.0 or 6.2 are the preferred versions. DOS 6.*x* contains a number of enhancements, commands, and features not found in earlier versions.

West Student Data Disks

Throughout the text, you will need several practice files. They are provided on your Instructor's Key Disk. We have suggested that the 44 practice files be placed on each student workstation in a directory named C:\WESTDATA.DS6. If they are available elsewhere, your instructor will tell you. During the course of completing the Guided Activities, you will need 8–10 practice disks, which you will label as West Student Data Disk #1, #2, #3, and so on.

We know that not all courses will require students to complete all units or all Guided Activities. The book may be tailored to the needs of a specific curriculum. Therefore, we have tried to make it possible for you to skip selected Guided Activities or selected units by keeping you posted regarding which files should be on each West Student Data Disk at the beginning of each unit. In most cases, each West Student Data Disk (#1, #2, #3, and so on) can be re-created with just a few steps. Watch for specific instructions in case you have not completed all previous Guided Activities. Further, most of the data disks are not used for more than 2 to 3 units totally.

Acknowledgments

I would like to express my appreciation for the support of the following West Publishing Company staff: Rick Leyh, Editor, and Jessica Evans, Developmental Editor. I appreciate their support, encouragement, and the opportunity to create this text.

Sincere thanks to Lisa Labrecque and Lisa Auer (Project Managers), Mark Woodworth (Copy Editor), Lisa Bravo (Page Makeup), and Andrea Fox (Proofreader) for their assistance in preparing this volume. I appreciate the professionalism, support, assistance, and humor with which they change a bundle of disk files and manuscript pages into an easy-to-read, well-designed, consistent learning tool. They add immeasurable quality to the book you hold in your hands. Thank you!

I would also like to express my sincere appreciation to the three most important people in my life: My lifelong partner, Joan, and my two Kansas State University Wildcats, Jennifer Anne and Jodi Elizabeth Bacon. Finally, to my Dad, Paul Junior Bacon, I dedicate this book—"I am your child, whatever I am you taught me to be."

J.P.B.
Overland Park, Kansas
September 1993

Publisher's Note

This book is part of THE MICROCOMPUTING SERIES. This popular series provides the most comprehensive list of books dealing with microcomputer applications software. We have expanded the number of software topics and provided a flexible set of instructional materials for all courses. This unique series includes five different types of books.

1. *West's Microcomputing Custom Editions* give instructors the power to create a spiral-bound microcomputer applications book especially for their course. Instructors can select the applications they want to teach and the amount of material they want to cover for each application—essentials or intermediate length. The following titles are available for the 1994 Microcomputing Series custom editions program:

Understanding Information Systems	*Lotus 1-2-3 Release 2.2*
Understanding Networks	*Lotus 1-2-3 Release 2.3*
DOS (3.x) and System	*Lotus 1-2-3 Release 2.4*
DOS 5 and System	*Lotus 1-2-3 Release 3*
DOS 6 and System	*Lotus 1-2-3 for Windows Release 4*
Windows 3.0	*Microsoft Excel 3*
Windows 3.1	*Microsoft Excel 4*
WordPerfect 5.0	*Quattro Pro 4*
WordPerfect 5.1	*Quattro Pro 5 for Windows*
WordPerfect 6.0	*dBASE III Plus*
WordPerfect for Windows (Release 5.1 and 5.2)	*dBASE IV Version 1.0/1.1/1.5*
	dBASE IV Version 2.0
WordPerfect 6.0 for Windows	*Paradox 3.5*
Microsoft Word for Windows Version 1.1	*Paradox 4.5 for Windows*
Microsoft Word for Windows Version 2.0	*Microsoft Access*
PageMaker 4	
Lotus 1-2-3 Release 2.01	

For more information about *West's Microcomputing Custom Editions*, please contact your local West Representative, or call West Publishing Company at 508-388-6685.

2. General concepts books for teaching basic hardware and software philosophy and applications are available separately or in combination with hands-on applications. These books provide students with a general overview of computer fundamentals including history, social issues, and a synopsis of software and hardware applications. These books include *Understanding Information Systems*, by Steven C. Ross.

3. A series of hands-on laboratory tutorials (*Understanding and Using*) are software specific and cover a wide range of individual packages. These tutorials, written at an introductory level, combine tutorials with complete reference guides. A complete list of series titles can be found on the following pages.

4. Several larger volumes combining DOS with three application software packages are available in different combinations. These texts are titled *Understanding and Using Application Software*. They condense components of the individual lab manuals and add conceptual coverage for courses that require both software tutorials and microcomputer concepts in a single volume.

5. A series of advanced-level, hands-on lab manuals provide students with a strong project/systems orientation. These include *Understanding and Using Lotus 1-2-3: Advanced Techniques Releases 2.2 and 2.3*, by Judith C. Simon.

THE MICROCOMPUTING SERIES has been successful in providing you with a full range of applications books to suit your individual needs. We remain committed to excellence in offering the widest variety of current software packages. In addition, we are committed to producing microcomputing texts that provide you both the coverage you desire and also the level and format most appropriate for your students. The Acquisitions Editor of the series is Nancy Hill-Whilton of West Educational Publishing; the Consulting Editor is Steve Ross of Western Washington University. We are always planning for the future in this series. Please send us your comments and suggestions:

Nancy Hill-Whilton
West Educational Publishing
Hamilton Gateway Building
5 Market Square
Amesbury, MA 01913

Steve Ross
Associate Professor/MIS
College of Business and Economics
Western Washington University
Bellingham, Washington 98225
Electronic Mail: STEVEROSS@WWU.EDU

We now offer these books in THE MICROCOMPUTING SERIES:

General Concepts

Understanding Information Systems
by Steven C. Ross

Understanding Computer Information Systems
by Paul W. Ross, H. Paul Haiduk, H. Willis Means, and Robert B. Sloger

Operating Systems/Environments

Understanding and Using Microsoft Windows 3.1
by Steven C. Ross and Ronald W. Maestas

Understanding and Using Microsoft Windows 3.0
by Steven C. Ross and Ronald W. Maestas

Understanding and Using MS-DOS 6.x
by Jonathan P. Bacon

Understanding and Using MS-DOS/PC DOS 5.0
by Jonathan P. Bacon

Understanding and Using MS-DOS/PC DOS 4.0
by Jonathan P. Bacon

Networks

Understanding Networks
by E. Joseph Guay

Word Processors

Understanding and Using WordPerfect 6.0 for Windows
by Jonathan P. Bacon

Understanding and Using WordPerfect for Windows (5.1 and 5.2)
by Jonathan P. Bacon

Understanding and Using Microsoft Word for Windows 2.0
by Larry Lozuk and Emily M. Ketcham

Understanding and Using Microsoft Word for Windows (1.1)
by Larry Lozuk

Understanding and Using WordPerfect 6.0
by Jonathan P. Bacon and Robert G. Sindt

Understanding and Using WordPerfect 5.1
by Jonathan P. Bacon and Cody T. Copeland

Understanding and Using WordPerfect 5.0
by Patsy H. Lund

Desktop Publishing

Understanding and Using PageMaker 4
by John R. Nicholson

Spreadsheet Software

Understanding and Using Quattro Pro 5 for Windows
by Larry D. Smith

Understanding and Using Microsoft Excel 4
by Steven C. Ross and Stephen V. Hutson

Understanding and Using Microsoft Excel 3
by Steven C. Ross and Stephen V. Hutson

Understanding and Using Lotus 1-2-3 for Windows Release 4
by Steven C. Ross and Alan H. Bauld

Understanding and Using Quattro Pro 4
by Steven C. Ross and Stephen V. Hutson

Understanding and Using Lotus 1-2-3 Release 2.01
by Steven C. Ross

Understanding and Using Lotus 1-2-3 Release 2.2
by Steven C. Ross

Understanding and Using Lotus 1-2-3 Release 2.3 and Release 2.4
by Steven C. Ross

Understanding and Using Lotus 1-2-3 Release 3
by Steven C. Ross

*Understanding and Using Lotus 1-2-3: Advanced Techniques
Releases 2.2 and 2.3*
by Judith C. Simon

Database Management Software

Understanding and Using Microsoft Access
by Bruce J. McLaren

Understanding and Using Paradox 4.5 for Windows
by Larry D. Smith

Understanding and Using Paradox 3.5
by Larry D. Smith

Understanding and Using dBASE III Plus, 2nd Edition
by Steven C. Ross

Understanding and Using dBASE IV Version 2.0
by Steven C. Ross

Understanding and Using dBASE IV
by Steven C. Ross

Integrated Software

Understanding and Using Microsoft Works for Windows
by Gary Bitter

Understanding and Using Microsoft Works 3.0 for the PC
by Gary Bitter

Understanding and Using Microsoft Works 3.0 for the Macintosh
by Gary Bitter

Understanding and Using ClarisWorks
by Gary Bitter

Understanding and Using Microsoft Works 2.0 on the Macintosh
by Gary Bitter

Understanding and Using Microsoft Works 2.0 on the IBM PC
by Gary Bitter

Combined Books

Essentials of Application Software, Volume 1: DOS, WordPerfect 5.0/5.1, Lotus 1-2-3 Release 2.2, dBASE III Plus
by Steven C. Ross, Jonathan P. Bacon, and Cody T. Copeland

Understanding and Using Application Software, Volume 4: DOS, WordPerfect 5.0, Lotus 1-2-3 Release 2, dBASE IV
by Patsy H. Lund, Jonathan P. Bacon, and Steven C. Ross

Understanding and Using Application Software, Volume 5: DOS, WordPerfect 5.0/5.1, Lotus 1-2-3 Release 2.2, dBASE III Plus
by Steven C. Ross, Jonathan P. Bacon, and Cody T. Copeland

Advanced Books

Understanding and Using Lotus 1-2-3: Advanced Techniques Releases 2.2 and 2.3
by Judith C. Simon

Jonathan Paul Bacon is currently the manager of the Academic Computing Technologies Group and coordinates efforts to promote use of multimedia and instructional computing at Johnson County Community College, Overland Park, Kansas. During his 16 years at JCCC, he served as Manager of User Information Systems, Director of Student Development and Counseling, and Director of Student Activities. He has worked in microcomputer and mainframe support, staff development and technical training, consulting, and programming for JCCC programs and staff. He has also served as a consultant for community agencies, business, and industry.

Bacon was instrumental in developing the curriculum for the JCCC Microcomputer Training Center, which currently trains over four thousand business and industry students each year. He has written training materials for courses on Lotus 1-2-3, MS-DOS/PC DOS, Multimate, MultiPlan, PFS:File, PFS:Write, Smart 3.1, SmartWare II, and WordStar.

Bacon has written or coauthored ten other West Publishing textbooks: *Understanding and Using MS-DOS/PC DOS: A Complete Guide*, *Understanding and Using MS-DOS/PC DOS: A Hard Disk Edition*, *Understanding and Using MS-DOS/PC DOS 4.0*, *Understanding and Using MS-DOS/PC DOS 5.0*, *Understanding and Using Application Software Volume 4* and *Volume 5*, *Understanding and Using WordPerfect 5.1*, *Understanding and Using WordPerfect for Windows*, *Essentials of Application Software Volume 1*, and *Understanding and Using Microsoft Word*. Bacon also is the author of *Mastering SmartWare II* (Sybex). He has, over the past ten years, been an electronic and print columnist for *Smart Times*, the Heartland Windows Users Group Newsletter, and numerous other publications.

Bacon also serves an ex officio role on the Steering Committee and is former Program Chair for the Heartland Windows Users Group and formerly served on the Instructional Technology Steering Committee for the Silicon Prairie Technology Association.

Jonathan Paul Bacon earned a B.A. in English literature and an M.A. in student personnel work, both from Michigan State University at East Lansing. He has also completed a wide range of studies in data processing. His experience includes curriculum design for several credit courses offered at JCCC in the microcomputer application curriculum.

Overview of MS-DOS

An Introduction to Operating Systems

■ **PART ONE** of this text provides an overview of the functions provided by a micro-computer operating system—specifically, Microsoft DOS (MS-DOS). The single unit in Part One explores the process of booting a computer, forms of issuing DOS com-mands, computer language syntax, and internal versus external DOS commands. Such foundational concepts as guidelines for file names, the component parts of a file name, the use of wild card characters, and drive designations are also covered.

   Once the background information in Part One is understood, you can proceed to Part Two, where basic DOS commands are introduced through hands-on Guided Activities and Exercises.

An Introduction to Operating Systems

At the completion of this unit, you should be able to

1. explain the function of a microcomputer or personal computer disk operating system,

2. explain the process followed when a computer is booted,

3. explain why computer language syntax is important,

4. define the difference between internal and external DOS commands,

5. list the guidelines for creating file names under DOS,

6. define the different parts of a file name,

7. recognize acceptable DOS file names,

8. indicate the function of the DOS prompt,

9. list the keystrokes to change the default drive,

10. explain how to issue DOS commands.

An Introduction to Operating Systems

On the surface, a microcomputer appears to be a miraculous little machine with mysterious insides. It may seem as if putting a floppy disk in the drive and hitting the appropriate keystroke is all that is required to master the technology. However, your ease of use is contingent on the accuracy of meticulous, step-by-step instructions that tell the computer how to behave like one.

These instructions are referred to as the *operating system (OS)*. The OS must kick into operation from the second the computer system is powered up and must handle additional instructions as required. The computer must know how to respond to keyboard *input*, read directions from memory or a storage device (such as a disk), and wait for further instructions.

From the point of view of a mainframe computer, a subset of its operating system is the *disk operating system (DOS)*. Mainframe DOS handles only the basic input and *output* operations between the *central processing unit (CPU)* and the disk drives. But, in the world of microcomputers, the operating system has become synonymous with DOS, which (significantly) rhymes with "boss." When referring to DOS, most microcomputer users are talking about the entire operating system.

The IBM *personal computer (PC)* family of microcomputers and *compatibles* use what is referred to as IBM Personal Computer DOS (*PC DOS*) or Microsoft DOS (*MS-DOS*). Microsoft Corporation is the firm that initially developed PC DOS for IBM computers and MS-DOS for manufacturers of compatibles. As of this writing, only MS-DOS 6.0 is available; IBM has not released a comparable version of PC DOS.

Word processors, data managers, accounting programs, and all other applications programs are written to run with a specific operating system. Operating systems, in turn, are written to take advantage of a specific microprocessor. The following personal computers use the microprocessors listed:

Microcomputer	Microprocessor Chip
Apple	MOS Technology 6502 and 65C02
Commodore Amiga	Motorola 68000
Macintosh	Motorola 68000, 68020, 68030, and 68040
IBM PC, XT	Intel 8088 and 8086
IBM PC/AT	Intel 80286
IBM PS/2	Intel 80286, 80386, 80486, and Pentium

An application program written for the Apple Macintosh or another non-DOS compatible machine will not run on the IBM PC unless the program is rewritten to use the IBM operating system and hardware. The reverse is also true. PC DOS and MS-DOS were designed to use the features of the 8088 microprocessor and its descendants (80286, 80386, 80486, and Pentium).

IBM compatibles exist because their manufacturers use the same basic operating system, or one that closely duplicates the operating system's set of instructions. Part of DOS, called the *basic input/output system* (BIOS), is contained in *ROM (read-only memory)*. ROM microchips contain circuitry patterns with embedded instructions. Each time electric current moves through the circuitry, the same functions are performed. Some of these ROM chips include the instructions that form the BIOS, or the interface between the OS and the specific hardware being used. This portion of the OS is so automatic that most users rarely concern themselves with it.

Booting Your System, and the Power-On Self-Test

An example of a ROM-based portion of DOS is the ***power-on self-test (POST)***. When a DOS-based PC is initially started (***booted***), it conducts a power-on self-test that takes 3 to 90 seconds—depending on how much ***random access memory* (*RAM*)** is installed in the computer, the speed of the microprocessor, and the kind of hardware components installed.

The process of starting up or turning on your computer is referred to as *booting your system*. The term comes from the concept of "pulling oneself up by one's bootstraps." The expression means that the person is a self-starter and tackles tasks without the assistance of anyone or anything.

Microcomputers entered the computing arena as freestanding, self-starting terminals. They booted themselves independent of any mainframe computer. Prior to 1981, you worked on a terminal connected to a mainframe (hidden away in a distant room). If the system was "down" or out of commission, you were stranded with no computing power. In that light, PCs are like people "pulling themselves up by their bootstraps"—they do not depend on a larger computer system to boot. Thus, the term "booting your system" evolved.

The POST checks memory and tries to ensure that the system is OK before proceeding. Next, the POST checks the hardware configuration, such as determining if a keyboard and printer are attached. With an IBM microcomputer, if everything is functional, the system generates a single beep. A second beep means a problem was encountered, such as a bad memory chip or unattached keyboard. Compatible computers may respond differently. Some may beep twice or more, to signal a specific problem, while others display an error message on the monitor screen.

The instructions for POST are included in ROM. Time after time, the computer will follow these instructions when it is booted. The POST is part of the operating system.

After the POST routine is completed, DOS instructs the computer to check disk drive A: for instructions. You will note that the in-use light on drive A: lights up at this point. If instructions are found on a disk, the computer reads them. If no disk is in the drive (and the system includes a hard disk drive), then the BIOS checks drive C: (the hard disk) for instructions. On an original IBM PC, XT, or AT computer, if computer-readable instructions are still not found, the BIOS takes over and reads a limited version of IBM Personal Computer ***Beginner's All-Purpose Symbolic Instruction Code*** (BASIC) into memory. This version of the BASIC programming language is stored in ROM.

With the introduction of the IBM PS/2 models, BASIC is no longer included in ROM on most models (there are a few exceptions to this). Instead, a PS/2 displays a screen message prompting you to insert a disk. When you boot a PC compatible (also called a ***clone***), you may encounter other responses. The most common is an error message indicating that no disk is in the drive. Clone manufacturers do not include ROM BASIC because it is proprietary ***firmware*** (software on a microchip) and, further, because QBasic is now packaged with MS-DOS.

NOTE *QBasic is a version of the BASIC computer language.*

Getting Started by Loading DOS

When the computer goes to drive A: and then subsequently to drive C:, it is looking for additional instructions or additional specialized portions of the software called DOS.

Loading DOS means that some of the DOS commands (referred to as ***internal DOS commands***) are read from disk into the computer's working memory. You must load DOS before you can use any application software or any of the system's utilities. If you load DOS and take no further action, the computer is said to be *at the DOS level* and the ***DOS prompt*** (such as C>) will appear on your monitor screen. In other words, you can execute DOS commands but no application program is yet loaded.

DOS is almost always installed on a new computer's hard drive, so bootable floppy disks are seldom used, except in emergency situations where a hard disk has failed. The first Guided Activity in this text (in Unit 2) walks you through the process of booting your computer and arriving at the DOS prompt.

Types of Personal Computers

The original IBM PC was based on the 8088 microprocessor, as was the original IBM XT. Subsequently, IBM released the Enhanced XT and the AT, both using the 80286 microprocessor.

Figure 1.1 shows a typical PC setup, including a system unit with two disk drives (stacked on top of each other), monitor, keyboard, and attached printer. Today, most computers are sold with a mouse, which is used to point, click, and select commands and options displayed on the monitor screen.

In April 1987, IBM decided to abandon the old PC architecture and proceed instead with manufacturing and marketing the new ***Personal System/2 (PS/2)*** family

FIGURE 1.1
Typical personal computer (desktop unit) configuration with laser printer

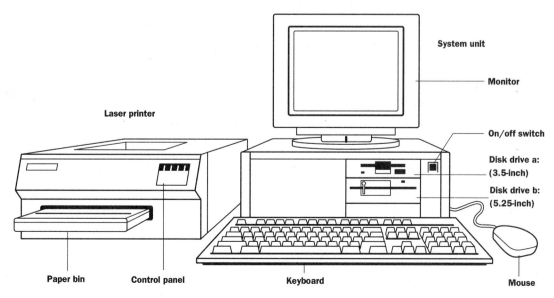

System unit

Monitor

On/off switch

Disk drive a: (3.5-inch)

Disk drive b: (5.25-inch)

Laser printer

Paper bin   Control panel   Keyboard   Mouse

of computers. Figure 1.2 illustrates a typical PS/2 system with a 3.5-inch disk drive, a 5.25-inch disk drive, and an internal hard disk. PS/2 systems and computers from other vendors are available in desktop units (as shown in Figure 1.1) and tower units (shown in Figure 1.2). By the end of 1993, many PC manufacturers were also including CD ROM drives (shown in Figure 1.2) in the systems sold.

FIGURE 1.2
Typical personal computer (tower unit) configuration

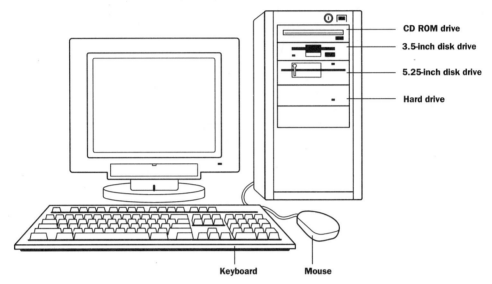

IBM continues to release new models to fill in the gaps in the PS/2 line of computers. Table 1.1 includes a sampling of the IBM PS/2 line. In the table, you will find information on the microprocessor (Processor) used by each system, the speed in *megahertz* (MHz), maximum system memory (RAM), number of slots, and typical hard disk sizes. These figures are supplied by IBM and may change as new systems are released and enhanced.

TABLE 1.1
Data on PS/2 computers

MODEL	PROCESSOR	MHz	RAM	SLOTS	HARD DISK SIZE
25**	8086/80286	8–10	512K–16MB	1–2	0–40MB
30E	80286	10	1–16MB	3	45MB
30*	8086	8	640KB	3	20MB
30–286	80286	10	1–16MB	3	0–20MB
35SX	80386sx	20	2–16MB	3	40MB
40SX	80386sx	20	2–16MB	5	40–80MB
50*	80286	10	16MB	3	20–60MB
50Z*	80286	10	16MB	3	30–60MB
55SX	80386sx	16	16MB	3	40–80MB
56SX	80386sx	20	4–16MB	3	40–80MB
56SLC	80386SLC	20	4–16MB	3	80–160MB
57SX	80386SX	20	4–16MB	5	80–160MB
57SLC	80386SLC	20	4–16MB	7	80–160MB
60*	80286	10	16MB	3	44–185MB

	MODEL	PROCESSOR	MHz	RAM	SLOTS	HARD DISK SIZE
TABLE 1.1 *(continued)*	70	80386	20–25	4–16MB	3	80–160MB
	70–386	80386	16–25	16MB	3	60–160MB
	P70	80386	20	4–16MB	2	60–120MB
	P75	80486	33	8–16MB	4	160–400MB
	80	80386	20–25	4–16MB	7	80–320MB
	90SX	80486sx	25	4–64MB	3	80–160MB
	90	80486	33–50	8–64MB	3	160–400MB
	95SX	80486sx	25	8–64MB	6	160–400MB
	95	80486	33–50	8–64MB	8	400MB–1GB

KB = Kilobytes, MB = Megabytes, GB = Gigabytes

*Discontinued model.

**Although the original model 25 has been discontinued, IBM offers about 17 variations of the model 25. Some use the 8086 microprocessor and others use the 80286. The slower machines with less hard disk and memory capacity use the 8086 processor.

All of the PS/2 models as well as PC and AT compatibles (from companies like Compaq, Dell, Gateway, and Northgate) can run PC DOS or MS-DOS 6.x.

The Importance of the Disk Operating System

DOS is the most crucial software you will ever own. Without it, the personal computer can only sit and look pretty. DOS has been described as a go-between, a traffic cop, or the boss of the computer. In fact, DOS is the manager of communications (or data transfer) between the computer and its internal/external parts such as memory, printers, disk drives, and the video display. Figure 1.3 shows some of the functions performed by the operating system.

The operating system handles basic instructions such as telling the computer how to retrieve, store, or delete data from the disk. These instructions are written in machine language, yet you can perform similar operations by using DOS commands such as COPY, DISKCOPY, and ERASE. Software developers also execute these commands from within their products to copy, delete, or save data.

Even if you intend only to use prepackaged software, a basic understanding of the DOS commands is essential. Without understanding DOS, you cannot do even simple maintenance activities such as duplicating data disks and erasing unwanted files from a disk.

FIGURE 1.3

Functions of the
operating system

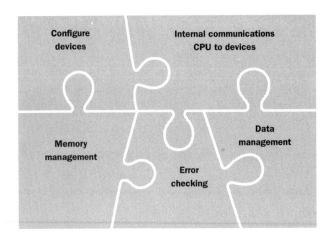

Computer Language Syntax: The Order That Promotes Understanding

Any spoken or written language requires that users follow certain conventions. There are rules for singular versus plural subjects. Guidelines are established to define what is present tense or past tense. Even the *syntax* or order of the language is critical.

Syntax is simply the way in which words, phrases, and ideas are put together, either verbally or on paper. We use language to communicate with computers; and because the machine's ability to understand language is limited, the required syntax with computers is even more exacting than in colloquial speech. We cannot assume the machine can guess our intentions based on body language, voice inflections, or familiarity.

An example of using syntax in the English language might clarify its use with computers. Mary Ellen, Pat, and Buddy are watching television when Pat becomes overwhelmed by a thirst for a cola. She knows there are no soft drinks in the refrigerator. Pat says, "Get," but the obvious question is "get what?" To clarify the command, Pat says, "Get a cola." Further clarification is still needed. Is she offering Mary Ellen and Buddy a cola, and if so, where are the colas?

The command must be expanded to include "get me a cola," and yet she still has not clarified where the cola is. Further, whom is Pat talking to? Will Mary Ellen or Buddy get the cola? In "computer talk," those additional modifiers are either *parameters* or *switches*.

The terms parameter and switch are often used interchangeably. In the strictest sense, a parameter identifies the object (file, drive, and so on) that DOS will act upon. A switch modifies the action by turning on or off specific functions of the command.

Pat's problem is the lack of modifiers or parameters. Another problem might be the sequence in which she states the command.

The following commands include the same words and, though one sounds like baby talk, the meanings are clear but very different:

"Mary Ellen go to the store and get me a cola."
"Me go to the store and get Mary Ellen a cola."

Further, the same words would probably be indecipherable if ordered as:

"Store to Mary Ellen the go me cola a get and."

Syntax makes all the difference. The same words are used, but in the last phrase their order defies understanding.

Computer language syntax must follow a specified order or the computer is left saying "Bad Command or File name"—its equivalent of "huh??" Commands must be modified by the use of parameters or switches. In the following *command form* (which is also referred to as a *command line*), everything after the command "COPY" is a parameter.

```
COPY a:FILE-A b:FILE-A
```

It says to the computer, "Copy the file named FILE-A from the disk in drive A: to the disk in drive B:." It might be helpful to note that with DOS, if two *file names* are listed on a command line, the first is always a *source file* and the second is the *target file*. This is a PC DOS/MS-DOS syntax convention. The first file is the FROM file and the second is the TO file. So, in the above example, the copy is FROM a:FILE-A TO b:FILE-A. If a file were being renamed, the REN command (short for RENAME) would be used. To change the file from HELP to ASSIST would require the following command line:

```
REN a:HELP ASSIST
```

When we discuss syntax, the following abbreviations will be used:

d: represents a disk drive name, such as the a: or b: drive. DOS parameters or switches are not case-sensitive; they may be upper- or lowercase, so A: or B: is also acceptable. If the computer system has a hard disk, it is usually referred to as drive c: (or C:).

s: represents the *source disk*; for example, in the COPY command, the disk from which a copy is being made.

t: represents the *target disk*; for example, in the COPY command, the disk to which a copy is being made.

In most DOS operations, the original disk is called the source disk and the recipient of a specific DOS operation is the target disk.

Issuing DOS Commands

Several guidelines on issuing DOS commands may be helpful as you proceed through the following units.

- A DOS command must be spelled correctly, using the syntax described throughout this text, including any spaces within the command line. A space will follow each command or file name, just as words in English are separated by spaces.

- Commands may be typed in either uppercase or lowercase. For clarity, DOS commands are printed in uppercase in this text, but they are not *case-sensitive*. Capitalization is not required. Further, to clarify spacing, text to be entered looks more like typewritten characters than typeset characters in this text (such as COPY A:*.* B:).

- After typing a DOS command line, you must press ⏎Enter. This tells the computer to begin executing the command. The ⏎Enter key is sometimes labeled as the ⏎Return key on some keyboards.

- If the command you type contains a typographical error, a missing space, an extra space, or other error (such as indicating the wrong drive), the error message "Bad command or file name" will appear when you press ⏎Enter. If this prompt does appear, simply retype the command correctly and try again. Screen messages are printed within quote marks.

Internal Versus External DOS Commands

Perhaps the most difficult concept for the novice PC user to grasp is the difference between internal and *external DOS commands*.

When we discuss file name extensions, you will find that files with a .COM or .EXE *extension* on the DOS disk are external commands. In this usage, "external" simply means that the command must be read from disk in order to be executed. It is external to working memory (RAM) until the file is read into memory.

NOTE *Storage (memory) is measured using bytes, kilobytes, megabytes, and gigabytes. These terms are used when discussing RAM (working memory), as well as hard disk and floppy disk space. One byte can represent one character such as a letter or number. One kilobyte (KB) equals 1,024 bytes of data. One megabyte (MB) equals 1,024 kilobytes, or 1,048,576 characters or bytes. One gigabyte (GB) equals 1,024 megabytes of storage.*

Internal DOS commands are loaded when the system is booted (or reloaded when the current application is exited) and are always resident in working memory. By "working memory," we mean random-access memory (RAM). The original IBM PC came with 64KB. The more recent Revision "B" PC includes a minimum of 256 *kilobytes* (KB) of memory, and can be upgraded to 640KB. 640KB is the maximum memory addressable at one time by the 8086 or 8088 microprocessor and versions of DOS prior to 4.*x*. A portion of that memory is consumed by loading DOS. The COMMAND.COM file includes instructions for the DOS command processor (that is, that "thing" which processes commands). With PC DOS, COMMAND.COM automatically loads DBLSPACE.BIN, IO.SYS, and MSDOS.SYS, three hidden files that contain additional portions of DOS. Once they are loaded, the internal DOS commands are accessible from the keyboard.

NOTE *Hidden files are files that will not show in a directory listing when you invoke the DIR command. DIR is one of the first commands you learn in Unit 2. Microsoft has hidden these files so that the novice user will not accidentally erase them or attempt to modify them.*

The following analogy (shared by Professor Kevin R. Parker of New Mexico Junior College) might help clarify internal versus external DOS commands. Internal DOS commands are like words that you know. When you hear a familiar word, you know its meaning because it is stored in your mind. External DOS commands are like unfamiliar words. To understand (process) the word, you must look it up in a dictionary, just as DOS must "look up" an external command on the DOS disk or in the DOS directory on a hard disk.

NOTE *Both internal and external DOS commands are available only when the DOS prompt (A> or B> or C>) is displayed on the screen. That prompt literally means "ready for your command."*

Using File Names, Extensions, Paths, and Drive Designators

DOS stores all information it is given (whether data or programs) in files. In order to save, modify, or retrieve the file, DOS must know its name. Guidelines for file names must be understood before we proceed to discuss specific DOS commands. Even beginning computer users must use file names—they are unavoidable. Every time data is saved to disk, or an application program (like a word processor) is loaded, a file name must be used. The ***complete file name*** is referred to as a ***file specification*** and follows this form:

```
[d:][path]filename[.ext]
```

The file specification (also called the "filespec") is composed of four parts:

- The drive designation (d:)

- The path name (path)

- The file name

- The extension (.ext)

NOTE *When square brackets are used, they signify an optional parameter or switch or path for the file name.*

The File Naming Conventions

DOS 2.1 and later versions use the following guidelines for the file name. File names are used with DOS to identify specific data, text, or application files. A file name must be no longer than eight characters. The following groups of characters may be used in a file name or extension:

Capital alphabetic characters	A–Z
Lowercase alphabetic characters	a–z
Numeric characters	0–9
Special characters	! @ # $ % & ( ) - _ { } ' '

Notice that the Spacebar character and a period (.) are not listed in the table. They cannot be used in a file name. Spaces are used as *delimiters* (separators) between a DOS command and any parameters that might be needed (such as one or more file names). Unless a DOS command is entered without any parameters, it is always followed by a space. The period serves as a delimiter (separator) between the file name and any extension attached to the file name.

You will encounter two exceptions to this rule as you learn DOS. First, a command without any parameters (such as DIR) does not have to be followed by a space. Second, any command followed by a backslash (\) or slash (/) character does not require a space. Examples would include commands like DIR/P and CD\DOS. Don't worry about the meaning of these commands until they are introduced in later units.

Table 1.2 lists the DOS reserved characters—that is, characters that may not be used in a file name because they are reserved for other purposes in DOS.

TABLE 1.2
DOS reserved characters

Asterisk	*
Backslash	\
Blanks or spaces	
Colon	:
Comma	,
Concatenation character	|
Double quote	"
Equal sign	=
Greater-than sign	>
Less-than sign	<
Period	.
Plus sign	+
Question mark	?
Semicolon	;
Slash	/
Square brackets	[ ]

Following the above guidelines, acceptable file names could include:

```
&G#$DX98
HUH!
PICKLES
```

File names should describe the contents of the file they identify. Thus, PICKLES would be an acceptable file name for a letter of complaint regarding a spoiled jar of pickles purchased at a local supermarket. The first two file names are not very descriptive of the file's contents, even though they are acceptable file names. Special characters are often avoided in the file name, unless they contribute to the descriptive nature of the file name.

The File Name Extension

The extension is a one-, two-, or three-character add-on to the file name. It is not required by DOS, but is often helpful. The extension always follows a delimiter (a period) and is tacked onto the end of the file name. Acceptable or legal file names with extensions would include:

```
LETTER.DOC
COST.WS
ORDER.BAS
```

Note that there are also a few *reserved words* in DOS. You may not call a file by these names: AUX, CLOCK$, COM1, COM2, COM3, COM4, CON, CON:, LPT1, LPT2, LPT3, LST, NUL, or PRN. These reserved words represent physical devices attached to your computer system. File names are logical devices used to identify data and program code. The operating system does not allow you to reference a logical device by a physical device name—which would confuse the operating system.

File names are not required to be eight characters long, nor are extensions required to be three characters long. Those are maximum limits. Since file names cannot exceed eight characters, you must often truncate (shorten) words to fit the character limitation. A memo detailing the company's equipment replacement schedule could be saved under the file name EQUIPMNT, REPLACEM, or SCHEDULE. In each case, the topic of the memo is truncated and reflected in the file name.

Some application programs automatically attach extensions to the files created by the user. For example, word processors often append a .DOC extension to documents created. The user does not even see the extension when files are listed from within these word processors. When an application program automatically backs up files, a .BAK extension is often added to revised text files.

Various spreadsheet programs automatically add file extensions to the worksheets created, such as .WKS or .WS. When files are printed to disk rather than to a printer, a typical extension used is .PRN.

Database software often assigns either a .DB or .DBF extension for database files. Other associated files may use such extensions as .DFR for a report definition, .DFQ for a query definition, and .PIX for a physical index file.

In each case outlined above (and in Table 1.3), the extension is automatically added by the software to differentiate between types of files. Table 1.3 lists file name extensions for several popular application software programs.

TABLE 1.3
*DOS application
software
extensions*

Access	.MDB
dBASE II	.DB2
dBASE III	.DBF
dBASE III+	.DBF
dBASE IV	.DBF
FileMaker Pro	.FM
IBM Filing Assistant	.PFS
Lotus 1-2-3, version 1A	.WKS
Lotus 1-2-3, version 2.01/2.2	.WK1
Lotus 1-2-3, educational version	.WKE
Lotus 1-2-3, version 3.*x*	.WK3
Paradox	.DB
PowerPoint	.PPT
Quattro Pro	.WQ1
Quattro Pro for Windows	.WKQ
ToolBook	.TBK
Word 5.5	.DOC
Word for Windows	.DOC
WordPerfect	(user defines the extension)
WordPerfect for Windows 6.0	.WPD (unless defined otherwise by user)
Microsoft Works Communications	.WCM
Microsoft Works Database	.WDB
Microsoft Works Spreadsheet	.WKS
Microsoft Works Word Processor	.WPS

DOS File Name Extensions

DOS has its own set of extensions, used for special function files. The most common DOS assigned file extensions are as follows:

.BAK   for a DOS-created backup file
.BAS   for a BASIC language file
.BAT   for a batch processing file
.COM   for an external DOS command or program file

.EXE	for an executable program or command file
.HEX	for a file used with the DEBUG command
.MAP	for a file used with the LINK command
.OBJ	for an object code file created by a compiler
.REL	for an object code file created by an assembler
.TMP	for a temporary file created by DOS

NOTE *The .COM files on the DOS disk are really special communication files. They correspond to the standard DOS external commands already discussed. Each .COM file contains raw machine-language code (instructions).*

Whenever a DOS external command is entered (such as CHKDSK, DISKCOPY, or DISKCOMP), DOS immediately checks to see if there is a .COM file by that file name on the disk in the default or specified drive. If such a file is located, the machine-language instructions contained in the file are loaded into memory and control of the system is passed to those instructions.

If no .COM file is found, then DOS checks first for an .EXE file, then for a .BAT file by the name entered. To execute files with these three types of extensions (.BAT, .COM, and .EXE), you do not need to enter the extension, only the file name. However, if you have three files with the same name but different extensions (.BAT, .COM, and .EXE) on the same disk, you can select which file to execute by including the extension when you enter the file name at the DOS prompt.

The Drive Designation

In the earlier discussion of syntax, it was pointed out that Mary Ellen and Buddy needed to be told where to go to obtain a cola for Pat.

Similarly, DOS must know where commands are located, where files are stored, and where specified actions are required. A personal computer typically has one or two disk drives. Usually the left-hand drive or the top drive (if the drives are stacked) is "drive A." The formal name is A: (the colon is a required part of the name, though orally we refer to "drive A").

If a second disk drive is included with the computer, it is referred to as "drive B." On an enhanced PC, IBM XT, AT, or PS/2, the first hard disk drive is referred to as drive C:. Depending upon the configuration of your PC system, you may have additional drives labeled D: through Z:.

NOTE *Though drive A: is typically the top or left drive and drive B: is the bottom or right, these drive locations may be reversed.*

Referring to the cola example, we might say, "Get a cola," although "Go to the store and get a cola" is more precise. The computer needs similar clarification. For a program file to be executed, DOS needs to know whether the executable file is on drive A:, B:, C:, or D:. The *drive designation* accomplishes this task. It communicates to the computer where commands to be executed are located.

The Default Drive or Logged-On Drive

In some ways, DOS makes life easy for the user. The DOS prompt (also called a *system prompt*) will always display the *default drive* or the logged-on drive. The terms are synonymous. On a floppy drive system, after you boot the computer with a disk in drive A:, the DOS prompt will appear as:

```
A>
```

On a hard disk system, if booted with no disk in drive A:, the DOS prompt would appear as:

```
C>
```

What does this mean for the user? It means that a command or file may be accessed from the default drive without using the drive designation. Two keystrokes are saved. The difference in keystrokes is demonstrated by the following two command lines. They have the same results if the default drive is C:.

```
FORMAT A:
C:FORMAT A:
```

In computing, any reference to the default drive means that any actions or commands will be executed on that drive—*unless* you indicate otherwise on the command line. In essence, the *default* is an assumed target, source, selection, or choice that is automatically used, unless you stipulate otherwise.

By simply typing in the drive designation (only) at the DOS prompt, you can change the default drive (also called the logged-on drive). If you are logged on to drive C:, the DOS prompt appears as:

```
C>
```

If you type B: and press the ⏎Enter key, also referred to as the ⏎Return key or carriage return, the prompt switches to:

```
B>
```

The Path

As you begin to work with external DOS commands in later units, you will find that you can identify the *path* to the command and still execute it—even if the command is not in the current directory or drive. The PATH command and the concept of directories and subdirectories are covered more fully in later units. For now, realize that a path can be specified. It simply tells the operating system which "route" (or path) should be taken to find a command, file name, or data.

The Complete File Name

A completely assembled file name might appear as:

```
A:\DOCS\LETTER3.DOC
```

This would be an appropriate file name for a letter created by a word processor using the .DOC extension and stored in the \DOCS directory (the backslash character represents the root directory under which all subdirectories begin) on drive A:.

In summary, the complete file name equals:

```
[Drive Designation] + [Path] + [Filename] + [Extension]
```

Global Wild Card Characters

Two characters are reserved for a special use and may not be used in the file name or extension. These characters are the question mark (?) and the asterisk (*). They are referred to as *global characters* or global *wild card characters*. Either term signifies that they may be substituted for one or more characters in a file name. The question mark substitutes for one character; the asterisk may substitute for one or more characters.

Depending on how you structure file names, these wild card characters may be very helpful. For example, it would be helpful when backing up specific files if you formed a habit of using common characters in files with common data.

Files storing a series of letters might be named:

```
LETTER1.DOC
LETTER2.DOC
LETTER3.DOC
LETTER4.DOC
```

When backing up the files to disk, all of the LETTER files could be copied with one command rather than several. The DOS COPY command (covered later in the text) duplicates the specified files. By using the ? wild card, the following command would copy every file from drive A: to drive B: that begins with LETTER and ends with a single character (any character, not just 1 through 9) and has a .DOC extension:

```
COPY A:LETTER?.DOC B:
```

Wild card characters are discussed further in the Guided Activities of upcoming units. For now, remember that:

- ? means that any character may occupy that position in a file name.

- * means that any character may occupy that position and the remaining positions in the file name or extension.

- The ? and * characters may not be used as part of the actual file name assigned to a document or disk file.

Disk-Handling Guidelines

Whether working with DOS, an application program, or data disks, you should be aware that the careful handling of floppy disks is crucial. Disks are the tools of the computing trade. If you fail to handle these tools properly, trouble and inconvenience will follow.

If a computer includes a hard disk system, you still must work with floppy disks. The most obvious use of disks is to *archive* (back up or make a spare copy of) application program disks and to back up data files. You cannot avoid working with disks—so it is best to learn how to use rather than abuse them.

The surface of the disk must be protected from any element or activity that might damage it. Damage can occur by exposing the surface to contaminants (dust, dirt, fingerprints, liquids), physical damage (folding, creasing, bending, heavy objects, indentations from writing tools), heat (direct and prolonged sunlight, or temperatures above 125 degrees F), cold (below 50 degrees F), and magnetic fields (small motors, stereo speakers, magnets, nonelectronic ringing telephones, televisions). A fairly new hazard is the microwave oven. If you place a floppy disk on top of a microwave and then use the appliance, your goose may be cooked but your data may be lost.

Another kind of disk protection is necessary to prevent accidental erasure or modification of important files on your disk. It is called *write protection*.

The 5.25-inch disk is packaged differently than the newer 3.5-inch disk. The 5.25-inch is typically sealed in a black plastic jacket with a window through which the disk drive read-write head accesses data. The easiest method of damaging a disk is to contaminate the magnetic oxide surface through that window. Each 5.25-inch disk comes with a paper envelope. To further protect the recording surface, the disk should always be housed in its envelope when not in use.

Figure 1.4 identifies the parts of a 5.25-inch disk, including the disk envelope, permanent protective jacket, and write-protection notch; remove the tab when you want to write data to the disk. To writeprotect this type of disk, simply use the write-protection tab (a small piece of self-adhesive tape) to cover the write-protection notch; remove the tab when you want to write data to the disk.

The 3.5-inch disk comes in a permanent rigid plastic container. It includes a small plastic slide to write-protect the disk. The 3.5-inch disk is constructed with a spring-loaded metal cover that protects the disk access area from damage. The disk drive retracts the cover when the disk is inserted in the drive. You should never open the cover manually as damage may occur to the recording surface. Each 3.5-inch disk may come with a clear plastic envelope, but not always. The parts of the 3.5-inch disk are identified in Figure 1.5. To write-protect this type of disk, move the small plastic slide on the back to cover the hole in the disk cover; or uncover the hole to remove write protection.

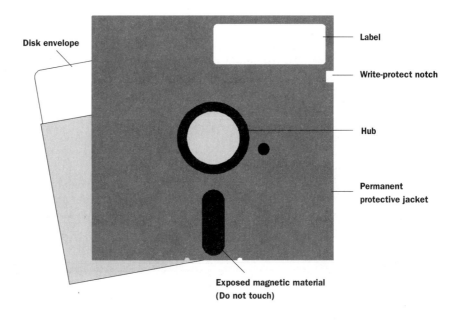

Disk envelope

Label

Write-protect notch

Hub

Permanent
protective jacket

Exposed magnetic material
(Do not touch)

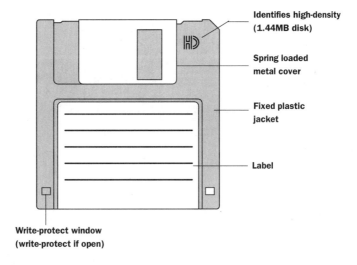

Identifies high-density
(1.44MB disk)

Spring loaded
metal cover

Fixed plastic
jacket

Label

Write-protect window
(write-protect if open)

Check Figure 1.6 for a listing of important disk-handling guidelines. These rules apply to all types of disks. Careful adherence to these guidelines will save you problems in the future.

FIGURE 1.6
*Disk-handling
guidelines*

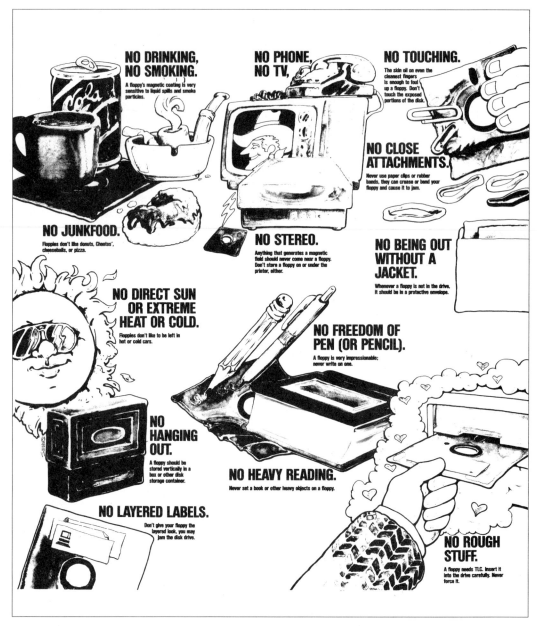

Basic Assumptions

PC DOS/MS-DOS is a standard operating system. While standards do exist, there is still phenomenal diversity when you consider the computer equipment currently installed in homes, schools, colleges, businesses, and industry. While we have attempted to make this text applicable to a wide variety of users, certain assumptions were made. The Guided Activities throughout this text are constructed with the following assumptions about your computer system and the software needed:

- Access to an IBM PC, XT, AT, Personal System/2 (PS/2), or compatible computer

- Access to DOS version 6.*x*

- Access to a system with at least one floppy disk drive and a hard disk

Each Guided Activity will not instruct you to boot your PC system. We'll cover booting your computer in the next unit and then assume that you can start your computer for each subsequent Guided Activity. Unit 2 details the process and provides the basic knowledge you need to complete the activities in following units.

Summary

In this unit you learned about the role of a personal computer disk operating system and discovered what happens when a computer is booted. The unit also discussed computer language syntax, the difference between internal and external DOS commands, guidelines for creating file names, and the careful handling of disks.

Review Questions

The answers to even-numbered questions are contained in Appendix A.

1. What is the difference between the operating system on a mainframe and DOS on an IBM PC?

2. Define DOS.

3. Who developed IBM PC DOS and MS-DOS?

4. Where is DOS stored for use by the computer?

5. Can application programs (such as word processors, spreadsheets, and data managers) be run without DOS?

6. Why is syntax important to a computer user?

7. When may internal and external DOS commands be executed?

8. What is the maximum number of characters that may be used in a file name? In an extension?

9. Name the two DOS wild card characters? Can they be used when naming a file? Why?

10. Which of the following are not legal file names?

    LETTER\TO\MOTHER.TXT
    FINAL.LTR
    CALLHOME.DOC
    $%&9441!.BAK
    1.BAT
    COMMAND.COMM
    12345678.*90

11. How does the user change the default drive?

12. What is the difference between the default drive and the logged-on drive?

13. What is meant by "case-sensitive"? Is DOS case-sensitive when naming a file or executing a DOS command?

14. Why is NEWSNOTE.DOC a better file name than &$123NTE.DOC?

15. Explain what is meant by "booting your system."

16. What is the difference between the DOS prompt and the system prompt?

Exercises

Where appropriate, Exercises are included within the text. Your instructor will tell you which exercises to complete and what materials (disks or printouts) should be handed in.

1. Write-protect one of your disks and show it to your instructor. Be prepared to demonstrate how to remove the write protection.

2. Submit a list of ten legal and descriptive file names to your instructor. Follow each file name with a "pretend" description of the contents of the file.

Key Terms

The following terms are introduced in this unit. Be sure you know what each of them means.

Archive
Basic input/output
  system (BIOS)
Beginner's All-Purpose
  Symbolic Instruction
  Code (BASIC)
Boot
Case-sensitive
Clone
Command form
Command line
Compatible
Complete file name
Central processing unit
  (CPU)
Default drive
Delimiter
Disk operating system
  (DOS)

DOS prompt
Drive designation
Extension
External DOS command
File specification
File name
Firmware
Global character
Input
Internal DOS command
Kilobyte
Megahertz (MHz)
MS-DOS
Operating system (OS)
Output
Parameter
Path
PC DOS
Personal computer (PC)

Personal System/2 (PS/2)
Power-on self-test (POST)
Random access memory
  (RAM)
Read-only memory
  (ROM)
Reserved word
Source disk
Source file
Switch
Syntax
System prompt
Target disk
Target file
Wild card character
Write protection

Basic DOS Commands

II

■ **PART TWO** of *Understanding and Using MS-DOS 6.x* covers the commonly used disk operating system (DOS) commands. Personal computer users must be able to copy, delete, and rename files. Further, they must format disks that will store data created by various application programs. Secretaries, managers, CEOs, and other users must be able to use the fundamental commands introduced in Part Two. Doing so does not require a programming background—only a desire to efficiently manage tasks on your computer. These basic commands are essential for all users.

The fundamental DOS commands fall into four groups: housekeeping, disk preparation, file management, and disk management commands.

Unit 2 introduces commands that enable you to set the system date and time, clear the monitor screen, and see a listing of files on a disk. Unit 3 covers such tasks as preparing a disk for use, making a disk bootable, and creating a copy of an existing disk. Unit 4 explores copying, deleting, undeleting, renaming, and comparing files. Unit 5 discusses how to organize files into directories and move among those directories. Finally, Unit 6 introduces you to two new commands (added with DOS 6) that enable you to modify your hard disk by moving or deleting directories and subdirectories of files. When you have finished Part Two, you will know all of the "everyday DOS commands."

Housekeeping Commands

Learning Objectives

At the completion of this unit, you should be able to

1. locate the function keys on your keyboard,
2. identify the toggle keys on your keyboard,
3. know how to boot your personal computer system,
4. know how to warm boot your system,
5. set the default drive,
6. use the CLS command to clear the monitor screen,
7. use the DATE command to set or update the system date,
8. use the DIR command to display a listing of files,
9. use the PROMPT command to change the system prompt,
10. use the TIME command to set or update the system time,
11. use the on-line Help reference to access additional information on DOS commands.

Important Commands

CLS

DATE

DIR

HELP

PROMPT

TIME

Introductory Concepts and Housekeeping Commands

If you were to purchase a new house or rent an apartment, your first action would be to get the necessary keys, enter the home or apartment, and figure out how to turn on the lights, furnace, air conditioning, and water. It would be important to know if there is a trick to unlocking a certain door, where your mail is delivered, and when you must follow certain procedures as an owner or tenant (for example, paying rent or property tax). All of this information would be required before you begin housekeeping chores. For instance, you cannot fill the refrigerator with food until you get the keys, enter the dwelling, and turn on the power.

There are certain introductory concepts you must learn before working with a personal computer, as well. Some are as simple as determining how to turn on the system unit and the monitor. Others may be more complex, such as adjusting to the similarities and dissimilarities between your computer's keyboard and any typewriter or other computer keyboard you have used in the past.

NOTE *Throughout the text, four terms are used interchangeably. They are* computer, personal computer, PC *(an abbreviation for personal computer), and* microcomputer *(originally used to designate a small version of a computer at a time when mainframe computers were the predominant type). You may also hear the PC referred to as a* desktop PC, desktop unit, *or* workstation *(connected to a network). In each case, we are talking about a desktop or tower system unit connected to a keyboard and monitor, primarily used by a single worker to accomplish specific computing tasks such as word processing, database management, desktop publishing, graphics creation, accounting-type activities (with a spreadsheet), or telecommunications.*

This unit is devoted to covering both the introductory concepts and the housekeeping chores. The first portion explores such topics as PC keyboards, function keys, loading DOS, starting, and restarting your personal computer. If you are familiar with PCs, you can quickly skim this material.

The final portion of the unit covers some basic DOS housekeeping commands. They are "housekeeping" actions in the sense that each is a common maintenance activity—just like washing dishes, vacuuming the floor, and checking the cupboards for food.

The Keyboard

There are several type of keyboards produced for DOS-based personal computers. International Business Machines Corporation (IBM) has produced and distributed four varieties of keyboards in the United States, as listed below:

- United States Enhanced PC keyboard, 101 keys

- United States AT keyboard, 84 keys

FIGURE 2.1
101-key keyboard

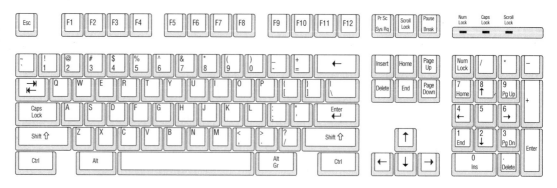

- United States XT keyboard, 83 keys

- United States Convertible keyboard, 58 keys

The original IBM PC used the keyboard that is labeled as the United States XT keyboard. However, since that time IBM and most manufacturers of DOS compatible computers have standardized on using the 101-key keyboard. There may be slight variations from one 101-key keyboard to the next, but most look similar to the keyboard in Figure 2.1.

Appendix C in the *Microsoft MS-DOS 6 User's Guide* includes layouts of 20 different keyboards currently used internationally on DOS-based computers. Countries or regions listed in the manual include Belgium, Canada, Croatia/Slovenia/Serbia (Yugoslavia), Czech Republic, Denmark, France, Germany, Hungary, Italy, Latin America, Netherlands, Norway, Poland, Portugal, Slovakia, Spain, Sweden/Finland, Switzerland, United Kingdom, and the United States.

The IBM original PC keyboard had 83 keys, about 40 more than most typewriters. It is illustrated in Figure 2.2. On the original PC and XT keyboards, symbols or **mnemonics** ("assisting-the-memory" associations) are used rather than text characters to identify the keys.

FIGURE 2.2
The original IBM-PC keyboard

NOTE *PC keyboards are also referenced by other names. For instance, you may read of references to the following keyboards:*

*The 5151 keyboard includes separate numeric and **cursor movement pads** with the function keys (F1 through F10) placed along the left end of the keyboard. This is like the United States AT keyboard.*

The 5060 keyboard has the same layout as the United States XT keyboard, except that the Shift and Enter keys have been enlarged.

The 101-key enhanced keyboard is a generic or compatible version of the United States Enhanced PC keyboard. It has 101 keys, including function keys F11 *and* F12 *and separate numeric and cursor movement keypads.*

Conventions and Keys Used in This Text

Beginning with this unit, Guided Activities are used that require you to enter information using the keyboard. We have established a number of typographical conventions that will make it easy for you to know exactly which keys to press.

The word *press* is used whenever you are instructed to push a single key. For instance, if you are instructed to press the *Enter* key or the *Return* key in order to enter a paragraph mark or hard return, the instructions will read

Press the Enter key.

The *Enter* key inserts a line feed/carriage return character, often called a paragraph mark or hard return, into a document or is used to signal the transmittal of a DOS command to the computer. On some keyboards, this key is called the *Enter* key, while others label it the *Return* key. The original PC keyboard designated it with a right-angle arrow; in this text, it is always referred to with the graphic symbol: Enter.

In the Guided Activities, the term *type* is used to indicate that one or more characters must be entered using the keyboard—just as you would on a typewriter. If you are instructed to *type* a character in uppercase, you will need to hold down the Shift key and press the designated key—the same as on a typewriter. The characters to be typed are shown in a `typewriter-style type font`.

The keys that control cursor movement are designated in the following manner:

↑	Up arrow key
↓	Down arrow key
→	Right arrow key
←	Left arrow key
Home	Home key
End	End key
PgDn	Page down key
PgUp	Page up key

Other keys on the keyboard are noted in the text as follows:

Alt	Alternate key
Backspace	Backspace key
CapsLock	Capital Letter lock key
Ctrl	Control key
Del	Delete key
Enter	Enter or Return key
Esc	Escape key
F1	Function key labeled F1
F2	Function key labeled F2
F3	Function key labeled F3
F4	Function key labeled F4

[F5]	Function key labeled F5
[F6]	Function key labeled F6
[F7]	Function key labeled F7
[F8]	Function key labeled F8
[F9]	Function key labeled F9
[F10]	Function key labeled F0
[F11]	Function key labeled F11
[F12]	Function key labeled F12
[Ins]	Insert key
[Num Lock]	Number Lock key
[Pause]	Pause/Break key
[Prt Sc]	Print Screen key
[Shift]	Shift key
[Spacebar]	Spacebar key
[Tab]	Tab key

Function Keys

Depending on your keyboard, the *function keys* are located in two rows along the left edge of the keyboard or in a single row across the top of the keyboard. Function keys are often used in application software packages (such as a word processor) to invoke specific commands or features. Some of the function keys have special uses when pressed at the DOS level. When the 101-key keyboard was first introduced, it increased the number of function keys from 10 to 12. The 12-function key style is now the de facto standard on most keyboards.

Multiple Key Combinations

On a typewriter, the [Shift] key is used in conjunction with a letter key to produce an uppercase letter. The same is true on a computer. Like the [Shift] key, the [Ctrl] key and the [Alt] key act as modifying keys. If either is used in conjunction with a second key, the action of the original key is modified. These keys are manipulated in the same manner as the [Shift] key. For example, if you are instructed to press [Alt][M], you would hold down the [Alt] key, press the [M] key once, and then release the [Alt] key.

In this textbook, if keys are to be pressed consecutively (rather than simultaneously), the keys noted will be separated by commas, such as

Press the [Alt][F], [X] keys.

Using Toggle Keys

Toggle keys act as on-off switches, like a pressable light switch. Press them once and they are activated; press them a second time to deactivate them. Examples of toggle keys include the [Num Lock] key (which toggles the numeric keypad between entering numbers and moving the cursor), the [Ctrl][Prt Sc] combination (which turns on the print mode where all text on the monitor screen is also sent to the printer), and the [Caps Lock] key (which causes all letters typed to appear in uppercase).

Caps Lock Key

As mentioned above, the [CapsLock] key shifts all alphabetic characters (a…z) to upper-case (A…Z). It has no effect on nonalphabetic keyboard characters. This is unlike the shift lock on a typewriter, which locks all keys into shifted characters (that is, the characters on the top of each key or capital letters). The [CapsLock] key is a toggle key.

Numeric Keypad Keys

The numeric pad is located on the right side of the keyboard and is configured like a 10-key calculator pad. It serves a dual purpose: as a cursor movement pad and as a 10-key numeric pad. When it is operating as a cursor movement pad, you would use the keys with arrows on them. They are referred to as arrow keys or as the [↑], [↓], [←], and [→] keys. The other keys used for cursor movement (on the keypad) are referred to by the text that appears on the key (that is, as the [Home], [PgUp], [PgDn], [End], [Del], and [Ins] keys).

When the keys on the numeric keypad move the cursor, you can activate the numeric entry function by pressing [NumLock] (a toggle) once. Most of these keys have minimal use when operating at the DOS prompt, but are used by application programs for cursor movement and entering numbers (especially in a spreadsheet or accounting program).

The cursor movement keys ([↑], [→], [PgUp], [Home], and so on) are repeated on a separate pad on the newer 101-key keyboard. The keys on this cursor movement pad can be used whether the [NumLock] key is toggled on or off.

Loading DOS

Loading DOS is as simple as turning on the power switch on your personal computer. When you load DOS, you place some of its programs in memory (RAM). A computer must load DOS before it can run either an application program or any of the operating system's programs. Most personal computers contain a small program stored in ROM that enables the computer to load DOS. This program is called the **bootstrap loader** and it begins operation as soon as you turn on the power switch to your computer. Thus, loading DOS is also called "booting the system."

Reading the DOS Prompt

Once you have successfully booted your computer, the DOS prompt appears. The DOS prompt (also called the system prompt) indicates that the computer is ready to respond to a command entered at the keyboard. The basic DOS prompt includes the default drive name (A:, B:, or C:) followed by a greater-than sign. On a single- or dual-drive system (where the default drive is A:) the prompt will appear as

```
A>
```

On a hard disk system where the single hard disk is designated as drive C:, the prompt will appear as

C>

The prompt indicates the default drive—that is, the disk drive where DOS will automatically look for data, an executable file, or a program file. Simply typing a different drive letter (followed by a colon) will change the default drive to the drive indicated.

The drive letter displayed is called the *drive designator*. The most common drive designations you will encounter include:

A: the first floppy drive attached to your computer system
B: the second floppy drive attached to your system
C: the first hard drive attached to your system
D: the second hard drive attached to your system or a CD-ROM drive
E: often a CD-ROM drive, if you have two hard drives attached to your system
F: a network drive, if your system is attached to a network

NOTE *In this text, we assume that you have booted from a hard disk and that the hard disk is drive C:. Unless otherwise indicated, the default drive will be C:.*

Correcting a Typing Mistake Before Pressing the Enter Key

As you begin using DOS commands, it is important for you to know how to correct misspelled entries. The Backspace key or ← arrow key can be used to correct typing errors at the DOS prompt. As the Backspace or the ← key is pressed, the right-most character after the DOS prompt (also called the *command line*) is erased.

If a line has several errors, it is easier to press the Esc key and retype the entire command line. When you press the Esc key at the DOS prompt, a backslash (\) character will appear. The cursor will move down one line on the screen but will not redisplay the prompt. Even though the command line with the error(s) still appears on the screen, it is deleted from memory. The system then waits for you to type the corrected command and press the Enter key to execute the command.

NOTE *If the NumLock key is toggled on, the ← arrow key on the numeric key pad produces the number 4 rather than erasing the right-most character on the command line. In fact, each of the arrow keys on the numeric key pad will produce numbers. If the arrow keys are producing numbers, simply press NumLock once. However, if you have a 101-key keyboard with two separate pads (one a 10-key numeric pad and the other a cursor movement pad), you can use the cursor movement pad whether the NumLock key is toggled on or off.*

Stopping a Command in Progress

There may be times when you need to terminate a DOS command before it completes. Most commands may be interrupted by using the following process:

- Press Ctrl Break simultaneously.

- Release both keys.

- The DOS prompt will reappear and you can type another command.

After you press [Ctrl][Break], execution of the command will halt as soon as the central processing unit (CPU) recognizes the break signal. Depending on the command that you are attempting to interrupt, you may see an immediate response, or the execution of the command may continue to completion.

On earlier keyboards the [Break] key notation can be found on the [Scroll Lock] key. The top of the key says "Scroll Lock" while the front face of the key is labeled "Break." The PS/2 and most 101-key keyboards have a separate key for the Pause/Break function and the Scroll Lock function. In this latter case, you will want to use the key with the Break label.

You can also press the [Ctrl][C] (for "cancel") key combination instead of [Ctrl][Break]. These two key combinations have identical results.

Booting Your PC

The steps required to start your PC are simple and straightforward. They are provided in Guided Activity 2.1. Before completing that activity, however, you need some background information.

Most PC systems include a hard drive on which DOS, application programs, and data files are stored. DOS is typically installed on the hard disk to make it easy to load the operating system and begin computing tasks. Unless your PC is configured otherwise, the bootstrap program looks at drive A: first to see if there is a bootable floppy disk in the drive. This is a holdover from the ancient days of PC computing (all of a dozen years ago!) when every system had one or two floppy drives (but no hard drives) and DOS was loaded from drive A:. If you try to boot your system with a data disk in drive A: that does not include the needed system files, the screen will display an *error message* and you must remove the disk before you can boot your system. In summary, assuming that your system has a hard drive with DOS installed on it, you should be sure that drive A: does not hold a floppy disk when you first boot your PC.

Booting your PC simply means turning on the power switch. On an IBM PC, XT, or AT the switch is located at the back of the right side of the system unit (the box under the monitor). With the PS/2 the switch is located on the right front of the system unit. Some monitors are powered on at the same time as the system unit; however, other monitors have their own power switch. Check to be sure the monitor is turned on. When the switch is pressed toward the bottom of the system unit, the computer is turned off. When its pressed up, the computer is turned on. The power switch on your PC may be labeled with the 0 and 1 symbols to indicate the On and Off positions. The 0 represents the Off position and 1 is used to identify the On position.

When your computer is first powered-up, it goes through a power-on self-test (POST) that can take from 3 to 90 seconds, depending on the speed of the machine. When the test is complete, the computer checks drive A: for a disk. If none is present, it goes to the hard disk and tries to read portions of DOS into memory.

On newer PC compatibles and IBM PS/2 computers, the date and time are automatically saved and maintained by the computer—even when turned off. This is possible because the computer includes a battery that powers the CMOS—that part of the computer operating system that includes date, time, and your system's configuration. If you are *not* prompted to enter date and time, you can probably assume that your computer maintains an internal date and time clock.

GUIDED ACTIVITY 2.1

Starting Up (Booting) Your Personal Computer

In this Guided Activity, you will start up your PC. We assume that your workstation is equipped with one or two floppy disk drives and a hard disk.

NOTE *If you are working on a network workstation or in a computing lab, ask your instructor how to access the DOS prompt. In a network environment (whether in the classroom or office) or in a computing lab, your computer may display a menu when it is first booted. Accessing the DOS prompt may be one of the options on that menu. Even stand-alone workstations may use a menu system. When in doubt, ask your instructor.*

You may also find that your workstation automatically loads Windows—a graphical user interface that uses icons, windows, and menus to make the operating system easier to use. If this occurs, ask your instructor how to exit Windows to the DOS prompt. Do not *complete the Guided Activities in this text from within Windows.*

1. Be sure that floppy disk drive A: is empty.

2. Turn on your personal computer.

3. Watch the monitor screen until the DOS prompt appears.

4. If needed, adjust the contrast controls on the monitor to a comfortable level. Most monitors have at least a brightness and contrast knob.

5. If prompted for date, enter it and then press the ⌨Enter key.

   The DATE command will be discussed later in this unit. For now, simply enter the date using the format M-D-YY or MM-DD-YYYY where MM or M equals the number of the month, DD or D equals the day of the month, and YY represents the year. For instance, September 12, 1994, would be entered as

   9-22-94

6. If prompted for time, enter it and then press the ⌨Enter key.

   The TIME command will be discussed later in this unit. For now, simply enter the time using the format HH:MM on a 12-hour basis. In other words, 8:15 a.m. is entered as 8:15, and 2:44 p.m. is entered as 2:44p. The p is added for any "after noon" times.

7. Type VER and press ⌨Enter to display the current version of DOS in use.

Unless your computer has an AUTOEXEC.BAT file (discussed in Unit 11), which automatically executes certain DOS commands or loads a menu, the monitor should now display the DOS prompt shown in Figure 2.3.

FIGURE 2.3
The DOS prompt after booting your system

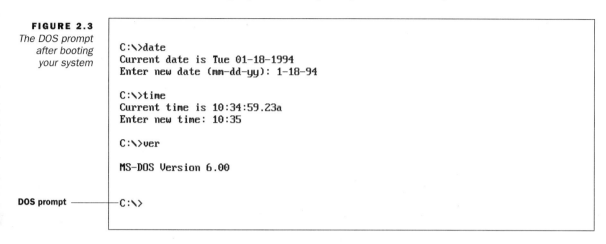

```
C:\>date
Current date is Tue 01-18-1994
Enter new date (mm-dd-yy): 1-18-94

C:\>time
Current time is 10:34:59.23a
Enter new time: 10:35

C:\>ver

MS-DOS Version 6.00


C:\>
```

DOS prompt ————— C:\>

If you see the DOS prompt, continue with the remaining steps in this Guided Activity. If you do not see the DOS prompt, proceed to the next Guided Activity.

8. Type PROMPT PG and press [Enter].

The last step changes the DOS prompt to indicate the current drive and subdirectory. It may not be neccessary on your computer, depending on the appearance of your DOS prompt. Later in the text, the PROMPT command is discussed further. At this point, the default directory should be the *root directory* and the DOS prompt should appear as

   C:\>

The backslash (\) indicates the beginning or root directory on your disk.

The preceding steps will prepare the system for any of the Guided Activities in this text. *These steps will not be repeated in each Guided Activity.*

GUIDED ACTIVITY 2.2

Exiting from the DOS Shell

This Guided Activity enables you to exit from the version 6.0 DOS Shell (discussed later in the text). If your screen appears similar to Figure 2.4, your computer is set up to automatically load the DOS Shell when it is turned on. If your screen does not appear similar to Figure 2.4 and you do not have the DOS prompt displayed on the screen, ask your instructor for assistance.

1. Press the [Alt] key once.

2. Type F to select the File command.

3. Type X to select the Exit option.

```
                                        MS-DOS Shell
     File  Options  View  Tree  Help
     C:\
     ⊟A    ⊟B    ■C    □D    ⊚E    □G    □H

    ┌──────── Directory Tree ────────┐┌──────────── C:\*.* ────────────┐
    │ 📁 C:\                       ↑ ││ 📇 AUTOEXEC.BAK      656  05-11-93 ↑│
    │   ├─⊞ ACCESS                   ││ ☐  AUTOEXEC.BAT      657  05-13-93 │
    │   ├─⊞ APW                      ││ 📇 AUTOEXEC.B~K      611  05-11-93 │
    │   ├─📁 ARC                     ││ 📇 CHKLIST .MS       216  02-21-93 │
    │   ├─📁 ARIS                    ││ ☐  COMMAND .COM   52,925  03-10-93 │
    │   ├─⊞ ASCEND                   ││ 📇 CONFIG  .BAK      325  04-08-93 │
    │   ├─📁 AW                      ││ 📇 CONFIG  .B~K      316  04-16-93 │
    │   ├─📁 BACKIT                  ││ 📇 CONFIG  .SYS      351  05-11-93 │
    │   └─📁 BIN                   ↓ ││ 📇 DBLSPACE.ERR      304  01-09-93 ↓│
    ├────────────────────────────── Main ──────────────────────────────┤
    │ ☐  Command Prompt                                                ↑│
    │ ☐  Editor                                                         │
    │ ☐  MS-DOS QBasic                                                  │
    │ ▦  Disk Utilities                                                 │
    │                                                                   │
    │                                                                  ↓│
    └───────────────────────────────────────────────────────────────────┘
     F10=Actions   Shift+F9=Command Prompt                        8:28a
```

The DOS prompt should appear at this point and look similar to the following:

    C>

You have simply exited from the DOS Shell by completing the last three steps.

4. Type PROMPT PG and press the [Enter] key.

    The last step changes the DOS prompt to indicate the current drive and subdirectory. Later in the text, the PROMPT command is discussed further. At this point, the default directory should be the *root directory* and the DOS prompt appears as

    C:\>

    The backslash (\) indicates the beginning or root directory on your disk.

    The preceding steps will prepare the system for any of the Guided Activities in this text. *These steps will not be repeated in each Guided Activity.*

Changing the Default Drive

There will be times when you want to change the default drive at the DOS level. Remember that DOS commands are executed on the default drive unless you include another drive designation. Before you try these steps, you must have a formatted disk (to be discussed soon in this unit) inserted in the designated drive. If no disk is present, you will see an error message similar to that shown in Figure 2.5. After explaining how to change drives, we'll discuss how to recover from an error when the drive does not have a disk in it.

The following steps are listed as a reference, not as a Guided Activity. Do not complete these steps until you have read further and have formatted a disk. *Each of the following steps will work only if you have the designated drive attached to your system.*

FIGURE 2.5

*Using the Fail
option*

```
C:\>A:


Not ready reading drive A
Abort, Retry, Fail?F
Current drive is no longer valid>
Not ready reading drive A
Abort, Retry, Fail?
Abort, Retry, Fail?f
```

The process to change the default drive to drive A: is as follows:

- Be sure that a formatted disk is in drive A:.

- At the DOS prompt, type A:

- Press the [Enter] key.

The process to change the default drive to drive B: is as follows:

- Be sure that a formatted disk is in drive B:.

- At the DOS prompt, type B:

- Press the [Enter] key.

The process to change the default drive to drive C: (your hard disk) is as follows.

- At the DOS prompt, type C:

- Press the [Enter] key.

Recovering from the Drive "Not Ready" Error Message

If you attempt to change the default drive to drive A: and that drive does not have a formatted disk in it, you will see a message that states

```
Not ready reading drive A
Abort, Retry, Fail?
```

A similar message appears if you attempt to use other DOS commands that act upon a drive without a formatted disk in it.

To recover from this error message, you can do one of the following:

- Type A to select the Abort option, whereupon control returns to the previous default drive.

If the above step does not work and your computer continues trying to read drive A:, complete the following steps.

- Insert a disk in the target drive (drive A: in this example), then

- Type R to select the Retry option, whereupon you should be logged onto the new drive.

If either of the first two actions is not successful and you do not see the DOS prompt, try the next option.

- Type F to select the Fail option. (The Fail option means that your computer system will continue to execute commands as best it can, even if the drive is not ready. The results can be unpredictable, and selecting this option is not recommended unless you cannot get the Abort or Retry options to work. The Fail option is recommended only if you continue on with the next step, which resets the default drive to your hard disk, drive C:.)

- When the message "Current drive is no longer valid>" appears (as shown in Figure 2.6), type a valid drive designation such as C: and press [Enter].

After completing the second step above, your screen should appear as shown in Figure 2.6. You can now proceed to execute other DOS commands.

Just remember, when your screen appears as shown in Figure 2.6, you can type the drive designation (A:, B:, C:, D:, and so on) for any drive that is ready and then press the [Enter] key.

FIGURE 2.6
Screen activity after switching back to a valid drive

```
C:\>A:


Not ready reading drive A
Abort, Retry, Fail?F
Current drive is no longer valid>C:

C:\>
```

Warm Booting Your Computer System

A *warm boot* restarts your computer electronically rather than mechanically (as in a cold boot, or turning the system off and then back on). It saves time by eliminating the power-on self-test (POST) routine on most computers and also reduces wear and tear on the system's mechanical parts. Further, you reduce the possibility of damaging the electronic parts of your system by an electrical surge that may accompany turning the machine off and then back on.

There may be occasions when you wish to restart your computer without turning it off. This can occur when the PC system appears to lock up or you encounter other problems. In a microcomputer training lab, you may find another program already loaded on the computer you are assigned to use. Unless you are familiar with the program, you will not know how to exit the program. The following procedure can be used, but only if you cannot exit the program in a normal fashion—that is, using a command within the program to exit or quit.

Warm Booting a Hard Disk System

The procedure for restarting a hard disk system is outlined in these steps.

- Clear drive A: of any disk it may contain.

- To reboot your system and load DOS, press [Ctrl][Alt][Del]; that is, hold down the [Ctrl] and [Alt] keys, then press the [Del] key once. After pressing the [Del] key once, release the [Ctrl] and [Alt] keys.

- When the in-use disk drive light goes off, the DOS prompt (C>) will be displayed on the screen, unless the system is set up to automatically load the DOS Shell. The DOS Shell was introduced in version 4.0. For all Guided Activities in this text, we assume the DOS Shell is not automatically installed. If the DOS Shell appears when you start your system, exit from the DOS Shell as shown in Guided Activity 2.2.

- If necessary, adjust the contrast and brightness controls on the monitor if the text is too bright, too faded, or not visible.

Shutdown Procedures

When finished with the computer, it is critical to exit properly from any application program in use. Here are some guidelines:

- Make sure you have followed the regular exit procedure for the program you are using. This allows your application to close files properly and complete any housekeeping procedures needed (such as warning you if you have modified a file without subsequently saving the revised document). Failure to follow such procedures can result in the loss of data.

- Unless you are using a menu system, after exiting an application program you will automatically return to the DOS level and see the DOS prompt. Before removing any disks, be sure that the red in-use light (for each disk drive) is not lit.

CAUTION *Disks should* always *be removed from the disk drives before the system unit is turned off.*

- If you know that you or someone else will be using the system within a short period of time, it is advisable to leave the system on (to minimize wear and tear on the mechanical parts and potential damage to the electronic parts of the computer). If the machine is left on, turn down the contrast control button on the monitor. This protects the monitor from having an image burned into the screen. Software that automatically blanks your screen after a predetermined time period (one to ten minutes) may be used, eliminating the need to dim the screen with the contrast or brightness dial. Common *screen saver programs* sold commercially include Burnout, After Dark, Intermission, and VGA Dimmer.

Housekeeping Commands

In a symbolic sense, at this point you have found the key to your computing kingdom, entered your apartment (or house), turned on the lights, and are now ready to take up "housekeeping." The remainder of this unit covers five common DOS commands: DIR (the directory command), CLS (to clear the screen), PROMPT (to alter your DOS prompt), DATE, and TIME (to alter the system date and time, respectively).

Setting Up Your Data Disk

To get involved in hands-on activities as soon as possible, you will first need to format and copy several files using two additional DOS commands: FORMAT and COPY. These commands are explored in more detail in the following units. At this time, do not worry about how or why they work. In the following Guided Activity, follow the directions carefully and you will create your own copy of West Student Data Disk #1 with specific files that are needed to complete the Guided Activities in this text.

GUIDED ACTIVITY 2.3

Setting Up Your Data Disk

In this Guided Activity, you will format a blank, new disk and then copy files to it from your computer's hard disk. You will use DOS commands that have not been explained yet—that is OK. Simply follow the step-by-step directions. *If any of these steps should be changed or modified, your instructor will tell you.* By the time you finish the following two units, you will be exposed to the commands used in this Guided Activity and understand how and why they are used here.

NOTE *It is important that you include the A: in the following command line!*

1. At the DOS prompt, type FORMAT A:/U and press 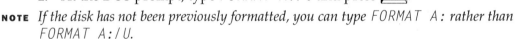.

NOTE *If the disk has not been previously formatted, you can type* FORMAT A: *rather than* FORMAT A:/U.

2. When you see the screen message prompting you to insert a disk in drive A: (as shown in Figure 2.7), insert a blank disk into drive A:.

FIGURE 2.7
Initial FORMAT command prompt

```
C:\>FORMAT A:/U
Insert new diskette for drive A:
and press ENTER when ready...
```

Be sure the disk in drive A: does not include files that you or anyone else will need. All files on the disk will be erased if you proceed.

3. After the disk is in the drive, press the [Enter] key to proceed.

   As the disk is formatted, you will see a screen prompt indicating the percentage of the disk that is formatted.

4. After seeing a "Format complete" message, you are prompted for a volume label. Type your last name followed by a space and then your first name, then press [Enter]. You can only use 11 characters in a volume label; DOS simply drops any extra characters.

   When the "Format another (Y/N)?" prompt appears, your screen will appear similar to Figure 2.8.

FIGURE 2.8
The FORMAT command screen messages

```
C:\>FORMAT A:/U
Insert new diskette for drive A:
and press ENTER when ready...

Formatting 1.44M
Format complete.

Volume label (11 characters, ENTER for none)? BACON JONATHAN

    1457664 bytes total disk space
    1457664 bytes available on disk

       512 bytes in each allocation unit.
      2847 allocation units available on disk.

Volume Serial Number is 0937-1203

Format another (Y/N)?
```

5. When prompted to "Format another (Y/N)?", type N and press [Enter].

6. You have formatted your West Student Data Disk #1. Now remove the disk, write the following data on a label (using a felt tip pen only), then attach the label to the disk.

   - West Student Data Disk #1

   - Your full name

   - The course number and title

   - Your instructor's name

7. Place the disk back in drive A: and continue.

   In the following steps, you will copy files to the disk.

8. At the DOS prompt, type CD\WESTDATA.DS6 and press the [Enter] key.

The CD command will be discussed later, in Unit 5. The command you entered changes the current directory to a subdirectory where your instructor has stored 44 files needed to proceed with subsequent Guided Activities. If your instructor has stored these files on a different drive or in a different subdirectory, your instructor will tell you how to change the command in step 8.

Your DOS prompt should appear as C:\WESTDATA.DS6.

9. Type COPY *.* A:/V and press the [Enter] key.

You will see a list of files as they are copied. When the process concludes, the screen displays the message

    44 file(s) copied

10. Type CD\ and press the [Enter] key to return to the root directory on your hard drive.

You are now ready to continue with the subsequent Guided Activities in this text.

The Directory Command: What's on That Disk?

When you go to a restaurant, you expect to see a menu to determine which foods are available. When you play a phonograph record or compact disc, you look for a listing of songs—and may select a single track or side rather than the entire sound track. Large office buildings include a ground-floor directory of all offices and services. As a consumer or user, you expect some kind of listing or directory information. DOS is no different. To find a program or data on disk, you must be able to view a list and select your option.

FIGURE 2.9
Directory listing generated by the DIR command

```
C:\>DIR A:

 Volume in drive A is DATADISK
 Volume Serial Number is 3071-13EB
 Directory of A:\

MISC     ZIP    24327 10-13-91   8:17p
CHANGING PM4      225 05-08-93   7:31p
PUBLISH  TXT      265 10-04-88   7:59p
SAYING   TXT      193 10-04-88   7:51p
STRATS2  DOC     4019 10-13-91   8:02p
STRATS1  DOC     4074 10-13-91   8:04p
STRATS1  TXT     2056 10-19-91   3:15p
STRATS2  TXT     1908 10-19-91   3:15p
HUMOROUS PM4       91 05-08-93   7:41p
WAR      DOC     1946 10-13-91   8:24p
WAR      WP      1244 10-13-91   8:24p
WAR      TXT      121 01-18-94  11:19a
        12 file(s)     40469 bytes
                      676864 bytes free

C:\>
```

The basic DIR (directory) command provides five columns of information regarding files on the target disk. Figure 2.9 displays a typical directory listing for a 720KB disk. The first two columns indicate the file name and extension, respectively. Notice that when the file name and extension are listed, the space character rather than a period is used as a delimiter. Additionally, the DIR command displays the size of the file in bytes (column 3), the *creation date* (column 4), and *creation time* (column 5).

NOTE *Beginning with DOS version 6.2, numbers greater than one thousand that are displayed by the DIR command will include commas as the thousands separator. Figure 2.9 was captured using DOS 6.0. As an example, if that figure had been captured using DOS 6.2, the bytes free at the bottom of the screen should appear as 676,864 rather than 676864.*

The file creation date indicates when the file was first created or the last date the file was altered. Likewise, the file creation time indicates the last time the file was altered. The accuracy of this date and time stamp is contingent on the accuracy of the system's date and time. (Setting the system date and time is discussed shortly.) At the beginning of the directory listing, the volume label of the disk is indicated, followed on the second line by a randomly assigned serial number. At the end of the directory listing, the command indicates how many files are present, how many bytes are used by the files on the disk, and how many bytes are still available.

NOTE *Not all disks are given a volume label when formatted. Unlike the DIR command listing shown in Figure 2.9 (which has a volume label of DATADISK), if no label was assigned when the disk was formatted, the DIR command will indicate that the "Volume in drive…has no label."*

Stopping That Scrolling Screen

If the directory listing created by executing the DIR command is more than 22 lines, the first part of the information will scroll off the screen (the screen actually can display 25 lines, but only 22 file names at a time). Unless you are a speed reader, you cannot see the detail on the first few files. To assist in solving the problem, DOS allows you to *suspend* the scrolling by pressing the [Ctrl][S] key combination or by pressing the [Pause] key. Remember that the [Ctrl] key is used like the [Shift] key: press it down and hold it while you press the second key once.

The specific process is as follows:

- Hold down the [Ctrl] key with one finger

- Press S

- Release the [Ctrl] key

To allow DOS to resume displaying the remainder of the DIR command listing, press any key on the keyboard. The [Ctrl][S] key combination works to stop the scrolling on any DOS command that generates a screen listing.

On a fast personal computer (running 16 MHz or faster), using the [Ctrl][S] key combination or the [Pause] key is not very effective. The text can scroll off the screen before you can press the keys. In the next section of this unit, we'll discuss a more effective method of pausing the information generated on the screen by the DIR command.

DIR Command Switches

Prior to the release of DOS 5.0, only two switches were available for use with the DIR command (the new switches are covered later in this unit). The first displays a horizontally oriented file listing (a "wide" listing). When you add the /W switch to the DIR command, as shown in Figure 2.10, less data is displayed on each file, but more files are listed per screen. Notice that the data on file size plus the date and time stamp information are not displayed. To see a horizontal listing of all files on drive A:, the command form would be

```
DIR A:/W
```

An additional switch avoids the need to use the [Ctrl][S] keys to suspend the scrolling of the screen display. The /P switch causes the output from the DIR command to pause once it fills the monitor screen. This is referred to as *page mode*, because one page (screen) of text is displayed at a time. You can press any key to cause the next page of the listing to scroll onto the screen. When using the /P switch, 22–23 lines of the detail will be displayed before the scrolling pauses. The last line on the screen prompts you to "Press any key to continue…" with the directory listing. The syntax required to use this command for a page-at-a-time directory listing of drive C: would be

```
DIR C:/P
```

The /P and /W switches can be used together.

FIGURE 2.10
Typical horizontal file listing caused by the DIR/W command

```
C:\>DIR A:/W

 Volume in drive A has no label
 Volume Serial Number is 2318-18DE
 Directory of A:\

ALIGN.DOC       BECOMING.TXT    CLASSES.DB      CLASSES.DBS     MISC.ZIP
DIDYUNO.PM4     MOM1.DOC        DASHIT-1.DOC    WAR.DOC         DIET.BAK
DINOSAUR.DOC    FAMOUS.DB       FAMOUS.DBS      FLAGS.BAK       FLAGS.DOC
INDEFENS.DOC    JUNK.DB         JUNK.DBS        MOM2.BAK        CHANGING.PM4
MOM3.BAK        DIET.DOC        MONSTERS        MYSTERY.TXT     MOM2.DOC
PUBLISH.BAK     MOM3.DOC        SAYING.TXT      HUMOROUS.PM4    WIN_MODE.DOC
ALIGN.WP        PUBLISH.TXT     TODOLIST.DOC    WINNEWS1.DOC    TRUCKIN.TXT
DINOSAUR.WP     STRATS2.DOC     STRATS1.DOC     STRATS1.TXT     WAR.WP
PAPER.WP        STRATS2.TXT     PAPER.TXT       WAR.TXT
        44 file(s)        65766 bytes
                        1379328 bytes free

C:\>
```

GUIDED ACTIVITY 2.4

Listing Files with the DIR Command

In this Guided Activity, you will use the DIR command to view a listing of all files on West Student Data Disk #1, created earlier in this unit. In this activity, you are assumed to be logged on to drive C: (your hard disk).

FIGURE 2.11
*The end of the
DIR command
screen listing*

```
MYSTERY   TXT       91 10-06-88    7:03p
MOM2      DOC      667 10-04-88    7:44p
PUBLISH   BAK      255 10-04-88    7:54p
MOM3      DOC     1536 10-04-88    7:43p
SAYING    TXT      193 10-04-88    7:51p
HUMOROUS  PM4       91 05-08-93    7:41p
WIN_MODE  DOC     1429 10-12-91    9:18p
ALIGN     WP      2377 10-12-91    9:49p
PUBLISH   TXT      265 10-04-88    7:59p
TODOLIST  DOC       74 05-08-93    7:59p
WINNEWS1  DOC       23 05-08-93    7:56p
TRUCKIN   TXT      719 07-13-89    8:11a
DINOSAUR  WP        24 05-08-93    7:52p
STRATS2   DOC     4019 10-13-91    8:02p
STRATS1   DOC     4074 10-13-91    8:04p
STRATS1   TXT     2056 10-19-91    3:15p
WAR       WP      1244 10-13-91    8:24p
PAPER     WP      2879 05-08-93   11:23a
STRATS2   TXT     1908 10-19-91    3:15p
PAPER     TXT     1043 05-08-93   11:29a
WAR       TXT      121 01-18-94   11:19a
        44 file(s)       65766 bytes
                       1379328 bytes free

C:\>
```

1. Place West Student Data Disk #1 in drive A:.

2. To view the DOS files on drive A:, type `DIR A:` and press the ⎆Enter key.

   You will see a list of DOS file names scroll by on your monitor screen. The end of the list appears as shown in Figure 2.11.

NOTE *Remember that beginning with DOS version 6.2, numbers greater than one thousand that are displayed by the DIR command include commas as the thousands separator.*

GUIDED ACTIVITY 2.5

Listing Files Horizontally

In this Guided Activity, you will use the DIR command with the /W switch to display a horizontal listing of files on West Student Data Disk #1.

1. Place West Student Data Disk #1 in drive A:.

2. Type `DIR A:/W` and press ⎆Enter.

CHECKPOINT 2A What effect does the /W switch have on the DIR command?

Your screen will appear similar to Figure 2.10 when you use the DIR/W command.

GUIDED ACTIVITY 2.6

Using the DIR Command Paging Option

In this Guided Activity, you will use the DIR command with the page switch (/P). This switch invokes the page mode, displaying a full screen of text and then stopping. To continue the listing of files, press any key.

1. Type DIR A:/P and press [Enter].

    The volume label, volume serial number, directory path, and 19 files are displayed, then the screen suspends the scrolling and waits for you to press any key before resuming the listing.

CHECKPOINT 2B What effect does the /P switch have on the DIR command?

2. Press any key to continue and another 22 files are listed.

3. Press any key to continue and the remaining files are listed on the screen.

Clearing Clutter from the Console

As you work with the DIR command, you will find that the monitor screen displays the results of each DOS command executed. It shows you the directory listing, the DOS prompt, error messages, and the like. Soon you will realize that the screen displays a historical view of what has happened on your computer—at least until the old data scrolls off-screen. The bottom line of data is the most recent. Periodically, you may wish to clear the residue of old commands, rather than wait for the text to scroll off the screen. The CLS (clear screen) command clears the text from the screen and moves the DOS prompt (and cursor) to the *home position* on the screen. The home position is the upper-left-hand corner of the screen. Basically, the CLS command is used to clear the screen of unwanted characters or text to give you a clean slate for your work.

GUIDED ACTIVITY 2.7

Clearing the Monitor Screen

In this Guided Activity, you generate an error message and use the CLS command to clear the screen.

1. Type I DON'T KNOW THE FILE NAME at the DOS prompt.

2. Press [Enter].

3. The screen will respond with:

        Bad command or file name

    The words "I DON'T KNOW THE FILE NAME" are not recognized by the operating system as a command or file name, so DOS displays the above error message.

4. Type CLS and press the [Enter] key.

CHECKPOINT 2C Why did you use the CLS command?

The DOS prompt and cursor are now the only items on the screen.

HELP and FASTHELP: Two DOS Help Features

DOS 6.0 continues a trend begun with the addition of an *on-line Help* feature to DOS 5.0. The trend is to provide users with assistance and clarification without their having to turn to a shelf full of user's manuals. This is a common trend by many software manufacturers.

Fast Help for Users

For instance, with DOS 5.*x* or 6.*x*, if you are uncertain about the syntax or action of a specific DOS command, you can type the command name (or abbreviation) followed by the /? switch at the DOS prompt. The displayed information will clarify the purpose of the command and detail the parameters or switches that can be used with it. If you want to know more about the DIR command and see a complete listing of all of its switches, you can type

    DIR/?

and then press [Enter]. The result would be the text displayed in Figure 2.12.

Beginning with DOS 6.*x*, this type of help is called *fast help* and can also be invoked by using the FASTHELP command followed by a single parameter, which is

FIGURE 2.12
Screen response after issuing the DIR/? command or the FASTHELP DIR command

```
Displays a list of files and subdirectories in a directory.

DIR [drive:][path][filename] [/P] [/W] [/A[[:]attribs]] [/O[[:]sortord]]
    [/S] [/B] [/L] [/C[H]]

  [drive:][path][filename]  Specifies drive, directory, and/or files to list.
  /P        Pauses after each screenful of information.
  /W        Uses wide list format.
  /A        Displays files with specified attributes.
  attribs   D  Directories   R  Read-only files      H  Hidden files
            S  System files  A  Files ready to archive  -  Prefix meaning "not"
  /O        List by files in sorted order.
  sortord   N  By name (alphabetic)    S  By size (smallest first)
            E  By extension (alphabetic)  D  By date & time (earliest first)
            G  Group directories first   -  Prefix to reverse order
            C  By compression ratio (smallest first)
  /S        Displays files in specified directory and all subdirectories.
  /B        Uses bare format (no heading information or summary).
  /L        Uses lowercase.
  /C[H]     Displays file compression ratio; /CH uses host allocation unit size.

Switches may be preset in the DIRCMD environment variable.  Override
preset switches by prefixing any switch with - (hyphen)--for example, /-W.

C:\>
```

the name of the command that you want help with. For example, if you want fast help on the DIR command, at the DOS prompt you can type

FASTHELP DIR

and then press ⟦Enter⟧. The results are identical to using the /? switch, as shown in Figure 2.12.

You can also use the DOS 6.x FASTHELP command, without a parameter, to display a list of all DOS commands and a brief description of their function. If you type FASTHELP at the DOS prompt, your screen will display the first of several screens of text, as shown in Figure 2.13. Press any key to display the next page of the list of DOS commands—until the DOS prompt appears again.

FIGURE 2.13

The first screen of the FASTHELP command listings

```
For more information on a specific command, type FASTHELP command-name.
APPEND    Allows programs to open data files in specified directories as if
          they were in the current directory.
ATTRIB    Displays or changes file attributes.
BREAK     Sets or clears extended CTRL+C checking.
CD        Displays the name of or changes the current directory.
CHCP      Displays or sets the active code page number.
CHDIR     Displays the name of or changes the current directory.
CHKDSK    Checks a disk and displays a status report.
CLS       Clears the screen.
COMMAND   Starts a new instance of the MS-DOS command interpreter.
COMP      Compares the contents of two files or sets of files.
COPY      Copies one or more files to another location.
CTTY      Changes the terminal device used to control your system.
DATE      Displays or sets the date.
DBLSPACE  Sets up or configures DoubleSpace compressed drives.
DEBUG     Starts Debug, a program testing and editing tool.
DEFRAG    Reorganizes the files on a disk to optimize the disk.
DEL       Deletes one or more files.
DELOLDOS  Deletes the OLD_DOS.1 directory and the files it contains.
DELTREE   Deletes a directory and all the files and subdirectories in it.
DIR       Displays a list of files and subdirectories in a directory.
DISKCOMP  Compares the contents of two floppy disks.
---More---
```

The HELP Command: More Detail

Beginning with DOS 6.0, a more detailed on-line Help feature is available by using the HELP command. Like the FASTHELP command, HELP requires a single parameter, which is the name of the command you seek to learn about. HELP command messages are more detailed than the FASTHELP information. To display information on the DIR command, at the DOS prompt you can type

HELP DIR

and then press ⟦Enter⟧. The initial HELP command screen results for the DIR command are displayed in Figure 2.14.

FIGURE 2.14
The Help screen for the DIR command

Menu bar

Click here to "jump" to Notes section

Contents button

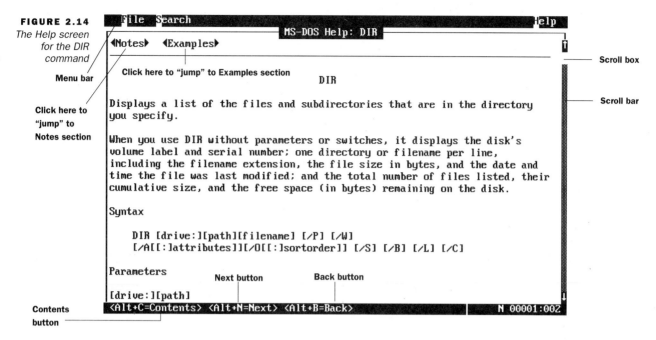

FIGURE 2.15
The HELP command Contents page

Menu bar

Jumps

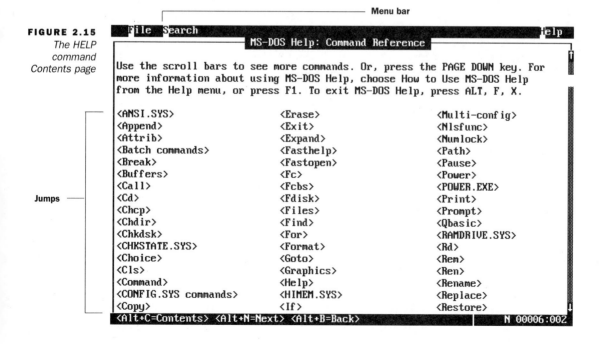

The HELP command is a complete on-line reference work. As with a dictionary or encyclopedia, you must know how to navigate within the reference to maximize its use. Understanding the structure of the on-line reference will help you learn to navigate effectively within the program.

Like any reference work, the HELP command has a table of contents. It can be displayed by typing HELP at the DOS prompt—without any parameter. Once invoked, the Contents page appears as shown in Figure 2.15.

Each command listed on the Contents page has an on-line reference that includes three sections of information:

- A Syntax section

- A Notes section

- An Examples section

Once you invoke the HELP command followed by a command name (such as HELP DIR), or once you select a command listed on the Contents page, the first screen encountered (shown in Figure 2.14) is the first page of the Syntax section. The Syntax section includes:

- A description of the command and its uses

- The command's syntax

- Each of the parameters or switches that work with the command

- Related DOS commands

The Notes section includes hints, clues, and information related to the command, while the Examples section provides specific examples of how to use the command with its more common parameters or switches.

Before viewing the list of keys that can be used to navigate through the Help reference, you need to understand that the HELP command uses character-based Jumps or buttons. Some of these Jumps are labeled in Figures 2.14 and 2.15. They are surrounded by greater-than and less-than symbols, as shown below:

```
<Notes>
<Examples>
```

NOTE *If you are using DOS 6.2, the HELP command Contents page has a new Jump at the top of the screen named* <What's New in MS-DOS 6.2?>.

Jumps are used throughout the on-line Help reference to allow you to "jump" to a specific topic or selection. Each screen also includes three buttons, located at the bottom of the screen. They are labeled on Figure 2.14 as follows:

`<Alt+C=Contents>`	the Contents button
`<Alt+N=Next>`	the Next button
`<Alt+B=Back>`	the Back button

Each HELP command screen will include one or more Jumps plus the three buttons listed. The following keystrokes are used to navigate through the on-line HELP command reference.

`[Tab]`	Moves to the next Jump (always moves from top of the page to the bottom, and from the left to the right)
`[Shift][Tab]`	Moves to the previous Jump
`[Enter]`	When the cursor has selected a Jump, pressing [Enter] moves to the selected topic and displays the desired help text on the screen

Additionally, if the text continues off the screen (as it does in Figure 2.14), you can use the cursor movement keys (⬆, ⬇, PgUp, PgDn, and so on) to scroll through the text.

You can also use the quick-key combinations for the three buttons (at the bottom of the screen) to move through the on-line reference. These keystrokes are as follows:

Alt C   to go to the Contents page

Alt N   to go to the next page

Alt B   to go back to the previous page

The on-line reference is structured just like a book. The commands are listed alphabetically, and within the "pages" for each command the Syntax section is listed first, followed by the Notes section, and concluding with the Examples section. For example, if you are on the Syntax page of the DIR command, Alt N will take you to the Notes section. If you press Alt N again, the Examples section is displayed. Pressing Alt N a third time will display the first page (Syntax section) of the next DOS command in alphabetical order. If you are viewing information on the DIR command, DISKCOMP is next in the on-line reference (DISKCOMP is covered in Unit 3).

You can use a mouse to navigate quickly through the on-line HELP command reference. To do so, simply point (with the mouse pointer) to the button or Jump you want, and click once. With a mouse, you can also use the scroll bar (right edge of the screen) to scroll through the text of each section. To do this, simply point at the scroll box (identified in Figure 2.14), click and hold the left mouse button, and drag the scroll box down (to move toward the end of the text) or up (to move toward the beginning of the text).

Printing Help Screen Information

At times, you may want a printed copy of the HELP command information. You can print the text from any Help screen by following these *keyboard* steps:

- Go to the Help screen you want to print.

- Press the Alt key.

- Type F to select the File command.

- Type P to select the Print option.

If using a *mouse*, simply complete these steps:

- Go to the Help screen you want to print.

- Point at the File command on the menu bar (identified in Figure 2.14) with the mouse pointer.

- Click the left button once.

- A menu will drop down and include a Print option.

- Click once on the Print option.

Exiting the HELP Command

When you are done searching for information using the HELP command, you must exit the on-line reference and return to the DOS prompt to execute another DOS command or load an application program. To exit the HELP command screen, you select the File command from the menu bar at the top of the screen and then select the Exit option. The *keyboard* process is as follows:

- Press the [Alt] key.

- Type F to select the File command.

- Type X to select the Exit option.

If using a *mouse*, simply complete these steps.

- Point at the File command on the menu bar with the mouse pointer.

- Click the left button once.

- When the menu drops down, click once on the Exit option.

GUIDED ACTIVITY 2.8

Using the HELP Command

In this Guided Activity, you will use the HELP command to learn more about the DIR command, then print the help topic. The HELP command will be used for all Documention Research questions posed in this textbook.

1. At the DOS prompt, type HELP and press the [Enter] key.

2. When the contents screen appears, press the [PgDn] key once.

3. Press the [↓] key until the <Dir> Jump button is selected, and then press the [Enter] key.

   Your screen should appear similar to Figure 2.14.

4. To exit the Help on-line reference, press [Alt][F], which selects the File command.

5. Type X to select the Exit option.

   In the following steps, you take a more direct route to the DIR command Help screens.

6. Type HELP DIR at the DOS prompt and press the [Enter] key.

7. Press the [PgDn] key until you have scanned through all the Syntax section text. A diamond in the middle of the screen, as shown in Figure 2.16, indicates the end of the text.

CHECKPOINT 2D How many Jumps are in the Syntax section of the DIR command help information?

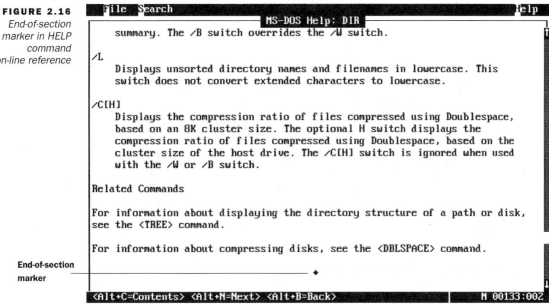

**End-of-section
marker**

8. Press 〔Alt〕〔N〕 or click on the Next button to move to the Notes section.

9. Scroll through the Notes section by pressing the 〔PgDn〕 key.

10. Press 〔Alt〕〔N〕 or click on the Next button to move to the Examples section.

11. Scroll through the Examples section by pressing the 〔PgDn〕 key.

12. Press 〔Alt〕〔C〕 or click on the Contents button to move to the Contents page.

13. Scroll through the Contents screen by pressing the 〔PgDn〕 key.

14. Press 〔Ctrl〕〔Home〕 to move back to the beginning of the list of commands.

15. Locate the <Dir> Jump button and select it again.

16. Move to the Examples section for the DIR command.

17. Press 〔Alt〕〔F〕 to select the File command.

18. Type P to select the Print option.

19. When the Print dialog box appears (shown in Figure 2.17), be sure the "Printer on…" radio button is selected. By default it should be. If it is not selected, which means the File radio button is selected, press the 〔↑〕 key once to select it.

20. Be sure that the printer is on and has paper loaded correctly, then press the 〔Enter〕 key or click on the OK button to start the pages printing.

21. Press 〔Alt〕〔F〕, 〔X〕 to select the File Exit command and return to the DOS prompt.

FIGURE 2.17
Print dialog box

Radio buttons
(only one can be
selected at a time)

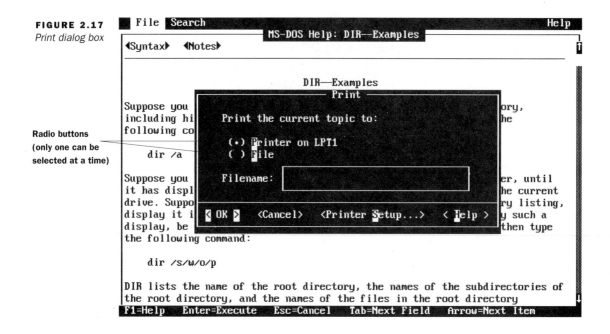

New DIR Command Switches

Beginning with DOS 5.0, several additional features were added to the DIR command. As shown in Figure 2.12 (using the fast help feature), you can now sort directory listings by name, extension, size, and date and time. You can also group subdirectories together at the beginning of the list. Additionally, beginning with DOS 6.0, you can sort files by the compression ratio. Compression ratios are discussed in Unit 3.

To order a directory listing, you must use the /O: switch followed by a character that signals the type of sort desired. The following switches accomplish these tasks:

/o:n Sorts by file name in alphabetical order.

/o:-n Sorts by file name in reverse alphabetical order.

/o:e Sorts by the file's extension in alphabetical order.

/o:-e Sorts by the file's extension in reverse alphabetical order.

/o:g Groups subdirectories first.

/o:-g Groups subdirectories last.

/o:s Sorts by file size (smallest first).

/o:-s Sorts by file size (largest first).

/o:d Sorts by date and time (earliest first).

/o:-d Sorts by date and time (most recent first).

/o:c Sorts by compression ratio (smallest to greatest compression).

/o:-c Sorts by compression ratio (greatest to smallest compression).

Keep in mind that the colon (:) is optional. You can choose not to use it if you wish. In the following Guided Activity, you use the colon only in the first couple of steps.

GUIDED ACTIVITY 2.9

Using the DIR Command Sort Options

In this Guided Activity, you will use the DIR command sort switches to display a listing of files in alphabetical order, in reverse alphabetical order, by file size, and in order by date.

1. With West Student Data Disk #1 in drive A:, type A: to log on to drive A:.

2. Type CLS and press the ⏎Enter key.

All of the following commands are effected on drive A:.

3. Type DIR D*.* and press the ⏎Enter key.

Notice that when you used the wild card character after the letter "D" you produced a list of all files (shown in Figure 2.18) beginning with the letter "D", but not in alphabetical order. You will use this same group of files in the following steps, but will sort them using the DIR command switches.

FIGURE 2.18
Listing of files beginning with letter "D"

```
A:\>DIR D*.*

 Volume in drive A has no label
 Volume Serial Number is 2318-18DE
 Directory of A:\

DIDYUNO  PM4        63 05-08-93    7:19p
DASHIT-1 DOC        18 05-12-93    8:12a
DIET     BAK      2560 11-10-87   11:54a
DINOSAUR DOC        26 05-08-93    7:51p
DIET     DOC      1310 08-15-91    8:15a
DINOSAUR WP         24 05-08-93    7:52p
        6 file(s)       4001 bytes
                     1379328 bytes free

A:\>
```

NOTE *In the following steps, the Order switch is the letter O, not the number zero (0).*

4. Type DIR D*.*/O:N and press the ⏎Enter key.

The files beginning with "D" are now in alphabetical order.

5. Type DIR D*.*/O:-N and press the ⏎Enter key.

The files beginning with "D" are now in reverse alphabetical order.

6. Type DIR D*.*/O:E and press the [Enter] key.

   The files beginning with "D" are now in order alphabetically by the extension. In the next and subsequent steps, we drop the colon.

7. Type DIR D*.*/OE and press the [Enter] key.

CHECKPOINT 2E What is the difference between the results of steps 6 and 7?

   In each of the subsequent steps, watch the results and notice how each switch works.

8. Type DIR D*.*/O-E and press the [Enter] key.

9. Type DIR D*.*/OS and press the [Enter] key.

10. Type DIR D*.*/O-S and press the [Enter] key.

11. Type DIR D*.*/OD and press the [Enter] key.

12. Type DIR D*.*/O-D and press the [Enter] key.

   You can also combine these switches with some of the ones you learned earlier. In the following steps, you first do a wide listing of files in alphabetical order and then use the /P switch with the switch that sorts the file names by size (using both the smallest first and largest first switches).

13. Type DIR *.*/ON/W and press the [Enter] key.

   Notice that the alphabetical listing goes left to right across the screen.

14. Type DIR/ON/W and press the [Enter] key.

CHECKPOINT 2F Is there any difference between the results of steps 13 and 14? Why or why not?

15. Type DIR/OS/P and press the [Enter] key.

16. Press any key until the listing is complete.

17. Type DIR/O-S/P and press the [Enter] key.

18. Press any key until the listing is complete (the screen displays the total number of files and bytes used).

Setting the System Date and Time

The DATE and TIME commands can be used either to set or to change, respectively, the system date or the system time. By "system date and time" we mean those values stored by the computer to represent the current date and the current time of day. Both the DATE and TIME commands are internal DOS commands and can be executed at any time the DOS prompt is displayed.

Early PCs did not have internal clocks and the user was required to enter the date and time whenever the machine was booted. That is seldom the case today. Your computer system likely has a battery-powered internal clock (called the *system clock*), and you probably are not prompted to enter date and time when booting the system. However, if you *are* prompted when starting your system, it is because the AUTOEXEC.BAT file (discussed in a later unit) includes the DATE and TIME commands.

Even with a battery-powered internal clock, the DATE and TIME commands are still useful and are used to correct or reset the date and time—such as when your geographical area goes on or off daylight savings time.

With or without an internal clock, once you use the TIME and DATE commands to establish the system time and date, those values are incremented automatically by the system. That is, the time and date will continue to be updated automatically. If you set the system time at 8:00 a.m. and work on your system for two hours, a check of the system time at the end of the two hours would show a current system time of 10:00 a.m. At the appropriate time (12 midnight), if your system remains on or has an internal battery-powered clock, the system date will change too. On computers with an internal battery-powered clock, the date and time remain current even after the power is turned off—as long as the computer's internal battery can power the internal clock.

Whenever a file is created, modified, or saved, the file is date- and time-stamped with the system date and time. Remember the listing under the DIR command? Those times and dates are derived from the system clock. If the system date and time are accurate, the date and time stamp will be accurate. When you begin copying files from one machine to another, often the only method of determining the most recent version is to check the date and time stamp for the file. Of course, this method works only if the system time and date were accurate when the file was saved to disk.

When your computer system prompts you for the current date and time, if the displayed date and time are accurate, you can take a shortcut and hit the [Enter] key to bypass entering the data. In the short run, it saves you time. In the long run, unless the displayed date and time are accurate, it defeats the purpose of date- and time-stamping your files.

The DATE Command

The DATE command is invoked at the DOS prompt by typing

```
DATE
```

followed by pressing the [Enter] key. The system displays the "Current date is" message and prompts you to "Enter new date (mm-dd-yy):." The DATE command takes entries in the following formats:

```
DD/MM/YY  or  DD/MM/YYYY
DD.MM.YY  or  DD.MM.YYYY
DD-MM-YY  or  DD-MM-YYYY
```

In these examples, DD represents the day of the month, MM is the number representing the month, and YY or YYYY is the year; that is, either 1994 or 94 may be entered for the year 1994. If the day of the month or the month itself can be accurately represented by a single digit, you do not need to pad it out with a leading zero. For instance, January 8, 1994, can be entered in any of the following formats:

```
01/08/94
1/08/1994
01/08/94
1/8/1994
01.8.94
1.8.1994
1-8-94
01-08-94
01-8-1994
```

The day, month, and year may be separated by a period, slash, or hyphen; it doesn't matter. The only valid dates recognized by DOS 6.*x* (and likewise DOS 4.*x* and DOS 5.*x*) are in the range beginning January 1, 1980, and ending December 31, 2099. Any year before 1980 is "prehistoric" in personal computer terms.

The TIME Command

The TIME command is invoked at the DOS prompt by typing

```
TIME
```

followed by pressing the [Enter] key. The system displays the "Current time is" message and prompts you to "Enter new time:." Beginning with DOS 4.*x*, you can respond to the TIME command using either a 12- or 24-hour format. That means that you can respond by listing the time as:

```
HH:MM or HH:MM or HH:MM:SS.hh
HH:MMA or HH:MMP or HH:MM:SS.hhA
```

In this form, HH represents the hours, MM the minutes, SS the seconds, and hh the hundredths of seconds. Seconds and hundredths of seconds are optional. If the time is after noon, you can enter the time on a 12-hour basis and include the "P" option. Or times can be entered on a 24-hour clock (military time) basis. For example, 9:15 p.m. can be entered as either

```
9:15p or 21:15
```

and 10:26 a.m. can be entered as either

```
10:26 or 10:26a
```

Like the DATE command, if the hours or minutes or seconds or hundredths of seconds can be accurately represented by a single digit, there is no need to pad the number out with a leading zero. The hours, minutes, and seconds can be separated from each other by periods or colons. The seconds and hundredths of seconds must be separated by a period. Thus, 7.09 seconds after 1:05 p.m. may be entered using any of these formats

```
13:05:07.09
13.5.7.9
1:05:07.09p
1:5:7.9p
1.5.7.9p
```

Remember, if your computer does not include an internal clock, changing the date or time only resets it for the current work session (that is, until the PC is turned off). Most computers now include an internal clock so that once you reset the date and time, it is stored by the computer—even if you turn the machine off, the time keeps ticking.

GUIDED ACTIVITY 2.10

Changing the System Date

In this Guided Activity, you modify the system date and experiment with different acceptable formats for entering the current date.

1. If you are not logged on drive C:, type C: and press the [Enter] key.

2. Type DATE and press the [Enter] key.

   The screen response for the DATE command will be similar to the following:

   ```
   C:\>DATE
   Current date is Tue 09-22-1994
   Enter new date (mm-dd-yy):
   ```

3. Type 01/01/80 and press the [Enter] key.

4. Type DATE and press the [Enter] key.

   The date is now set to 01-01-1980, based on the action you took in step 3.

5. Type 9.9.99 and press the [Enter] key.

6. Type DATE and press the [Enter] key.

   The new date is now listed as 09-09-1999. Notice that either the slash, period, or dash may be used as delimiters between the day, month, and year designations—but DOS will always display the dash format.

7. Type 13-30-94 and press the [Enter] key.

   DOS responds with an "Invalid date" error message and prompts you to "Enter new date." DOS cannot deal with a month 13 (neither can most people). It is an error and you are given the opportunity to correct it.

8. Type 01/01/01

   Ideally, this should be the date January 1, 2001.

9. Press the [Enter] key.

    DOS again responds with an error message. It cannot recognize a date beyond the year 1999 unless you enter all four digits of the year past 2000. DOS also cannot recognize a date prior to January 1, 1980.

10. Type 01-01-2001 and press the [Enter] key.

11. Type DATE and press the [Enter] key.

    The year 2001 was accepted and stored.

12. Enter today's date and press the [Enter] key.

CHECKPOINT 2G Why should you complete the last step?

GUIDED ACTIVITY 2.11

Changing the System Time

In this Guided Activity, the TIME command is used to set and update the system time.

1. Type TIME and press the [Enter] key.

    DOS will respond with the system time and prompt you to "Enter new time."

2. Type 10/30 and press the [Enter] key.

    DOS will give you an error message:

    ```
    Invalid time
    Enter new time:
    ```

    The time would have been acceptable if entered with a colon or period. The slash is an unacceptable delimiter between the number of hours and minutes.

3. Type 9:15p and press the [Enter] key.

NOTE *The p option is not accepted by versions of DOS prior to 4.x.*

4. Type TIME and press the [Enter] key.

    The time is now set. Since a few seconds have passed, the time should be in the range of 9:15:18:87p.

5. Enter the current time and press the [Enter] key.

CHECKPOINT 2H Why should you complete the last step?

Summary

In this unit, you learned to set the current date and time that will be stored and automatically incremented by your computer system. You also learned to boot your computer system, access on-line Help, clear the screen (and move the cursor to the home position on the screen), and display a listing of files on a disk in a variety of ways. These are fundamental tasks that you will use time and again as you work with your computer and its operating system.

Command Review

In this unit, you learned about several DOS commands. Most have optional parameters or switches. We have tried to cover both the common and the rarely used forms of each command. The following forms of this unit's commands are the most frequently used and should be reviewed carefully.

CLS	Clears the monitor screen and moves the DOS prompt and cursor to the home position (upper-left-hand corner).
DATE	Prompts you to set or change the system date.
DIR	Lists files on the current disk drive including file names, date and time created, size in bytes, total number of files, and total bytes free on the disk.
DIR/P	Causes the screen to stop scrolling after approximately 23 lines of information about the current drive are displayed.
DIR/W	Displays a horizontal directory of files on the current drive. Lists only file names, total number of files, bytes used, and bytes free on the disk.
HELP	Accesses the on-line Help reference that provides information on all DOS commands. The on-line Help screens list parameters, notes, and examples for each command.
PROMPT PG	Changes the DOS prompt to display the current path and drive, and concludes the DOS prompt with the greater-than sign.
TIME	Prompts you to set or change the current time.

Review Questions

The answers to even-numbered questions are contained in Appendix A.

1. What are function keys and where are they located?

2. Three keys on the PC keyboard are always used in combination with other keys. Name these three keys.

3. What is a toggle key? Name two toggle keys.

4. What does "warm booting" your system mean? What are the advantages of a warm boot?

5. Which command displays the creation date and creation time of a file?

6. Which command displays the size of a file in bytes?

7. What information is lost by using the /W switch with the DIR command?

8. Which switch causes the DIR command to pause after displaying a full screen of file names?

9. Define the home position.

10. Which DOS command moves the system prompt to the home position?

11. Which characters can be used as delimiters in both the DOS DATE and TIME commands?

12. Why is it important for your system date and time to be accurate?

13. Why would you enter a DOS command at the DOS prompt followed by the /? parameter?

14. Does DOS 6.*x* include an on-line Help reference? If so, how would you access the Contents page/screen?

15. How would you access, from the DOS prompt, a list of parameters for a DOS command, review notes on the command, and see examples of how the command can be used?

16. What is invoked (name it) when you use the /? parameter?

Key Terms

The following terms are introduced in this unit. Be sure you know what each of them means.

Bootstrap loader	Error message	Page mode
Command line	Fast help	Root directory
Creation date	Function key	Screen saver program
Creation time	Home position	System clock
Cursor movement pad	Mnemonic	Toggle key
Drive designator	On-line Help	Warm boot

Documentation Research

Documentation Research questions are included at the end of most units to encourage you to explore and discover the additional features available with DOS 6.*x*. All Documentation Research questions within the text can be answered by using the on-line reference (accessed by using the HELP command). Review Guided Activity 2.8 if you are unsure how to use the HELP command.

1. Identify which command, HELP or FASTHELP, has the less detailed display of information. Identify a source other than the textbook for your conclusion.

2. What does FASTHELP have to say about the CLS command?

3. How many related commands are listed for the DATE command? Name them.

4. How many related commands are listed for the TIME command? Name them.

5. How many parameters or switches are listed for the DATE command?

Disk Preparation Commands

Learning Objectives

At the completion of this unit, you should be able to

1. explain the uses of the FORMAT command,

2. format a nonsystem disk,

3. format a system disk,

4. preset the volume label when formatting a disk,

5. transfer the DOS files with the SYS command,

6. create a duplicate disk with the DISKCOPY command,

7. compare a newly created disk with the original,

8. understand the structure of a disk as a recording medium,

9. understand the benefits of disk compression,

10. compress files on a floppy disk.

Important Commands

DBLSPACE

DISKCOMP

DISKCOPY

FORMAT

SYS

All About Floppy Disks

When the IBM PC was introduced in 1981, *floppy disks* came in one size and variety—the *single-sided, single-density* 5.25-inch disk. Since that time, *double-sided*, *double-density*, *quad-density*, and *high-density* disks have appeared in both the 5.25-inch and 3.5-inch disk varieties. With the diversification in types of disks and disk drives, one fact remains constant: a disk is useless plastic and mylar unless it can store data, and it cannot do that until its surface is properly prepared. The largest percentage of floppy disks are sold over-the-counter *unformatted*. Preformatted disks are available, but the more common practice is to purchase unformatted disks and then format them on your machine.

Parts of a Disk

A disk must be *formatted* or *initialized* before use; that is, the surface must be prepared to hold data. The surface has no physical grooves, yet the magnetic placement of data and system files on a disk follows very rigid rules. For instance, each 720KB disk drive must read and write data in the same way as every other 720KB drive or there would be no way to transport programs or data from one machine to another. The same requirement holds for every other capacity disk drive.

Data on a disk is stored on *tracks* composed of tiny positive magnetic charges (each one represented by the binary value 1) or the absence of a magnetic charge (represented by the binary value 0). A computer's disk drive is built to read these charges from the tracks on the iron oxide surface of the disk. Although a disk can be compared theoretically to a phonograph record that stores music or sound, there are three important differences between a disk and a phonograph record.

First, the phonograph record comes with a removable jacket. To play the record, you remove the platter from the jacket. All varieties of PC disks come with a nonremovable jacket.

Figure 3.1 shows an exploded view of a 3.5-inch disk. The fixed plastic jacket protects the recording surface from damage and debris.

The second difference relates to how data is stored. The phonograph record stores sound in physical grooves; a disk has only magnetic tracks, not physical grooves on its surface.

FIGURE 3.1
*Exploded view
of a 3.5-inch
disk*

Finally, the sound on a phonograph is intended to be played sequentially; that is, from the first sound on the outer track to the final sound on the inside track. A disk can be read sequentially, but most often data is accessed in a random fashion. The tracks on a disk are divided into *sectors*, as well as ***allocation units*** (also called ***clusters***). Figure 3.2 shows the 40 concentric tracks of a 5.25-inch disk. A complete file may be stored in allocation units scattered around the disk on several tracks. Don't worry, the computer has a mechanism for remembering where all the parts of a file are stored. That mechanism is discussed shortly in the text.

Tracks and Sectors and Clusters and Things

The 360KB disk has 40 tracks, numbered 0 through 39 (as shown in Figure 3.2). The quad-density drive (1.2MB) found in the IBM AT and compatibles has 80

FIGURE 3.2
*Concentric
recording tracks
on a disk*

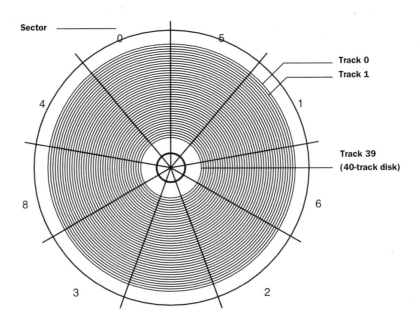

tracks—double the number found on a double-density disk. IBM PS/2 models use 3.5-inch disks (720KB, 1.44MB, or 2.88MB), which also have 80 tracks. The newest type of drive reads and stores data on a 2.88MB disk. It was introduced with the IBM PS/2 model 57 in 1991.

The concentric magnetic tracks run parallel to each other, as opposed to the corkscrew or spiral pattern found on a phonograph record. Each track is divided into sectors, or "sections of the track." On the 360KB and 720KB disks, there are 9 sectors per track, while the high-density 1.2MB disk has 15 sectors per track. Each sector contains 512 bytes. The smallest unit of disk space that a program can write to is called a cluster or allocation unit. An allocation unit is composed of two sectors (1KB) on a 360KB or 720KB disk and one sector (512 bytes) on a 1.2MB or 1.44MB disk (see Table 3.1). Hard disks use different variations, depending on the formatting scheme used. A hard disk may have one, two, or more sectors per cluster.

TABLE 3.1
Disk types with storage capacity and other information

TYPE OF DISK	360KB	720KB	1.2MB	1.44MB
STATISTICS FOR DATA DISKS				
Total bytes of disk space	362,496	730,112	1,213,952	1,457,664
Bytes in each allocation unit	1,024	1,024	512	512
Allocation units free on disk	354	713	2,371	2,847
Sectors per cluster	2	2	1	1
Tracks	40	80	80	80
Sectors per track	9	9	15	18
STATISTICS FOR SYSTEM DISK (IF DIFFERENT FROM ABOVE)				
Bytes used by three hidden system files	132,096	132,096	131,072	131,072
COMMAND.COM size	53,248	53,248	53,248	53,248
Allocation units free on disk	173	596	2,011	2,487

With the release of DOS 6.2, the operating system increased in size. Table 3.1 lists the data for DOS 6.0. With version 6.2, COMMAND.COM increased to 54,619 bytes and the three hidden system files increased in size to 142,950 bytes. As a result, the number of allocation units free on disk diminished to 159 (360KB disk), 518 (720KB disk), 1,983 (1.2MB disk), and 2,459 (1.44MB disk). All other data in Table 3.1 is the same for versions 6.0 and 6.2.

Remember that we are dealing with double-sided media. DOS considers the bottom of the disk (the side without the label) as side 0 and the top of the disk as side 1. Each side has a like number of tracks, sectors, and allocation units. For example, on a 360KB disk, the sectors are numbered 0 through 17, with sectors 0 through 8 on side 0 and tracks 9 through 17 on side 1. DOS numbers each cluster or allocation unit and uses that number to reference a specific area on the disk.

Zero for Zero: The Boot Record

Every disk has a *boot record* stored on side 0, track 0, sector 0. The boot record includes such data as the version of DOS on the disk, some basic error messages, and the names of any hidden system files stored on the disk. If the disk is a system disk, its boot record includes a small program that loads the system files and transfers control to them. The system files for MS-DOS 6.*x* are named IO.SYS, MSDOS.SYS, DBLSPACE.BIN, and COMMAND.COM. If no system files are on the disk, the boot record causes the following error message to appear.

```
Non-System disk or disk error
Replace and strike any key when ready
```

On a floppy-based system, if you see this message the disk in drive A: should be replaced by a *bootable* disk. If your system has a hard disk and you see the message, it could indicate one of two situations—the latter more serious than the first:

- You have a nonsystem disk in drive A:. DOS was unable to access the hard disk (drive C:) to find the system files because it encountered a disk in drive A:. In this case, open drive A:. On a 5.25-inch drive, unlatch it and press any key on the keyboard. On a 3.5-inch drive, press the disk eject button and then press any key. It is not really necessary to remove the disk. With the drive door open or unlatched, the disk will not be read.

- If there is no disk in drive A: and you still see the message, it means that the hard disk is not bootable. This could result from accidentally erasing the system files, damage to the disk, corruption of the system files or boot record, or loss of your system configuration in CMOS. Any of these can be a serious problem.

The cure for the latter occurrence is to reinstall the system files, using the SYS command (discussed at the end of this unit), which also copies COMMAND.COM to the root directory. If your hard disk has been damaged, there is still the possibility of booting the system off a floppy disk in drive A:, backing up all data, and then reformatting the hard disk. Often the use of the FORMAT command will cure the problem by marking bad sections of the disk as unusable (this should only be done after first attempting to back up as much data from the disk as possible). The worst problem would occur if the physical location where the boot record should be (side 0, track 0, sector 0) is damaged. In such a case, the disk is unusable as a system disk—this applies to both floppy and hard disks—unless a utility program is used to relocate the boot sector.

There Is FAT on Your Disk

The four sectors following the boot record are reserved for the *file allocation table* (FAT). The disk actually holds a duplicate record of the FAT because it is so essential to the operation of the disk. DOS does not use the second copy, but file/disk recovery utilities do use the second FAT in order to reconstruct the first file allocation table (should it be damaged). The FAT includes linked lists of all clusters or allocation units on the disk. In a sense, it is a map of the entire disk. This map includes an indication of which allocation units are bad (bad sectors are not used to store data), already in use (allocated), or free for use (nonallocated).

Each *bit* in the file allocation table represents an allocation unit on the disk. If the allocation unit is not currently allocated to a file or damaged, the bit stores that information. If the cluster is currently used by a file, the bit in the FAT will indicate the next allocation unit used by the file. In other words, the FAT includes forward-only pointers to each part of the file stored on disk.

When DOS stores files on disk, it looks for the first free allocation unit and begins saving the file in that allocation unit. Let us assume that each allocation unit on the disk contains two sectors of 512 bytes each, so each unit can store 1KB of data. If your file is just under 64KB in length, it will take 64 allocation units to store the total file. After saving, moving, deleting, modifying, and resaving files on a disk, there is a good chance that 64 *contiguous* (adjoining) sectors will not be found. Therefore, DOS starts at the beginning of the disk and stores the file piece-by-piece until the entire file is stored. The pointers in the FAT relieve worry about where the file is stored; it can be *fragmented* all over the disk and can still be retrieved if the FAT is OK. However, the more fragmented a file is, the slower it is loaded. There are commercial programs like Disk Optimizer, Norton's Speed Disk, and PC Tools that copy and recopy files until they are in contiguous sectors, thus speeding up access (read/write) time. Beginning with DOS 6.0, the operating system itself comes with a new utility program called DEFRAG. It can be used to optimize or defragment your hard disk or any disk. DEFRAG will be discussed in Unit 8.

If dealing with a floppy disk, you can unfragment files (without using DEFRAG) by simply formatting a new disk and then copying all files from the old disk to the new one. When files are first copied to a new disk, they are placed in contiguous sectors. It is only after copying, deleting, and recopying files that fragmentation occurs.

The Disk's Directory Table

The *directory table* is stored on disk immediately after the FAT. Using a 5.25-inch double-density disk as an example, the directory table includes sectors 5 through 11—seven sectors. Each directory listing provides information on one file on the disk. If your disk has a volume label, it uses one entry in the table. Each subdirectory (to be discussed more in later units) takes up an entry, as does each file on the disk.

Each entry uses 32 bytes to store information on a file, subdirectory, or volume label. Since each sector includes 512 bytes, each of the directory table sectors can include 16 entries. The 5.25-inch 360KB disk uses 7 sectors for the table for a total of 112 entries (16 entries times 7 sectors equals 112). On the 360KB disk you cannot have more than 112 files in the root directory, minus one for every subdirectory and minus one for the volume label, if used. As you might expect, when using a 1.2MB disk, the number of directory table sectors is doubled (to 14) and the number of file entries in the table increases to 224.

NOTE   *You can store more than 112 files on a 360KB disk by using subdirectories. Creating a subdirectory requires you to use one of the 112 file entries, but each subdirectory can store an unlimited number of file entries. The greater constraint on disk storage is disk space (bytes free) rather than the number of acceptable directory entries.*

TABLE 3.2
*Breakdown of
bytes in a
directory listing*

BYTE NUMBER	DESCRIPTION OF USE
0–7	Eight-character file name
8–10	Three-character file extension
11	The attribute byte. It indicates if the file is a hidden file, is a system file, or was modified since last backed up by the DOS BACKUP command. Each of the eights bits in this byte represent a different attribute. For instance, if the second bit is on (a binary 1, rather than a binary 0), the file is a hidden file. If the third bit is on (a binary 1), then the file is a system file. When you create a document file (using a word processor), both bits 2 and 3 are turned off because the file is neither a hidden file nor a system file.
12–21	Not used. Reserved for a future version of DOS.
22–23	Stores creation time. Two bytes (16 bits) can store the hexadecimal numbers to reflect the creation time within a two-second interval. That is, there are 86,400 seconds per day (24 hours times 60 minutes times 60 seconds). A two-place number to the power of 16 (using the hexadecimal numbering system) can store a number up to 65,536. That cannot quite handle a number representing every second in a day, but it can represent every other second in a day.
24–25	Stores the creation date. These two bytes are broken into 16 bits. The first seven bits can represent any year between 1980 and 1999. The next four bits represent the month and the final five bits represent the day of the month.
26–27	Is a pointer that points to the first allocation unit in the FAT where the file's data is stored.
28–31	Indicates the length of the file in bytes.

Each directory entry is 32 bytes long. Table 3.2 indicates the breakdown of each 32-byte entry, byte by byte.

As you can see, the DIR command gets its data from the directory table. The information on the boot record, FAT, and directory table is rather technical. It is presented to help you understand that the rules within DOS all have a necessary purpose. File names can only be eight characters in length because that is the maximum space allotted for the information in the directory table. File name extensions are limited for the same reason. As newer versions of DOS are released, the exact location of these tables may change. Further, the information in the tables may be enhanced or changed (remember those 10 unused bytes in the 32-byte directory table entry?). To memorize the exact number of sectors per track for each type of disk media is far less important than understanding how a disk is constructed and why.

Preparing a Disk with the FORMAT Command

The FORMAT command is the program provided by DOS to prepare the surface of a disk or hard disk to store data. Whether you use a hard disk, a 5.25-inch or 3.5-inch disk, you must use the FORMAT command before data can be stored on the *medium*. As such, it is one of the most essential DOS commands. Formatting a disk prepares the surface of the disk by creating magnetic tracks and removing any existing data. During the formatting process, DOS checks the surface of the disk for any blemishes or construction defects. If portions of the surface are flawed and cannot store data, the bad sectors or allocation units are marked as unusable. These bad sectors are never used by the computer when storing data to the disk. DOS uses two tables (already discussed) to keep track of files you store and the space still available to be used on the disk. The directory table and the FAT are created by the FORMAT command. After the disk is formatted, you will see a display on your monitor screen indicating the number of usable bytes, number of bytes in bad sectors, and total number of bytes on the disk.

NOTE *The FORMAT command erases all data from a disk. If you have any doubts about whether the contents are still needed, do not format the disk. Instead, use the DIR command to review the files and determine if they still have value to you. Even with the addition of the UNFORMAT command (introduced with DOS 5.0 and discussed later in Unit 7), you run the risk of not being able to retrieve files if you accidentally format the disk they are stored on.*

There are several optional forms of the FORMAT command. The options concern the physical format and density of the disk and whether it will be bootable after formatting. DOS often provides different variations of the same command. You indicate which variation you desire by using a parameter or switch. Parameters are items that clarify a DOS command by indicating the object (drive or file) that the DOS command will act upon. A switch turns on or off specific features of the command.

Often the computer needs additional information to tell the system exactly what is to be done. Some parameters are required, others are optional. If you do not include some parameters, a default value will be used by DOS.

In the following examples of the FORMAT command, you would substitute for the *d:* the drive that contains the disk to be formatted. Switches are separated from the DOS command with a slash (/) followed by one of several characters.

As you work through the Guided Activities, remember that FORMAT is an external DOS command. It must be available on disk before you can use it. In this text, we assume that you are working on a computer with a hard disk and that a PATH command statement (discussed in Unit 5) has been issued to enable the operating system to locate the DOS external commands. We assume that the DOS commands are in a separate directory (probably C:\DOS, C:\DOS6, or C:\DOS-V6) on your hard disk. If you cannot execute the DOS commands as outlined in the following activities, ask your instructor for assistance.

NOTE *If no PATH command had been issued and your DOS files are located in the C:\DOS subdirectory, you would have to precede all DOS external commands with the path to the command file. For instance: C:\DOS\FORMAT A:. Or you can issue the PATH command by typing* PATH=C:\DOS *and pressing the* ⏎Enter *key.*

Common FORMAT Parameters and Switches

Despite the vast array of possible FORMAT command parameters, there are really only a few that are practical for everyday use. Typically, you will need to know how to format the following types of disk:

- Hard disk

- 360KB 5.25-inch disk

- 1.2MB 5.25-inch disk

- 720KB 3.5-inch disk

- 1.44MB 3.5-inch disk

- 2.88MB 3.5-inch disk

You will probably also want to know how to use the quick-format option.

For the disk types listed above, you will want to create either a disk with the system files or a nonbootable disk. Nonbootable disks are used to store data. They have more free bytes because the two hidden system files and COMMAND.COM are not present. Bootable disks are used to boot the computer and load a specific application program when using a floppy disk-based system; that is, a PC without a hard disk.

Common versions of the FORMAT command available with DOS version 6.x are listed in Table 3.3.

TABLE 3.3 *Common versions of the FORMAT command*	**FORMAT d:** Creates a nonsystem 9 or 15 sector-per-track formatted disk. A nonsystem disk cannot be used to start (boot) your computer. It lacks several crucial files including COMMAND.COM (which contains the internal DOS commands). Beginning with DOS version 4.x, this form of the FORMAT command automatically asks for a volume label for the newly formatted disk. Earlier versions of DOS only prompted for a label if the /V switch was used. After attaching the volume label during the FORMAT process, you will see it displayed whenever you use the DIR or CHKDSK commands. CHKDSK is covered in Unit 7.
	FORMAT d:/Q Executes a quick format. This command can only be used on a disk that was previously formatted. It is a fast method of deleting existing files on the disk and reinitializing the disk.
	FORMAT d:/S Creates a bootable formatted disk (with the DOS operating system installed on it). A bootable disk can be used to start up your personal computer. With this switch, three hidden system files are installed on the disk. MS-DOS names the three system files IO.SYS, MSDOS.SYS, and DBLSPACE. Additionally, COMMAND.COM is installed. The three hidden files are not normally listed when you execute the DIR command—unless you use the /AH switch.
	FORMAT d:/U Performs an unconditional format. Once you format a disk with the /U switch, existing data on the disk cannot be retrieved because unformatting data is not preserved.

TABLE 3.3 *Continued*	FORMAT d:/V:name	Creates a formatted disk with the volume *name* indicated after the /V switch. (You would ordinarily use your name, the organization name, or other text identifier here.) The label cannot exceed 11 characters.

FORMAT d:/F:size	180KB SS 5.25-inch	/F:160, /F:180
	360KB DD 5.25-inch	/F:160, /F:180, /F:320, /F:360
	720KB DD 3.5-inch	cannot use /F switch
	1.2MB QD 5.25-inch	/F:160, /F:180, /F:320, /F:360, /F:1200
	1.44MB QD 3.5-inch	/F:720, /F:1440
	2.88MB HD 3.5-inch	/F:720, /F:1440, /F:2880

Creates a disk with storage in kilobytes corresponding to the size specified after the /F switch. You can format some disks to hold less storage (in memory) than the maximum memory the drive can read/write.

Formatting Low-Density Disks in High-Density Drives

You should be aware that when formatting different capacity disks in various types of disk drives, you need to use the /F: FORMAT command switch. For instance, this command switch is used to format a double-density disk in a high-density drive. Table 3.4 indicates which types of drives can format which types of disks and the FORMAT command switches that should be used. Each of the following examples assumes that the disk to be formatted is in drive A:.

TABLE 3.4
Types of disks that can be formatted in various floppy drives, plus the FORMAT commands and switches

DOUBLE-DENSITY 5.25-INCH DISK DRIVE	
360KB 5.25-inch disk	FORMAT A:
1.2MB 5.25-inch disk	cannot format
720KB 3.5-inch disk	cannot format
1.44MB 3.5-inch disk	cannot format
2.88MB 3.5-inch disk	cannot format

QUAD-DENSITY 5.25-INCH DISK DRIVE	
360KB 5.25-inch disk	FORMAT A:/F:360
1.2MB 5.25-inch disk	FORMAT A:
720KB 3.5-inch disk	cannot format
1.44MB 3.5-inch disk	cannot format
2.88MB 3.5-inch disk	cannot format

TABLE 3.4 *Continued*	**DOUBLE-DENSITY 3.5-INCH DISK DRIVE**	
	360KB 5.25-inch disk	cannot format
	1.2MB 5.25-inch disk	cannot format
	720KB 3.5-inch disk	FORMAT A:
	1.44MB 3.5-inch disk	cannot format
	2.88MB 3.5-inch disk	cannot format
	QUAD-DENSITY 3.5-INCH DISK DRIVE	
	360KB 5.25-inch disk	cannot format
	1.2MB 5.25-inch disk	cannot format
	720KB 3.5-inch disk	FORMAT A:/F:720
	1.44MB 3.5-inch disk	FORMAT A:
	2.88MB 3.5-inch disk	cannot format
	HIGH-DENSITY 3.5-INCH DISK DRIVE	
	360KB 5.25-inch disk	cannot format
	1.2MB 5.25-inch disk	cannot format
	720KB 3.5-inch disk	FORMAT A:/F:720
	1.44MB 3.5-inch disk	FORMAT A:/F:1440
	2.88MB 3.5-inch disk	FORMAT A:

Prior to DOS 5.0, the terms "quad-density" and "high-density" were often used interchangeably. With the introduction of the 2.88MB drive and disk, this is no longer the case. The 2.88MB disk is now referred to as a high-density disk. The 1.44MB and 1.2MB disks are referred to as quad-density disks.

Note that all of the FORMAT command switches listed in Table 3.3 can be combined. For instance, you could format a 720KB system disk with a volume label on a quad-density drive by using the command form

```
FORMAT d:/F:720/S/V:name
```

Keep in mind that the 160KB, 180KB, and 320KB sizes are used only with out-of-date systems and software. They are maintained only because of the computer industry's commitment to upward compatibility for customers.

Formatting a Hard Disk

The process of formatting a hard disk, sometimes referred to as a fixed disk, is an important function of DOS. When an organization or computer dealer initially sets up a hard disk, the FORMAT command is used in combination with FDISK to format and partition the disk. For more information on formatting your hard disk, refer to the *Microsoft MS-DOS 6 User's Guide*.

Though this book deals with DOS 6.x, you should understand that older versions of DOS are not as "forgiving" as DOS 6.0. When using earlier versions of the FOR-MAT command (version 3.1 and earlier) on a personal computer with a hard disk, *proceed with extreme caution*. If you are logged on to the hard disk drive and fail to specify a target drive for the FORMAT command, the hard disk is formatted and all data stored on it is lost. The loss of all data stored on your hard disk can be catastrophic—unless you have a recent backup (the MSBACKUP and RESTORE commands will be discussed in Unit 10). If you attempt to format a hard disk with DOS 4.x or later, you are prompted to enter the volume label of the hard disk. This is a safety check to prevent accidental formatting of a hard disk and the subsequent loss of all data on the drive.

With version 5.0 and 6.0, if you accidentally try to format your hard drive (drive C: in the following example), you will see the message

```
WARNING, ALL DATA ON NON-REMOVABLE DISK
DRIVE C: WILL BE LOST!
Proceed with Format (Y/N)?
```

If you do not want to reformat your hard drive (and thus lose all files), press N to abort the process.

If you have used the DOS 6.x DBLSPACE command to compress your data (DBLSPACE is covered later in this unit), you will get a slightly different message when you try to format a *compressed volume*. If you invoke the FORMAT command (with drive C: as the target), DOS will display the message

```
You must use "DBLSPACE /FORMAT C:" to format that drive
```

Using the FORMAT Command to Create a Data Disk

Before you can save data on a disk, it must be formatted or initialized. Data disks are often referred to as nonsystem disks because they do not include the system files. If you do not need to boot your computer from a floppy disk, installing the system files consumes disk space that could otherwise be used for data.

The steps required to format a nonsystem (data) disk and a bootable (system) disk are almost identical except for the parameters or switches used on the command line. The following steps are used to format a data disk.

- At the DOS prompt, type FORMAT A: and press Enter.

NOTE *If you are trying to format a 3.5-inch 720KB disk in a 1.44MB drive, you must type FORMAT A:/F:720. If you are trying to format a 5.25-inch 360KB disk in a 1.2MB drive, you must type FORMAT A:/F:360. In all other cases, simply type FORMAT A:.*

You will be prompted to

```
Insert new diskette for drive A:
and press ENTER when ready...
```

- Follow the directions and press Enter after you have inserted a blank disk in drive A:.

Notice that the in-use light goes on for drive A: and the screen displays the message "Checking existing disk format."

If you attempt to format a low-density disk in a high- or quad-density drive (or vice versa) without using the /F switch, you will see an error message similar to Figure 3.3.

FIGURE 3.3
Different format than specified message

```
C:\>FORMAT A:
Insert new diskette for drive A:
and press ENTER when ready...

Checking existing disk format.
Existing format differs from that specified.
This disk cannot be unformatted.
Proceed with Format (Y/N)?
```

If you tell DOS to proceed with the format anyway, you will see an error message as shown in Figure 3.4.

FIGURE 3.4
Format failure message

```
C:\>FORMAT A:
Insert new diskette for drive A:
and press ENTER when ready...

Checking existing disk format.
Existing format differs from that specified.
This disk cannot be unformatted.
Proceed with Format (Y/N)?Y
Formatting 1.44M
Invalid media or Track 0 bad - disk unusable.
Format terminated.
Format another (Y/N)?
```

If the disk was not previously formatted, the error message is slightly different and appears similar to Figure 3.5.

To correct the situation, see Table 3.3 and use the proper /F switch.

If the disk has been previously formatted, you will see the message "Saving UNFORMAT information" as shown in Figure 3.6. This information enables you to use the UNFORMAT command and *attempt* to retrieve data from a disk that was accidentally formatted. The UNFORMAT command is covered later in the text.

FIGURE 3.5
*Format failure
message on an
unformatted disk*

```
C:\>FORMAT A:
Insert new diskette for drive A:
and press ENTER when ready...

Checking existing disk format.
Formatting 1.44M
Invalid media or Track 0 bad - disk unusable.
Format terminated.
Format another (Y/N)?
```

FIGURE 3.6
*The saving
UNFORMAT
information
message*

```
C:\>FORMAT A:
Insert new diskette for drive A:
and press ENTER when ready...

Checking existing disk format.
Saving UNFORMAT information.
Verifying 1.44M
Format complete.

Volume label (11 characters, ENTER for none)?
```

If the disk has never been formatted, the FORMAT command proceeds to the next step—which is to display the disk capacity with a message such as

    Formatting 1.44M

If the disk has been previously formatted, the FORMAT command proceeds to verify that the disk type matches the form of the FORMAT used. You will see a message such as

    Verifying 1.44M

The screen will begin to display a running tally of how much of the disk is formatted. The message will indicate, for instance, "50 percent completed." After the last cylinder on the disk is formatted, you will see the message "Format complete" and will be prompted as shown in Figure 3.6 with the following message:

    Volume label (11 characters, ENTER for none)?

- Type a volume label and then press Enter.

If you press Enter without typing a label name, no volume label is written to the disk. To give a disk a volume label, simply type up to 11 characters and then press Enter. The volume label will be displayed each time you use the DIR command on the disk. Spaces are acceptable in volume names (in addition to letters and numbers), but periods are not.

NOTE *You can add or change a volume label later by using the LABEL command. For example, to set the volume label for a disk in drive A: to TESTDISK, type LABEL A: TESTDISK.*

FIGURE 3.7
*Formatting
messages after
creating a
nonsystem disk*

```
C:\>FORMAT A:
Insert new diskette for drive A:
and press ENTER when ready...

Checking existing disk format.
Saving UNFORMAT information.
Verifying 1.44M
Format complete.

Volume label (11 characters, ENTER for none)? BACON JONATHAN

    1,457,664 bytes total disk space
    1,457,664 bytes available on disk

        512 bytes in each allocation unit.
      2,847 allocation units available on disk.

Volume Serial Number is 3A6E-12D1

Format another (Y/N)?
```

When formatting is complete, your screen appears similar to Figure 3.7. The detail in Figure 3.7 is generated by formatting a 3.5-inch disk in a high-capacity (1.44MB) drive. Depending upon the type of disk you are formatting, the number of bytes and allocation units will vary, as shown in Table 3.1.

At the end of the formatting process, the screen lists the number of total bytes on the disk, the number of bytes in each allocation unit, and the number of free bytes and allocation units. If bad sectors are found, the quantity is listed. Bad sectors indicate that defects were found on the disk's surface. DOS will not store data at those locations. The number of bytes in bad sectors is based on those sections of the disk surface that are irregular or otherwise cannot be used to store data.

NOTE *Beginning with DOS 6.2, the FORMAT command (like the DIR, MEM, and CHKDSK commands) displays all numbers larger than one thousand with commas. Figure 3.7 was created using DOS version 6.2 while Figure 3.8 was created using version 6.0. Notice the different ways in which the total bytes of disk space are listed. In Figure 3.7, the total is listed as 1,457,664 while Figure 3.8 displays the total as 1457664.*

Figure 3.8 shows a listing of 746,496 bytes in bad sectors on a 1.44MB 3.5-inch disk. This disk had a scratch on its recording surface. On a floppy disk, the loss of 10–20 percent of your storage space to bad sectors is not crucial unless you intend to use the disk to back up programs or data that require the full capacity of the disk. Some users advocate discarding a floppy disk with any bad sectors, but the disk can still be used for backing up small data files or programs.

The final prompt, shown in Figure 3.7, appears after the disk is formatted and inquires whether you want to format another disk.

- If done formatting, type N to quit the FORMAT command, then press ⏎Enter.

- The DOS prompt reappears at this point and you can execute another DOS command.

FIGURE 3.8
*Formatted
nonsystem disk
with bad sectors*

```
C:\>FORMAT A:/U
Insert new diskette for drive A:
and press ENTER when ready...

Formatting 1.44M
Format complete.

Volume label (11 characters, ENTER for none)?

   1457664 bytes total disk space
    746496 bytes in bad sectors
    711168 bytes available on disk

       512 bytes in each allocation unit.
      1389 allocation units available on disk.

Volume Serial Number is 3C3E-1BD5

Format another (Y/N)?
```

MATCHING DISK AND DRIVE SIZES

Whether you are creating a data disk or a bootable disk, it is important to use a disk that matches the type of drive attached to your computer. The "size" match is obvious; you cannot put a 3.5-inch disk in a 5.25-inch drive or vice versa. The required "capacity" match is less obvious. If you are formatting a high-density disk in a high-density drive, no switch is needed to tell the system that the disk matches the drive's capacity. However, if you attempt to format a low-density disk in a high-density drive, you must use the /F switch (see Table 3.3). If you do not use the /F switch (and tell DOS to "Proceed with Format"), the disk will be unreadable on any computer other than the one it was formatted on .

The steps in this unit's Guided Activities assume that you are using a disk that matches your drive's capacity. For example, the following disks match the drives listed:

360KB 5.25-inch disk	use in a low-density 5.25-inch drive
720KB 3.5-inch disk	use in a low-density 3.5-inch drive
1.2MB 5.25-inch disk	use in a quad-density 5.25-inch drive
1.44MB 3.5-inch disk	use in a quad-density 3.5-inch drive
2.88MB 3.5-inch disk	use in a high-density 3.5-inch drive

If uncertain whether your disk type matches the drive type, ask your instructor which type of disk you will need.

GUIDED ACTIVITY 3.1

Formatting a Nonsystem Disk

In this Guided Activity, the FORMAT command is used to create a nonsystem disk in disk drive A:. You may use either a 5.25-inch or 3.5-inch disk for this activity. Depending upon the type of disk and drive, the total number of bytes and allocation units listed on your screen images will vary.

1. Boot your computer system.

NOTE *If you are trying to format a 3.5-inch 720KB disk in a 1.44MB drive, you must type FORMAT A:/F:720. If you are trying to format a 5.25-inch 360KB disk in a 1.2MB drive, you must type FORMAT A:/F:360. In all other cases, simply type FORMAT A:.*

2. At the DOS prompt, type FORMAT A: and press ⌈Enter⌉.

CHECKPOINT 3A How would you change the command in step 2 to format a disk in drive B:?

When completing the next step, do not use the disk labeled West Student Data Disk #1 (which was formatted in Unit 2).

3. When prompted, insert a new disk in drive A: and press ⌈Enter⌉.

4. When prompted for a volume label, type your last name first, then press the ⌈Spacebar⌉ and type your first name.

If your name is longer than 11 characters, the ending characters (beyond the first 11) will be dropped from the volume label. Spaces are acceptable in volume names (in addition to letters and numbers), but periods are not.

5. After entering the volume label, press ⌈Enter⌉.

6. When the screen message asks if you want to format another disk, type N to quit the FORMAT command, then press ⌈Enter⌉.

CHECKPOINT 3B What would happen if you typed Y in step 6?

7. Remove the disk, write the following information on a label (using a felt tip pen), and place the label on the disk.

   - West Student Data Disk #2

   - Your full name

   - Course title and number

   - Your instructor's name

8. Reinsert the disk in drive A:.

9. Type DIR A: to see a listing of files on the newly formatted disk and press ⌈Enter⌉.

Because this disk is newly formatted, no files are found, but the volume label and volume serial number are displayed.

Formatting a System Disk

Formatting a system disk is almost identical to formatting a data disk, except you must use the /S switch to indicate that you want the system files transferred to the new disk. Once you enter the FORMAT /S command at the DOS prompt, you will be prompted to place a disk in the target drive and then press ⌈Enter⌉.

If the disk has been previously formatted, you will see the message "Saving UNFORMAT information." Next, the screen will begin to give you a running tally of how much of the disk is formatted. The percentage statement will be replaced by a "Format complete" message when the surface of the disk is initialized.

After the "Format complete" message, the system seems to pause. During this time, the three hidden system files (IO.SYS, MSDOS.SYS, and DBLSPACE.BIN) are copied to the target disk along with the COMMAND.COM file. When done copying the system files, the "System transferred" message appears. Figure 3.9 shows the screen response after the initialization process is complete.

FIGURE 3.9
Screen activity when formatting a bootable system disk

```
C:\>FORMAT A:/S
Insert new diskette for drive A:
and press ENTER when ready...

Checking existing disk format.
Saving UNFORMAT information.
Verifying 1.44M
Format complete.
System transferred

Volume label (11 characters, ENTER for none)?
```

When the formatting is complete, the screen responds by listing the total number of bytes on the disk, bytes used by the hidden system files, bytes used by user files (COMMAND.COM), bytes available on disk, the number of bytes in each allocation unit, and the number of available allocation units. These statistics are listed by disk type in Table 3.1. If bad sectors are found, they are also listed.

The detail in Figure 3.10 is generated by formatting a 3.5-inch disk in a 1.44MB drive. It shows 184,320 bytes used by the system files (IO.SYS, MSDOS.SYS, DBLSPACE.BIN, and COMMAND.COM).

NOTE *DOS 6.2 uses 198,656 bytes for the system files.*

The final prompt in Figure 3.10 inquires whether you want to format another disk. At this point, simply type N to not format another disk or type Y to proceed to format another disk.

If you were to execute the DIR command on the newly formatted system disk, only one file name would be listed. That file is COMMAND.COM, one of the system files. The other three files are hidden files and are only visible when using the DIR command with the /AH switch as shown below:

    DIR A:/AH

Figure 3.10 displays the number of bytes used by system files, while Figure 3.11 displays the results of the DIR command on the formatted system disk. Also shown by Figure 3.11 are the results of using the DIR A:/AH command.

NOTE *Figure 3.11 displays the results of using DOS 6.0. The files are larger when using DOS 6.2.*

FIGURE 3.10

Formatting messages after creating a 1.44MB system disk

```
C:\>FORMAT A:/S
Insert new diskette for drive A:
and press ENTER when ready...

Checking existing disk format.
Saving UNFORMAT information.
Verifying 1.44M
Format complete.
System transferred

Volume label (11 characters, ENTER for none)? SYSTEM DISK

    1457664 bytes total disk space
     184320 bytes used by system
    1273344 bytes available on disk

        512 bytes in each allocation unit.
       2487 allocation units available on disk.

Volume Serial Number is 093C-1BF1

Format another (Y/N)?
```

FIGURE 3.11

DIR listings showing the COMMAND.COM file on a 1.44MB system disk and showing the hidden files (using the DIR A:/AH command)

```
C:\>DIR A:

 Volume in drive A is SYSTEM DISK
 Volume Serial Number is 093C-1BF1
 Directory of A:\

COMMAND  COM     52925 03-10-93   6:00a
        1 file(s)      52925 bytes
                     1273344 bytes free

C:\>DIR A:/AH

 Volume in drive A is SYSTEM DISK
 Volume Serial Number is 093C-1BF1
 Directory of A:\

IO       SYS     40470 03-10-93   6:00a
MSDOS    SYS     38138 03-10-93   6:00a
DBLSPACE BIN     51214 03-10-93   6:00a
        3 file(s)     129822 bytes
                     1273344 bytes free

C:\>
```

When formatting any size disk, the following files (some are hidden) consume the number of bytes shown (column one applies to DOS 6.0 and column two lists bytes for DOS 6.2):

COMMAND.COM	52,925	54,619
IO.SYS	40,470	40,566
MSDOS.SYS	38,138	38,138
DBLSPACE.BIN	51,214	64,246

What are the advantages of a system disk versus a nonsystem disk? The former is bootable because of the system files, but the latter can store more data and programs. If data storage is your main concern, format your disks as data disks—without the system files. However, it's a good idea to have one system disk to use in case of an emergency (such as the accidental deletion of the system files from your hard disk).

GUIDED ACTIVITY 3.2

Formatting a System Disk

In this Guided Activity, you will create a self-booting system disk. The /S switch is added to tell DOS to copy the three system files to the target disk. You may use either a 3.5-inch or 5.25-inch disk for this activity, depending on the type of disk drive you intend to use. The total bytes and allocation units listed for the formatted disk will vary, depending on the type and capacity of disk you use. In this Guided Activity, you will create West Student Data Disk #3. Do not use West Student Data Disk #1 or #2, which were formatted in the preceding Guided Activities.

1. At the DOS prompt, type CLS and press [Enter].

NOTE *If you are trying to format a 3.5-inch 720KB system disk in a 1.44MB drive, you must type FORMAT A:/S/F:720. If you are trying to format a 5.25-inch 360KB system disk in a 1.2MB drive, you must type FORMAT A:/S/F:360. In all other cases, simply type FORMAT A:/S.*

2. At the DOS prompt, type FORMAT A:/S and press [Enter].

3. When prompted, insert in drive A: a new disk that will become your West Student Data Disk #3 and press [Enter].

4. When prompted for a volume label, type SYSTEM DISK as the volume name and press [Enter].

CHECKPOINT 3C Would DOS accept a volume name of "SYSTEM DISK3" rather than "SYSTEMDISK3"?

5. When prompted, type N to quit the FORMAT command, then press [Enter].

6. Remove the disk, write the following information on a label (using a felt tip pen), and place the label on the disk.

   - West Student Data Disk #3
   - Your full name
   - Course title and number
   - Your instructor's name

7. Next, reinsert the disk in drive A:.

8. Type CLS and press [Enter] to clear the monitor screen.

9. Type DIR A: and press [Enter] to see a listing of files on the newly formatted disk.

Only the COMMAND.COM file is listed. Remember, the other three system files are hidden files and are not usually visible when using the DIR command.

Presetting the Volume Label When Formatting

The DOS 6.0 FORMAT command will always prompt you for a volume label unless you specify the volume name using the /V:*name* switch. If you use the /V:*name* switch, DOS will not prompt you for a volume name.

Figure 3.12 lists the screen messages generated by formatting a 3.5-inch disk in a high-capacity (1.44MB) drive. Notice that the volume label is entered on the command line and the FORMAT command does not prompt for a volume label.

FIGURE 3.12
Screen activity when using the /V:name switch

```
C:\>FORMAT A:/V:BACKUPDISK
Insert new diskette for drive A:
and press ENTER when ready...

Checking existing disk format.
Saving UNFORMAT information.
Verifying 1.44M
Format complete.


   1457664 bytes total disk space
   1457664 bytes available on disk

       512 bytes in each allocation unit.
      2847 allocation units available on disk.

Volume Serial Number is 214A-1CCB

Format another (Y/N)?
```

NOTE *DOS 6.x has an idiosyncrasy that affects the use of spaces in a volume label. In theory, you can include one or more space characters in a volume label, but if you use the FORMAT /V:labelname command format to establish the volume label (and include spaces in the proposed volume label), DOS returns an error message that reads "Too many parameters -". This would occur if you attempted to use the command form* FORMAT A:/V:DATA DISK 3. *In such a case, an alternative would be to substitute an underscore character instead of the spaces in the volume label so that the command would be entered as* FORMAT A:/V:DATA_DISK_3.

GUIDED ACTIVITY 3.3

Presetting the Volume Label When Formatting a Disk

In this Guided Activity, you will reformat West Student Data Disk #3 that you created in the last Guided Activity. When you format it, you will assign a volume label name of DATA_DISK_3. Be sure to use the disk used in the last Guided Activity. At the conclusion of the Guided Activity, you will use the DIR command to view the volume label. Although you may use any capacity disk for this activity, the screen displays reflect the formatting of a 3.5-inch disk in a 1.44MB drive.

1. At the DOS prompt, type CLS and press [Enter].

2. Type FORMAT A:/V:DATA_DISK_3 and press [Enter].

CHECKPOINT 3D Would DOS accept a volume label of "DATA DISK 3" in step 2 instead of "DATA_DISK-3"?

3. When prompted to "Insert new diskette for drive A: and press ENTER when ready...", insert West Student Data Disk #3 in drive A: and press [Enter].

4. When prompted, type N to quit the FORMAT command, then press [Enter].

5. At the DOS prompt, type CLS and press [Enter].

6. To see a listing of files on the newly formatted disk, type DIR A: and press [Enter].

Figure 3.13 indicates that no files are found, but the volume label is displayed.

FIGURE 3.13
DIR command listing on newly formatted nonsystem disk

```
C:\>DIR A:

Volume in drive A is DATA_DISK_3
Volume Serial Number is 143F-1CCF
Directory of A:\

File not found

C:\>
```

The SYS Command

The DOS system files must be present on a formatted disk if the disk is to be bootable. Prior to DOS 4.*x*, the hidden system files were always stored in the first two directory entries of the disk in contiguous sectors. In fact, IO.SYS was required to be at the beginning of the disk's data area; that is, stored right after the file allocation table and directory table on track zero. Beginning with DOS 4.*x*, these files are no longer required in contiguous sectors. Prior to DOS 4.*x*, a disk was formatted either with the /B option in order to use the SYS command on the disk at a later time (which reserved space for the hidden system files) or with the /S switch (which transferred the system files). DOS 4.*x*, 5.*x*, and 6.*x* do not have this requirement. In these later versions, the SYS command can transfer the system files to any formatted disk if there is sufficient space for them on the disk.

NOTE *Three of the system files (IO.SYS, MSDOS.SYS, and DBLSPACE.BIN) are often referred to as hidden DOS files—and they are. Technically, they are system files and are required in order to boot your system. The fact that they have an archive bit that is set to cause them not to appear in a directory listing also makes them hidden files. Of course, you can use the /AH switch with the DIR command to display just the hidden files.*

The SYS command enables you to transfer these hidden system files from a source disk to a target disk. It is used for three primary purposes:

- To add the DOS hidden system files to any formatted disk
- To update a formatted disk (with the system files) to a new version of DOS
- To copy COMMAND.COM to the formatted disk

The first use is most common when a software manufacturer sells you a program disk without DOS. If it provides you with the option of making the disk bootable, then you must use your copy of the SYS command to transfer the system files.

An example of the second purpose would be when you switch from an earlier version of DOS to version 6.x. Rather than reformat a bootable floppy disk or a hard disk, you could use the SYS command to overwrite the old system files with the new. To update to a later version of DOS you must

- Boot the system with the new version of DOS.
- Use the SYS command to transfer the system files.
- Overwrite the old DOS files with the new versions using the COPY command.

The syntax of the SYS command is

```
[s:][path]SYS t:
```

where s: is the source drive and t: is the target drive.

To copy the system files from a disk in drive A: to the hard disk (drive C:), you would enter this command form:

```
A:SYS C:
```

The SYS command also transfers the COMMAND.COM file but not any of the other DOS external command files. You must use the COPY command to accomplish that task.

GUIDED ACTIVITY 3.4

Transferring DOS System Files with the SYS Command

In this Guided Activity, use West Student Data Disk #3 (a nonsystem formatted disk) created earlier in this unit.

1. At the DOS prompt, type CLS and press [Enter].

2. Insert West Student Data Disk #3 in drive A:.

3. Type DIR A: and press [Enter].

    Notice that no files exists on this disk.

4. Before proceeding, be sure that you are logged on to the drive and directory with the DOS external commands or that a path has been established to the DOS sub-directory. If the following steps do not work, ask your instructor for assistance.

5. At the DOS prompt, type SYS A: and press [Enter].

    After several seconds, you will see the "System transferred" message on your screen.

6. Type DIR A: and press [Enter].

    Notice that now the COMMAND.COM file exists on the disk.

    Figure 3.14 shows the screen response when the SYS command is executed and the subsequent execution of the DIR command.

FIGURE 3.14
Screen responses generated by the SYS command

```
C:\>DIR A:

 Volume in drive A is DATA_DISK_3
 Volume Serial Number is 143F-1CCF
 Directory of A:\

File not found

C:\>SYS A:
System transferred

C:\>DIR A:

 Volume in drive A is DATA_DISK_3
 Volume Serial Number is 143F-1CCF
 Directory of A:\

COMMAND  COM     52925 03-10-93   6:00a
        1 file(s)       52925 bytes
                      1273344 bytes free

C:\>
```

You now have a bootable system disk. The next step will check to ensure that the disk is bootable.

7. Leave the disk in drive A: and press [Ctrl][Alt][Del] simultaneously.

    After the POST is completed, you will see the DATE and TIME command prompts. Respond to these by entering the correct date and time.

8. Remove the disk from drive A: and reboot your system from the hard disk by pressing the [Ctrl][Alt][Del] key combination.

The DISKCOPY Command

With one handy command, DISKCOPY, you can format and create a duplicate copy of a disk. This command can be very useful when making copies of new program disks (for archive purposes) or backing up data. DISKCOPY will format the target disk, if necessary. If the target disk is already formatted, the command proceeds to make a copy of the original disk. DISKCOPY goes track by track, sector by sector, to make an exact duplicate copy of the source disk on the target disk.

Four guidelines apply when using the DISKCOPY command:

- If the target disk has any data or program code on it, it will be overwritten by the new data from the source disk.

- When using the DISKCOPY command, the size and storage capacity of both source and target disks must be identical. Logically, you cannot copy (track by track and sector by sector) from a hard disk to a floppy disk, or from a 3.5-inch 1.44MB disk drive to a 5.25-inch 360KB disk drive. The disks must be of the same size (physical dimensions) and same storage capacity (in kilobytes or megabytes).

- The DISKCOPY command does not avoid bad sectors. If the source disk has sectors marked as bad, the same sectors will be marked bad on the target disk—even if they are good sectors on the target disk. If the target disk has bad sectors, good data from the source disk may be written to those sectors. The DISKCOPY command creates a track-by-track and sector-by-sector copy.

- Finally, the DISKCOPY command preserves file fragmentation. If the files on a disk have been modified extensively, they are most likely fragmented into sectors or allocation units in multiple locations on the disk. The ideal is for files to be saved to contiguous sectors. When files become fragmented, file access speed decreases. The read-write head must jump around the disk to find all sectors composing the file. The COPY command is more likely to write files to contiguous sectors, while the DISKCOPY command just recreates the existing fragmentation.

The syntax of the command follows.

```
[d:][path]DISKCOPY [s:] [t:]
```

DISKCOPY is an external DOS command. If it is stored on drive C: in the \DOS directory, and you wish to make an exact duplicate of the disk in drive A: (with the new copy in drive B:), use this command form:

```
C:\DOS\DISKCOPY A: B:
```

Most computers with a hard disk have a PATH command (discussed in a later unit) that enables you to use DOS external commands without changing to the DOS subdirectory or adding the path to the command (as shown above).

Keep in mind that if the DISKCOPY command parameters are accidentally reversed, the original disk will be overwritten by the data (or lack of data) on the target disk. The safest route is to write-protect the original disk before using the DISKCOPY command— and not let yourself be distracted during *any* disk-copying procedure.

If you only have a single disk drive, you can still use the DISKCOPY command. Simply enter the following command form at the DOS prompt and the screen prompts you to insert the source disks:

```
DISKCOPY A: A:
```

DOS 6.0 then reads the data from the source disk into working memory until no free RAM exists. When this occurs, DOS 6.0 prompts you to insert the target disk. After you insert the target disk, the data from memory is written to the disk.

DOS 6.0 will continue prompting you to swap disks until all data is transferred to the duplicate disk. Depending upon the RAM in your system unit, you may need to swap disks one, two, or three times to complete the process.

However, if you use DOS 6.2, the operating system uses the hard disk as a scratch area and you will not need to swap disks.

If you are logged on to a floppy drive on your system, you can avoid entering the parameters (disk drive designation) and enter only the command

```
DISKCOPY
```

You cannot omit the drive designation if you are logged on to a hard disk because DOS tries to use the default drive for the disk copy operation. If you try this, DOS responds with the error message:

```
Invalid drive specification
Specified drive does not exist
or is non-removable
```

"Non-removable" is the DOS term for a hard disk. A floppy disk is considered a removable disk.

The DISKCOPY Verify Switch

Beginning with DOS 5.0, a new switch (/V) was added to the DISKCOPY command. When you use this switch, every sector copied is also verified. The verification process causes the operating system to check that each sector on the new target disk matches each sector on the old source disk. If you copy class notes from another student, you will most likely verify that what you have written matches the original document. Verification ensures an exact match. The verification process slows down disk copying, but ensures an accurate duplication of all files on the disk.

GUIDED ACTIVITY 3.5

Making a Duplicate Disk

In this Guided Activity, the DISKCOPY command will be used to make a backup of your West Student Data Disk #1.

NOTE *From this point on in the text, we assume that you have completed several tasks before beginning each Guided Activity. You must have done the following:*

- Turned on your computer system

- Logged on to drive C: or your hard disk drive (unless instructed otherwise)

- Logged on to the directory containing the DOS commands or issued a PATH command so that you can access the external DOS commands

- Seen the DOS prompt displayed on the screen

In later units, we discuss directories and how to change directories. For now, if the external DOS commands cannot be executed, ask your instructor for assistance.

1. Insert West Student Data Disk #1 in drive A:, type DIR A: and press ⏎Enter.

   You should see a listing of 44 files on your screen.

2. Write-protect your West Student Data Disk #1 before continuing.

NOTE *It is always a good idea to write-protect your source disk so it does not accidentally get mixed up with the target disk and its files get overwritten when swapping disks.*

3. Type CLS and press ⏎Enter.

4. Type DISKCOPY A: A: and press ⏎Enter.

   You will be prompted to "Insert SOURCE diskette in drive A:" and then "Press any key to continue…".

5. West Student Data Disk #1 should still be in drive A:. This will serve as the source disk.

6. Press any key to continue.

7. When prompted to "Insert TARGET diskette in drive A:…" insert West Student Data Disk #2. This will serve as the target disk.

8. Press any key to continue.

9. With versions of DOS prior to 6.2, you may be prompted to insert the source and target disks again. Follow the screen prompts. However, if you are using DOS 6.2, the operating system uses the hard disk as a scratch area and you do not need to swap disks. Remember that if you are requested to insert the source disk, insert West Student Data Disk #1. If prompted for the target disk, insert West Student Data Disk #2.

10. When the copying process is complete, you will be prompted whether to "Copy another diskette (Y/N)?" Type N.

NOTE *If you are using DOS 6.2, the screen messages displayed will be a little different from Figure 3.15. The important change is that you will be prompted "Do you wish to write another duplicate of this disk (Y/N)?" If you type Y, you can make multiple duplicates of the same source disk without reinserting the source disk. Once you type N, you will see the screen prompt "Copy another diskette (Y/N)?" In this Guided Activity, type N.*

   Figure 3.15 shows the screen response for the DISKCOPY command. If the target disk is unformatted, you will see the message "Formatting while copying."

   Figure 3.15 displays the results of using a 3.5-inch 1.44MB disk and DOS 6.0. The number of disk swaps are different if you use another capacity disk.

11. With West Student Data Disk #2 in drive A:, type DIR A: and press ⏎Enter.

   Notice that the 44 files from West Student Data Disk #1 are now on the disk in drive A:.

FIGURE 3.15
*DISKCOPY
command
screen
messages*

```
Insert TARGET diskette in drive A:

Press any key to continue . . .

Insert SOURCE diskette in drive A:

Press any key to continue . . .

Insert TARGET diskette in drive A:

Press any key to continue . . .

Insert SOURCE diskette in drive A:

Press any key to continue . . .

Insert TARGET diskette in drive A:

Press any key to continue . . .

Volume Serial Number is 1CE6-1D2B

Copy another diskette (Y/N)? N

C:\>
```

CHECKPOINT 3E What was accomplished in the preceding Guided Activity?

CHECKPOINT 3F Why do you think the Guided Activity started by asking you to write-protect West Student Data Disk #1?

The DISKCOMP Command

A companion to the DISKCOPY command is the DISKCOMP (disk compare) command. It compares two disks track by track and sector by sector. If the duplicate (target) disk you made with DISKCOPY is not identical to the source (original) disk, you will be told by the DISKCOMP command. The DISKCOMP command is most effective *immediately* after using the DISKCOPY command, because once you modify any file on either the source or target disk, the comparison will fail. DISKCOMP cannot be used with the COPY command since COPY makes duplicate files on the target disk wherever space exists, while DISKCOPY makes the duplicate file on the same track and using the same sectors. Because DISKCOMP checks each sector on each track against the same sector on the same track of the other disk, it just won't work with duplicate files created using the COPY command (discussed in Unit 4).

The syntax of the command is

```
[d:][path]DISKCOMP [s:] [t:]
```

DISKCOMP, like DISKCOPY, is an external command. It must be available on the default drive, or you must preface the command with the path to the directory storing the command. If the command is in the \DOS directory on drive C: and you wish to compare a disk in drive A: to a disk in drive B:, the syntax of the command would be

```
C:\DOS\DISKCOMP A: B:
```

As mentioned earlier, most computers with a hard disk have a PATH command that enables you to use DOS external commands without changing to the DOS sub-directory or adding the path to the command (as shown above).

If the track-by-track comparison indicates that the disks are identical, you will see the message "Compare OK" as shown in Figure 3.16.

FIGURE 3.16
Screen response to a successful comparison of two disks

```
Comparing 80 tracks
18 sectors per track, 2 side(s)

Insert SECOND diskette in drive A:

Press any key to continue . . .

Insert FIRST diskette in drive A:

Press any key to continue . . .

Insert SECOND diskette in drive A:

Press any key to continue . . .

Insert FIRST diskette in drive A:

Press any key to continue . . .

Compare OK

Compare another diskette (Y/N) ?N

C:\>
```

If errors are detected, DISKCOMP will list the track (0 to 39 on a 360KB 5.25-inch disk or 0 to 79 on a 720KB disk) and the side (0 or 1) where the comparison(s) failed. Figure 3.17 shows the results of comparing two disks with identical files—except for one file that has a different date and time stamp.

CAUTION *Be careful of the similarity in spelling between the DISKCOPY and DISKCOMP commands. If you begin to compare two disks and accidentally type DISKCOPY, the data on the target disk will be overwritten by the data on the source disk.*

If you go to the trouble of backing up program and data disks using the DISKCOPY command, you owe it to yourself to complete the process by comparing the accuracy of the disk copy operation. DISKCOMP is your insurance that the copy was successful and accurate—track by track.

FIGURE 3.17
DISKCOMP command error listing

```
Compare error on
side 0, track 0

Compare error on
side 1, track 0

Compare error on
side 1, track 4

Insert FIRST diskette in drive A:

Press any key to continue . . .

Insert SECOND diskette in drive A:

Press any key to continue . . .

Insert FIRST diskette in drive A:

Press any key to continue . . .

Compare another diskette (Y/N) ?N

C:\>
```

GUIDED ACTIVITY 3.6

Comparing Two Disks

In this Guided Activity, you will compare the two disks used in the last Guided Activity.

1. Type DISKCOMP A: A:

CHECKPOINT 3G   If you were comparing a disk in drive A: with one in drive B:, how would you alter the command in step 1?

2. Press [Enter].

3. When prompted for the source disk, insert West Student Data Disk #1 in drive A:.

4. Follow the screen prompts. Be sure to insert West Student Data Disk #1 when prompted for the first disk and insert West Student Data Disk #2 when prompted for the second disk.

     When the comparison is complete, you should see the "Compare OK" message.

5. If you do not want to compare another disk, type N.

The Quick Format Command Switch

The quick format command switch (/Q) can only be used if the target disk has already been formatted once. The FORMAT /Q command form erases the file allocation table (FAT) and the root directory. It does not check for bad sectors on the disk, so it should only be used if you are sure the disk is in good condition.

GUIDED ACTIVITY 3.7

Using the Quick Format Switch

Earlier in this unit, we discussed the /Q switch that enables you to quickly format a disk that was previously formatted. In this Guided Activity, you use the quick format procedure on West Student Data Disk #3.

1. Set the default drive to drive C: and clear the screen.

2. Type FORMAT A:/Q and press Enter.

3. When prompted to insert a disk, place West Student Data Disk #3 in drive A:.

4. Press Enter to begin formatting the disk.

   Your screen will display the quick formatting message as shown in Figure 3.18.

5. When prompted for a volume label, type your last name first, followed by your first name, and then press Enter.

6. When prompted to "Format Another (Y/N)?", type N and press Enter.

CHECKPOINT 3H Why would you quick-format a disk?

FIGURE 3.18
The FORMAT/Q command screen activity

```
C:\>FORMAT A:/Q
Insert new diskette for drive A:
and press ENTER when ready...

Checking existing disk format.
Saving UNFORMAT information.
QuickFormatting 1.44M
Format complete.

Volume label (11 characters, ENTER for none)?
```

GUIDED ACTIVITY 3.8

Using the Unconditional FORMAT Command Switch

Earlier in this unit, we discussed the /U switch that enables you to format a previously formatted disk without saving the unformat data. In this Guided Activity, you use the unconditional format procedure on West Student Data Disk #3. After unconditionally formatting the disk, you will combine the /U and /Q switches to execute a quick unconditional format of a previously formatted disk.

1. Set the default drive to drive C: and clear the screen.

2. Type FORMAT A:/U and press Enter.

3. When prompted to insert a disk, place West Student Data Disk #3 in drive A:.

4. Press Enter to begin formatting the disk.

Your screen will indicate a percentage of the formatting complete and will continue incrementing until you see the "Format complete" message as shown in Figure 3.19.

FIGURE 3.19
The FORMAT/U
command
screen activity

```
C:\>FORMAT A:/U
Insert new diskette for drive A:
and press ENTER when ready...

Formatting 1.44M
Format complete.

Volume label (11 characters, ENTER for none)?
```

5. When prompted for a volume label, press [Enter].

6. When prompted to "Format Another (Y/N)?", type N and press [Enter].

7. Type CLS and press [Enter].

8. Type FORMAT A:/Q/U and press [Enter].

9. When prompted to insert a disk, leave West Student Data Disk #3 in drive A:.

10. Press [Enter] to begin formatting the disk.

   Your screen will display the unconditional quick-formatting messages as shown in Figure 3.20.

*FIGURE 3.20
The
FORMAT/Q/U
command
screen activity*

```
C:\>FORMAT A:/Q/U
Insert new diskette for drive A:
and press ENTER when ready...

Checking existing disk format.
QuickFormatting 1.44M
Format complete.

Volume label (11 characters, ENTER for none)?
```

11. When prompted for a volume label, type your last name first, followed by your first name, and then press [Enter].

12. When prompted to "QuickFormat Another (Y/N)?," type N and press [Enter].

Understanding DOS Disk Compression and the DBLSPACE Command

Disk compression utilities have become more and more necessary as applications became more powerful and feature-rich. The end result of disk compression is to store each application or data file in compressed form so that it uses the smallest amount of hard disk space.

With the appearance of Windows 3.*x*, the hard disk space required to install a typical application has increased dramatically. Early hard drives ranged from 10–20MB of storage, yet current Windows and Windows-like applications can require 12–20MB just for installation. In late 1993, although the average new consumer hard drive was 120–200MB in size, many systems require disk compression to increase their storage capacity to workable size. Though third-party vendors have offered disk compression utilities, this feature was not added to the operating system until the release of DOS 6.0.

The DOS 6 DBLSPACE command is used to perform the following functions. The actual command form used to accomplish each function in listed in parentheses. These are only the more common uses of the command.

- To compress a hard disk drive or floppy disk (DBLSPACE /COMPRESS)
- To check the validity of the internal structure of a compressed drive (DBLSPACE /CHKDSK)
- To delete a compressed drive (DBLSPACE /DELETE)
- To format a compressed drive (DBLSPACE /FORMAT)
- To display information about a compressed drive (DBLSPACE /INFO)
- To display a list of compressed and uncompressed drives on your system (DBLSPACE /LIST)
- To mount a compressed drive and assign it a drive letter so that it can be accessed (DBLSPACE /MOUNT)
- To unmount a compressed drive so that it can no longer be accessed or identified by a drive letter (DBLSPACE /UNMOUNT)
- To change the size of an existing compressed drive (DBLSPACE /SIZE)
- To change the estimated compression ratio of an existing compressed drive (DBLSPACE /RATIO)

Issuing the DBLSPACE Command

You can invoke the DBLSPACE command without listing any parameters and the DoubleSpace program will start. It is a menu-driven utility program that can be used to set up compressed drives and work with them. Figure 3.21 shows the opening screen that appears if you simply enter the following command at the DOS prompt:

```
DBLSPACE
```

Once the opening screen appears, you can use a mouse click to select commands from the menu bar. For instance, Figure 3.22 displays the drop-down menu that would appear after you click on the Drive command on the menu bar.

Notice that each command on the drop-down menu corresponds with a parameter that can be added to the DBLSPACE command at the DOS prompt. If you want to have the DBLSPACE command perform only a specific task, you can use the parameters listed earlier in this section—such as the /COMPRESS, /FORMAT, or /INFO parameters.

FIGURE 3.21
*The opening
screen of the
DoubleSpace
utility program*

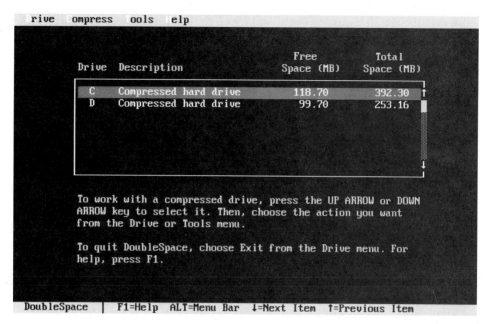

In this textbook, you will only use the DBLSPACE command to compress a
floppy disk. *Do not use the command to compress your computer's hard drive,* for the following reasons:

- Your workstation's hard drive may already be compressed.

- To compress a 100–200MB hard drive can take 6–8 hours or longer.

- Some programs cannot use compressed hard disk space (the most common example is the permanent swap file used by Windows 3.*x*).

FIGURE 3.22
*The Drive
command
drop-down menu*

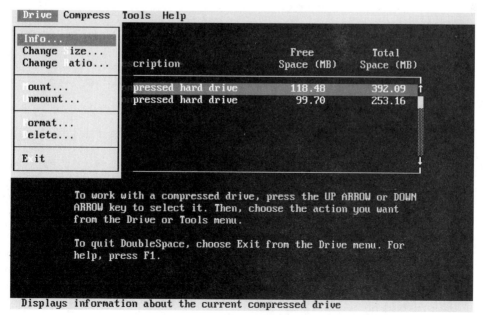

- DBLSPACE cannot compress a drive that is almost or completely full. Many instructional computing labs have filled their hard drives with required application programs and might not have sufficient "working space" to permit compression.

- If your workstation has a hard disk compressed by a third-party vendor's product, special precautions must be made before trying to convert it.

- It's not "nice" to compress someone else's hard drive without the individual's permission!

Compressing a Disk

Compressing any disk can increase the storage space on that disk from 50 to 100 percent. For instance, a 100MB hard drive, after compression by the DBLSPACE command, will typically store 150 to 200MB of data. The actual amount of gain is dependent on how much space is reserved for uncompressed files (such as the Windows 3.x permanent swap file) and the type of files that are compressed. Typically, text files (created by a text editor or word processor) can be compressed more than graphic files (artwork, graphs, charts, and line art), video files, or audio files.

The form of the DBLSPACE command that is used to compress a disk includes entering the command at the DOS prompt followed by the /COMPRESS parameter (which can be abbreviated to /COM) and then followed by the drive to be compressed. If you are compressing a floppy disk in drive A:, the command form would be

```
DBLSPACE /COMPRESS A:
```

or

```
DBLSPACE /COM A:
```

DBLSPACE COMMAND GUIDELINES

The following guidelines apply whenever using the DBLSPACE command to compress a disk:

- To compress a hard drive, it must have at least 1.2MB of free space—preferably more.

- To compress a floppy drive, it must have at least 500KB of free space.

- You can compress a disk before it has files stored on it or after you have already saved files to it.

- The fewer files on the disk, the faster it will be compressed.

- DBLSPACE cannot compress a 360KB disk, only larger sized floppy disks.

- You cannot run DBLSPACE from a DOS window inside Windows.

If you want to reserve a specific amount of disk space for uncompressed files, you can add the /RESERVE parameter to the command line. For instance, to reserve 20MB of a 120MB hard drive (drive C:) for uncompressed files, you would use the command line

```
DBLSPACE /COMPRESS C: /RESERVE=20
```

The /RESERVE parameter can be abbreviated to /RES as shown below:

```
DBLSPACE /COM C: /RES=20
```

GUIDED ACTIVITY 3.9

Compressing a Floppy Disk

In this Guided Activity, you will compress West Student Data Disk #1, which includes 44 files. This disk was created in Unit 2 and then used earlier in this unit as the source disk in a DISKCOPY operation. You will check the available disk space, both before and after compressing the disk. Finally, you will use the DBLSPACE command form to mount a compressed drive (so that it can be accessed by DOS).

1. Be sure to make West Student Data Disk #1 read/write enabled. Remember, in Guided Activity 3.5, you write-protected this disk. Before proceeding, you must remove the write-protection.

2. Insert West Student Data Disk #1 in drive A:.

3. At the C: prompt, type CLS and press Enter.

4. Type DIR A: and press Enter.

   If using a 1.44MB disk, it should list 44 files, using 65,766 bytes with 1,379,328 bytes free. If you are using a 720KB disk, the number of files and file size will be the same, but the bytes free will only be 636,928. If using a 1.2MB floppy disk, before compression there will be 1,135,616 bytes free.

5. At the DOS prompt, type DBLSPACE /COMPRESS A: and press Enter.

   NOTE *If you see a message that indicates "DoubleSpace cannot compress a floppy drive until you have installed DoubleSpace on your computer. To install DoubleSpace type DBLSPACE at the command prompt.", **do not proceed without instructions from your instructor**.*

   The screen will display a series of messages. The first indicates that

   ```
   DoubleSpace is running CHKDSK on drive A.
   ```

   The DBLSPACE command then scans the drive. Next, a screen message appears and indicates that "DoubleSpace is now compressing drive A." The screen includes the time the compression began, the current time, estimated finish time, time left in the conversion, and the file name of the current file being compressed. You will also see a bar representing the percentage of compression completed. Compressing the West Student Data Disk #1 files, whether stored on a 720KB, 1.2MB, or 1.44MB floppy disk, will take approximately 3–5 minutes.

   After completion, a message appears, stating that

   ```
   DoubleSpace is examining your system...
   ```

6. When the C: prompt reappears, type DIR A: and press Enter.

According to the DIR command, the 44 files are still listed on the disk and still use 65,766 bytes. However, the bytes free have jumped from 1,379,328 to 2,236,416 bytes on a 1.44MB disk, from 636,928 to 761,856 bytes on a 720KB disk, and from 1,135,616 to 1,753,088 bytes on a 1.2MB disk.

7. Type CHKDSK A: and press [Enter].

Figure 3.23 shows the results of the CHKDSK command. The 1.44MB floppy disk now can store approximately 2.6MB of data, a 1.2MB disk can store 2MB, and a 720KB disk can store approximately 1MB of data. The CHKDSK command is covered in Unit 7.

FIGURE 3.23

The CHKDSK command display for the compressed West Student Data Disk #1

```
C:\>CHKDSK A:

Volume BACON JONAT created 05-29-1993 8:18a
Volume Serial Number is 0FDA-3E3D

   2613248 bytes total disk space
    376832 bytes in 44 user files
   2236416 bytes available on disk

      8192 bytes in each allocation unit
       319 total allocation units on disk
       273 available allocation units on disk

    655360 total bytes memory
    496944 bytes free
DoubleSpace is scanning your computer for drive A's compressed volume file.
DoubleSpace is checking drive A.

DoubleSpace found no errors on drive A.

C:\>
```

NOTE *If you are using DOS 6.2, the operating system displays the following message (not shown in Figure 3.23) at the bottom of the screen:*
"Instead of using CHKDSK, try using SCANDISK. SCANDISK can reliably detect and fix a much wider range of disk problems. For more information, type HELP SCANDISK from the command prompt."

The remainder of this Guided Activity applies only to users of DOS version 6.0. Version 6.2 automatically mounts a compressed disk and treats it just like an uncompressed disk.

Because you have just completed compressing the disk in drive A:, it is accessible using any DOS command—for the duration of the current work session. If you were to reboot your computer, the compressed disk would not be accessible without first having the operating system mount it. The following steps reset the computer (so the disk is not mounted) and then mount it using the DBLSPACE /MOUNT command.

8. Remove the compressed disk from drive A:.

9. Reboot your computer by pressing [Ctrl][Alt][Del].

10. When the system reboots and the DOS prompt reappears, insert West Student Data Disk #1 in drive A:.

11. Type DIR A: and press Enter.

    Figure 3.24 displays the results. DOS 6.0 displays only a single READTHIS.TXT file that appears in the directory listing.

FIGURE 3.24

DIR listing on an unmounted, compressed disk

```
C:\>DIR A:

Volume in drive A is HOST_FOR_A
Volume Serial Number is 1454-1BE5
Directory of A:\

READTHIS TXT        350 05-29-93   8:20a
       1 file(s)            350 bytes
                          78336 bytes free


C:\>
```

If you were to load the file in a text editor or word processor, it would read:

> This disk has been compressed by MSDOS 6 DoubleSpace.
>
> To make this disk's contents accessible, change to the drive that contains it, and then type the following at the command prompt:
>
> DBLSPACE/MOUNT
>
> (If this file is located on a drive other than the drive that contains the compressed disk, then the disk has already been mounted).

12. Type CLS and press Enter.

13. To mount the disk in drive A:, type DBLSPACE /MOUNT A: and press Enter.

    The screen will indicate that

    > DoubleSpace is mounting drive A:

    After a few seconds, the message appears

    > DoubleSpace has mounted drive A:

14. At the DOS prompt, type DIR A: and press Enter.

    The 44 files are once again listed.

NOTE *With DOS 6.0, if you have a mounted compressed disk in a drive and swap another disk into that drive, the drive automatically becomes unmounted. If the new disk is also compressed, you would need to reexecute the DBLSPACE /MOUNT command in order to access the files on the new compressed disk.*

Summary

In this unit, you learned how to prepare a disk to store data and application programs (using the FORMAT command). You also learned the difference between a bootable disk with system files and a nonbootable data disk. The unit covered how to make a duplicate copy of a disk (using the DISKCOPY command) and how to compare the resulting disk with the source disk (using the DISKCOMP command). Finally, disk compression was discussed and you learned how to compress a disk so that it can store more files and data (using the DBLSPACE command) and how to mount a compressed disk to allow its files to be accessed.

Command Review

In this unit, you learned several DOS commands. Most have optional switches. We have tried to cover both the common and the rarely used forms of each command. The following forms of this unit's commands are the most frequently used and should be reviewed carefully.

DISKCOPY A: A:	Makes an exact duplicate in drive A: of the original (source) disk in drive A:. DOS will prompt you to insert the source disk and then the target disk at the appropriate times. The copy is made track by track and sector by sector.
DISKCOPY A: B:	Makes an exact duplicate in drive B: of the original (source) disk in drive A:. The copy is made track by track and sector by sector.
DISKCOMP A: B:	Compares the disk in drive A: to the disk in drive B:. This form of the command only works if both the A: and B: drives have the same storage capacity. The comparison is made track by track and sector by sector.
DBLSPACE	Loads the DoubleSpace program.
DBLSPACE /COMPRESS A:	Compresses data on the disk in drive A:
DBLSPACE /MOUNT A:	Mounts a compressed disk in drive A: so that files may be accessed by the operating system.
FORMAT A:	Prepares a disk in drive A: to store data or programs. System files are not copied to the disk.
FORMAT A:/S	Prepares a self-booting system disk to store data or programs.

FORMAT A:/F:720	Prepares a low-density 720KB disk in a high-density 3.5-inch drive (A:) to store data or programs. System files are not copied to the disk.
FORMAT A:/F:360	Prepares a low-density 360KB disk in a high-density 5.25-inch drive (A:) to store data or programs. System files are not copied to the disk.
SYS A:	Copies the two hidden system files to a disk in drive A:, thus making the disk bootable.

Review Questions

1. Why must a disk be formatted before use?

2. Which FORMAT command switch installs system files on a formatted disk?

3. Which FORMAT command switch makes a formatted disk bootable?

4. Which FORMAT command does not save unformatting data?

5. Which DOS command creates a duplicate disk?

6. Which DOS command would you use to verify that a duplicate disk is identical to the original disk?

7. Which DOS command would you use to do a quick format of a previously formatted disk in drive A:?

8. What does a switch or parameter do for a DOS command?

9. Name the six types of disk drives currently in use on PCs and compatibles.

10. Name the DOS command used to format a hard disk. A floppy disk?

11. Will DOS 6.x always prompt you for a volume label when formatting a disk?

12. Name five common floppy disk storage capacities.

13. What purpose does the SYS command serve?

14. Can the DISKCOPY command be used to copy from a hard disk to a 3.5-inch disk?

15. Can the DISKCOPY command be used to copy from a 5.25-inch disk to a 3.5-inch disk?

16. Can the DISKCOPY command be used to copy from a 720KB disk to a 1.2MB disk?

17. Does the DISKCOMP command compare files on different drives file by file, track by track, or directory by directory?

18. When is the most effective time to use the DISKCOMP command?

19. Why would you use the FORMAT/S command?

20. Can you combine a quick format with an unconditional format?

21. What is meant by an unconditional format?

22. Why would you use the FORMAT/Q command?

23. Why would you use the FORMAT/U command?

24. Name at least five reasons would you use the DBLSPACE command.

25. What does disk compression do?

26. Indicate the command that would be used to compress a floppy disk in drive B:.

27. Name the DBLSPACE command parameter that reserves uncompressed space on a compressed drive.

28. Why would you not be able to access files on a compressed floppy disk and instead only see a file named READTHIS.TXT?

Exercises

Whenever instructed to format a disk, use your last name (first) and then your first name (such as BACON JON) as the volume label unless instructed otherwise. If instructed to print data from the screen, be sure to write your full name, course number and section, course title, instructor's name, unit and exercise number, and today's date on the paper. Your instructor will indicate if the disk(s) created or printouts should be submitted for grading.

1. Format a disk with the DOS system files. Be sure the disk is bootable and includes the volume label SYSTEM-DISK.

NOTE *Before beginning the next Exercise, turn on your printer, press* Ctrl PrtSc *to turn the printer echo function on (anything displayed on your screen will be echoed to the printer). When done, press the on-line button and form feed the sheet so that you can eject or detach it and submit it to your instructor. Press* Ctrl PrtSc *to turn off the printer echo function. In the subsequent exercises, use this method when instructed to create a screen dump.*

2. Format a disk so as to maximize the data that can be stored on it (do not use DBLSPACE). Use your first initial and last name as the volume label. Submit a screen dump of the screen activity to your instructor.

3. Execute a quick format of the disk in Exercise 2 above and give it a new volume label (your last name first and then your first initial). Make a screen dump of the results of this exercise.

4. Format a nonsystem disk. Next, transfer the system files to the disk. Make a screen dump of the results of this exercise.

Key Terms

Allocation unit	Disk compression	Initialize
Bit	Double-density	Medium
Bootable	Double-sided	Quad-density
Boot record	File allocation table (FAT)	Sector
Cluster	Floppy disk	Single-density
Compressed volume	Formatted	Single-sided
Contiguous	Fragmented	Tracks
Directory table	High-density	Unformatted

Documentation Research

Documentation Research questions are included at the end of most units to encourage you to explore and discover the additional features available with DOS 6.x. All Documentation Research questions within the text can be answered by using the on-line reference (accessed by using the HELP command). Review Guided Activity 2.8 if you are unsure how to use the HELP command.)

1. The Help screen for DISKCOMP lists which DOS command as a related command?

2. Which FORMAT command switch should be used rather than the /N or /T switch?

3. Which FORMAT command switch causes DOS not to scan for bad sectors?

4. Which FORMAT command switch does not perform a "safe" format?

5. What is DBLSPACE.BIN?

6. Name the DBLSPACE parameter that is used to remove fragmentation from a compressed drive.

7. What does the abbreviation CVF represent? (*Hint: Check the DBLSPACE command.*)

8. Besides indicating the free and used space on a compressed disk, what other data is displayed by the DBLSPACE /INFO command?

Formatting a Blank Disk

In Unit 3, you learned how to format and copy a disk. You also learned how to change the volume label on a disk. In this application, you use all three skills.

1. Format a blank disk. Do not format it with system files—it should be a non-system, data disk. Use your first initial and last name as the volume label.

2. Make a duplicate of the disk without using the FORMAT command again.

3. Change the volume label of the second disk to be your first name only.

4. Submit both disks to your instructor. Be sure to write your name, course and section number, instructor's name, and today's date on the disk labels.

File Management Commands

Learning Objectives

At the completion of this unit, you should be able to

1. use the COPY command to copy one or more files to the same disk, another disk, the monitor screen, or a printer,

2. use the COPY command to combine two or more files into one file,

3. use the COMP command to compare one or more files,

4. use the REN command to change the name of a file,

5. use the DEL command to delete one or more files,

6. use the UNDELETE command to restore one or more files.

Important Commands

COMP

COPY

DEL

RENAME

UNDELETE

File Management Commands

The commands considered in this unit enable you to manage data stored on disk. Whenever you load an application program or create a document, spreadsheet, or database, you are executing DOS commands that create or work with files. A file is a common "container" in which the operating system stores program code and data. Some files (*system files*) contain code that tells the computer how to behave like a computer. These instructions are stored in files like IO.SYS, MSDOS.SYS, DBLSPACE.BIN, COMMAND.COM, and all the external DOS command files.

Other files (*program files*) provide instructions that tell the computer how to accomplish specific tasks—such as word processing, database management, and so on. When you run program files, they create additional files (*data files*) that store your data.

The more you use your computer, the more files you create. The commands described in this unit help you manage those data files. You will learn to copy, delete, rename, and compare files. These are the most basic tasks required to operate a personal computer—trying to do so without these skills is like seeking a job before you learn to read and write.

All of the file management commands (except COMP and UNDELETE) are internal DOS commands. This unit discusses the COMP, COPY, DEL, RENAME and UNDELETE commands.

The COPY Command

The COPY command is similar to the DISKCOPY command. As you learned in the last unit, DISKCOPY duplicates an entire disk track by track. The COPY command creates duplicate files byte by byte. The COPY command normally duplicates only one file at a time, yet by using the wild card characters, it can be told to duplicate multiple files with one execution of the command. Table 4.1 details the differences between the COPY command and the DISKCOPY command. Each of the eight differences provides additional insight into how DOS works.

TABLE 4.1
Comparison of the COPY and DISKCOPY commands

DISKCOPY A: B:	COPY A:*.* B:
External DOS command	Internal DOS command
Will format the target disk	Will not format the target disk
Destructive copy (overwrites other data on the disk)	Appends files to the target disk rather than overwriting all data
Will copy hidden and system files	Will not copy hidden or system files
Will not cross media (from high-density to low-density or from one sized disk to another)	Will cross media
Will not work with a hard disk drive	Will work with a hard disk drive
Copies track by track	Copies file by file (byte by byte)
Maintains disk fragmentation	Resequences files to eliminate disk fragmentation

The syntax of the command is

```
COPY [s]filename [t][filename]
```

This command syntax tells DOS to copy the first file listed (on the source drive) to the second file name listed (on the target drive). If you had a file on drive A: called TRYTHIS.DOC and wished to copy it to a disk in drive B:, the command form would be

```
COPY A:TRYTHIS.DOC B:TRYTHIS.DOC
```

In short, you are copying "from" drive A: "to" drive B: a file named TRYTHIS.DOC. DOS helps you save a few keystrokes by making some assumptions about the command you enter. For instance, if the default drive (as shown by the DOS prompt) is A:, the above command line could be simplified to

```
COPY TRYTHIS.DOC B:TRYTHIS.DOC
```

If you fail to enter the drive designation, DOS assumes that you mean the default drive (but you could not copy a file to the same name on the same drive). Likewise, if you omit the target disk file name parameter, DOS assumes that you wish to copy the file from drive A: to drive B: and keep the same file name. Assuming you are logged on to drive A: and wish to copy TRYTHIS.DOC to drive B: with the same name, you could simply enter

```
COPY TRYTHIS.DOC B:
```

Notice that the drive designation is assumed (to be the default drive) and the new file name on drive B: is assumed to be the same as it was on drive A: (TRYTHIS.DOC).

If you haven't already guessed, this leads into the capability of copying a file under one name on a drive to a different name on the same (or a different) disk. If TRYTHIS.DOC is on drive A: (the default drive) and you wish to copy it to a file called NOTHANKS.DOC on drive B:, the command line would be

```
COPY TRYTHIS.DOC B:NOTHANKS.DOC
```

The longer version of the command would also work:

```
COPY A:TRYTHIS.DOC B:NOTHANKS.DOC
```

One more example: If you want to duplicate TRYTHIS.DOC on drive A: under the name NOTHANKS.DOC, the command line would be

```
COPY TRYTHIS.DOC NOTHANKS.DOC
```

The important guidelines to remember are as follows:

- DOS assumes that all actions or commands are executed on the default drive (shown by the DOS prompt) unless you indicate otherwise.

- DOS assumes that the original file name is used for the new file created on the target disk, unless you indicate otherwise.

- You can copy a file to a different disk using the same or a different name.

- You can copy a file to the same disk using a different name.

- You cannot copy a file to the same disk using the same name—unless you copy to a different directory (directories are covered in Unit 5).

Using Wild Card Characters with the COPY Command

The wild card characters discussed in Unit 1 are very helpful with the COPY command. Let us assume that the disk in drive A: contains the following files:

```
NEWS1.DOC
NEWS2.DOC
NEWS3.DOC
NEWS4.DOC
NEWS5.DOC
```

You could use a series of commands to copy these files from drive A: to B:. The process would include typing five command lines and pressing the ⌨Enter key after each line.

```
COPY A:NEWS1.DOC B:
COPY A:NEWS2.DOC B:
COPY A:NEWS3.DOC B:
COPY A:NEWS4.DOC B:
COPY A:NEWS5.DOC B:
```

These command forms assume that the files will be called by the same names on drive B:. This is really a waste of time and energy. DOS provides a shortcut by using global wild card characters. The question mark (?) substitutes for a single character, and the asterisk (*) replaces all characters, in either the file specification or the extension. If these are the only files on the disk, you can use the following command line:

```
COPY A:*.* B:
```

This tells DOS to disregard both the file specification and the file extension, and to copy *all* files from A: to B:.

Let us complicate the matter by adding a few more files to the disk in drive A:.

NEWS1.DOC	NEWS3.BDC
NEWS1.BDC	NEWS4.DOC
NEWS2.DOC	NEWS4.BDC
NEWS2.BDC	NEWS5.DOC
NEWS3.DOC	NEWS5.BDC

The .BDC extension means that the file is a backup of the .DOC file with the same name. In this example, only the .DOC files should be copied to drive B:. Since all of the files you wish to copy have a common extension, you could use the asterisk to disregard the file specification, but stipulate the extension desired:

```
COPY A:*.DOC B:
```

In a similar fashion, if you want to copy only the two files NEWS4.DOC and NEWS4.BDC, you could use the wild card in place of the extension.

```
COPY A:NEWS4.* B:
```

Finally, consider the use of the question mark wild card. It allows even more selective copying. In this example, we will change the disks in drive A:. The new one includes the following files:

BUDGET89.DOC	BUDGET91.BDC	NEWS2.BDC
BUDGET89.WKS	BUDGET91.DOC	NEWS3.DOC
BUDGET90.DB	BUDGET91.WKS	NEWS4.DOC
BUDGET90.DBS	BUDGET92.DOC	NEWS5.BDC
BUDGET90.DOC	BUDGET92.WKS	NEWS5.DOC
BUDGET90.WKS		

Your task is to copy just the 1990 through 1992 budget worksheets and document files from the disk in drive A: to the disk in drive B:. You do not want to copy BUD-GET89.WKS, BUDGET89.DOC, or any of the NEWS files. The extensions on the 1990–92 files are different, so you must use the asterisk to accept any extension. However, using the question mark wild card character in the last character place of the file specification enables you to select the files you want to copy. A possible solution would be:

```
COPY A:BUDGET9?.* B:
```

What if you only want the database files (.DB and .DBS) and the document files (.DOC) for budget years 1990–92? The solution is to use the question mark wild card character in the file name extension. The command line would be:

```
COPY A:BUDGET9?.D?? B:
```

This command line says, in effect, "Copy any file that has BUDGET9 as the first seven characters of the file specification and D as the first character of the extension." This will eliminate the worksheet files (.WKS) and the backup document files (.BDC). Of course, you can also use the asterisk instead of the two question mark wild card characters. The following command line accomplishes the same task:

```
COPY A:BUDGET9?.D* B:
```

While you can use the question mark (?) wild card repeatedly to represent multiple characters (such as BUDGET9?.D??), it is more efficient to use the asterisk (*) wild card whenever multiple characters are involved.

Can You Verify That?

Two more keystrokes will buy you an insurance policy. Whenever you copy files, it makes sense to *verify* the results. When you add the /V switch, DOS finishes the copying process and then verifies that the original and duplicate files match. The process of verifying the accuracy of the copy slows the process down slightly, but not enough to be tedious. Once you have invested hours in creating a file, spending a few more seconds to verify the backup copy of that file should be a small price to pay for protecting the time already invested. Buy insurance and use the /V switch every time you copy files. To copy a file named SAVETHIS.TXT from drive C: to A: and verify the copy requires this command line:

```
COPY C:SAVETHIS.TXT A:/V
```

GUIDED ACTIVITY 4.1

Copying a File to Another Drive

In this Guided Activity, you copy files from the C:\WESTDATA.DS6 directory on drive C: to drive A:. Your instructor will advise you if the files are stored in a different location. You will need to use West Student Data Disk #3 in this activity. At this point, West Student Data Disk #3 is formatted but has no files stored on it.

1. Insert West Student Data Disk #3 in drive A:.

2. Change the default drive to C:.

3. Type CLS and press [Enter].

4. Type CD\WESTDATA.DS6 and press [Enter].

NOTE *You will learn about the CD command in Unit 5.*

If DOS displays the message "Invalid directory," ask your instructor for assistance.

5. Type DIR A: and press [Enter].

No files are on the disk.

CHECKPOINT 4A Why would you use the DIR command on a disk?

6. Type COPY C:MISC.ZIP A: and press [Enter].

The screen will display the message "1 file(s) copied."

7. Type DIR A: and press [Enter].

Figure 4.1 displays the screen as it should now appear.

NOTE *Remember, if you are using DOS 6.2, the column listing bytes used by each file will include commas in numbers above one thousand.*

8. Type CLS and press [Enter] to clear the screen.

In the following steps, you will practice the COPY command. Be sure you understand what you are doing and how the command must be executed.

9. Type COPY C:ALIGN.WP A: and press [Enter].

10. Copy ALIGN.WP from drive C: to drive A: again, without specifying drive C:.

NOTE *Beginning with DOS 6.2, if the file already exists on the target drive (as ALIGN.WP does), you will see an "Overwrite (Yes/No/All)?" screen message. To not overwrite the file on the target drive, type N. To overwrite the file on the target drive, type Y. If you are copying multiple files*

FIGURE 4.1
*DIR listing of
drive A: with
one file*

```
C:\>CD\WESTDATA.DS6

C:\WESTDATA.DS6>DIR A:

 Volume in drive A is BACON JONAT
 Volume Serial Number is 3A6A-1DCF
 Directory of A:\

File not found

C:\WESTDATA.DS6>COPY C:MISC.ZIP A:
        1 file(s) copied

C:\WESTDATA.DS6>DIR A:

 Volume in drive A is BACON JONAT
 Volume Serial Number is 3A6A-1DCF
 Directory of A:\

MISC     ZIP     24327 10-13-91   8:17p
        1 file(s)        24327 bytes
                       1433088 bytes free

C:\WESTDATA.DS6>
```

(using wild card characters), you can cause DOS to bypass the overwrite prompt by typing A to select the All option. The All option means that even if a file by the same name already appears on the target drive, DOS will overwrite the file with the identically named file from the source disk. This is the default setting with DOS prior to version 6.2.

If you see the overwrite message, type Y and press Enter.

CHECKPOINT 4B Do you understand why you can eliminate the reference to C:?

11. Copy the PAPER.WP file from drive C: to drive A:. Do not specify drive C: in the command. The command is similar to the command issued above. Do you understand why either form of the command works?

12. Type COPY WAR.WP A:/V and press Enter.

The /V switch verifies that the copy is made accurately, byte by byte.

NOTE *If using DOS 6.2, when you complete the next step you will see the prompt "Overwrite A:PAPER.WP (Yes/No/All)?" If this occurs, type Y and press Enter. Throughout these Guided Activities, when told to copy a file, type Y in response to the overwrite prompt, if it appears.*

13. Copy the PAPER.WP file to drive A: again.

NOTE *When you copied PAPER.WP to drive A: the second time, there was no warning message (unless you are using DOS 6.2). DOS does not warn you when you copy a file to a disk that contains a file with the same file name (in this case, PAPER.WP). The files could be completely different documents (with the same file name on different disks) and, after the copy process, one has been overwritten by the other.*

FIGURE 4.2
Directory listing of files copied to drive A:

```
C:\WESTDATA.DS6>DIR A:

 Volume in drive A is BACON JONAT
 Volume Serial Number is 3A6A-1DCF
 Directory of A:\

MISC     ZIP    24327 10-13-91   8:17p
ALIGN    WP      2377 10-12-91   9:49p
PAPER    WP      2879 05-08-93  11:23a
WAR      WP      1244 10-13-91   8:24p
        4 file(s)       30827 bytes
                      1425920 bytes free


C:\WESTDATA.DS6>
```

14. Type CLS and press [Enter] to clear the screen.

15. Type DIR A: and press [Enter].

    Your screen should appear similar to Figure 4.2.

GUIDED ACTIVITY 4.2

Copying Selected Files with the Wild Card Characters

In this Guided Activity, you use the wild card characters to copy selected files from C:\WESTDATA.DS6 to the disk in drive A:. In this and subsequent activities (until Guided Activity 4.7), we assume that you have continued directly from the last Guided Activity with West Student Data Disk #3 in drive A:.

1. Type CLS and press [Enter].

2. Type DIR MOM?.DOC and press [Enter].

   Three files are listed as meeting this file specification.

3. Type COPY MOM?.DOC A:/V and press [Enter].

CHECKPOINT 4C Will step 3 copy a file named MOM44.DOC to the disk in drive A:?

   The screen will display the message "3 file(s) copied."

4. Type DIR A: and press [Enter] to view the files on drive A:.

   Your screen should look like Figure 4.3. You now have seven files on the disk in drive A:.

5. Type CLS and press [Enter].

FIGURE 4.3
Screen display after using the COPY command

```
                    125181952 bytes free

C:\WESTDATA.DS6>COPY MOM?.DOC A:/V
MOM1.DOC
MOM2.DOC
MOM3.DOC
        3 file(s) copied

C:\WESTDATA.DS6>DIR A:

 Volume in drive A is BACON JONAT
 Volume Serial Number is 3A6A-1DCF
 Directory of A:\

MISC     ZIP     24327 10-13-91    8:17p
ALIGN    WP       2377 10-12-91    9:49p
PAPER    WP       2879 05-08-93   11:23a
WAR      WP       1244 10-13-91    8:24p
MOM1     DOC       419 10-04-88    7:28p
MOM2     DOC       667 10-04-88    7:44p
MOM3     DOC      1536 10-04-88    7:43p
        7 file(s)      33449 bytes
                     1422848 bytes free

C:\WESTDATA.DS6>
```

6. Type DIR A:*.TXT and press [Enter].

   No files exist on drive A: with the .TXT extension.

7. Type DIR C:*.TXT and press [Enter].

   Nine files are in the C:\WESTDATA.DS6 directory with the .TXT extension.

8. Type COPY *.TXT A:/V and press [Enter].

CHECKPOINT 4D Will the command in step 8 copy a file named NEWSLETR.TXT to the disk in drive A:?

   This will cause all files with the .TXT extension to be duplicated from drive C: to the disk in drive A:

9. Type CLS and press [Enter].

10. Type DIR A: and press [Enter].

CHECKPOINT 4E How would you display these files in order by their extension?

   Sixteen files are now displayed on your monitor screen as illustrated in Figure 4.4.

11. Type CLS and press [Enter].

12. Type DIR MOM?.* and press [Enter].

   Five files meet this file specification.

FIGURE 4.4
Sixteen files on the disk in drive A:

```
Volume in drive A is BACON JONAT
Volume Serial Number is 3A6A-1DCF
Directory of A:\

MISC     ZIP    24327 10-13-91    8:17p
ALIGN    WP      2377 10-12-91    9:49p
PAPER    WP      2879 05-08-93   11:23a
WAR      WP      1244 10-13-91    8:24p
MOM1     DOC      419 10-04-88    7:28p
MOM2     DOC      667 10-04-88    7:44p
MOM3     DOC     1536 10-04-88    7:43p
BECOMING TXT       53 10-04-88    7:22p
MYSTERY  TXT       91 10-06-88    7:03p
SAYING   TXT      193 10-04-88    7:51p
PUBLISH  TXT      265 10-04-88    7:59p
TRUCKIN  TXT      719 07-13-89    8:11a
STRATS1  TXT     2056 10-19-91    3:15p
STRATS2  TXT     1908 10-19-91    3:15p
PAPER    TXT     1043 05-08-93   11:29a
WAR      TXT      121 01-18-94   11:19a
        16 file(s)       39898 bytes
                       1413120 bytes free

C:\WESTDATA.DS6>
```

13. Type COPY MOM?.* A:/V and press [Enter].

NOTE *If using DOS 6.2, you will have to tell DOS to overwrite files that were copied to West Student Data Disk #3 in earlier Guided Activities. The easiest method is to type A to select the All option when the overwrite prompt appears.*

GUIDED ACTIVITY 4.3

Making a Duplicate File on the Same Disk

In this Guided Activity, we use the DOS COPY command to create a duplicate of an existing file. The difference between this and earlier Guided Activities is that the new file is given a new name so that it can coexist on the same disk as the original file.

1. With West Student Data Disk #3 in drive A:, type A:, and press [Enter] to change the default drive to A:.

2. Type CLS and press [Enter].

3. Type COPY BECOMING.TXT DREAMIT and press [Enter].

4. Type DIR and press [Enter].

Figure 4.5 shows the result of the COPY and DIR commands. The disk in drive A: now has a nineteenth file named DREAMIT. Notice that it does not have an extension. BECOMING.TXT is also on the disk.

FIGURE 4.5

*DIR listing after
using the COPY
command to
create a
duplicate file
with a new name*

```
Directory of A:\

MISC        ZIP      24327  10-13-91     8:17p
ALIGN       WP        2377  10-12-91     9:49p
PAPER       WP        2879  05-08-93    11:23a
WAR         WP        1244  10-13-91     8:24p
MOM1        DOC        419  10-04-88     7:28p
MOM2        DOC        667  10-04-88     7:44p
MOM3        DOC       1536  10-04-88     7:43p
BECOMING    TXT         53  10-04-88     7:22p
MYSTERY     TXT         91  10-06-88     7:03p
SAYING      TXT        193  10-04-88     7:51p
PUBLISH     TXT        265  10-04-88     7:59p
TRUCKIN     TXT        719  07-13-89     8:11a
STRATS1     TXT       2056  10-19-91     3:15p
STRATS2     TXT       1908  10-19-91     3:15p
PAPER       TXT       1043  05-08-93    11:29a
WAR         TXT        121  01-18-94    11:19a
MOM2        BAK        665  10-04-88     7:36p
MOM3        BAK        545  10-04-88     7:40p
DREAMIT                 53  10-04-88     7:22p
        19 file(s)       41161 bytes
                       1410560 bytes free

A:\>
```

GUIDED ACTIVITY 4.4

Copying All Files on a Disk with the Wild Card Character

In this Guided Activity, you will copy all files on C:\WESTDATA.DS6 to drive A:,
using the wild card character.

1. Type C: and press Enter.

2. The default directory should still be C:\WESTDATA.DS6 (set in Guided Activity
    4.1). If not, at the C: prompt, type CD\WESTDATA.DS6 and press Enter.

3. Type CLS and press Enter.

NOTE *If using DOS 6.2, you can add the /Y switch, which causes DOS to automatically overwrite
any files that exist on both the source and the target disks. To use this switch in the next step,
type COPY *.* A:/V/Y.*

4. Type COPY *.* A:/V and press Enter.

    The /V switch causes DOS to verify each copy.

    The screen will display the list of files as it copies them from drive A: to B:, using
    the global wild card characters (those standing for any and all characters in both
    file name and extension). Figure 4.6 shows the tail end of the screen activity.

FIGURE 4.6

*Results of using
the global wild
card characters
in the COPY
command*

```
MONSTERS
MYSTERY.TXT
MOM2.DOC
PUBLISH.BAK
MOM3.DOC
SAYING.TXT
HUMOROUS.PM4
WIN_MODE.DOC
ALIGN.WP
PUBLISH.TXT
TODOLIST.DOC
WINNEWS1.DOC
TRUCKIN.TXT
DINOSAUR.WP
STRATS2.DOC
STRATS1.DOC
STRATS1.TXT
WAR.WP
PAPER.WP
STRATS2.TXT
PAPER.TXT
WAR.TXT
        44 file(s) copied

C:\WESTDATA.DS6>
```

Copying Files to the Screen or Printer

The COPY command also provides a means of displaying the contents of a file on the screen or to the printer. In Unit 1, we briefly discussed DOS reserved words, and two of them come in handy now. *CON:* and *PRN* are, respectively, device names for the *console* (monitor screen) and a printer attached to *parallel port* 1 (LPT1:). These *device names* are discussed in greater depth later, in Unit 12. For now, just be aware that you can copy a file (usually meaning a text or document file) to the console or a printer by using these reserved words, which represent devices attached to the system unit.

GUIDED ACTIVITY 4.5

Copying a File to the Screen and to a Printer

In this Guided Activity, you will first copy a file to the printer attached to your system unit. Next, you will copy the same file to your monitor screen. West Student Data Disk #3 should be in drive A: for this Guided Activity.

NOTE *The following steps should work if you have a dot-matrix or laser printer, unless your laser printer is a PostScript printer. If you have a PostScript printer, complete only steps 1–2, then 5–10.*

1. Turn on your printer.

2. Type A: and press ⌨Enter to log on to drive A:.

3. Type CLS and press [Enter].

4. Type COPY SAYING.TXT PRN and press [Enter].

    Literally, this means "Copy from the default drive A: the file SAYING.TXT to the printer (PRN)."

5. Take your printer off line, press the form feed button, and put it back on line. Review the printed text.

    Next, you will copy the same file to the monitor screen.

6. Type COPY SAYING.TXT CON: and press [Enter].

    Literally, this means "Copy from the default drive A: the file SAYING.TXT to the console (CON:)."

    The screen display should match Figure 4.7.

FIGURE 4.7
Screen display after copying a file to the console

```
A:\>COPY SAYING.TXT PRN
        1 file(s) copied

A:\>COPY SAYING.TXT CON:
I DON'T CARE HOW
TALENTED, SKILLED,
OR TECHNICAL
YOU ARE.

IF YOU AREN'T A
PEOPLE PERSON, YOU
WON'T MAKE IT.

THAT'S WHAT
MAKES OR BREAKS A
SUCCESSFUL PERSON
IN ALL PROFESSIONS.
        1 file(s) copied

A:\>
```

7. Type CLS and press [Enter].

8. Type COPY PAPER.TXT CON: and press [Enter].

9. Type CLS and press [Enter].

10. Type COPY WAR.TXT CON: and press [Enter].

11. Use the previous steps and copy the PUBLISH.TXT document to your monitor screen.

12. Be sure your printer is turned on and on-line.

13. Type COPY STRATS1.TXT PRN: and press [Enter].

14. Take your printer off-line and form feed the page.

15. Be sure your printer is turned on again and on-line.

16. Type COPY STRATS2.TXT PRN: and press [Enter].

17. Take your printer off-line and form feed the page.

18. Be sure your printer is turned on again and on-line.

GUIDED ACTIVITY 4.6

Combining Files

In this Guided Activity, you will use the COPY command to combine two files. This is referred to as *file concatenation*. The files are concatenated (linked as in a chain) by placing + (the plus sign) between the file names. More than two files may be combined. Further, the text of the target file will include the text of all source files—in the order in which the files were listed on the command line. The resulting target file must have a new name, distinct from either source file, or the target file will overwrite one of the source files.

In this Guided Activity, the source files are on drive C: but the target (new file) will be on drive A:.

1. Type C: and press [Enter]. The current directory should be C:\WESTDATA.DS6.

2. Type CLS and press [Enter].

3. Type COPY SAYING.TXT+BECOMING.TXT A:NEWFILE and press [Enter].

4. Type DIR A:/W and press [Enter]. The NEWFILE file will be listed in a wide directory display (at the bottom of the list) on drive A:.

In the next few steps, you will display the text of the new file on the console.

5. Type COPY A:NEWFILE CON: and press [Enter].

The monitor screen will look like Figure 4.8.

Comparatively Speaking with the COMP Command

The COPY command is used to

- Transport files from one PC to another
- Share files with other users
- Back up crucial files

No matter what the reason, the accuracy of the copy is important. Just as the /V switch is used as insurance, DOS provides another method of comparing two copies of a file to determine if they are identical. The COMP command is a second safety net. It is used to compare the contents of a file (byte by byte) to a second file. When you use the wild card characters, the COMP command can also compare a group of

FIGURE 4.8
Results of combining two files

```
                    1378304 bytes free

C:\WESTDATA.DS6>COPY A:NEWFILE CON:
I DON'T CARE HOW
TALENTED, SKILLED,
OR TECHNICAL
YOU ARE.

IF YOU AREN'T A
PEOPLE PERSON, YOU
WON'T MAKE IT.

THAT'S WHAT
MAKES OR BREAKS A
SUCCESSFUL PERSON
IN ALL PROFESSIONS.


                We become

        what we think about.

        1 file(s) copied

C:\WESTDATA.DS6>
```

files to a second group of files. Ideally, you should use the COMP command immediately after using the COPY command to ensure the accuracy of the new copies.

The syntax of the command is

```
[d:][path]COMP [s:][filename] [t:][filename]
```

Do not forget that COMP is an external DOS command and must be accessible on disk.

NOTE *Beginning with DOS 6.0, the COMP command is not automatically installed when you install or upgrade DOS. It is available on the Supplemental Disk that can be ordered from Microsoft. Information on ordering the Supplemental Disk is available in the back of the Microsoft MS-DOS 6 User's Guide. If you are upgrading to DOS 6.x from a previous version, the COMP command will be available if it was already on your disk. The upgrade process does not delete the file.*

If you wish to compare the file TRUEBLUE.DB on drive C: (using the COMP command also located on C:) to the same file on drive A:, you would use the command line

```
COMP C:TRUEBLUE.DB A:
```

The same assumptions discussed under the COPY command are applicable to the COMP command. That is, DOS assumes the default drive unless another drive is specified, and DOS assumes that the file names to compare are identical—unless told otherwise. If the default drive is C:, the command line could be simplified to

```
COMP TRUEBLUE.DB A:
```

If each comparison made with COMP is successful, then you will see the following screen message:

```
Files compare OK
```

If the command discovers comparison errors, an error message will appear, indicating the location of mismatched bytes. The form of the message is

```
Compare error at OFFSET X
file 1 = XX
file 2 = XX
```

The offset indicates how many bytes from the beginning of the file the mismatch occurred. The next two lines indicate, in *hexadecimal*, the contents of the offending byte of data. That is, it lists, in hexadecimal code (which represents the letters and numbers you type in a document), the data from the first file and then the data from the second file. If ten mismatches occur, DOS terminates the comparison and gives you a message. Disk copy errors may result from a flaw in one of the disks (either the source or target), an electrical spike or power loss during the copying process, or a mechanical failure of the floppy disk drive. Errors are very infrequent and are cause for concern. To most users, *any* mismatch means that the file should simply be recopied. An example of a compare error is shown in Figure 4.9.

FIGURE 4.9
*Screen
messages
indicating
compare errors*

```
A:\>COMP A: B:
Comparing A:BECOMING.TXT and B:BECOMING.TXT...
Files are different sizes

Comparing A:MYSTERY.TXT and B:MYSTERY.TXT...
Compare error at OFFSET 0
file1 = 57
file2 = 4D
Compare error at OFFSET 32
file1 = 4D
file2 = 57
Compare error at OFFSET 4C
file1 = 6E
file2 = 6D

Compare more files (Y/N) ?
```

Finally, it should be noted that if you simply enter the command COMP with no file name or parameters, your computer will prompt you further for the "Name of first file to compare:". Once you type the first file name to compare and press Enter, you will be prompted for the "Name of second file to compare:". It saves time to enter all the parameters on the command line rather than just enter the COMP command. Since COMP is an external DOS command, entering COMP alone is really helpful only on a floppy disk-based system. In such a case, when you enter just COMP, the system loads the file and then gives you time to switch disks before entering the two files names or two drives to compare.

Using Wild Card Characters with the COMP Command

The global wild card characters can be used with the COMP command in the same manner as with the COPY command. If you have copied multiple files by using wild card characters, use the same format to invoke the COMP command. For example, you may have just copied all files from drive A: to B:, using the following command:

```
COPY A:*.* B:
```

You can then compare the same files by simply using the COMP command instead of the COPY command.

```
COMP A:*.* B:
```

In the discussion of the COPY command, we used an example disk with the following files:

```
NEWS1.DOC        NEWS3.BDC
NEWS1.BDC        NEWS4.DOC
NEWS2.DOC        NEWS4.BDC
NEWS2.BDC        NEWS5.DOC
NEWS3.DOC        NEWS5.BDC
```

To copy all the files ending with a .DOC extension, the command line was

```
COPY A:*.DOC B:
```

Immediately after using this form of the COPY command, you could compare the files with the following command line:

```
COMP A:*.DOC B:
```

The question mark wild card character may also be used with the COMP command. The following are two companion command lines. They will, respectively, copy a group of files and then compare the original and duplicate versions of the files.

```
COPY A:BUDGET9?.* B:
COMP A:BUDGET9?.* B:
```

TIP *The two commands listed above can be combined into a single command if you use the /V (verify) switch with the COPY command. The /V switch was discussed earlier in this unit. The combined command line would read* COPY A:BUDGET9?.* B:/V. *The verify switch performs the same function as executing the COMP command.*

When using the COMP command, you may see the message "EOF mark not found." The *end-of-file mark* is placed at the end of a file by pressing Ctrl Z or F6. For some files the EOF "tells" DOS the file is complete. Not all application programs use the EOF mark. When it is not found, it may not mean your files are incorrect. But if you are comparing program files that contain an EOF mark and you receive the error message, you would have cause for concern.

GUIDED ACTIVITY 4.7

Comparing Files with the COMP Command

In this Guided Activity, you will format a new disk, label it as West Student Data Disk #4, and then copy files from the C:\WESTDATA.DS6 directory to the disk. Finally, you will compare the files to be sure accurate copies were made.

You should be logged on to drive C:\WESTDATA.DS6 to begin this Guided Activity.

1. Format a new disk and label it as West Student Data Disk #4.

2. Be sure that West Student Data Disk #4 is in drive A:

3. Type CLS and press [Enter].

4. Type COPY PUBLISH.BAK A: and press [Enter].

5. Type DIR A: and press [Enter].

6. Type COMP PUBLISH.BAK A: and press [Enter].

7. Type N and press [Enter].

    Figure 4.10 shows the proper screen response.

8. Type CLS and press [Enter].

9. Type COPY CLASSES.* A: and press [Enter]. Two files are copied.

10. Type COMP CLASSES.* A: and press [Enter].

11. Type N and press [Enter].

    Figure 4.11 shows the screen response for the COMP command, using the global wild card character.

12. Type CLS and press [Enter].

FIGURE 4.10

Screen activity for the COMP command

```
C:\WESTDATA.DS6>COPY PUBLISH.BAK A:
        1 file(s) copied

C:\WESTDATA.DS6>DIR A:

 Volume in drive A is BACON JONAT
 Volume Serial Number is 1F55-1AF5
 Directory of A:\

PUBLISH  BAK       255 10-04-88   7:54p
        1 file(s)          255 bytes
                       1457152 bytes free

C:\WESTDATA.DS6>COMP PUBLISH.BAK A:
Comparing PUBLISH.BAK and A:PUBLISH.BAK...
Files compare OK

Compare more files (Y/N) ? N

C:\WESTDATA.DS6>
```

FIGURE 4.11
Screen responses when using the COMP command and wild card character

```
C:\WESTDATA.DS6>COPY CLASSES.* A:
CLASSES.DB
CLASSES.DBS
        2 file(s) copied

C:\WESTDATA.DS6>COMP CLASSES.* A:
Comparing CLASSES.DB and A:CLASSES.DB...
Files compare OK

Comparing CLASSES.DBS and A:CLASSES.DBS...
Files compare OK

Compare more files (Y/N) ? N

C:\WESTDATA.DS6>
```

I Want My Name Legally Changed, Said the File

DOS provides the RENAME command as the tool by which a file name may be changed. As with many DOS commands, there is a shorter version of the command, REN, which is used throughout the remainder of this text.

The syntax of the REN command is

```
REN [d:]oldfilename.ext newfilename.ext
```

The old and new file names and extensions are not optional. You must use the complete file name. For instance, suppose drive A: has a file named JUNK.DOC. To rename it to TREASURE.DOC, you must use this command line:

```
REN JUNK.DOC TREASURE.DOC
```

If you use the command line

```
REN JUNK.DOC TREASURE
```

and leave off the extension, the new file name will be TREASURE rather than TREA-SURE.DOC. File name extensions with some applications are important, so be sure that when you rename files you give them the same extension—unless you have a specific reason not to do so.

Wild card characters may also be used with the REN command, but *use them cautiously*. REN cannot rename a file to a name already in use on the disk. Figure 4.12 displays the error message indicating that a file named TREASURE.DOC already exists.

The REN command is an internal DOS command. As such, it does not require access to DOS files on disk to execute the command. The REN command allows you to change the name of your file.

One final note on the REN command. You never need to specify the drive designation for the new file name. DOS assumes it is the same drive as the drive for the old file name. In fact, REN can only rename a file on a specified drive to another name on the same drive. DOS will indignantly refuse to execute the REN command if the drive is repeated for the new file name (the screen will display an "invalid

FIGURE 4.12
*REN command
error message*

```
A:\>REN JUNK.DOC TREASURE.DOC
Duplicate file name or file not found

A:\>
```

parameter" error message). If you want to create a file on a different drive with a different name, use the COPY command—not the REN command.

GUIDED ACTIVITY 4.8

Changing a File Name

In this Guided Activity, you will first rename a single file, then use the global wild card characters to rename a group of files. West Student Data Disk #4 should still be in drive A:. At the beginning of this Guided Activity it contains only three files, PUBLISH.BAK, CLASSES.DB, and CLASSES.DBS. During the course of the activity, you will copy the remaining files from C:\WESTDATA.DS6 to West Student Data Disk #4.

1. Type A: and press [Enter] to change the logged-on drive to A:.

2. Type CLS and press [Enter].

    Be sure the DOS prompt shows the A: drive as the default drive.

3. Type REN PUBLISH.BAK PARISH.DOC and press [Enter].

4. Type DIR and press [Enter] to see the directory listing for drive A:.

    PUBLISH.BAK is now PARISH.DOC as shown in Figure 4.13.

5. Type C: and press [Enter] to change the default drive.

6. The default directory should be C:\WESTDATA.DS6. If not, type CD\WESTDATA.DS6 and press [Enter].

7. Type CLS and press [Enter].

FIGURE 4.13
*Directory
listing with
renamed file*

```
A:\>REN PUBLISH.BAK PARISH.DOC

A:\>DIR

 Volume in drive A is BACON JONAT
 Volume Serial Number is 1F55-1AF5
 Directory of A:\

PARISH   DOC        255 10-04-88    7:54p
CLASSES  DB         566 10-04-88    8:08p
CLASSES  DBS        485 01-01-80   12:30p
         3 file(s)        1306 bytes
                       1455616 bytes free

A:\>
```

8. Copy all files from the C:\WESTDATA.DS6 directory to the disk in drive A:
    (West Student Data Disk #4).

NOTE *If using DOS 6.2, be sure to add the /Y switch, which causes DOS to automatically overwrite any files that exist on both the source and the target disks.*

CHECKPOINT 4F Name the command that most efficiently accomplishes the task required in the last step.

9. Change the default drive to A:.

10. Type DIR DAD* and press Enter. There are no files meeting this specification.

11. Type CLS and press Enter.

12. Type REN MOM?.* DAD?.* and press Enter.

    This command line will rename each MOM file to a DAD file. Because of the use of the question mark wild card, all five files will be renamed, respectively, to

        DAD1.DOC
        DAD2.DOC
        DAD3.DOC
        DAD2.BAK
        DAD3.BAK

13. Type DIR DAD* and press Enter.

    Figure 4.14 shows the screen activity. Notice the new file names as a result of using the REN command.

FIGURE 4.14
New directory listing after using the REN command

```
A:\>REN MOM?.* DAD?.*

A:\>DIR DAD*

 Volume in drive A is BACON JONAT
 Volume Serial Number is 1F55-1AF5
 Directory of A:\

DAD1     DOC      419 10-04-88   7:28p
DAD2     BAK      665 10-04-88   7:36p
DAD3     BAK      545 10-04-88   7:40p
DAD2     DOC      667 10-04-88   7:44p
DAD3     DOC     1536 10-04-88   7:43p
        5 file(s)        3832 bytes
                     1378816 bytes free

A:\>
```

14. Type CLS and press Enter.

15. Type REN DIET.DOC NEWFILE1.TXT and press Enter.

16. Type DIR/W and press Enter.

    Notice that DIET.DOC no longer exists, but NEWFILE1.TXT does (column 3).

17. Type `REN INDEFENS.DOC NEWFILE2.TXT` and press [Enter].

18. Type `DIR/W` and press [Enter].

   Notice the change in the file name (column 2).

19. Type `REN WINNEWS1.DOC NEWFILE1.TXT` and press [Enter].

   Notice the error message: "Duplicate file name or file not found." You cannot rename a file to use a file name that is already in use in the target directory on the target disk.

The Second Most Destructive DOS Command

The DEL or ERASE command is second only to the FORMAT command in the havoc it can play on your data. If used indiscriminately, the DEL command can wipe out every file in a directory or on a disk before you can blink twice. On the other hand, if used wisely, it can quickly eliminate old files and free storage space for new documents, databases, and program files. The DEL and ERASE commands are identical, so it makes sense to use the shorter version, which saves keystrokes. Throughout the text, we ignore the ERASE command and only use DEL. Just remember that both commands are identical in syntax and results.

NOTE *You might assume that the DEL command is a shortened or mnemonic version of DELETE, but that is not the case. There is no DELETE command in MS-DOS.*

The syntax of the DEL command is

```
DEL [d:]filename.ext
```

For example, if you wish to eliminate a file on drive A: containing out-of-date data, called NOGOOD.TXT, the command form would be

```
DEL A:NOGOOD.TXT
```

If the file is on drive C: and your DOS prompt indicates that drive C: is the default drive, the command can be simplified to

```
DEL NOGOOD.TXT
```

Using Wild Card Characters with the DEL Command

Wild card characters can be used with the DEL command, just as they are with COPY, COMP, and REN. *Just be careful that you understand the results of the DEL command and use it with caution.* When a file is deleted, it cannot be restored without using the UNDELETE command. That command, introduced in DOS 5.0, only works if you use it before the deleted file is overwritten by a new file saved to the same sectors on the disk. The UNDELETE command is discussed shortly.

It is a safe practice always to use the same parameters with the DIR command, before using them with the DEL command. The DIR command provides a list of all files that will be deleted—if you substitute the DEL command for DIR. For example, if you enter

```
DIR LETTER.*
```

then DOS will display all files with the LETTER file name and any extension. If the list is acceptable (the files you want to delete), then you can enter

```
DEL LETTER.*
```

NOTE *The DEL command does not remove files from your disk; rather, it marks the appropriate allocation units (in the FAT) as free or nonallocated. In fact, the contents of the file(s) are still on the disk until other information is written over it. When using the DEL command, you should assume that you are permanently erasing the files, which was the case prior to DOS 5.x. When this was done in earlier versions of DOS, the files were literally inaccessible unless you used a special utility program like PC Tools or Norton Utilities to retrieve them. Even now, with the availablity of the UNDELETE command, once the allocation unit is marked as free, the next save operation may overwrite the data in the allocation unit, thus making the data irretrievable. Unerase utilities and the UNDELETE command are most effective if used* immediately *after the accidental erasure.*

The DEL Command Switch

The DEL command has a single switch. The /P switch causes DOS to prompt you before actually deleting any files from the disk. This switch can be very helpful when using global or wild card characters. It serves as an extra safety precaution. The syntax of this form of the command is

```
DEL [d:][path]filename[/P]
```

When you use the /P (prompt) switch, DOS will list each file name and inquire

```
Delete (Y/N)?
```

To delete all files with the .TXT extension from the disk in drive A:, you would execute the command

```
DEL A:*.TXT
```

If you wish to be prompted before the deletion of each file with the .TXT extension, use the command form

```
DEL A:*.TXT/P
```

As you become more expert in using DOS and learn good housekeeping habits, you may not need the warning prompt.

GUIDED ACTIVITY 4.9

Deleting Files

In this Guided Activity, you will delete a single file, a group of files, and all remaining files from the disk in drive A: (West Student Data Disk #4). By the time you complete this activity, the disk will once again be clear of all files. *Be sure that you have logged on to drive A: before you begin deleting files in this activity.*

1. Change the default drive to A:, if it is not already the default drive.

2. Type CLS and press [Enter].

3. Type DIR/W and press [Enter].

    You will see a wide listing of the files on drive A:. Notice the presence of the file STRATS1.DOC (column 4).

4. Type DEL STRATS1.DOC and press [Enter].

5. Type DIR/W/ON and press [Enter] and you will see an alphabetical listing of the files on drive A:.

✓ **CHECKPOINT 4G** What is the result of using the /W and /ON switches with the DIR command?

Notice that the STRATS1.DOC file is no longer listed. Also notice the existence of several files: DAD1.DOC, DAD2.DOC, DAD3.DOC, DAD2.BAK, and DAD3.BAK. In the next few steps, you will delete the .DOC versions of these files.

6. Type CLS and press [Enter].

7. Type DIR DAD?.DOC and press [Enter].

    Three files are listed.

8. Type DEL DAD?.DOC and press [Enter].

    This command deletes all files beginning with "DAD" no matter what the fourth character in the file is, if the file has a .DOC extension.

9. Type DIR DAD* and press [Enter].

    Notice the absence of these three files: DAD1.DOC, DAD2.DOC, and DAD3.DOC. However, the DAD files with the .BAK extension remain.

    In the next two steps, you will determine which files end with a .BAK extension on the disk and then delete them.

10. Type DIR *.BAK and press [Enter].

11. Type DEL *.BAK and press [Enter].

12. To see that the files are gone, type DIR *.BAK and press [Enter].

    Finally, the next two steps will cause the deletion of the remaining files on drive A:.

13. Type DIR A:*.* and press ⏎Enter

    Thirty-six files are currently on the disk.

14. Type DEL A:*.* and press ⏎Enter.

    DOS responds with the message, "All files in directory will be deleted! Are you sure (Y/N)?" Figure 4.15 displays this warning message. If you type Y for yes and press ⏎Enter, all the files on the disk in drive A: will be deleted.

FIGURE 4.15
*Warning
message issued
when using
the DEL *.*
command form*

```
MYSTERY   TXT       91 10-06-88   7:03p
SAYING    TXT      193 10-04-88   7:51p
HUMOROUS  PM4       91 05-08-93   7:41p
WIN_MODE  DOC     1429 10-12-91   9:18p
ALIGN     WP      2377 10-12-91   9:49p
PUBLISH   TXT      265 10-04-88   7:59p
TODOLIST  DOC       74 05-08-93   7:59p
WINNEWS1  DOC       23 05-08-93   7:56p
TRUCKIN   TXT      719 07-13-89   8:11a
DINOSAUR  WP        24 05-08-93   7:52p
STRATS2   DOC     4019 10-13-91   8:02p
STRATS1   TXT     2056 10-19-91   3:15p
WAR       WP      1244 10-13-91   8:24p
PAPER     WP      2879 05-08-93  11:23a
STRATS2   TXT     1908 10-19-91   3:15p
PAPER     TXT     1043 05-08-93  11:29a
WAR       TXT      121 01-18-94  11:19a
        36 file(s)       54391 bytes
                       1392128 bytes free

A:\>DEL A:*.*
All files in directory will be deleted!
Are you sure (Y/N)?Y

A:\>
```

15. Type Y and press ⏎Enter.

16. Type DIR and press ⏎Enter.

    The screen should respond by indicating that no files have been found on drive A:.

NOTE *You should continue with the next Guided Activity before you copy, delete, or otherwise further modify your West Student Data Disk #4.*

The UNDELETE Command

Prior to DOS 5.0, the operating system did not include an UNDELETE command. If you accidentally deleted one or more files, you had to go to a backup copy (possibly outdated) or use a third-party utility program like Norton Utilities, PC Tools, or Mace Utilities to attempt to recover the file. Beginning with DOS 5.*x*, this feature was made available as part of the operating system and eliminated the need to buy an additional utility program.

Normally, when a file is deleted, its entry in the file allocation table (FAT) is modified to indicate the deletion and free the file's allocation units for use with other files. That erasure can be restored and the file retrieved, by using the UNDELETE command.

Beginning with DOS 6.*x*, the UNDELETE command uses one of three levels of protecting files from accidental deletion. The three methods are called Delete Sentry, Delete Tracker (which uses a *deletion-tracking file*), and the standard method (sometimes referred to as the MS-DOS directory method).

Delete Sentry

Delete Sentry provides the highest level of protection. Whenever a file is "deleted," the data is simply moved from its current location to a hidden \SENTRY directory without changing the record of the file's location in the file allocation table.

NOTE *Directories are discussed in more depth in Unit 5. For now, consider a directory as a "file folder" in which you place one or more files.*

If you decide that you need the file and take steps to undelete it, DOS moves it back to its original location. Because you would rapidly run out of hard disk space if every deleted file was moved to the \SENTRY directory, the size of this directory is limited to 7 percent of your hard disk space. If a newly deleted file would push the directory beyond that limit, the oldest deleted files are purged until space is freed to accommodate the newly deleted file.

To use the Delete Sentry system, you must load a *memory-resident program*, which takes about 13.5KB of memory. A memory-resident program (also called terminate-and-stay-resident, or TSR) is an accessory or utility program designed to stay in RAM at all times; it often can be invoked with a keystroke or two. The Delete Sentry program is loaded by entering the following command at the DOS prompt:

    UNDELETE /S

This form of the UNDELETE command can also be entered every time you reboot your computer by using your system's AUTOEXEC.BAT file. This is a special file discussed in Unit 11.

If you enter UNDELETE /S, the Delete Sentry protection is available only for your current default drive. If you want this protection extended to another drive, you must add that drive letter after the /S parameter the next time you invoke the UNDELETE command. For instance, to add drive A: to Delete Sentry protection, enter the command as

    UNDELETE /SA

NOTE *The UNDELETE command documentation indicates that UNDELETE /S protects only the current default drive and that the /S parameter followed by a drive letter protects only the specified drive. However, the effect appears to be cumulative. If you first use the /S parameter and then later add a floppy drive letter after the /S parameter, UNDELETE appears to protect both the original default hard disk drive and the floppy drive added later. You cannot use two drive letters after a single execution of the UNDELETE command with the /S parameter; for example, UNDELETE /SCA will generate an "invalid parameters" message.*

Delete Tracker

The Delete Tracker system provides an intermediate level of protection against accidentally deleting files. This method stores information on deleted files and the allocation units they were assigned, in a hidden file called PCTRACKER.DEL. Delete Tracker is more accurate than the standard method (discussed next) but less accurate than using Delete Sentry. Delete Tracker requires 13.5KB of memory (it too is a memory-resident program) but requires far less hard disk space than Delete Sentry because it only adds one file to your system, the PCTRACKER.DEL file. The program is loaded by entering the following command at the DOS prompt:

```
UNDELETE /TC
```

Unlike the UNDELETE /S command form, this form of the command requires that you stipulate the drive on which you want the PCTRACKER.DEL file installed. The above command form places the PCTRACKER.DEL file on drive C:.

Delete Standard

The standard level of protection (also called the MS-DOS directory method or Delete Standard) is automatically available whenever you turn on your personal computer and without invoking the UNDELETE command to load a memory-resident module. It provides the lowest level of protection but is always available. It does not require either memory (RAM) or hard disk space. However, unlike with Delete Sentry, once you save a file that uses some or all of the allocation units formerly used by the deleted file, the file becomes irretrievable.

Determining the Protection Method

You can determine the protection method in use by using the /STATUS parameter with the UNDELETE command. For example, at the DOS prompt, you can type the following command to determine if Delete Sentry, Delete Tracker, or the Delete Standard method is in effect.

```
UNDELETE /STATUS
```

If Delete Sentry is in effect, your screen will appear similar to Figure 4.16. In this example, Delete Sentry is enabled for drives C: and D:, but would not protect files on floppy drives A: or B:.

FIGURE 4.16
The current delete protection method screen

```
A:\>UNDELETE /STATUS

UNDELETE - A delete protection facility
Copyright (C) 1987-1993 Central Point Software, Inc.
All rights reserved.

Delete Protection Method is Delete Sentry.
Enabled for drives : C D

A:\>
```

If you are using only the Delete Standard method, you can change the protection method by loading either the Delete Sentry or Delete Tracker module, as described above. However, if you want to change from one of the two memory-resident methods (Sentry or Tracker) to the other, or change to the standard protection method, you must first unload the memory-resident module. This is accomplished by entering the following command at the DOS prompt:

```
UNDELETE /UNLOAD
```

Undeleting Files

To unerase or restore a file named JUNK.DOC, you would use the UNDELETE command followed by the file name, such as

```
UNDELETE JUNK.DOC
```

If the file is not in the current directory, you must specify the path to the file.

```
UNDELETE C:\WESTDATA\JUNK.DOC
```

Two switches are most commonly used with this command (in addition to specifying the file name):

/LIST Lists the files available for undeletion but does not unerase them.

/ALL Attempts to recover all deleted files, without prompting for confirmation on each file.

NOTE *Deleted files have the first character of the file name erased in the DOS directory table. If DOS is not using the Delete Sentry or the Delete Tracker program during the undeletion process (unless you use the /ALL switch), you are prompted to supply the missing character. If you are unsure of the first character, you can type any character so long as it does not cause a duplicate file name to exist in the current directory on the target drive. If you use the /ALL switch, the UNDELETE command substitutes the pound sign (#) for the first character of the file name. If that causes a duplicate file name to exist, the command substitutes another character (%, &, - are the first choices) until it arrives at a legal and unique file name. You can then inspect the revived files and rename them as you wish.*

GUIDED ACTIVITY 4.10

Undeleting Files

In this Guided Activity, you undelete several files deleted on West Student Data Disk #4 in the last Guided Activity.

1. You should still be logged on to drive A:; type CLS and press Enter.

2. To check the delete protection status, type UNDELETE /STATUS, and press Enter.

3. After reviewing the screen message, type CLS and press Enter.

4. Type UNDELETE A:MYSTERY.TXT and press Enter.

5. When prompted "Undelete (Y/N)?," type Y.

If the Delete Sentry protection system is installed, you will not see the prompt in the next step. Delete Sentry already knows the first letter of the file name.

6. When prompted "Please type the first character of ?YSTERY. TXT:," type M.

If the command is successful, you will see the message

    File successfully undeleted.

Assuming that Delete Sentry protection is not installed, your screen will appear similar to Figure 4.17.

FIGURE 4.17
The UNDELETE command screen messages using the MS-DOS directory method (standard protection)

```
UNDELETE - A delete protection facility
Copyright (C) 1987-1993 Central Point Software, Inc.
All rights reserved.

Directory: A:\
File Specifications: MYSTERY.TXT

    Delete Sentry control file not found.

    Deletion-tracking file not found.

    MS-DOS directory contains     1 deleted files.
    Of those,     1 files may be recovered.

Using the MS-DOS directory method.

    ?YSTERY  TXT       91 10-06-88  7:03p  ...A  Undelete (Y/N)?Y
    Please type the first character for ?YSTERY .TXT: M

File successfully undeleted.


A:\>
```

If the Delete Sentry protection is installed, your screen will appear similar to Figure 4.18.

7. Type DIR and press [Enter].

The MYSTERY.TXT file once again appears in the directory listing.

8. Use the same process to undelete the following files on the disk in drive A:

        DAD1.DOC
        PAPER.TXT
        TRUCKIN.TXT
        ALIGN.WP

9. Type CLS and press [Enter].

10. Type DIR A: and press [Enter].

FIGURE 4.18
The UNDELETE command screen messages, using Delete Sentry

```
UNDELETE - A delete protection facility
Copyright (C) 1987-1993 Central Point Software, Inc.
All rights reserved.

Directory: A:\
File Specifications: MYSTERY.TXT

     Delete Sentry control file contains    1 deleted files.

     Deletion-tracking file not found.

     MS-DOS directory contains    2 deleted files.
     Of those,    0 files may be recovered.

Using the Delete Sentry method.

     MYSTERY  TXT      91 10-06-88  7:03p  ...A  Deleted: 5-31-93  7:19a
This file can be 100% undeleted. Undelete (Y/N)?Y

File successfully undeleted.



A:\>
```

Five files should be listed as shown in Figure 4.19.

FIGURE 4.19
Five undeleted files

```
A:\>DIR A:

Volume in drive A is BACON JONAT
Volume Serial Number is 1F55-1AF5
Directory of A:\

DAD1      DOC       419 10-04-88   7:28p
MYSTERY   TXT        91 10-06-88   7:03p
ALIGN     WP       2377 10-12-91   9:49p
TRUCKIN   TXT       719 07-13-89   8:11a
PAPER     TXT      1043 05-08-93  11:29a
          5 file(s)      4649 bytes
                      1451520 bytes free

A:\>
```

The global wild card characters (* or ?) can be used with the UNDELETE command. In the following steps, you will use a wild card character and the /ALL switch.

11. Type CLS and press [Enter].

12. Type UNDELETE A:*.WP/ALL and press [Enter].

Your screen should now appear similar to Figure 4.20.

13. Type CLS and press [Enter].

14. Type DIR and press [Enter].

FIGURE 4.20
The UNDELETE /ALL command activity

```
        Delete Sentry control file not found.

        Deletion-tracking file not found.

        MS-DOS directory contains     3 deleted files.
        Of those,    3 files may be recovered.

Using the MS-DOS directory method.

        ?INOSAUR WP          24  5-08-93  7:52p  ...A

File successfully undeleted.

        ?AR      WP        1244 10-13-91  8:24p  ...A

File successfully undeleted.

        ?APER    WP        2879  5-08-93 11:23a  ...A

File successfully undeleted.



A:\>
```

Eight of the previously deleted files are now unerased and displayed by the DIR command, as shown in Figure 4.21. Notice that all the files with the .WP extension (except ALIGN.WP) now begin with the # character. You can use the REN command to rename them back to their original file names and eliminate the # sign.

NOTE   *If using Delete Sentry, the files all have their original file names and none of them begin with the # sign.*

FIGURE 4.21
Undeleted files on disk in drive A:

```
A:\>DIR

  Volume in drive A is BACON JONAT
  Volume Serial Number is 1F55-1AF5
  Directory of A:\

DAD1     DOC      419 10-04-88    7:28p
MYSTERY  TXT       91 10-06-88    7:03p
ALIGN    WP      2377 10-12-91    9:49p
TRUCKIN  TXT      719 07-13-89    8:11a
#INOSAUR WP        24 05-08-93    7:52p
#AR      WP      1244 10-13-91    8:24p
#APER    WP      2879 05-08-93   11:23a
PAPER    TXT     1043 05-08-93   11:29a
        8 file(s)       8796 bytes
                     1446400 bytes free

A:\>
```

The DIR and UNDELETE Commands

When using the Delete Sentry program, you will find that executing the DIR command on a floppy disk may take an unusually long time. This occurs when you have deleted files and then do not use that particular disk for a few days. The delay is only experienced the first time you access the disk using the DIR command. Delete Sentry stores the deleted files in the \SENTRY directory until the erased files consume about 7 percent of the available disk space. When that level of disk space is used, Delete Sentry begins deleting the oldest files first to free up disk space.

It may appear that your system has "hung" (stopped working), but give the command a few extra seconds (10–20) to evaluate the previously erased files stored in the \SENTRY directory.

Summary

In this unit, you learned how to manage files on your disk, including the procedures to copy and compare them, rename them, delete them, and undelete them. These are the basic file management skills that all computer users must have.

Command Review

In this unit, you learned several DOS commands. Most have optional parameters or switches. We have tried to cover both the common and the rarely used forms of each command. The following forms of this unit's commands are the most frequently used and should be reviewed carefully.

COMP A:*.* C:	Compares all files on the disk in drive A: with like-named files on drive C:.
COPY A:FILE.DOC B:.	Copies the file FILE.DOC from the disk in drive A: to the disk in drive B:
COPY A:FILE.DOC B:/V	Copies and verifies that the file FILE.DOC was accurately copied to drive B:.
COPY *.* B:	Copies all files on the default drive to the disk in drive B:.
DEL A:OLDFILE.DOC	Deletes the file named OLDFILE.DOC from the disk in drive A:.
DEL A:*.*	Deletes all files from the disk in drive A:.
DEL A:*.*/P	Deletes all files from the disk in drive A: only after you respond "Y" to the prompt "Delete (Y/N)?" for each file.

REN A:ONE.TXT TWO.TXT	Renames the file ONE.TXT (on the disk in drive A:) to TWO.TXT.
UNDELETE A:LOSTFILE.DOC	Restores the accidentally erased file named LOSTFILE.DOC on drive A:.
UNDELETE A:*.*/ALL	Restores all accidentally erased files on the disk in drive A:.
UNDELETE /S	Turns on the Delete Sentry method of protection.

Review Questions

1. How would you copy all files from the disk in drive A: to a disk in drive B:?

2. How would you copy a file named THISONE.TXT on drive A: to the new file name THATONE.DOC on drive C:?

3. What is the result of using the /V switch with the COPY command?

4. Name the two wild card characters that may be used with the COPY command.

5. When using the following command line, what would be the name of the new file created? On which drive would it appear?

   ```
   COPY B:THIS.MSG A:OLD.MSG
   ```

6. How would you copy the file C:SCREEN.MSG to the monitor screen?

7. How would you copy the file B:PRINTER.MSG to the printer?

8. Name two reserved words.

9. How would you use the COPY command to combine two files into a new, third file?

10. What does the COMP command do?

11. What happens if a comparison of two files discovers mismatched bytes of data?

12. What is the difference between the COMP and DISKCOMP commands?

13. Which DOS command is used to change the name of a file?

14. Name the second most destructive DOS command. Name the first most destructive command.

15. Which command should always be used before using the DEL command with a wild card character?

16. How would you erase all the files on a disk with a single command?

17. Name the command that attempts to recover deleted files.

18. Which version of DOS introduced the UNDELETE command?

19. Name the form of the UNDELETE command that loads the memory-resident Delete Sentry protection system.

20. Name the three methods used by the UNDELETE command to restore files.

21. When undeleting a group of files, which character is used for the first character of the restored file?

22. How would you cause DOS to display a list of files that may be undeleted?

23. How would you determine which type of deletion protection is currently being used by your computer system?

24. Which form of the UNDELETE command will undelete files without prompting for each file?

25. How would you invoke Delete Sentry protection for a disk in drive A:?

Exercises

Whenever instructed to format a disk, use your last name (first) and then your first name (such as BACON JON) as the volume label. If instructed to print data from the screen, be sure to handwrite your full name, course number and section, course title, instructor's name, unit and exercise number, and today's date on the paper. Your instructor will indicate if the disk(s) created or printouts should be submitted for grading.

In the following Exercises, use a different disk for Exercises 1 and 2.

1. Copy all files from the \WESTDATA.DS6 directory with either a .DB or .DBS extension to a formatted disk in drive A:.

2. Copy all files from the \WESTDATA.DS6 directory beginning with the letter "D" to a formatted disk in drive A:.

3. Use `Ctrl` `PrtSc` to print any screen messages from the following activity to your printer. Place the disk created in Exercise 2 (above) in drive A:. Use the DEL command with a parameter that causes you to be prompted before each file is deleted. When prompted, do not delete any files.

4. In this exercise, you will be required to generate a printed copy of all screen activity. Use the CLS command before you begin. Take the disk created in Exercise 1 (above) and delete all files on the disk. Next, restore all the files, using a single execution of the appropriate DOS command.

5. Assume that you have just purchased a disk with several games on it. Start with a new disk and list all the commands you would use to prepare the disk to store files, and then transfer all the files from the original disk (in drive A:) to the new disk (in drive B:). Be sure to check that the original and duplicate files compare exactly. List all the DOS commands you would use and submit the list to your instructor.

Key Terms

CON:	End-of-file mark	Parallel port
Console	File concatenation	PRN
Deletion-tracking file	Hexadecimal	Verify
Device names	Memory-resident program	

Documentation Research

Documentation Research questions are included at the end of most units to encourage you to explore and discover the additional features available with DOS 6.x. All Documentation Research questions within the text can be answered by using the on-line reference (accessed by using the HELP command). Review Guided Activity 2.8 if you are unsure how to use the HELP command.

1. Name the switches available for use with the COPY command.

2. Does the COPY command have a /P switch available?

3. Does the on-line Help reference include information on the COMP command?

4. Does the fast help feature include information on the COMP command?

5. Name the COMP command switch that disregards differences in case between two files.

6. Name the COMP command switch that displays the line numbers of differences between two files.

7. According to the fast help for the REN command, what does the command do?

8. Name three commands listed by the DEL command Help screen that are related commands.

Copying and Renaming Files

In Unit 4, you learned how to copy and rename files. In this application you use those skills.

1. Format a blank disk. It should be formatted as a data disk, not a system disk.

2. Copy the following files from the WESTDATA.DS6 directory on your hard disk to the newly formatted disk in drive A:. Refer to Guided Activity 4.1 if you are unsure how to do this.

> TRUCKIN.TXT
> DIET.DOC
> DINOSAUR.WP

3. Rename each of the files on the disk in drive A:. The original file name is in the first column. Rename the file to use the file name in the second column.

> TRUCKIN.TXT   TRACKING
> DIET.DOC   WEIGHT.WP
> DINOSAUR.WP DINOSAUR.DOC

4. Submit the disk to your instructor. Be sure to write your name, course and section number, instructor's name, and today's date on the disk label.

Disk Management Commands (I)

5

Learning Objectives

At the completion of this unit, you should be able to

1. use the CHDIR or CD command to change to a different directory on a disk,

2. use the MKDIR or MD command to make a subdirectory on a disk,

3. use the PATH command to establish access to executable files on directories other than the current directory,

4. use the RMDIR or RD command to remove a directory from a disk,

5. use the TREE command to view the directories and files on a disk,

6. use the TREE command to list directories to a printer,

7. use the PROMPT command to change the DOS prompt.

Important Commands

CHDIR or CD

MKDIR or MD

PATH

PROMPT

RMDIR or RD

TREE

Hard Disk Management

In previous units, we have referred to *directories*, *subdirectories*, the root directory, and the path to a given command or file. Now it is time to consider these concepts more fully. Imagine that you have just been hired by a new company. The first day on the job, you find that your office has no file cabinets. Your predecessor left all the files in random stacks on your desk. What would be your first task?

Obviously, the office needs some organization. After verifying that each folder includes the data indicated by its label, you would probably begin organizing the files into groups. One stack of file folders might include files relating to a special project originated by your predecessor, another stack might be personnel folders for your staff. If your office works extensively with a specific department in the company, you might group all those files together. Yet another group might include minutes and agendas to meetings you regularly attend or chair.

You have the option of simply putting the folders in sequential order (if you can determine when your predecessor created each file), or you might order the file folders by size (the thin files up front and the thicker ones toward the back). Each of these options is less effective than grouping files alphabetically by topic.

The bottom line is that you will order and group the files in some functional way to make it easier to retrieve the data each contains. After grouping the files and ordering file cabinets, you might go a step further and select specific groups of files to go in specific file cabinet drawers. One set of drawers (probably with a lock for security) will contain the personnel files. Another set of drawers will contain files related to special projects. You may spend days organizing your office files, but the net gain is time. You will be able to find what you want, when you want it—and find it faster.

With the advent of DOS 2.*x*, PCs began turning away from reliance on floppy disk *storage* and moved toward the use of hard disk storage, sometimes referred to as *fixed-disk* storage. Whereas a low-density floppy disk can store up to 112 files containing a maximum of 360KB, the first hard disk systems offered by IBM could store 10MB of data—the equivalent of some 28.92 360KB disks of data. Immediately, organization became a problem. Just like the "new job" situation outlined above, it became necessary to bring order to the chaos. It is simply not feasible to store 10MB of data without creating "groups of files" and adding some hard disk management to personal computing.

Today, the 10MB hard disk is as obsolete as a flesh-and-blood dinosaur. The IBM AT was introduced with a 20MB hard disk. That storage capacity was quickly surpassed by drives ranging up to 1 *gigabyte* (one billion bytes) of data or more. The limit has yet to be reached. By summer 1993, a quick survey of firms in the Kansas City, Missouri area disclosed that most new purchases were for machines with at least 100–200MB of storage. Today, it is not unusual to find individual workstations with 300–600MB or more of hard disk storage space. Further, the average disk access speed had dropped from 61 to 10–19 *milliseconds* (*ms*) in speed, making file manipulation even faster.

Again, with such a volume of data, a system of organization becomes essential. Early on, Microsoft Corporation and IBM decided upon a system borrowing on the hierarchical directory structure used by UNIX and Microsoft's own XENIX platforms. DOS, UNIX, and XENIX each use a tree-structured system of directories.

Just as the only way to get nutriments into a tree is through the root, the only way to access data on a tree-structured directory is through the root directory. When you format either a floppy disk or a hard disk, you automatically create a single directory—the root directory. In most of the Guided Activities using drive A:, you were creating, storing, and deleting files in the root directory of the disk. First access is through the root directory, which is designated by the backslash character (\). Remember that the PROMPT command in past Guided Activities displayed the current directory? When you logged on to drive A:, after invoking the PROMPT PG command, the system prompt looked like

```
A:\>
```

The system prompt is indicating the default drive (A:) and the current directory (\ or the root directory). If you could only use the root directory, your hard disk would be like a desk with random, disorganized stacks of file folders. DOS provides the ability to make additional directories or subdirectories on either a floppy disk or a hard disk. The disk may be broken down into subdirectories that extend out from the root directory much like the branches of a tree extend from the root and trunk of the tree. Each subdirectory may be further broken into new subdirectories, and those in turn to new sub-subdirectories, and so on.

For clarification, we'll return to the earlier example of a disorganized office. The root directory is like a three-drawer file cabinet. All your files must be accessed through the cabinet. For organizational ease, you have decided to store personnel files in the top drawer, special project folders in the second drawer, and budget data in the third drawer. The drawers in the file cabinet are like directories (or subdirectories to the root directory) on a hard disk. If you open the top drawer of the file cabinet, you will find numerous file folders, each identified with a staff member's name running the gamut from Appleseed to Zonker (usually in alphabetical order unless you have made a conscious decision to order by employee number or Social Security number). Those file folders are like files (each with a file name) on your hard disk.

Figure 5.1 illustrates the file cabinet and how its physical structure is divided into topical compartments (subdirectories).

If you had an enormous group of personnel files, you might use stiff, heavy, cardboard letter dividers between the As, Bs, Cs, and so on. These dividers would make it easier to find specific staff folders. On a hard disk, these additional divisions would be equivalent to new subdirectories. Figure 5.2 maps out the file cabinet as if it were a hard disk with subdirectories.

NOTE *Subdirectory names are similar to file names. They are limited to eight characters followed by a three character extension. That is why the PERSONNEL directory in the above illustration is listed as PERSONNE.L. The final letter follows a period and is the same as a one-character file name extension.*

FIGURE 5.1
*Physical view of
a file cabinet*

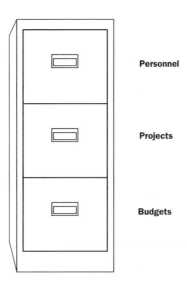

Personnel

Projects

Budgets

FIGURE 5.2
*Logical map of
the file cabinet*

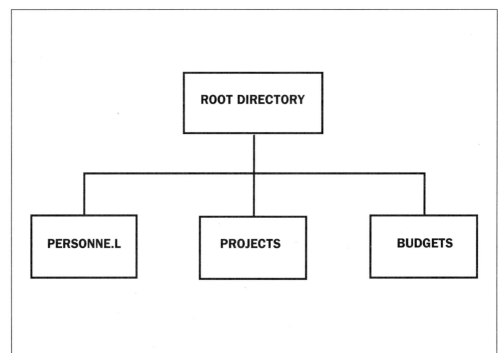

Directories Versus Subdirectories

In computing literature, you will find references to directories, subdirectories, and parent directories. In the above example, the root directory is clearly labeled. It has three subdirectories: PERSONNE.L, PROJECTS, and BUDGETS. Each is a sub-directory of the root directory. However, each could also be considered a directory in its own right. If we were to add three subdirectories under PROJECTS called ACQUISIT.ION (acquisitions), MERGERS, and DIVESTME.NTS (divestments), they would each be subdirectories of the directory called PROJECTS. With the exception of the root directory, every directory on a hard disk is also a subdirectory. Further, each may be a directory with subdirectories. In the example of the PROJECTS directory, it is considered the **parent directory** to the three subdirectories under it. The terms *directory* and *subdirectory* represent relationships. Among families, one person may be a mother, daughter, aunt, and grandparent—all at the same time. Files are stored in a directory, but that directory may also be a subdirectory at the same time. The title only depicts the relationship of one directory to another.

Directories are created to store a group of files. When you use the DIR command to display a directory listing, it shows the files in the current directory. Soon, you will discover how to change directories and how to move among the "branches" of the tree—represented by the various directories and subdirectories.

Before explaining how directories are created, removed, or accessed, let us look at a typical tree structure for a hard disk. In the example of Figure 5.3, four subdirectories exist under the root directory. They are called DOS, UTILITIE.S, EXCEL, and WPWIN. The image in Figure 5.3 is a screen display made using the DOS TREE command.

FIGURE 5.3
Typical hard disk tree structure

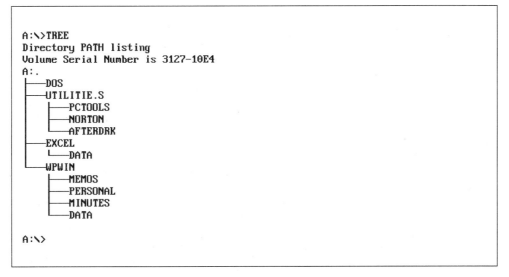

```
A:\>TREE
Directory PATH listing
Volume Serial Number is 3127-10E4
A:.
├───DOS
├───UTILITIE.S
│       ├───PCTOOLS
│       ├───NORTON
│       └───AFTERDRK
├───EXCEL
│       └───DATA
└───WPWIN
        ├───MEMOS
        ├───PERSONAL
        ├───MINUTES
        └───DATA

A:\>
```

Many software packages instruct you to install their files in a directory separate from other programs. Further, many application programs now come with INSTALL or SETUP programs that automatically create the necessary directories and install the *program files* in those directories. In the example displayed in Figure 5.3, the WordPerfect 5.2 for Windows program files are copied to the \WPWIN directory, DOS files are stored in the \DOS directory, Microsoft Excel program files are found in the \EXCEL directory, and various utility program files are installed under the \UTILITIE.S directory. In fact, under the \UTILITIE.S directory are subdirectories for PC Tools (PCTOOLS), Norton Utilities (NORTON), and After Dark (AFTERDRK, a screen saver).

Two approaches are common when determining where to store your **data files** (text files, document files, data base files, and spreadsheet files). They can be stored

- In a subdirectory directly under the directory where the program files are located

  or

- In a subdirectory directly under the root directory

Because of the logic in grouping similar files and subdirectories together, the first option has merit. For instance, in Figure 5.3, the word processing files created with WordPerfect for Windows are stored in one of three subdirectories: MEMOS stores all memos, PERSONAL stores personal notes and letters, MINUTES stores minutes to meetings, and DATA stores all other document files. The Excel worksheet files are stored in a subdirectory called DATA (notice that the subdirectory names do not have to be distinctive if they have different parent directories). This strategy is used to help organize files on the disk and simplify access to specific files. It keeps data from the various application programs separate so that data may be backed up to floppy disks easily without also (unnecessarily) backing up program files.

As an added benefit, since the DEL command only operates on the current or specified directory, splitting files into logical subdirectories also minimizes the loss if you should accidentally delete files.

Further, you receive an additional bonus when a hard disk is broken into directories. The root directory of any hard drive has a finite number of files that it can store. For example, the IBM AT 30MB hard disk can only contain 512 files in the root directory. Even though that amount exceeds the limitation of 360KB and 1.2MB floppy disks (respectively, they may only store 112 and 224 files in the root directory), it is a handicap. The limitation can be overcome by creating subdirectories to the root directory.

The root directory is the only directory that is not stored in the disk's data area; that is, as a typical directory listing. It is stored in the system area of the disk immediately following the file allocation table. It is fixed in size—thus the limitation on the number of files that can be recorded in the root directory. An entry listed in the root directory can be either a file (like COMMAND.COM, AUTOEXEC.BAT, or CONFIG.SYS) or a subdirectory listing (like \WPWIN, \EXCEL, \DOS, and so on). The subdirectory listing is just like a file that can be any size and can be increased or diminished in size. Each file listed in a subdirectory is listed in the subdirectory file. This process effectively increases the potential number of files on your disk to a near-infinite number.

Three Little Commands to Build, Move, and Destroy

Now you know basically how a hard disk can be structured and why such a structure is desirable. All that remains is to learn to use the hard disk management commands that allow you to create, remove, and move between directories.

Using the MD Command

The MKDIR (make directory) command is used to create a subdirectory under the current directory. Immediately after formatting a disk, only the root directory exists. While in the root directory, you can use the MKDIR command to create one or more subdirectories. The syntax of the command is

```
MKDIR [d:][subdirectory][\][...][\]subdirectory
```

or

```
MD [d:][subdirectory][\][...][\]subdirectory
```

When a path includes more than one directory name, each of the directories must be separated by a backslash (\) character. MD is an abbreviated form of the MKDIR command. To save a few keystrokes, we will use the shortened version throughout the text. To create a subdirectory under the root directory called WPWIN, you would type

```
MD WPWIN
```

Once you press [Enter], the subdirectory will be created.

Using the CD Command

To move to the new WPWIN directory (to add files or just look around), you would use the CHDIR (change directory) command. It can be abbreviated to CD. The syntax of the command is

```
CD [subdirectory][\][...][\]subdirectory
```

The CD command can only be used to access an existing directory. Directories are created either with the MD command or during the installation of an application program. Even if an application program itself creates a directory during the installation process, it does so (invisibly) by using the DOS MD command. To change to the newly created C:\WPWIN directory, you would enter

```
CD\WPWIN
```

or

```
CD WPWIN
```

The first example is used to change to the C:\WPWIN directory from *any* directory on the disk. The second example (without the backslash character) can only be used to change to a subdirectory (called WPWIN) under the current directory.

NOTE *The CD command may be entered without any parameters to display the current or default drive and directory path. Executing the CD command to determine the current drive and path is unnecessary if you invoked the PROMPT PG command when booting your system.*

Suppose you wish to create a subdirectory under C:\WPWIN called MEMOS. The command line is entered as

```
MD MEMOS
```

This command assumes that you are in the C:\WPWIN directory. If you were in the root directory, the MEMOS subdirectory would be created under the root (C:\MEMOS) rather than under the WPWIN directory (C:\WPWIN\MEMOS). To move to the C:\WPWIN\MEMOS subdirectory from the C:\WPWIN directory, you would enter

```
CD MEMOS
```

You could have created the C:\WPWIN\MEMOS subdirectory while in the root directory (C:\) by entering the following, more precise, command line at the DOS prompt.

```
MD \WPWIN\MEMOS
```

The CD command has one more form, using two periods, that can help move up one directory (or level) in the directory tree at a time.

```
CD..
```

or

```
CD ..
```

This form may be used to change from the current directory to its parent directory. If the current directory is C:\WPWIN\MEMOS, the CD.. command form changes the current directory to

```
C:\WPWIN
```

Do not use the backslash character if you have changed directories to the parent directory under which you wish to add a new subdirectory. The backslash tells DOS to start from the root directory in creating, removing, or changing directories. If you fail to specify a drive, DOS assumes that the new directory is on the default drive.

Using the RD Command

Finally, the RMDIR (remove directory) command enables you to remove a directory. This command may be abbreviated to RD. The syntax is

```
RD [d:][path]subdirectory
```

Several guidelines must be followed in order to remove a subdirectory using the RD command:

- You cannot remove the current directory (as shown by the DOS prompt).

- The default directory cannot be a directory under the one you wish to remove.

- To remove a directory, it must be empty of files. Further, there must be no subdirectories under it and no subdirectories to any of its subdirectories. Only the . and .. files that display in a directory listing may remain in a directory to be deleted. The . file simply refers to the current directory and .. refers to the parent directory of the current directory. These are not really files—you cannot delete them.

- Hidden files must be removed from a directory you wish to remove. Hidden files are typically created by copy-protected software. Be sure to uninstall any copy-protected software before attempting to delete files and remove the directory.

- You can only delete one directory at a time.

- Finally, the root directory cannot be deleted.

To remove the C:\WPWIN\MEMOS directory, you would need to delete any files it contains, move to the C:\WPWIN directory (CD\WPWIN), and type

```
RD MEMOS
```

The most common practice is to remove a subdirectory while the current directory is its parent directory. This is not a requirement. In the preceding example, you could delete C:\WPWIN\MEMOS from the root directory by using the following command line.

```
RD C:\WPWIN\MEMOS
```

or

```
RD \WPWIN\MEMOS
```

You could also remove a directory from another drive by specifying the drive designation and directory path. For instance, if the default drive is A:, you could delete the \WPWIN\MEMOS directory on drive C: by entering

```
RD C:\WPWIN\MEMOS
```

Using the DIR Command to List Subdirectories

Directories are stored just like files in the directory listing. In fact, they are special-purpose files. When you invoke the DIR command, you will see the subdirectories under the current directory listed as files. They are set apart by the way in which they are listed (with a <DIR> identifier). Figure 5.4 displays a DIR listing with subdirectories.

NOTE *You can use the command* DIR *. *to obtain a list of all subdirectories to the current directory on your disk, unless the subdirectory name has an extension such as UTILITIE.S (the extension is .S). This will also display any files without extensions, but this may be a quick method of determining the subdirectories currently available under the current directory. Of course with DOS 5.0 or 6.0, you can also use the* DIR/OS *or* DIR/O-S *command forms to list, respectively, all subdirectories at the beginning or ending of the directory listing.*

The disk in drive A: contains four subdirectories. They are named DOS, UTILITIE.S, EXCEL, and WPWIN. Each is displayed with a <DIR> extension rather than a three-character extension. You can give a directory an extension—but usually should not. To give a directory an extension means that you must enter *both* the directory name *and* the extension each time you wish to change directories.

FIGURE 5.4
DIR listing with subdirectories

```
A:\>DIR

 Volume in drive A has no label
 Volume Serial Number is 3127-10E4
 Directory of A:\

DOS          <DIR>       10-20-91    1:09p
UTILITIE S   <DIR>       10-20-91    1:09p
EXCEL        <DIR>       10-20-91    1:09p
WPWIN        <DIR>       10-20-91    1:10p
BECOMING TXT          53 10-04-88    7:22p
MISC     ZIP       24327 10-13-91    8:17p
MONSTERS             84 10-06-88    7:04p
PAPER    TXT       1026 10-12-91    9:48p
PUBLISH  BAK        255 10-04-88    7:54p
PUBLISH  TXT        265 10-04-88    7:59p
       10 file(s)        26010 bytes
                        687104 bytes free

A:\>
```

The PROMPT Command: A Brief Review

In an earlier unit, we briefly discussed the PROMPT command. At that time, we only covered its most common form:

```
PROMPT $P$G
```

That form displays the current drive and directory path. As you begin moving around the disk, it will be important to know where you are in the maze created by directories and subdirectories. If you use the PROMPT PG command in your AUTOEXEC.BAT file (discussed later, in Unit 11), you can always look at the DOS prompt to determine your default, or current, drive and directory path. At the end of this unit, we will revisit the PROMPT command and explore its additional uses.

Climbing the DOS Tree

There is a basic difference between the branches of a tree and the branches of your hard disk structure as represented by the directories. In DOS, you cannot jump from one directory (branch) to another without specifying a path through the root directory.

Another analogy might help. The root directory is like the front hallway to your home. Your home has only one entrance. To get to any room, you must pass through the front hallway. Further, each room has a single entrance. This approximates the tree-structured setup created by DOS. In Figure 5.5, a strangely structured house is pictured.

FIGURE 5.5
House illustration as an analogy of disk navigation

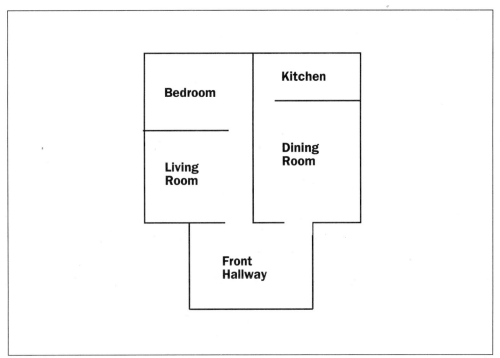

If you are working in the kitchen, you must go to the bedroom by going through the dining room, into the front hallway, through the living room, and then to the bedroom. DOS uses this kind of path concept, but with a slight twist. If the default directory path is in the kitchen (\FRONTHALL\DININGROOM \KITCHEN), then DOS assumes that the program files and data files are in the kitchen. Every time DOS needs to access files, it enters the house by the front hall (the equivalent of the root directory) and checks the kitchen. If the desired file is not in the kitchen (the default *path name*), you must tell DOS where to go starting from the front hallway—not from the kitchen.

The PATH command is based on the concept of mapping out how to get from the front hallway (the root directory and drive) to where you want to be to invoke a program file or executable file. On a tree, it would be like going back to the ground (root) every time you decided to climb another branch of the tree.

Stating the Path of Least Resistance

A path by definition is nothing more than a trail or road map. It begins at the root directory and tells DOS where to find *executable files*.

If you assume that the strangely structured house is a hard disk, you might find a situation where you want to execute a command called SLEEP.EXE in the bedroom. In DOS, you can invoke any executable file from any directory on the disk *if* you state the path to the executable file.

NOTE *An executable file will always end with one of three file extensions: .EXE, .COM, or .BAT. You do not need to enter the extension when invoking an executable file. Just as you can type* INSTALL *to invoke INSTALL.BAT, you need only type* WORD *to invoke WORD.EXE or WORD.COM.*

To execute the SLEEP.EXE command while still in the kitchen, you would have to indicate the drive (HOME: in this example) and indicate the directory path. It would look like

```
HOME:\FRONTHALL\LIVINGROOM\BEDROOM\SLEEP
```

Remember that DOS always starts from the root directory (\FRONTHALL) when it looks for executable files. In the above example, you simply prefaced the command to be executed with the path to the file.

Back in the real world of DOS, suppose the default directory path is the root directory. You want to execute the DOS external command FORMAT. It is stored in the C:\DOS directory. Without using the PATH command or stating the path, you cannot execute the command by typing FORMAT at the DOS prompt (C:\>). You would have to state the path to the command:

```
C:\DOS\FORMAT A:
```

That command line is not difficult to enter at the DOS prompt, but the longer the path, the more of a hassle it can be. For instance, to load PC Tools, you might end up with a command line like

```
C:\UTILITIE.S\TOOLS\PCTOOLS
```

In this case, the PCTOOLS.EXE file is stored in a subdirectory called TOOLS under the UTILITIE.S directory. The longer the path, the greater the risk of typing errors—with unintended consequences.

The PATH command is used by DOS to create a ready-to-use path from the root directory to any commonly used executable files. It allows DOS to find the files even if they are not on the current directory path or drive. If you are in C:\WPWIN\DATA and invoke the FORMAT command, DOS first checks the current drive and directory for the FORMAT file. If it is not found, DOS begins checking, in order, each path listed by the PATH command. The syntax of the command is

```
PATH [d:][path];[...];[d:][path]
```

The PATH command is an internal DOS command and can be invoked at the DOS prompt. However, the most efficient way to use the PATH command is to place it in your AUTOEXEC.BAT file (this special file is discussed later, in Unit 11). That way, it is invoked each time you boot your computer system.

If you wish to have DOS check the C:\DOS directory, you would enter

```
PATH C:\DOS
```

If you also want DOS to check the C:\WPWIN directory (after checking C:\DOS), the command would be

```
PATH C:\DOS;C:\WPWIN
```

Each path in the PATH command must be separated by a semicolon from the other paths listed. DOS does not limit the number of directories referenced in the PATH command statement; however, the search path cannot be over 127 characters long (about one and a half lines).

GUIDED ACTIVITY 5.1

Creating Subdirectories

In this Guided Activity, you will use West Student Data Disk #2 in drive A: and create several subdirectories on the disk.

1. Insert West Student Data Disk #2 in drive A:.

NOTE *West Student Data Disk #2 should include copies of all files from the C:\WESTDATA.DS6 directory on your workstation. No additional files are on the disk; so, if needed, you can re-create Disk #2 by formatting a disk and copying all 44 files from C:\WESTDATA.DS6 to the new disk.*

2. Change the default drive to drive A:.

3. Type CLS and press [Enter].

4. At the DOS prompt, type PROMPT PG and press [Enter].

5. Type DIR and press [Enter].

    Notice that all 44 files from the C:\WESTDATA.DS6 directory exist on the disk.

6. Type CLS and press [Enter] to clear the monitor screen.

7. Type MD PROGRAMS to create a \PROGRAMS subdirectory and press [Enter].

8. Type MD DOS to create a \DOS subdirectory and press [Enter].

9. Type MD TEST to create a \TEST subdirectory and press [Enter].

CHECKPOINT 5A Which directory is currently the default directory?

10. Type DIR and press [Enter].

    Three new directories appear at the end of the directory listing, as shown in Figure 5.6.

FIGURE 5.6

*Directory listing
with three new
directories*

```
MOM3       DOC        1,536 10-04-88    7:43p
SAYING     TXT          193 10-04-88    7:51p
HUMOROUS   PM4           91 05-08-93    7:41p
WIN_MODE   DOC        1,429 10-12-91    9:18p
ALIGN      WP         2,377 10-12-91    9:49p
PUBLISH    TXT          265 10-04-88    7:59p
TODOLIST   DOC           74 05-08-93    7:59p
WINNEWS1   DOC           23 05-08-93    7:56p
TRUCKIN    TXT          719 07-13-89    8:11a
DINOSAUR   WP            24 05-08-93    7:52p
STRATS2    DOC        4,019 10-13-91    8:02p
STRATS1    DOC        4,074 10-13-91    8:04p
STRATS1    TXT        2,056 10-19-91    3:15p
WAR        WP         1,244 10-13-91    8:24p
PAPER      WP         2,879 05-08-93   11:23a
STRATS2    TXT        1,908 10-19-91    3:15p
PAPER      TXT        1,043 05-08-93   11:29a
WAR        TXT          121 01-18-94   11:19a
PROGRAMS     <DIR>          12-03-93    6:27p
DOS          <DIR>          12-03-93    6:27p
TEST         <DIR>          12-03-93    6:27p
        47 file(s)         65,766 bytes
                        1,377,792 bytes free

A:\>
```

The TREE Command

DOS provides a command to display the structure of directories and subdirectories on a disk. That command is the TREE command. The syntax for the command is

```
[d:][path]TREE [t:][path][/A][/F]
```

To view a list of the current directory and all its directories, you would enter

```
TREE
```

TREE is an external DOS command and must be available on disk. If TREE is stored in the C:\DOS directory, you must invoke the PATH command to establish a path to that directory. To execute the command without using the PATH command, you must include the path and drive as shown below.

```
C:\DOS\TREE
```

In most cases, a PATH command is executed in the AUTOEXEC.BAT file when you boot your computer. Execution of that PATH command commonly establishes a path to your DOS commands.

A typical screen display after invoking the TREE command is shown in Figure 5.7. Directories are displayed on the screen in the order in which they were created, not alphabetical order.

If you are familiar with earlier versions of DOS (2.x and 3.x), you will be surprised at the graphic presentation in Figure 5.7 of the directories and subdirectories. Earlier versions of DOS used an indented listing. Beginning with DOS 4.x the TREE command uses block graphics characters.

FIGURE 5.7
*TREE command
listing*

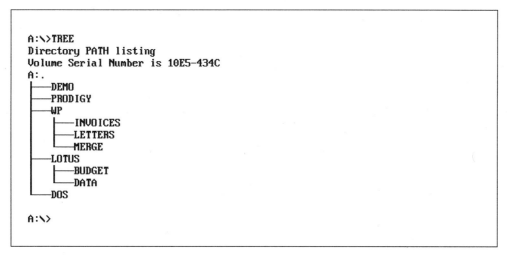

```
A:\>TREE
Directory PATH listing
Volume Serial Number is 10E5-434C
A:.
    ├──DEMO
    ├──PRODIGY
    ├──WP
    │   ├──INVOICES
    │   ├──LETTERS
    │   └──MERGE
    ├──LOTUS
    │   ├──BUDGET
    │   └──DATA
    └──DOS

A:\>
```

For the following examples, assume that you have invoked the PATH command and can access all DOS commands from the current directory. If you wish to see a TREE listing for a disk in drive A: (and the default drive is C:), you would enter

    TREE A:

You can also indicate a parent directory in the TREE command. If you do, DOS displays only the subdirectories under the indicated parent directory. If drive C: has a WPWIN directory, you could view the subdirectories under C:\WPWIN by entering the following:

    TREE C:\WPWIN

GUIDED ACTIVITY 5.2

Creating, Removing, and Moving Between Subdirectories

In this Guided Activity, you continue making new subdirectories and move from one directory to another. You use an external DOS command, therefore you must have a PATH command issued that opens a path to the directory (on your hard drive) where the DOS commands are stored. If you find that the TREE command does not execute, ask your instructor for assistance.

1. With West Student Data Disk #2 still in drive A:, log on to drive A:.

2. Type CLS and press [Enter].

3. Type TREE and press [Enter].

   Your screen should appear similar to Figure 5.8 and display three directories created in the last Guided Activity.

4. Type CLS and press [Enter].

5. Type MD\PROGRAMS\WORDS to create a subdirectory under \PROGRAMS called WORDS.

FIGURE 5.8
*The TREE
command
display*

```
A:\>TREE
Directory PATH listing for Volume BACON JONAT
Volume Serial Number is 0FD2-0F68
A:.
├───PROGRAMS
├───DOS
└───TEST


A:\>
```

6. Press ⏎Enter.

7. Type MD\PROGRAMS\DATA to create a subdirectory under \PROGRAMS called DATA.

8. Press ⏎Enter.

9. Type TREE and press ⏎Enter.

   Figure 5.9 displays the TREE listing invoked by the last step. Three directory listings are displayed on the screen plus the two new subdirectories under \PROGRAMS. No files are included in the listing.

FIGURE 5.9
*TREE command
listing of three
directory
listings
and their
subdirectories*

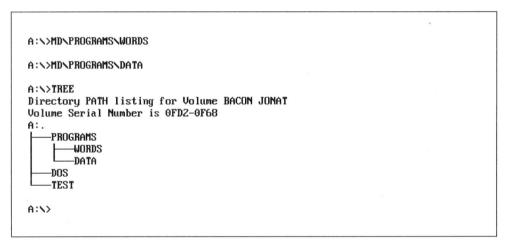

```
A:\>MD\PROGRAMS\WORDS

A:\>MD\PROGRAMS\DATA

A:\>TREE
Directory PATH listing for Volume BACON JONAT
Volume Serial Number is 0FD2-0F68
A:.
├───PROGRAMS
│   ├───WORDS
│   └───DATA
├───DOS
└───TEST


A:\>
```

10. Type CLS and press ⏎Enter.

11. Type CD\PROGRAMS to change to the \PROGRAMS directory and press ⏎Enter.

CHECKPOINT 5B Indicate an alternative method of entering the command in step 11.

12. Type DIR and press ⏎Enter to view the files in the \PROGRAMS directory.

    Figure 5.10 displays the two new subdirectories, \WORDS and \DATA. Notice that four files or subdirectories are listed. The . and .. files represent, respectively, the current directory and the parent directory.

FIGURE 5.10
DIR command listing of \PROGRAMS subdirectories

```
A:\>CD\PROGRAMS

A:\PROGRAMS>DIR

 Volume in drive A is BACON JONAT
 Volume Serial Number is 0FD2-0F68
 Directory of A:\PROGRAMS

 .            <DIR>      05-31-93    2:10p
 ..           <DIR>      05-31-93    2:10p
 WORDS        <DIR>      05-31-93    2:14p
 DATA         <DIR>      05-31-93    2:14p
        4 file(s)            0 bytes
                      1376768 bytes free

A:\PROGRAMS>
```

13. Type MD JUNK to create a JUNK subdirectory under the current directory and press [Enter].

14. Type CLS and press [Enter].

15. Type DIR\PROGRAMS and press [Enter].

    Notice the addition of the new subdirectory to the DIR listing.

16. Type TREE and press [Enter].

    This shows a different representation of the same disk structure.

17. Type CD.. and press [Enter].

NOTE *Entering CD\ will accomplish the same thing (because the current directory is immediately under the root directory). However, the results would be different if the current directory was not immediately under the root directory.*

    The system prompt displayed in Figure 5.11 indicates that you have changed the current directory to be the parent directory of \PROGRAMS—which is the root directory.

18. Type CLS and press [Enter].

19. Type CD\PROGRAMS\WORDS to change directories and press [Enter].

20. Type COPY A:*.DOC A:/V to copy all files with the .DOC extension (in the root directory on drive A:) to the WORDS subdirectory on drive A:.

21. Press [Enter].

    Fifteen files are listed as copied from the root directory on drive A: to the A:\PROGRAMS\WORDS directory as shown in Figure 5.12.

CHECKPOINT 5C Is it possible to remove the A:\PROGRAMS\WORDS directory without deleting files in that directory?

FIGURE 5.11
*DIR command
listing and
tree of
A:\PROGRAMS*

```
A:\PROGRAMS>DIR\PROGRAMS

 Volume in drive A is BACON JONAT
 Volume Serial Number is 0FD2-0F68
 Directory of A:\PROGRAMS

 .              <DIR>      05-31-93    2:10p
 ..             <DIR>      05-31-93    2:10p
 WORDS          <DIR>      05-31-93    2:14p
 DATA           <DIR>      05-31-93    2:14p
 JUNK           <DIR>      05-31-93    2:15p
         5 file(s)            0 bytes
                       1376256 bytes free

A:\PROGRAMS>TREE
Directory PATH listing for Volume BACON JONAT
Volume Serial Number is 0FD2-0F68
A:.
├───WORDS
├───DATA
└───JUNK

A:\PROGRAMS>CD..

A:\>
```

22. Type DIR and press Enter to view the files in the subdirectory.

    The DIR listing shows 17 files; 2 of these are the hidden files (. and ..) representing the current and parent directories.

23. Type CD\ and press Enter to change the current directory to the root directory.

24. Type CLS and press Enter.

FIGURE 5.12
*Fifteen files
copied to
A:\PROGRAMS
\WORDS
subdirectory*

```
A:\>CD\PROGRAMS\WORDS

A:\PROGRAMS\WORDS>COPY A:\*.DOC A:/V
A:\ALIGN.DOC
A:\MOM1.DOC
A:\DASHIT-1.DOC
A:\WAR.DOC
A:\DINOSAUR.DOC
A:\FLAGS.DOC
A:\INDEFENS.DOC
A:\DIET.DOC
A:\MOM2.DOC
A:\MOM3.DOC
A:\WIN_MODE.DOC
A:\TODOLIST.DOC
A:\WINNEWS1.DOC
A:\STRATS2.DOC
A:\STRATS1.DOC
        15 file(s) copied

A:\PROGRAMS\WORDS>
```

25. Type RD\ and press [Enter].

The screen displays the error message "Attempt to remove current directory - \."
You cannot remove the current directory, nor can you *ever* remove the root directory.

26. Type RD\PROGRAMS\JUNK and press [Enter] to remove the named subdirectory.

27. Type DIR\PROGRAMS and press [Enter].

The JUNK subdirectory is gone.

GUIDED ACTIVITY 5.3

Creating and Removing Directories

In this Guided Activity, you explore an easier method of adding and deleting subdirectories. Rather than typing out the path for the new directories, you simply move
to the parent directory and execute the RD or MD command.

1. With West Student Data Disk #2 still in drive A:, log onto drive A:.

2. Type CLS and press [Enter].

3. Type CD TEST and press [Enter].

4. Type TREE and press [Enter].

Your screen should appear similar to Figure 5.13 and indicate that "no subdirectories exist" to the \TEST directory.

FIGURE 5.13
No subdirectories under \TEST

```
A:\>CD TEST

A:\TEST>TREE
Directory PATH listing for Volume BACON JONAT
Volume Serial Number is 0FD2-0F68
A:.
No sub-directories exist


A:\TEST>
```

5. Type CLS and press [Enter].

6. Type MD CLASSONE and press [Enter].

7. Type TREE and press [Enter].

8. Type MD CLASSTWO and press [Enter].

9. Type MD NOCLASS and press [Enter].

10. Type CLS and press [Enter].

11. Type TREE and press [Enter].

    Your screen should appear similar to Figure 5.14 and display the three sub-directories under \TEST.

```
A:\TEST>TREE
Directory PATH listing for Volume BACON JONAT
Volume Serial Number is 0FD2-0F68
A:.
├──CLASSONE
├──CLASSTWO
└──NOCLASS

A:\TEST>
```

12. Type RD NOCLASS and press [Enter].

13. Type TREE and press [Enter].

    Your screen should appear similar to Figure 5.15 and display the two remaining subdirectories under \TEST.

```
A:\TEST>TREE
Directory PATH listing for Volume BACON JONAT
Volume Serial Number is 0FD2-0F68
A:.
├──CLASSONE
├──CLASSTWO
└──NOCLASS

A:\TEST>RD NOCLASS

A:\TEST>TREE
Directory PATH listing for Volume BACON JONAT
Volume Serial Number is 0FD2-0F68
A:.
├──CLASSONE ───────────── Directories after deleting the NOCLASS directory
└──CLASSTWO

A:\TEST>
```

14. Remove the CLASSONE and CLASSTWO subdirectories.

15. Type TREE and press [Enter].

    There are no longer any subdirectories under the \TEST directory.

16. Switch to the root directory on drive A:.

The TREE Files Switch

When you add the /F switch, DOS will list (to your monitor screen) the directories, subdirectories, and all their associated files. To view a listing of all directories, subdirectories, and files (from the root directory), use the following command line:

```
TREE A:/F
```

The TREE command, especially with the /F switch, is not the most useful command. If you have numerous files and subdirectories, the list speeds by, unless you are quick at pressing the [Pause] key. Further, most of the data that TREE offers is available when using the DIR command.

The TREE Command: One Screen at a Time

DOS includes several *pipes* and *filters*. One filter that might be helpful here is the MORE command. The following form will display one page of the TREE listing at a time, similar to the page mode of the DIR command. DOS will prompt you to press a key to view the next page of the TREE listing. This will continue until the entire listing has been displayed to the screen. The form is

```
TREE | MORE
```

NOTE *The **piping symbol** (|) usually shows up on the computer keyboard as a broken vertical line, but on the monitor and when printed, it appears as a solid vertical line.*

The same filter could be used with the /F switch to generate a page-at-a-time listing from the TREE command.

```
TREE /F | MORE
```

Redirecting the TREE Listing to a Printer

Another useful option, when trying to absorb and study a long TREE listing (especially when using the /F switch), is to *redirect* the output from the screen to your printer. Assuming that you have a parallel printer attached to parallel port 1 (LPT1:), you can enter the following command line:

```
TREE /F >PRN
```

Be sure your printer is turned on, is on line, and has paper loaded, then enter the above command line.

USING UNIVERSAL GRAPHICS RATHER THAN BLOCK GRAPHICS CHARACTERS

When redirecting the TREE command listing to your printer, you may wish to use the universal set of graphics characters rather than the block graphics characters. The universal set of graphics characters includes the following:

```
+ - | \
```

When using the universal graphics characters, DOS substitutes these crude symbols for the finer block graphics characters. The substitutions are listed in Table 5.1.

TABLE 5.1
*Universal
graphics
characters*

+	is used instead of right angles
–	is used instead of horizontal lines
\	is used instead of corners
|	is used instead of vertical lines

You can choose to use these characters rather than the better-looking block graphics if your printer does not support block graphics or in order to speed up the printing process.

The /A switch is used to generate a TREE listing (to the screen or printer), using the universal set of graphics characters. To get a TREE command listing for the disk in drive A: you would enter the following:

```
TREE A:/A
```

This screen listing would be redirected to the printer by using the command

```
TREE A:/A >PRN
```

The /A switch may be combined with the /F switch to get a listing of all files, using the universal set of graphics characters. You have the option of displaying the list to the printer or the monitor screen as shown below:

```
TREE A:/A/F >PRN
TREE A:/A/F >CON:
```

GUIDED ACTIVITY 5.4

Seeing the Trees Through the Forest

In this Guided Activity, you will use the TREE command to view the structure of the disk created in the last Guided Activity.

Be sure that West Student Data Disk #2 is in drive A:. Also be sure that A: is the default drive. In this exercise you must set the PATH command to equal C:\DOS (or wherever your DOS files are stored) if the TREE command does not work.

1. Type CLS and press Enter.

2. Type TREE and press Enter.

    The monitor screen should display the disk structure shown in Figure 5.16.

    To see the structure of the hard disk on your computer, complete the next step.

3. Type TREE C:\ and press Enter.

    If the TREE command list is more than a screen long, you can execute the following command to examine the structure more closely. If you use the following

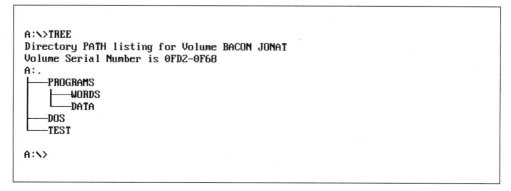

FIGURE 5.16
TREE display for West Student Data Disk #2

```
A:\>TREE
Directory PATH listing for Volume BACON JONAT
Volume Serial Number is 0FD2-0F68
A:.
    ┌───PROGRAMS
    │       ├───WORDS
    │       └───DATA
    ├───DOS
    └───TEST

A:\>
```

command, you must press any key to see the next full screen. Continue pressing a key until you see the DOS prompt again.

4. Type TREE C:\|MORE and press ⏎Enter. Press any key until the DOS prompt reappears.

NOTE *On your computer's keyboard, the concatenation character (used in the previous step) is usually a broken vertical line rather than a solid vertical line (as shown in the text).*

5. Type CLS and press ⏎Enter.

6. Type TREE/F and press ⏎Enter to display the tree structure plus associated files.

CHECKPOINT 5D The TREE command executed in step 5 displays the structure for the disk in which drive?

Figure 5.17 displays the end of the tree structure plus the files associated with each directory.

FIGURE 5.17
End of the file structure displayed by using the TREE/F command

```
│   WAR.TXT
│
├───PROGRAMS
│       ├───WORDS
│       │       ALIGN.DOC
│       │       MOM1.DOC
│       │       DASHIT-1.DOC
│       │       WAR.DOC
│       │       DINOSAUR.DOC
│       │       FLAGS.DOC
│       │       INDEFENS.DOC
│       │       DIET.DOC
│       │       MOM2.DOC
│       │       MOM3.DOC
│       │       WIN_MODE.DOC
│       │       TODOLIST.DOC
│       │       WINNEWS1.DOC
│       │       STRATS2.DOC
│       │       STRATS1.DOC
│       │
│       └───DATA
├───DOS
└───TEST

A:\>
```

7. Type CLS and press [Enter].

8. Type TREE/F/A and press [Enter].

   Notice the difference between the display using block graphics and the universal set of graphics characters.

9. Type CLS and press [Enter].

10. Type MD\TEST\PM to create a new subdirectory for PageMaker application files and press [Enter].

11. Type TREE/F and press [Enter].

    The PM subdirectory has been added to the display, but it does not include any files yet.

12. Type COPY A:*.PM4 A:\TEST\PM/V and press [Enter].

    The screen will display a message indicating that three files were copied.

13. Type TREE/F and press [Enter].

    The three files DIDYUNO.PM4, CHANGING.PM4, and HUMOROUS.PM4 were copied from the root directory of West Student Data Disk #2 to the \TEST\PM directory on the disk. The disk structure displayed by the TREE/F command now includes the three new files. Figure 5.18 shows the messages displayed by your monitor screen.

14. Type TREE/A/F and press [Enter] to see a tree display using the universal graphics characters.

FIGURE 5.18
The new TREE/F command listing

```
                    MOM1.DOC
                    DASHIT-1.DOC
                    WAR.DOC
                    DINOSAUR.DOC
                    FLAGS.DOC
                    INDEFENS.DOC
                    DIET.DOC
                    MOM2.DOC
                    MOM3.DOC
                    WIN_MODE.DOC
                    TODOLIST.DOC
                    WINNEWS1.DOC
                    STRATS2.DOC
                    STRATS1.DOC
            └──DATA
    ├─DOS
    └─TEST
        └──PM
                    DIDYUNO.PM4
                    CHANGING.PM4
                    HUMOROUS.PM4

A:\>
```

FIGURE 5.19

*TREE/A/F listing
using universal
graphics
characters*

```
 |   |        MOM1.DOC
 |   |        DASHIT-1.DOC
 |   |        WAR.DOC
 |   |        DINOSAUR.DOC
 |   |        FLAGS.DOC
 |   |        INDEFENS.DOC
 |   |        DIET.DOC
 |   |        MOM2.DOC
 |   |        MOM3.DOC
 |   |        WIN_MODE.DOC
 |   |        TODOLIST.DOC
 |   |        WINNEWS1.DOC
 |   |        STRATS2.DOC
 |   |        STRATS1.DOC
 |   |
 |   \---DATA
 +---DOS
 \---TEST
     \---PM
             DIDYUNO.PM4
             CHANGING.PM4
             HUMOROUS.PM4


A:\>
```

Figure 5.19 shows the same tree structure as Figure 5.18, but this time using the universal graphics characters.

Tips on Hard Disk Organization

Effective organization of several megabytes of data on a hard disk is a learned skill. You learn what works and what doesn't through trial and error. A few tips might save you some time:

- Keep only required files in the root directory. A well-organized root directory would have only three files (COMMAND.COM, AUTOEXEC.BAT, CONFIG.SYS), plus all the subdirectories you create under it. There is seldom cause to place other files in the root directory.

- Keep directory names as short and meaningful as possible. It will minimize the typing required to access files. For instance, UTIL is not only acceptable but a better directory name than UTILITIE.S or UTILITYS. You save several keystrokes every time you change directories or use other DOS commands that require the path name. Some users give two-letter names to all subdirectories: for example, UT (utilities), DB (database), SS (spreadsheet), WP (word processing), and so on.

- In your PATH command, place the directories you access most often at the beginning of the command line. If DOS does not find the command you invoke in the current directory, it begins checking directories in the order listed in the PATH command. Typically, the path to external DOS commands is listed first. For instance, in the following PATH command, DOS would seek an executable file first in the current directory, second in C:\DOS, third in C:\UTIL, and finally in C:\WPWIN:

```
PATH C:\DOS;C:\UTIL;C:\WPWIN
```

- It is wise to always store data files separately from the program files. This makes it easier to make periodic backups of your data. For example, you could store Microsoft Word in C:\WORD, then store the Word document files in a subdirectory under C:\WORD (such as C:\WORD\TEXT).

- Many users set up a \BATCH directory with a batch file created to invoke each of their application programs. This makes it easy to load a program, because the batch file changes the directory, loads the program, and then upon exiting the program automatically changes back to the \BATCH directory. Such an approach minimizes the use of the CHDIR command. The batch files do all the work for you. Batch files are discussed later, in Unit 11.

The PROMPT Command Revisited

The standard "plain vanilla" version of the DOS prompt includes the drive designator and a greater-than sign. Respectively, the DOS prompts for drives A:, B:, and C: are displayed below.

```
A>
B>
C>
```

The PROMPT command can be used to change the DOS prompt by following the command with text or special *meta-strings*. The meta-strings used by the PROMPT command are listed in Table 5.2. Note that each meta-string character must be preceded by the dollar sign ($) character. If you fail to precede the meta-string with a dollar sign, the text itself is used for the DOS prompt.

In Figure 5.20, you can see that the DOS prompt has been changed each time the PROMPT command was executed. After each execution of the PROMPT command, the [Enter] key is pressed to show how the prompt looks by itself on a line. Then the new form of the PROMPT command is entered and executed. The prompt begins as the standard prompt form and is altered to the following forms:

- Displays the time using the PROMPT $T command form

- Displays time and date using the PROMPT $T $D command form

- Displays the version number using the PROMPT $V command form

- Displays the text HI FOLKS! using the PROMPT HI FOLKS! command form (by omitting the dollar sign, the text following the PROMPT command is displayed)

- Displays the text WHAT NOW? on the next line by using the PROMPT WHAT NOW? $_ command form

TABLE 5.2	$$	Displays the dollar sign
PROMPT	$_	The underscore character generates a carriage return/line feed that moves the cursor to the start of a new line
command		
meta-strings	$B	Displays the vertical bar
	$D	Displays the system date
	$E	Displays the escape character*
	$G	Displays the greater-than sign
	$H	Backspaces one character and deletes that character*
	$L	Displays the less-than sign
	$N	Displays the default drive
	$P	Displays the directory on the default drive
	$Q	Displays the equal sign
	$T	Displays the system time
	$V	Displays the DOS version number

* to use these options, the ANSI.SYS file must be loaded in the root directory when the system is booted. Further, the DEVICE=ANSI.SYS command line must be in the CONFIG.SYS file.

- Displays the current drive path followed by the greater-than sign using the PROMPT PG command form (in this example the path is the root directory, signified by the backslash character)

Unless you use the $_ meta-string, the cursor will remain on the same line as the DOS prompt. The $_ meta-string moves the cursor down one line under the DOS prompt.

FIGURE 5.20
Examples of the PROMPT command using different meta-strings

```
A:\>PROMPT $T

16:24:43.84
16:24:51.26PROMPT $T $D

16:25:00.48 Mon 05-31-1993
16:25:01.86 Mon 05-31-1993PROMPT $V

MS-DOS Version 6.00
MS-DOS Version 6.00PROMPT HI FOLKS!

HI FOLKS!
HI FOLKS!PROMPT WHAT NOW? $_

WHAT NOW?

WHAT NOW?
PROMPT $P$G

A:\>
A:\>
```

GUIDED ACTIVITY 5.5

Modifying the System Prompt

In this Guided Activity, the PROMPT command is used to change your DOS prompt.

1. Type C L S and press [Enter].

2. Type PROMPT OK and press [Enter].

   The DOS prompt has been altered to read:

   > OK

3. Type PROMPT OK NG and press [Enter].

   The DOS prompt has been altered to read:

   > OK A>

   The $N meta-string displays the current (default) drive, while the $G displays the greater-than sign.

4. Type PROMPT and press [Enter] to reset the DOS prompt to the default setting.

5. Type PROMPT PG and press [Enter] to display the current drive and path followed by the greater-than sign as the DOS prompt.

CHECKPOINT 5E   Why would you execute the PROMPT PG command form rather than just the PROMPT command with no parameters?

Summary

In this unit, you learned how to create directories (using the MD or MKDIR command), remove directories (using the RD or RMDIR command), and maneuver through the directory tree structure (using the CD or CHDIR command). You also discovered how to generate a graphical picture of your disk's tree structure (using the TREE command). The PATH command was introduced to enable you to set a path to executable files in directories other than the default one. Finally, you learned how to use some additional meta-strings with the PROMPT command that enable you to change the form of the DOS prompt.

Command Review

In this unit, you learned several DOS commands. Most have optional parameters or switches. We have tried to cover both the common and the rarely used forms of each command. The following forms of this unit's commands are the most frequently used and should be reviewed carefully.

CD ..	Switches the default directory path from the current directory to its parent directory.
CD\	Switches the default directory path from the current directory to the root directory.
CD DOS	Switches the directory path to the DOS subdirectory if it exists under the current directory.
CD\DOS	Switches the directory path to the \DOS subdirectory.
MD DOS	Makes a new subdirectory named DOS under the current directory.
PATH ;	Resets the path to only search the current directory for executable files.
PATH C:\DOS	Opens a path to executable files in the C:\DOS subdirectory.
PROMPT	Resets the DOS prompt to show just the current drive and a greater-than sign.
RD TRASH	Removes a subdirectory named TRASH that is under the current directory.
RD\TRASH	Removes a subdirectory named TRASH under the root directory.
TREE	Lists the current directory and all its subdirectories.
TREE/F	Lists the current directory, all its associated files, plus all subdirectories under the current directory and their associated files.

Review Questions

1. How many files can be stored in the root directory of a 360KB floppy disk?
2. Why is it necessary to manage or organize files on a hard disk?
3. How many files can be stored in the root directory of a 1.2MB floppy disk?
4. How many files can be stored in the root directory of a 30MB hard disk?
5. What is a fixed disk?
6. What is the difference between a directory and a subdirectory?
7. What is a parent directory?
8. How would you create a subdirectory under the root directory named GAMES?

9. Which of the following are legal subdirectory names?

    87654321
    WPWIN.DIR
    DIRECTORY

10. How would you change from the root directory to the \WPWIN\DATA directory on drive B:?

11. How would you create a root directory on a disk?

12. If the default drive and directory path is C:\UTIL\PCTOOLS, how would you erase a subdirectory named \LOTUS\DATA on drive A:?

13. If the default drive and directory path is C:\UTIL\PCTOOLS, how would you erase the PCTOOLS subdirectory on drive C:?

14. Which DOS command (and what form of the command) would display the current directory path and drive as part of the system prompt?

15. If you have executable files in three directories (C:\DOS, C:\BATCH, and C:\UTIL\TEST), list the DOS command and its form that would give access to these directories from any directory on your disk.

16. How would you reset the path so that DOS only checks the current directory for executable files?

17. How would you display all directories, subdirectories, and their associated files on disk A: to the monitor screen?

18. What is the difference between the following two forms of the TREE command?

    ```
    TREE /A
    TREE >PRN
    ```

19. What does the TREE/F command do?

20. What is the function of the PROMPT command?

21. Define a meta-string. How is it used in DOS?

22. List at least three meta-strings and their results.

Exercises

Whenever instructed to format a disk, use your last name (first) and then your first name (such as BACON JON) as the volume label. If instructed to print data from the screen, be sure to write your full name, course number and section, course title, instructor's name, unit and exercise number, and today's date on the paper. Your instructor will indicate if the disk(s) created or printouts should be submitted for grading.

1. Format a disk and then create the directories shown in Figure 5.21.

FIGURE 5.21

Directories to duplicate on a floppy disk

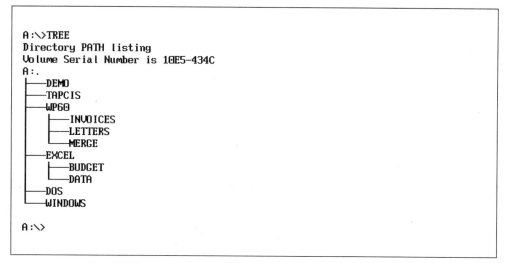

```
A:\>TREE
Directory PATH listing
Volume Serial Number is 10E5-434C
A:.
├────DEMO
├────TAPCIS
├────WP60
│    ├────INVOICES
│    ├────LETTERS
│    └────MERGE
├────EXCEL
│    ├────BUDGET
│    └────DATA
├────DOS
└────WINDOWS

A:\>
```

2. Use the TREE command to output the disk structure (created in Exercise 1 above) to your printer.

3. Use the appropriate DOS command to set a path to the following directories:

   \DOS
   \WESTDATA.DOS
   \WP

   After executing the command, screen dump the screen activity to your printer.

4. Change the DOS prompt to "WHAT NOW, MY DEAR WATSON?" and print the screen messages to the printer. The messages should indicate the command used to change the DOS prompt and the result of executing the command.

5. Create at least five subdirectories on a formatted floppy disk. The disk's volume label should include your first initial and surname (up to 11 characters). The tree structure must be at least two subdirectories deep (under the root directory). Send the tree structure of your disk to the printer.

Key Terms

Data file	Meta-string	Program file
Directory	Milliseconds (ms)	Redirect
Executable file	Parent directory	Storage
Filter	Path name	Subdirectory
Fixed-disk	Pipe	
Gigabyte	Piping symbol	

Documentation Research

Documentation Research questions are included at the end of most units to encourage you to explore and discover the additional features available with DOS 6.x. All Documentation Research questions within the text can be answered by using the on-line reference (accessed by using the HELP command). Review Guided Activity 2.8 if you are unsure how to use the HELP command.

1. Name the five commands listed as related commands on the RMDIR command Help screen.

2. According to the TREE command Help screen (examples section), how would you display the names of all subdirectories on the disk in your current drive?

3. According to the TREE command Help screen (examples section), how would you display, one screen at a time, the names of all subdirectories on drive C:?

4. According to the PROMPT command Help screen, are there character strings (meta-strings) listed on the Help screen that are not listed in this unit (Table 5.2)?

5. What does the PROMPT command Help screen call the vertical line generated by the $B meta-string?

APPLICATION

Creating Multiple Subdirectories

In this application, you create several subdirectories on a floppy disk.

1. Format a blank disk without the DOS system files.

2. Create the following directories on the disk:

> \MENU
> \WP51\COLUMNS
> \PM4
> \EXCEL\DATA
> \DOS
> \UTIL\NORTON

3. Submit the disk to your instructor. Be sure to write your name, course and section number, instructor's name, and today's date on the disk label.

Disk Management Commands (II)

Learning Objectives

At the completion of this unit, you should be able to

1. use the MOVE command to move one or more files from one directory to another on the same disk,

2. use the DELTREE command to delete all files in a directory plus any of its subordinate subdirectories.

Important Commands

DELTREE

MOVE

Using the MOVE Command

If you haven't yet, you someday will want to move one or more files from one directory to another. Earlier versions of DOS allowed you only to move a file from one directory on a disk to another by copying the file to its new location, comparing the two files to be sure the copy was identical, and then returning to the original file to erase it. Beginning with DOS 6.0, you can accomplish with one command what formerly required three.

The new MOVE command can be used to

- Move one or more files from one directory to another on the same disk

- Move one file from one directory to another on the same disk and rename it in the process

- Create a new directory and move one or more files to it from an existing directory

- Rename a directory without changing its position in the disk's *directory tree*

NOTE *You cannot move a file (using the MOVE command) from one disk to another.*

The syntax for the MOVE command is

```
MOVE [drive:][path]file name destination
```

The destination can consist of a drive letter and a colon, a path, a file name, or a combination of these elements.

FIGURE 6.1

Example of directory tree

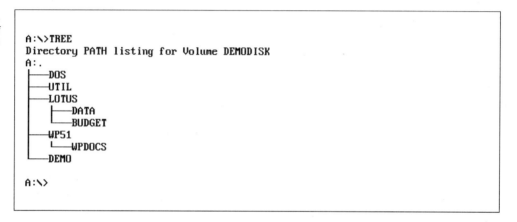

```
A:\>TREE
Directory PATH listing for Volume DEMODISK
A:.
├───DOS
├───UTIL
├───LOTUS
│   ├───DATA
│   └───BUDGET
├───WP51
│   └───WPDOCS
└───DEMO

A:\>
```

Figure 6.1 will be used to illustrate how the MOVE command can be used. In the first few examples, we'll assume that the default drive and path is the root directory and that that is where the file to be moved is located.

First, using the tree structure shown in Figure 6.1, you can move a single file (named EXAMPLE.DOC) from one directory (the root directory) to another directory (A:\DEMO) using the following command form:

```
MOVE EXAMPLE.DOC A:\DEMO\EXAMPLE.DOC
```

The command can also be shortened to indicate only the target directory, as in the following example.

```
MOVE EXAMPLE.DOC A:\DEMO
```

NOTE *The DOS 6.0 and DOS 6.2 MOVE commands have one important difference. Whenever you move a file from one location to another using the DOS 6.0 version, the MOVE command will without warning overwrite an existing file with the same name in the target directory. When using the DOS 6.0 MOVE command, you must be cautious that you do not accidentally overwrite files. However, when using the DOS 6.2 MOVE command, you cannot accidentally overwrite files. Overwrite protection is built into the new version of the MOVE command, just like the new DOS 6.2 version of the COPY command.*

When using the MOVE command, it is not necessary to use the drive designation, if you are logged on to the drive where files are being moved. For instance, the previous command can be further shortened to include just the path but not the drive designation, such as

```
MOVE EXAMPLE.DOC \DEMO
```

You can also use the command to move more than one file at a time. The following command form would move three files (LETTER.DOC, MEMO.DOC, and REPORT.DOC) from the root directory to the \WP51\WPDOCS directory.

```
MOVE LETTER.DOC,MEMO.DOC,REPORT.DOC A:\WP51\WPDOCS
```

or

```
MOVE LETTER.DOC,MEMO.DOC,REPORT.DOC \WP51\WPDOCS
```

When you move more than one file, you only stipulate the directory where you want the files moved to. The MOVE command cannot copy multiple files to a single file name, so listing anything other than a directory would cause the following error message to appear

```
Cannot move multiple files to a single file
```

You can move all files in any directory to any other directory on a disk. For instance, using the *directory tree structure* in Figure 6.1, you can move all files from A:\LOTUS\DATA to A:\WP51\WPDOCS using the following command form:

```
MOVE A:\LOTUS\DATA\*.* A:\WP51\WPDOCS
```

or

```
MOVE \LOTUS\DATA\*.* \WP51\WPDOCS
```

NOTE *In the last example, if the A:\WP51\WPDOCS directory does not exist, you can still issue the command and DOS will create the new directory. After issuing the MOVE command, you would be prompted with the message "Make directory "a:\wp51\wpdocs"? [y/n]." If you press Y, the new directory will be created and the files copied to it from A:\LOTUS\DATA. Of course, even if you were to move a single file from an existing directory to a nonexistent directory, DOS would issue the prompt and enable you to create the new directory.*

Finally, you can rename a directory by using the following command form:

```
MOVE A:\DEMO A:\POWERUP
```

or

```
MOVE \DEMO \POWERUP
```

NOTE *When renaming a directory using the MOVE command, the default path cannot be the directory being renamed. In other words, you cannot be logged on to the \DEMO directory if you try to rename it to \POWERUP.*

However, you cannot rename a directory and change its position in the directory tree. For example, the following command will not work.

```
MOVE A:\DEMO A:\LOTUS\DEMO
```

If you attempt to change the directories' position in the tree structure (as shown in the last example), DOS issues one of the following error messages:

```
Unable to open source
```

or

```
Cannot move [file name] - no such file or directory
```

GUIDED ACTIVITY 6.1

Using the MOVE Command

In this Guided Activity, you will move files from one directory to another and experiment with several ways to use the MOVE command.

1. Insert West Student Data Disk #2 into drive A:.

NOTE *The disk, if you have completed all previous activities in the text, would include all 44 files from the C:\WESTDATA.DS6 directory in its root directory. Additionally, the 15 files from the C:\WESTDATA.DS6 directory with a .DOC extension would be saved in the \PROGRAMS\ WORDS directory and 3 files with a .PM4 extension would be saved in the \TEST\PM direc-tory. The remainder of the disk tree structure would match the structure shown in Figure 6.2.*

FIGURE 6.2
The West Student Data Disk #2 disk structure at the beginning of this unit

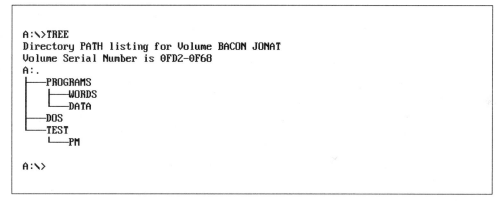

```
A:\>TREE
Directory PATH listing for Volume BACON JONAT
Volume Serial Number is 0FD2-0F68
A:.
├───PROGRAMS
│   ├───WORDS
│   └───DATA
├───DOS
└───TEST
    └───PM

A:\>
```

2. Log on to drive A:.

3. Type CLS and press [Enter].

The following step will display the file structure of the disk and the files in each directory. It uses the MORE filter (discussed in Unit 12) to display the results of the TREE command, one page at a time.

4. Type TREE/F|MORE and press [Enter].

5. Press any key twice until you see the listing of 15 files in the A:\PROGRAMS \WORDS directory.

Notice the TODOLIST.DOC file. You will move it shortly. Also notice that the A:\PROGRAMS\DATA directory has no files in it.

6. Press any key again to see the end of the TREE command listing.

7. Type CD\PROGRAMS\WORDS and press [Enter] to change to the new subdirectory.

    In the next step, you will move a single file.

8. Type MOVE TODOLIST.DOC \PROGRAMS\DATA and press [Enter].

    Notice the screen message as shown in Figure 6.3.

The MOVE command screen message

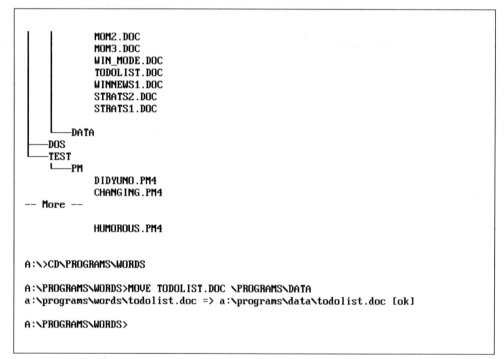

```
                    MOM2.DOC
                    MOM3.DOC
                    WIN_MODE.DOC
                    TODOLIST.DOC
                    WINNEWS1.DOC
                    STRATS2.DOC
                    STRATS1.DOC

          ——DATA
      ——DOS
      ——TEST
          └——PM
                    DIDYUNO.PM4
                    CHANGING.PM4
-- More --

                    HUMOROUS.PM4


A:\>CD\PROGRAMS\WORDS

A:\PROGRAMS\WORDS>MOVE TODOLIST.DOC \PROGRAMS\DATA
a:\programs\words\todolist.doc => a:\programs\data\todolist.doc [ok]

A:\PROGRAMS\WORDS>
```

9. Type CD\PROGRAMS\DATA and press [Enter] to move to the target directory of the move operation (in the last step).

10. Type DIR and press [Enter].

    The TODOLIST.DOC file is now in the A:\PROGRAMS\DATA directory.

11. Type CD\PROGRAMS\WORDS and press [Enter]

12. Using step 8 as a guide, move the following files, one at a time, to A:\PROGRAMS\DATA.

        WAR.DOC
        DINOSAUR.DOC
        WIN_MODE.DOC

CHECKPOINT 6A From the current directory, how would you move FLAGS.DOC to the TEST\PM directory?

13. Type CLS and press Enter.

14. When done, type DIR A:\PROGRAMS\DATA and press Enter.

     The directory should now hold four files as shown in Figure 6.4.

FIGURE 6.4
*Four files in
A:\PROGRAMS
\DATA directory*

```
A:\PROGRAMS\WORDS>DIR A:\PROGRAMS\DATA

Volume in drive A is BACON JONAT
Volume Serial Number is 0FD2-0F68
Directory of A:\PROGRAMS\DATA

.              <DIR>      05-31-93   2:14p
..             <DIR>      05-31-93   2:14p
TODOLIST DOC       74 05-08-93   7:59p
WAR      DOC     1946 10-13-91   8:24p
DINOSAUR DOC       26 05-08-93   7:51p
WIN_MODE DOC     1429 10-12-91   9:18p
        6 file(s)       3475 bytes
                     1350144 bytes free

A:\PROGRAMS\WORDS>
```

In the following steps, you will move all files beginning with the letter S to a new directory (that does not currently exist).

15. Type CLS and press Enter.

16. Type MOVE S*.* \PROGRAMS\WORDS\STRATS and press Enter.

     After you execute the command, your screen should appear as shown in Figure 6.5.

FIGURE 6.5
*Moving multiple
files with the
MOVE command
and at the same
time creating a
new directory*

```
A:\PROGRAMS\WORDS>MOVE S*.* \PROGRAMS\WORDS\STRATS
Make directory "a:\programs\words\strats"? [yn]
```

17. Type Y and press Enter in response to the screen message.

18. Type DIR and press Enter.

CHECKPOINT 6B Are there any files (not counting subdirectories) in the current directory beginning with S? Why or why not?

     In the next step, you will move all remaining files in A:\PROGRAMS\WORDS to A:\DOS.

19. Type MOVE *.* \DOS and press Enter.

20. Type DIR and press Enter.

     The current directory will no longer have any files, just the \STRATS subdirectory.

In the following steps, you will rename a directory from \TEST\PM to \TEST\PM4.

21. Type CD\ to return to the root directory.

22. Type CLS and press [Enter].

23. Type TREE and press [Enter] to see the current directory structure as shown in Figure 6.6.

FIGURE 6.6
The TREE command before renaming a directory

```
A:\>TREE
Directory PATH listing for Volume BACON JONAT
Volume Serial Number is 0FD2-0F68
A:.
├───PROGRAMS
│   ├───WORDS
│   │   └───STRATS
│   └───DATA
├───DOS
└───TEST
    └───PM


A:\>
```

24. Type MOVE \TEST\PM \TEST\PM4 and press [Enter]

25. Type TREE and press [Enter] to see the new directory structure as modified in the last step and shown in Figure 6.7.

FIGURE 6.7
The TREE command after renaming a directory

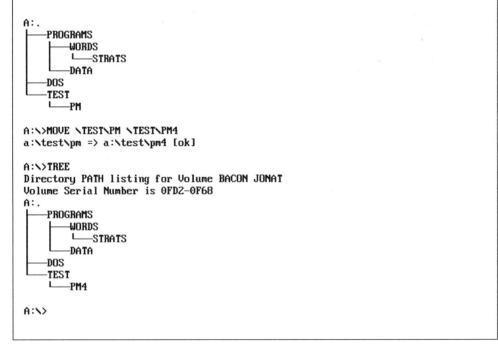

```
A:.
├───PROGRAMS
│   ├───WORDS
│   │   └───STRATS
│   └───DATA
├───DOS
└───TEST
    └───PM

A:\>MOVE \TEST\PM \TEST\PM4
a:\test\pm => a:\test\pm4 [ok]

A:\>TREE
Directory PATH listing for Volume BACON JONAT
Volume Serial Number is 0FD2-0F68
A:.
├───PROGRAMS
│   ├───WORDS
│   │   └───STRATS
│   └───DATA
├───DOS
└───TEST
    └───PM4


A:\>
```

Using DELTREE to Remove a Directory and Its Files

As you work with computers, occasions will occur when you would like to delete a directory and all of its files. Your motivation may be to remove an application from your hard disk or just to clean it up by deleting old files that are no longer needed.

In some cases, the files and directories to delete may be several levels deep. Prior to DOS 6.0, to remove the A:\LOTUS directory (shown in Figure 6.1) you would have to go to the lowest subdirectory level (\LOTUS\DATA) of the "branch" you want to delete, delete the files in that subdirectory, and then use the RD command to remove it. Next you would have to repeat the process in the next lowest level sub-directory (in this case the \LOTUS\BUDGET subdirectory), including deleting files and then removing the subdirectory. You would have to repeat the process until all directories to be deleted were empty (no files) and you would have to remove each subdirectory before you could delete its parent directory. The process was time con-suming, especially if the directories were nested several levels deep.

Beginning with DOS 6.0, you can use a single command, DELTREE, to remove a specified directory, its files, and all of its subdirectories including files in those sub-directories. The syntax of the command is

```
DELTREE [/Y] [drive:]path
```

The only required parameter is the path that you want removed. For example, if you want to eliminate the DEMO directory shown in Figure 6.1, while logged on the root directory, you would enter the following command at the DOS prompt:

```
DELTREE DEMO
```

If you wanted to delete the \DEMO directory from some location other than the root directory, you could enter the command form

```
DELTREE \DEMO
```

NOTE *You cannot be logged on to the directory you are trying to delete, nor can the current path be one of the subdirectories under the directory being deleted. If you try to delete the default directory, no error message appears, the command appears to work, but the directory will not be deleted. If you attempt to use the DELTREE command to remove a parent directory of the default directory, other subdirectories under the specified directory will be removed, but the path from the specified directory to the default directory and files in the default directory will be spared. The results will appear to be unpredictable, so it is best never to try to remove the current default drive or any directory above it in the directory tree structure.*

It does not matter if the \DEMO directory contains files—either of the above ver-sions of the DELTREE command will automatically remove the directory and all files it contains.

Let's look at a second example. If you want to remove the \LOTUS directory (shown in Figure 6.1) including its subdirectories (\LOTUS\BUDGET and \LOTUS\DATA) and all files in the \LOTUS directory and its subdirectories, you can enter a single command

```
DELTREE \LOTUS
```

or, from the root directory, enter

```
DELTREE LOTUS
```

DELTREE and Hidden or System Files

In Unit 4, you learned about the DEL command, which is used to erase one or more files in a specified directory. However, the DEL command cannot eliminate files that are marked as either hidden or system files. So far we have only discussed a few files that fall in this category, such as the IO.SYS, MSDOS.SYS, and DBLSPACE.BIN files. As long as a file is marked as hidden or a system file, the DEL command cannot erase it, but the DELTREE command can. Some games, and other programs, create hidden files—often as a means of protecting the software from unauthorized duplication. Simply be aware that using the DELTREE command will delete all files in the directory whether the file is a regular data file, program file, hidden file, or system file.

DELTREE Warning

When you invoke the DELTREE command, you will see a screen message that warns you that the specified directory will be deleted, if you type Y and press [Enter]. If you were attempting to delete the \DEMO directory, the message would read

```
Delete directory "\demo" and all its subdirectories? [yn]
```

At this point if you type Y, the deletion occurs, and if you type N, the DELTREE command is aborted. If you proceed with deleting the directory, DOS responds with the message shown in Figure 6.8.

FIGURE 6.8
DELTREE command messages

```
A:\>TREE
Directory PATH listing for Volume DEMODISK
A:.
├───DOS
├───UTIL
├───LOTUS
│   ├───DATA
│   └───BUDGET
├───WP51
│   └───WPDOCS
└───DEMO

A:\>DELTREE \DEMO
Delete directory "\demo" and all its subdirectories? [yn] y
Deleting \demo...

A:\>
```

If you are sure that you want to erase the directory, its subdirectory, and all of its files, you can add the /Y switch to the DELTREE command and you will not see the prompt shown in Figure 6.8. The actual command form would look like

```
DELTREE /Y \DEMO
```

NOTE *The /Y switch must precede the path (\DEMO in this example), not follow it. In other words,* `DELTREE \DEMO /Y` *will not work.*

Using Wild Card Characters with the DELTREE Command

You can use the global wild card characters with the DELTREE command but should *do so with great caution*. If the specified DELTREE parameter (path) matches both one or more directories and one or more file names, all will be removed. For instance, the following command form, if entered in the root directory, would delete all of the following files (assuming they are all in the root directory) and all the listed directories (assuming they are immediately under the root directory). The command form would be

```
DELTREE WP*
```

The affected (deleted) files and directories would be

```
WP{WPC}.TRE       \WP60
WPWIN.BAT         \WPC
WP51.BAT          \WPWIN
\WP51
```

If you decide to use a global wild card character with the DELTREE command, first use the parameter with the DIR command to see which files and directories will be affected. In the above example, it would be wise to first issue the following command form

```
DIR WP*
```

If it lists files or directories that you do not want to eliminate, don't use that wild card with the DELTREE command.

GUIDED ACTIVITY 6.2

Using the DEL and DELTREE Commands

In this Guided Activity, you will first delete all files stored in the root directory of West Student Data Disk #2, using the DEL command. Remember that the DEL command erases files in the current directory but does not alter the directory tree structure. Next you will use the TREE command to view the structure of the disk (its directories and subdirectories). Finally, you use the DELTREE command to remove directories with all files in those directories.

1. Be sure that West Student Data Disk #2 is still in drive A: and that the root directory of drive A: is the default drive.

   Your DOS prompt should appear as A:\.

2. In the root directory, type `DIR` and press [Enter].

   The DIR command listing displays 47 files, 3 of which are directory listings.

3. Type `DEL *.*` and press [Enter].

4. When prompted "All files in directory will be deleted! Are you sure (Y/N)?," type Y and press [Enter].

    The last two steps delete all files in the root directory.

5. Type DIR and press [Enter].

    Your screen should appear similar to Figure 6.9.

```
PAPER     TXT      1043 05-08-93   11:29a
WAR       TXT       121 01-18-94   11:19a
PROGRAMS       <DIR>      06-04-93    8:27a
DOS            <DIR>      06-04-93    8:27a
TEST           <DIR>      06-04-93    8:28a
          47 file(s)        65766 bytes
                          1339392 bytes free


A:\>DEL *.*
All files in directory will be deleted!
Are you sure (Y/N)?Y

A:\>DIR


 Volume in drive A is BACON JONAT
 Volume Serial Number is 0FD2-0F68
 Directory of A:\

PROGRAMS       <DIR>      06-04-93    8:27a
DOS            <DIR>      06-04-93    8:27a
TEST           <DIR>      06-04-93    8:28a
           3 file(s)            0 bytes
                          1411584 bytes free


A:\>
```

6. Type CLS and press [Enter].

7. To display the directory tree structure of the disk in drive A:, type TREE and press [Enter].

    Your screen should appear similar to Figure 6.10. Notice that the \DOS directory is under the root directory.

```
A:\>TREE
Directory PATH listing for Volume BACON JONAT
Volume Serial Number is 0FD2-0F68
A:.
├───PROGRAMS
│   ├───WORDS
│   │   └───STRATS
│   └───DATA
├───DOS
└───TEST
    └───PM4


A:\>
```

8. To see the files in each directory, type TREE/F and press [Enter].

Your screen should appear similar to Figure 6.11. Notice that the \DOS directory includes nine files—all ending with the .DOC extension.

FIGURE 6.11
The end of the TREE/F command listing for drive A:

```
    └──DATA
            TODOLIST.DOC
            WAR.DOC
            DINOSAUR.DOC
            WIN_MODE.DOC

   ┌──DOS
   │        ALIGN.DOC
   │        MOM1.DOC
   │        DASHIT-1.DOC
   │        FLAGS.DOC
   │        INDEFENS.DOC
   │        DIET.DOC
   │        MOM2.DOC
   │        MOM3.DOC
   │        WINNEWS1.DOC
   └──TEST
      └──PM4
               DIDYUNO.PM4
               CHANGING.PM4
               HUMOROUS.PM4


A:\>
```

In the next two steps, with one command you will remove the \DOS directory (which can be done with the RD command if the directory is free of files) and erase all files in the directory (which normally would be accomplished using the DEL command).

9. Type DELTREE \DOS and press [Enter].

10. When prompted whether to delete the directory, type Y and press [Enter].

11. Type CLS and press [Enter].

12. To see the revised directory structure, type TREE/F and press [Enter].

Compare the screen in Figure 6.12 with the screen in Figure 6.11. Notice the absence of the \DOS directory and its files in Figure 6.12.

In Figure 6.12, you will see that the \TEST directory has no files stored in it, but it does have a subdirectory (\PM4) that contains three files (all with the .PM4 extension). In the following steps, you will remove both the \TEST directory and its subdirectory (including the three files) with a single DOS command.

13. To remove the \TEST directory and all its subdirectories and files, type DELTREE \TEST and press [Enter].

14. When prompted whether to delete the directory, type Y and press [Enter].

FIGURE 6.12
*The directory
tree structure
after deleting
the \DOS
directory*

```
A:\>TREE/F
Directory PATH listing for Volume BACON JONAT
Volume Serial Number is 0FD2-0F68
A:.
    ├──PROGRAMS
    │   ├──WORDS
    │   │   └──STRATS
    │   │           STRATS2.DOC
    │   │           STRATS1.DOC
    │   │
    │   └──DATA
    │           TODOLIST.DOC
    │           WAR.DOC
    │           DINOSAUR.DOC
    │           WIN_MODE.DOC
    │
    └──TEST
        └──PM4
                DIDYUNO.PM4
                CHANGING.PM4
                HUMOROUS.PM4


A:\>
```

15. Type C L S and press [Enter].

16. Type T R E E / F and press [Enter].

Your screen should appear similar to Figure 6.13.

FIGURE 6.13
*The directory
tree structure
after deleting
the \TEST
directory*

```
A:\>TREE/F
Directory PATH listing for Volume BACON JONAT
Volume Serial Number is 0FD2-0F68
A:.
    └──PROGRAMS
        ├──WORDS
        │   └──STRATS
        │           STRATS2.DOC
        │           STRATS1.DOC
        │
        └──DATA
                TODOLIST.DOC
                WAR.DOC
                DINOSAUR.DOC
                WIN_MODE.DOC


A:\>
```

✓ **CHECKPOINT 6C** What single command can be used to delete all files on West Student Data Disk #2 without using the FORMAT command?

Summary

In this unit, you learned to use two commands that are very helpful when working with a simple or complex directory tree structure on a disk. These commands (MOVE and DELTREE) enable you to, respectively, move files from one directory to another on a single disk and delete entire branches of the directory tree structure. Both commands have their dangers and should be used with careful planning and forethought.

Command Review

In this unit, you learned several DOS commands. Most have optional parameters or switches. We have tried to cover both the common and the rarely used forms of each command. The following forms of this unit's commands are the most frequently used and should be reviewed carefully.

DELTREE \DATA	Removes the \DATA directory and all of its files and subdirectories.
MOVE \JUNK \DATA	Renames the \JUNK directory to \DATA.
MOVE TEXTFILE \DATA	Moves the TEXTFILE file from the current directory to the \DATA directory.
MOVE TEXT.ONE,TEXT.TWO, TEXT.DOC \WPDOCS	Moves three files (TEXT.ONE, TEXT.TWO, and TEXT.DOC) to the \WPDOCS directory.

Review Questions

1. Which DOS command can be used to move one or more files from one directory to another on the same disk?

2. Which DOS command can be used to rename a directory?

3. Can the MOVE command create a new directory?

4. Is the following command a valid command? Explain. `MOVE \DOS \DOS6\OLD`

5. Indicate the command form that would be used to move the LETTER2.DOC file from the current directory to the \WPWIN\WPDOCS directory.

6. Indicate the command form that would be used to move two files (MEMO.WP and LETTER.WP) from the current directory to the \WPWIN\WPDOCS directory.

7. If you move the CHARTER.DOC file from one directory to another one that already has a file named CHARTER.DOC, what happens?

8. Why would you use the DELTREE command?

9. Name the only DELTREE command switch.

10. Name the kinds of files that the DELTREE command can erase but the DEL command cannot.

11. What happens when you try to delete the current (default) directory with the DELTREE command?

12. Can you delete IO.SYS and DBLSPACE.BIN, using the DELTREE command?

13. What is the danger of using global wild card characters with the DELTREE command?

14. From the root directory, how would you erase the \JUNK directory and all files in the directory?

15. Can you delete the \JUNK directory and all files in it using the DELTREE command but not delete the \JUNK\OLDSTUF directory?

Exercises

Whenever instructed to format a disk, use your last name (first) and then your first name (such as BACON JON) as the volume label. If instructed to print data from the screen, be sure to write your full name, course number and section, course title, instructor's name, unit and exercise number, and today's date on the paper. Your instructor will indicate if the disk(s) created or printouts should be submitted for grading.

1. Copy all files from C:\WESTDATA.DS6 to West Student Exercise Disk A. Create three directories on the disk as listed below:

   \DOCFILES
   \TXTFILES
   \ZIPFILES

   While completing this exercise, send the screen messages to your printer and submit the printout to your instructor.

2. Use the disk from Exercise 1 (above) and complete the following activities:

   - Move all files with the .DOC extension to \DOCFILES.
   - Move all files with the .TXT extension to \TXTFILES.
   - Move all files with the .ZIP extension to \ZIPFILES.

   How many files remain in the root directory, excluding directory listings?

   - Erase all remaining files in the root directory.

   How many files remain on the disk?

   Submit the disk and the answers to the above questions to your instructor.

Key Terms

Directory tree
Directory tree structure

Documentation Research

Documentation Research questions are included at the end of most units to encourage you to explore and discover the additional features available with DOS 6.*x*. All Documentation Research questions within the text can be answered by using the on-line reference (accessed by using the HELP command). Review Guided Activity 2.8 if you are unsure how to use the HELP command.

1. Name the two related commands listed on the DELTREE command Help screen.

2. Can the DELTREE command erase read-only attribute files?

3. If you are moving more than one file with the MOVE command, according to the Syntax Help screen, what must the destination be?

4. What example is used on the MOVE command Help screen in the discussion of renaming a directory?

Changing Your Disk Structure

In this application, you create several directories on a floppy disk and then move files from the root directory to those new directories.

1. Format a blank disk without the DOS system files.

2. Copy all 44 files from the C:\WESTDATA.DS6 directory to your floppy disk.

3. Create the following directories on the disk:

> \ALDUS\PM4
> \WP51\DOCS
> \EXCEL\DATA
> \DOS
> \PARADOX\DATABASE

4. Move the files with the specified extension (the first column) from the root directory to the directory listed (in the second column):

> | .WP | \WP51\DOCS |
> | .PM4 | \ALDUS\PM4 |
> | .DB | \PARADOX\DATABASE |
> | .DBS | \PARADOX\DATABASE |

5. Use the DISKCOPY command to make a second copy of the disk.

6. Use the appropriate command to change \PARADOX to \FMPRO on the second disk.

7. Remove the \PM4 subdirectory but not the \ALDUS directory on the second disk.

8. Submit both disks to your instructor. Be sure to write your name, course and section number, instructor's name, and today's date on each disk's label.

Intermediate DOS Commands

III

■ **PART THREE** of the text covers DOS commands for the intermediate user. Each of the commands goes beyond the needs of the novice user, who is mainly concerned with using application programs, formatting disks, and storing data files.

In Unit 7, you will explore the new UNFORMAT command (introduced in DOS 5.0). Unit 8 introduces four new commands offered for the first time with DOS 6. They include utilities to defragment a disk, provide antivirus protection, and diagnose problems. The new DOS Edit program (introduced with DOS 5) is covered in Unit 9, while disaster recovery commands are covered in Unit 10.

7 DOS Utility Commands (I)

Learning Objectives

At the completion of this unit, you should be able to

1. use the CHKDSK command to determine the total amount of disk space in bytes, bytes available on a disk, the total memory available in the computer, and the amount of memory currently used by DOS and application programs,

2. use the CHKDSK command with the /V and /F switches,

3. use the UNFORMAT command to restore data on a disk that has been accidentally reformatted.

Important Commands

CHKDSK

UNFORMAT

The CHKDSK Command

After you execute the FORMAT command and successfully format a disk (or hard disk), several bits of information are displayed:

- Total disk space in bytes
- Total bytes in *bad sectors* (if any)
- Total bytes available on the disk

- Total bytes in each allocation unit

- Total allocation units on the disk

- The volume serial number

   The CHKDSK command displays the same list of data but adds the following:

- Volume label name, if available

- Date and time the disk was created (formatted)

- Number of user files on the disk

- Number of *hidden files* on the disk (these are most often system files)

- Total bytes in memory (this is RAM rather than disk storage)

- Total bytes in memory free

   In essence, this "informational" command checks the disk's directories, files, directory table, and file allocation table. If there are lost clusters, the CHKDSK command will warn you. *Lost clusters* are allocation units that contain data but are not associated with files in the file allocation table. They occur when the computer loses power (power loss or surge), when you fail to exit properly from an application and the files are not closed, or when an application does not function correctly.

   The syntax of the command is

```
CHKDSK [d:] [/F] [/V]
```

   The CHKDSK command is an external DOS command. To execute the command, you must have access to the CHKDSK.EXE file on disk. Assuming that the CHKDSK.EXE file is in the default drive and path, you could check the disk in drive A: with the command

```
CHKDSK A:
```

   You can also check a specific file by using the file name on the command line. For instance, if you wish to check the file named STORIES.DOC on a disk in drive A:, you would enter

```
CHKDSK A:STORIES.DOC
```

Disk-Related Information

   In Figure 7.1, the CHKDSK command is executed on a 720KB 3.5-inch disk in drive A:. Notice that this particular disk has a volume label (DISK 1), a serial number (1567-0DE4), and a creation date and time of June 5, 1993 (06-5-1993), at 8:02 a.m. The CHKDSK command also indicates that the disk has 3 directories (one is the hidden \SENTRY directory used to store deleted files) using 3,072 bytes plus 46 user files that consume 102,400 bytes. 624,640 bytes are still available for use on the disk.

NOTE   *If you are using DOS 6.2, the operating system displays the following message (not shown in Figure 7.1 or 7.2) at the bottom of the screen:*

FIGURE 7.1
*Results of
executing the
CHKDSK
command*

```
C:\>CHKDSK A:

Volume DISK 1      created 06-05-1993 8:02a
Volume Serial Number is 1567-0DE4

    730112 bytes total disk space
      3072 bytes in 3 directories
    102400 bytes in 46 user files
    624640 bytes available on disk

      1024 bytes in each allocation unit
       713 total allocation units on disk
       610 available allocation units on disk

    655360 total bytes memory
    515488 bytes free

C:\>
```

"Instead of using CHKDSK, try using SCANDISK. SCANDISK can reliably detect and fix a much wider range of disk problems. For more information, type HELP SCANDISK from the command prompt."

SCANDISK is a new utility added with DOS version 6.2. It is a disk analysis and repair tool that checks the target drive for any errors and corrects the errors found.

Memory-Related Information

The 655,360 total bytes in memory (that equates to 640KB, since a kilobyte is actually 1,024 bytes) indicates the total amount of RAM available for use by DOS and any application programs. The bottom two lines of data generated by the CHKDSK command do not refer to disk storage, but to the internal working memory (RAM) of the personal computer.

The bytes free in memory equal 515,488. The difference between bytes free and total bytes in memory equals the amount being used by DOS, background applications, and memory-resident programs. The latter are technically called ***terminate-and-stay-resident (TSR)*** programs. They include calculators, emulators, note pads, phone dialers, and other utility programs that in effect are terminated programs that stay resident in memory—thus occupying RAM even when not in use. The advantage to using them is that TSR programs can be invoked at a keystroke without taking the time to reload them.

NOTE   *The CHKDSK command displays four blocks of information, each separated from the next by a blank line on the screen (refer to Figure 7.1). The top block provides header information such as the volume name and volume serial number. The next block displays data on floppy or hard disk space and provides a count of files and directories on the disk. The third block lists details on the number of allocation units on the disk. The fourth and final block concerns the internal working memory of the PC; that is, random access memory (RAM). If you need to know how much storage is still available on your disk, look at the second, not the fourth, block.*

Another CHKDSK command listing is shown in Figure 7.2. In this case, no volume label name is listed, but three hidden files and one user file are indicated. This

FIGURE 7.2
*Results of
CHKDSK
command on a
bootable disk*

```
C:\>CHKDSK A:
Volume Serial Number is 1546-0FD4

   1457664 bytes total disk space
    131072 bytes in 3 hidden files
     53248 bytes in 1 user files
   1273344 bytes available on disk

       512 bytes in each allocation unit
      2847 total allocation units on disk
      2487 available allocation units on disk

    655360 total bytes memory
    515488 bytes free

C:\>
```

display was generated by executing the CHKDSK command on a bootable 1.44MB disk with only one user file: COMMAND.COM.

The three hidden files are IO.SYS, MSDOS.SYS, and DBLSPACE.BIN (the three DOS system files). Together these three files use 131,072 bytes (if using DOS 6.0) and 142,950 bytes (if using DOS 6.2). The single user file listed is COMMAND.COM. Its size varies depending on whether you use DOS 6.0 (53,249 bytes) or DOS 6.2 (54,619 bytes in size).

CHKDSK Optional Switches

The CHKDSK command has two switches available in DOS version 6.*x*:

CHKDSK/F Fixes any errors found in the directory or file allocation table.

CHKDSK/V Displays all files with their path names (on the default drive or drive specified) as CHKDSK checks the files. Unlike the standard DIR command, the CHKDSK command does display hidden files if used with the /V switch.

The output of the CHKDSK command does not display files and directories unless the /V switch is used. The listing in Figure 7.3 was generated by adding the /V switch. Each file on the bootable disk is shown, including the path to that file. If you run the CHKDSK command on a hard disk, you will get pages and pages of file listings that will scroll up the screen faster than you can read them. Unfortunately, there is no /P switch (as we used with the DIR command) to force output to stop after each page.

Two options include suspending the output with the [Ctrl] [S] key combination, or redirecting the output to a printer (using [Ctrl] [P] to toggle the printer option on or off). Another option is the use of the MORE filter, which is discussed in Unit 12. It can be used to force CHKDSK to display one screen of data at a time.

The /V switch is not practical, unless you use it with a disk containing seven or fewer files (because the file listing will scroll off the screen). Also, CHKDSK/V does not give you other data (file creation date and time, or size in bytes) that is available from the DIR command. CHKDSK is more useful when you want to check the available storage space on your disk or request a status report on the amount of internal working memory in your system (both free and total available).

FIGURE 7.3

*Output from the
CHKDSK
command,
using the /V
switch*

```
C:\>CHKDSK A:/V
Volume Serial Number is 1546-0FD4
Directory A:\
A:\IO.SYS
A:\MSDOS.SYS
A:\COMMAND.COM
A:\DBLSPACE.BIN

   1457664 bytes total disk space
    131072 bytes in 3 hidden files
     53248 bytes in 1 user files
   1273344 bytes available on disk

       512 bytes in each allocation unit
      2847 total allocation units on disk
      2487 available allocation units on disk

    655360 total bytes memory
    515488 bytes free

C:\>
```

The other and final purpose of CHKDSK is to troubleshoot your files looking for lost clusters. When you add the /F switch, the CHKDSK command will fix errors found in the directory or file allocation table. The way in which the fix is made is simple. DOS takes the lost cluster(s) and changes each one into a separate and distinct file. They are given names such as

```
FILE0000.CHK
FILE0001.CHK
FILE0002.CHK
FILE0003.CHK
```

Once CHKDSK has created these separate files, you can try to load them with your word processor (assuming they originally were part of a document file) to see if any part of the file is retrievable. Often, you will find that the .CHK files do not have retrievable data—in which case, the best action is to simply delete them. By deleting these files, you make more disk space available and unclutter your root directory.

It is usually wise to perform the CHKDSK command without the /F switch first. Then, if lost clusters are found, execute the command again with the /F switch. Lost clusters are turned into files (FILE0001.CHK, and so on) only when you use the /F switch. Sometimes it is preferable to use a file recovery program rather than CHKDSK/F. The CHKDSK command creates separate files out of each group of lost clusters, while file recovery programs typically try to reassemble the original file. Norton Utilities or PC Tools are just two examples of programs that enable you to unerase files or reattach lost clusters.

TIP *The two best defenses against lost clusters are action-oriented. First, always exit properly from all software programs, and never turn off your personal computer until you are back at the DOS prompt. Second, make periodic backups. In Unit 10, the whole area of backing up files is explored further.*

GUIDED ACTIVITY 7.1

Using the CHKDSK Command

In this Guided Activity, you will use the CHKDSK command on each of the four West Student Data Disks (#1, #2, #3, and #4).

1. Insert West Student Data Disk #1 in drive A:.

NOTE *This is the disk that you compressed using the DBLSPACE command. If you are using DOS 6.0, it will react differently than the other noncompressed West Student Data Disks. If you are using DOS 6.2, a compressed disk is automatically mounted without issuing the DBLSPACE /MOUNT command form indicated in step 7. Further, when you issue the CHKDSK command in step 4, your screen will display the CHKDSK data shown in the middle of Figure 7.5 rather than listing the HOST_FOR_A data shown in Figure 7.4. Steps 7 and 9 are required only if you are using DOS 6.0, not version 6.2.*

2. Be sure you are logged on to the root directory of drive C:.

3. Type CLS and press Enter.

NOTE *If you are using MS-DOS 6.2, jump to step 8. You do not need to complete steps 4 through 7.*

4. Type CHKDSK A: and press Enter.

CHECKPOINT 7A How would you change the command in step 3 to act upon your hard drive (assuming it is drive C:)?

Figure 7.4 shows the screen response for the CHKDSK command when using DOS 6.0. According to the screen, the West Student Data Disk #1 in drive A: was formatted with the label HOST_FOR_A. That is not the label you gave the file when you formatted it. Further, the CHKDSK listing indicates that the disk includes 1 hidden file (1,378,816 bytes) and 1 user file (512 bytes). Actually, you are seeing the CHKDSK response to a compressed but unmounted drive. The volume label, HOST_FOR_A, is the clue that you are looking at an unmounted, double-spaced disk when using DOS 6.0.

FIGURE 7.4
CHKDSK screen activity for a compressed but unmounted disk when using DOS 6.0.

```
C:\>CHKDSK A:

Volume HOST_FOR_A  created 05-29-1993 8:18a
Volume Serial Number is 1454-1BE5

  1457664 bytes total disk space
  1378816 bytes in 1 hidden files
      512 bytes in 1 user files
    78336 bytes available on disk

      512 bytes in each allocation unit
     2847 total allocation units on disk
      153 available allocation units on disk

   655360 total bytes memory
   515488 bytes free

C:\>
```

5. Type CLS and press ⏎Enter⏎.

6. Type DIR A: and press ⏎Enter⏎.

Notice that a single file, READTHIS.TXT, is listed. If you were to load this file into a text editor or word processing program, it would indicate that the disk in drive A: is compressed and must be mounted—as directed in the next step.

7. Type DBLSPACE /MOUNT A: and press ⏎Enter⏎.

8. Type CHKDSK A: and press ⏎Enter⏎.

Your screen should now appear similar to Figure 7.5. According to the CHKDSK command shown in Figure 7.5, the West Student Data Disk #1 in drive A: was formatted with the label BACON JONAT on 05-29-1993 at 8:18 a.m. There are 44 user files and no directories indicated by the CHKDSK command. If CHKDSK only finds a root directory on a disk, it does not list the number of directories. If other directories are found, CHKDSK lists the number. CHKDSK may indicate one more directory than you expect—this is because the disk may have a hidden \SENTRY directory, used by the Delete Sentry system (discussed in conjunction with the UNDELETE command in Unit 4). The amount of total memory or bytes free may vary, depending on the amount of RAM in your computer.

Before moving on to the next student data disk, it is best to unmount the disk in drive A:.

NOTE *If you are using MS-DOS 6.2, please skip the next step. It is not required since version 6.2 automatically mounts and dismounts a compressed disk.*

9. Type DBLSPACE /UNMOUNT A: and press ⏎Enter⏎.

FIGURE 7.5
The CHKDSK command screen based on West Student Data Disk #1

```
C:\>DBLSPACE /MOUNT A:
DoubleSpace is mounting drive A.
DoubleSpace has mounted drive A.

C:\>CHKDSK A:

Volume BACON JONAT created 05-29-1993 8:18a
Volume Serial Number is 0FDA-3E3D

  2613248 bytes total disk space
   376832 bytes in 44 user files
  2236416 bytes available on disk

     8192 bytes in each allocation unit
      319 total allocation units on disk
      273 available allocation units on disk

   655360 total bytes memory
   515488 bytes free
DoubleSpace is scanning your computer for drive A's compressed volume file.
DoubleSpace is checking drive A.

DoubleSpace found no errors on drive A.

C:\>
```

10. Remove the disk from drive A: and insert West Student Data Disk #2.

11. Type CLS and press [Enter]

12. Type CHKDSK A: and press [Enter].

Notice that this disk only has 4 or 5 directories, but may have between 6 and 175 user files. This disk was used in earlier units to discuss deleting and undeleting files. If the Delete Sentry system was used to protect the deleted files, the disk now contains a hidden directory called \SENTRY, which in turn contains copies of all deleted files. The disk also includes four visible directories as listed:

```
\PROGRAMS
\WORDS
\WORDS\STRATS
\DATA
```

NOTE *If you have not used the Delete Sentry system, the disk will include a total of 4 directories and 6 files.*

If present, you'll see the deleted files and directories in the next Guided Activity.

13. Insert West Student Data Disk #3 in drive A:.

14. Type CLS and press [Enter].

15. Type CHKDSK A: and press [Enter].

This disk has no directories listed, but does list 46 user files.

NOTE *If your computer has Delete Sentry active, you may find 1 directory and up to 68 user files listed by the CHKDSK command. If a directory is listed, it is the \SENTRY directory and the 68 user files include 46 visible files and up to 22 deleted files.*

16. Insert West Student Data Disk #4 in drive A:.

17. Type CLS and press [Enter].

18. Type CHKDSK A: and press [Enter].

The CHKDSK display lists 8 files and no directories.

NOTE *If your computer has Delete Sentry active, you may find 1 directory and up to 48 user files listed by the CHKDSK command.*

GUIDED ACTIVITY 7.2

Using CHKDSK with the /V Switch

In this Guided Activity, you will use the CHKDSK command with the /V switch to view the files and their paths on the disk. You will need the West Student Data Disks.

1. Be sure West Student Data Disk #4 is still in drive A:.

2. Type CLS and press [Enter].

3. Type CHKDSK A:/V and press [Enter].

FIGURE 7.6
Screen activity when using the CHKDSK /V command

```
Directory A:\
Directory A:\SENTRY
A:\SENTRY\CONTROL.FIL
A:\MYSTERY.TXT
A:\DAD1.DOC
A:\PAPER.TXT
A:\TRUCKIN.TXT
A:\ALIGN.WP
A:\#INOSAUR.WP
A:\#AR.WP
A:\#APER.WP

   1457664 bytes total disk space
       512 bytes in 1 directories
     12288 bytes in 9 user files
   1444864 bytes available on disk

       512 bytes in each allocation unit
      2847 total allocation units on disk
      2822 available allocation units on disk

    655360 total bytes memory
    515488 bytes free

C:\>
```

Assuming that Delete Sentry is active, the disk in drive A: may appear similar to Figure 7.6. The single directory in Figure 7.6 is the hidden \SENTRY directory and the file in the directory is CONTROL.FIL—which is used by the Delete Sentry system. Your disk may have additional files with such file names as #A1B2N1A.MS.

4. Type CLS and press Enter.

5. With West Student Data Disk #4 still in drive A:, type SYS A: and press Enter to make it a bootable system disk.

6. Type CHKDSK A:/V|MORE and press Enter.

NOTE *You have used the MORE filter earlier in the text. It causes the output from a command to pause when the screen is full—until you press any key to make it continue.*

Notice that IO.SYS and MSDOS.SYS are listed on the first screen of the CHKDSK command display.

7. Press any key to continue until the DOS prompt appears.

Your screen should appear similar to Figure 7.7 and indicates that three hidden files (MSDOS.SYS, IO.SYS, and DBLSPACE.BIN) plus COMMAND.COM and user files exist on the disk.

8. Insert West Student Data Disk #3 in drive A:.

9. Type CLS and press Enter.

10. Type CHKDSK A:/V and press Enter.

FIGURE 7.7

Displaying hidden system files and COMMAND.COM on a system disk

```
A:\ALIGN.WP
A:\#INOSAUR.WP
A:\#AR.WP
A:\#APER.WP
Directory A:\SENTRY
A:\SENTRY\CONTROL.FIL
A:\DBLSPACE.BIN
A:\COMMAND.COM

   1457664 bytes total disk space
    131072 bytes in 3 hidden files
       512 bytes in 1 directories
     65536 bytes in 10 user files
   1260544 bytes available on disk
-- More --


       512 bytes in each allocation unit
      2847 total allocation units on disk
      2462 available allocation units on disk

    655360 total bytes memory
    515488 bytes free

C:\>
```

The end of the CHKDSK display lists some of the 46 user files on the disk including STRATS1.DOC, STRATS2.DOC, and NEWFILE.

11. Insert West Student Data Disk #2 in drive A:.

12. Type CLS and press [Enter].

13. Type CHKDSK A:/V|MORE and press [Enter].

The MORE filter causes the CHKDSK command display to pause when the screen is full. On the first screen, you will see the files in the \PROGRAMS \WORDS, the \PROGRAMS\WORDS\STRATS, and the \PROGRAMS\DATA directories, and the beginning of the file list for the \SENTRY directory (if you are using Delete Sentry).

14. Press any key.

The next screen displays additional files in the \SENTRY directory. This directory is used by the Delete Sentry system to store copies of all deleted files—thus enabling you to undelete them.

15. Press any key until the end of the CHKDSK command display appears.

The last page of the CHKDSK command display appears similar to Figure 7.8. It lists the summary data on the number of files, directories, and bytes available.

FIGURE 7.8
*The end of the
CHKDSK
A:/V\MORE
command listing*

```
A:\SENTRY\#A1B2FYT.MS
A:\SENTRY\#A1B2FYU.MS
A:\SENTRY\#A1B2FYV.MS
A:\SENTRY\#A1B2FYW.MS
A:\SENTRY\#A1B2FYX.MS
A:\SENTRY\#A1B2FYY.MS
A:\SENTRY\#A1B2FYZ.MS
A:\SENTRY\#A1B2FZ1.MS
A:\SENTRY\#A1B2FZ2.MS

   1457664 bytes total disk space
      7168 bytes in 4 directories
    310272 bytes in 175 user files
   1140224 bytes available on disk

       512 bytes in each allocation unit
      2847 total allocation units on disk
      2227 available allocation units on disk
-- More --


    655360 total bytes memory
    515488 bytes free

C:\>
```

The UNFORMAT and MIRROR Commands

Recall that the FORMAT command erases all data from a disk. The command must be used carefully because of its destructive nature. Beginning with DOS 5.0, accidentally formatting a disk may not be as catastrophic as it once was. The UNFORMAT command is a close relative of the UNDELETE command. It enables you to attempt to recover all data on an accidentally formatted hard disk or floppy disk. Though the existence of this new command is no license to be careless when formatting disks, it does help in case of error.

The UNFORMAT command uses information stored when the target disk is formatted (accidentally or otherwise) using the FORMAT command. Remember, when you formatted disks earlier, you saw a message indicating

        Saving UNFORMAT Information.

This data is stored by a program called MIRROR that is automatically invoked when you use the FORMAT command (unless you add the /U switch). Though the FORMAT command invokes the MIRROR program, you obviously do not want to reformat a hard drive just to create unformat data. To create or update the *unformat information* on either a hard disk or floppy disk, you can type MIRROR at the DOS prompt.

The MIRROR command actually has three functions:

- It creates a backup copy of a hard disk's partition tables (using the /PARTN switch).

- It creates a file to assist the UNFORMAT command that is used to recover data on a formatted disk (as discussed in this section).

- It performs deletion-tracking, which assists the UNDELETE command in restoring deleted files (by using the /Td: switch and parameter—where you substitute the target drive for d:).

When using any form of the MIRROR command, you must be logged on to the drive to be mirrored or you must specify the target drive. For example, the following command form creates unformat information for the disk in drive A:.

```
MIRROR A:
```

The data stored by the MIRROR command is placed in a file named MIRROR.FIL or UNFORMAT.DAT. That file cannot be erased using the DEL command.

The UNFORMAT command defaults to using data created by the MIRROR command. If MIRROR command data does not exist, you can use the following command form to attempt to unformat your disk, using information in the root directory and the file allocation table.

```
UNFORMAT A:/U
```

It is unlikely that the previous command will work, but as a last resort, it should be attempted.

GUIDED ACTIVITY 7.3

Unformatting a Floppy Disk

In this Guided Activity, you first reformat West Student Data Disk #3 using the FORMAT command and then use the UNFORMAT command to restore the data on the disk. Then you repeat the process using West Student Data Disk #4.

1. Insert West Student Data Disk #3 in drive A:.

   Be sure you are logged on to drive C:.

2. Type DIR A: and press [Enter].

   A list of 46 files appears.

NOTE *This disk contains all 44 files from the C:\WESTDATA.DS6 directory (some were renamed back in Unit 4) plus two files called DREAMIT and NEWFILE (created in earlier units). If your disk does not exactly match this, that is OK. Just be sure that you know how many files are on the disk, so that you can verify the number after formatting and after unformatting the disk.*

CHECKPOINT 7B Why would you use the DIR command on a disk before using the FORMAT command?

3. Type FORMAT A: and press [Enter].

   Follow screen directions to format the disk and assign it a volume label of UNFORMATEST.

4. After the volume label is entered and you are prompted to "Format another (Y/N)?," type N and press [Enter].

5. Type DIR A: and press [Enter]. The disk should have no files listed.

6. Type CLS and press [Enter].

   Now you will attempt to restore the disk to its earlier state, using the UNFORMAT command.

7. Type UNFORMAT A: and press [Enter].

8. When prompted "Insert disk to rebuild in drive A: and press ENTER when ready," be sure that West Student Data Disk #3 is in drive A: and then press [Enter].

9. When prompted "Are you sure you want to update the system area of your drive A (Y/N)?," type Y.

   When the UNFORMAT command is done, your screen appears similar to Figure 7.9.

FIGURE 7.9
Screen results
of UNFORMAT
command

```
Restores the system area of your disk by using the image file created
by the MIRROR command.

    WARNING !!        WARNING !!

This command should be used only to recover from the inadvertent use of
the FORMAT command or the RECOVER command.  Any other use of the UNFORMAT
command may cause you to lose data!  Files modified since the MIRROR image
file was created may be lost.

Searching disk for MIRROR image.

The last time the MIRROR or FORMAT command was used was at 11:13 on 06-05-93.

The MIRROR image file has been validated.

Are you sure you want to update the system area of your drive A (Y/N)? Y

The system area of drive A has been rebuilt.

You may need to restart the system.

C:\>
```

10. Type DIR A: and press [Enter]. The files displayed in step 2 should be listed once again.

    In the following steps, you will format and then unformat West Student Data Disk #4.

11. Insert West Student Data Disk #4 in drive A:.

12. Type CLS and press [Enter].

13. Type DIR A: and press [Enter].

FIGURE 7.10
*West Student
Data Disk #4
files*

```
C:\>DIR A:

 Volume in drive A is BACON JONAT
 Volume Serial Number is 1F55-1AF5
 Directory of A:\

MYSTERY  TXT        91 10-06-88    7:03p
DAD1     DOC       419 10-04-88    7:28p
PAPER    TXT      1043 05-08-93   11:29a
TRUCKIN  TXT       719 07-13-89    8:11a
ALIGN    WP       2377 10-12-91    9:49p
#INOSAUR WP         24 05-08-93    7:52p
#AR      WP       1244 10-13-91    8:24p
#APER    WP       2879 05-08-93   11:23a
COMMAND  COM     52925 03-10-93    6:00a
          9 file(s)        61721 bytes
                         1260544 bytes free

C:\>
```

The disk contains 9 files, one of which is COMMAND.COM. Remember that this disk was made bootable earlier in this unit. Your screen should appear similar to Figure 7.10.

The files on this disk should include:

MYSTERY.TXT	TRUCKIN.TXT	#AR.WP
DAD1.DOC	ALIGN.WP	#APER.WP
PAPER.TXT	#INOSAUR.WP	COMMAND.COM

NOTE *If you are using the Delete Sentry system, the three files beginning with a pound sign (#INOSAUR.WP, #AR.WP, and #APER.WP) will be named DINOSAUR.WP, WAR.WP, and PAPER.WP, respectively. If using DOS 6.2, the size of the COMMAND.COM file will be 54,619 bytes rather than 52,925. Further, the order in which the DIR command lists the files on the disk may vary.*

If your disk does not match exactly, you can copy any eight files to the disk and then make it bootable, using the SYS command.

14. Type FORMAT A:/Q and press [Enter].

   Follow screen directions to format the disk and assign it a volume label of REFORMATTED.

15. After the volume label is entered and you are prompted to "QuickFormat another (Y/N)?," type N and press [Enter].

16. Type DIR A: and press [Enter]. The disk should have no files.

   Now you will attempt to restore the disk, using the UNFORMAT command.

17. Type CLS and press [Enter].

18. Type UNFORMAT A: and press [Enter].

19. When prompted to "Insert disk to rebuild in drive A:," be sure that West Student Data Disk #4 is in drive A: and then press `Enter`.

20. When prompted "Are you sure you want to update the system area of your drive A (Y/N)?," type Y.

    When the UNFORMAT command is done, your screen appears similar to Figure 7.11.

21. Type DIR A: and press `Enter`. The files displayed in step 13 should be listed once again.

FIGURE 7.11
Screen results of UNFORMAT command

```
Restores the system area of your disk by using the image file created
by the MIRROR command.

    WARNING !!         WARNING !!

This command should be used only to recover from the inadvertent use of
the FORMAT command or the RECOVER command.  Any other use of the UNFORMAT
command may cause you to lose data!  Files modified since the MIRROR image
file was created may be lost.

Searching disk for MIRROR image.

The last time the MIRROR or FORMAT command was used was at 11:17 on 06-05-93.

The MIRROR image file has been validated.

Are you sure you want to update the system area of your drive A (Y/N)? Y

The system area of drive A has been rebuilt.

You may need to restart the system.

C:\>
```

Summary

In this unit, you learned how to display a status report on a floppy or hard disk using the CHKDSK command and how to use that command to correct lost clusters. You also discovered how to use the UNFORMAT and MIRROR commands, which attempt to restore an accidentally formatted disk.

Command Review

In this unit, you learned about several DOS commands. Most have optional switches. We have tried to cover both the common and the rarely used forms of each command. The following forms of this unit's commands are the most frequently used and should be reviewed carefully.

CHKDSK A:	Provides a status report on the internal working memory and disk storage contained on the disk in drive A:.
CHKDSK A:/F	Provides a status report on the internal working memory and disk storage contained on the disk in drive A:, and fixes lost clusters by making them into individual files.
UNFORMAT A:	Restores the directory structure and files on an accidentally formatted disk in drive A:.

Review Questions

1. What happens if the CHKDSK /F command finds lost clusters?
2. What are the four blocks of data provided by the CHKDSK command?
3. Name two CHKDSK optional switches.
4. Of the four types of data provided by the CHKDSK command, which is not provided when the FORMAT command finishes its work?
5. Does the CHKDSK command list the number of hidden files on a disk?
6. Does the CHKDSK command indicate the total bytes of RAM available?
7. Does the CHKDSK command indicate the number of directories on a disk?
8. What is a TSR program?
9. What causes the creation of a file named FILE0000.CHK?
10. When were the UNFORMAT and MIRROR commands introduced to DOS users?
11. Name the three functions of the MIRROR command.
12. Which two DOS commands save unformat information?
13. Can you use the UNFORMAT command on a hard disk or just a floppy disk?

Exercises

Whenever instructed to format a disk, use your last name (first) and then your first name (such as BACON JON) as the volume label. If instructed to print data from the screen, be sure to write your full name, course number and section, course title, instructor's name, unit and exercise number, and today's date on the paper. Your instructor will indicate if the disk(s) created or printouts should be submitted for grading.

1. Format a disk as a system disk and use the CHKDSK command to view the hidden DOS files. Make a screen dump of the screen messages.
2. Use the CHKDSK command to display all files on West Student Data Disk #1. Print the results to a printer.

3. Use the CHKDSK command to display the files and directories on West Student Data Disk #2. Print the results to a printer.

4. Format a disk with the DOS system files. Be sure the disk is bootable and includes the volume label SYSTEM-DISK. Copy any three files from the \WESTDATA.DS6 directory to the disk. Format the disk again and then unformat the disk while capturing screen messages to a printer.

Key Terms

Bad sector   Terminate-and-stay-resident (TSR)
Hidden file   Unformat information
Lost cluster

Documentation Research

Documentation Research questions are included at the end of most units to encourage you to explore and discover the additional features available with DOS 6.x. All Documentation Research questions within the text can be answered by using the on-line reference (accessed by using the HELP command). Review Guided Activity 2.8 if you are unsure how to use the HELP command.

1. Does the CHKDSK command verify that your files can be read accurately if it returns no errors?

2. Can the UNFORMAT command be used to restore network drives that have been accidentally formatted?

3. Which command is listed as a related command on the CHKDSK command Help screen?

4. Which command is listed as a related command on the UNFORMAT command Help screen?

5. Name two times when the CHKDSK command should not be run.

DOS Utility Commands (II)

Learning Objectives

At the completion of this unit, you should be able to

1. defragment or optimize a disk using the DOS DEFRAG command,

2. name two DOS commands that assist in protecting your system from a computer virus,

3. protect your system from a virus, using the Microsoft Anti-Virus program,

4. use the Microsoft Diagnostics program to list technical details on your computer system.

Important Commands

DEFRAG

MSAV

MSD

VSAFE

Healthy Computer Systems

The more you use a personal computer, the more you will find it an indispensable tool. Like any tool, it must be cared for and provided with routine maintenance or you may find that your system's "health" fails at the most inopportune time. In this unit, you will learn about four new commands introduced with DOS 6.0. Each of the four—DEFRAG, MSAV, MSD, VSAFE—can be used to keep your system healthy or to give it a periodic checkup.

Disk Fragmentation

When your computer saves files to disk, it saves them in allocation units (sometimes called clusters). The size of the cluster or allocation unit varies, depending on the size of the disk. Both 512- and 1,024-byte allocation units are common. When a file is stored on disk, it uses the entire allocation unit(s), not just a part of an allocation unit. For instance, if your file is 640 bytes in size (assuming a 512-byte allocation unit), the file will use 2 allocation units. Though the file is only 640 bytes in size, it will use 1,024 bytes of disk space—because no other file can use the unused portion of the second allocation unit.

DOS always tries to save a file in contiguous allocation units, that is, in clusters that would be read sequentially by the read-write head of the drive. If the file requires 10 contiguous allocation units but only 7 are available, the operating system will store the first part of the file in the first available 7 contiguous clusters it finds. DOS will then search for the next (hopefully) 3 contiguous allocation units. When files are not stored in contiguous allocation units, they are said to be fragmented. They can still be read by DOS, but it takes longer because the file must be accessed (read) at multiple locations on the disk rather than just a single location. The end result is that *disk access speed* is reduced as the disk becomes more and more fragmented. Disk access speed is the time it takes to locate each allocation unit used by a file and read it into memory.

As you save files to the disk, modify those files (which can either increase or decrease the storage space used on the disk), and delete old files, your disk becomes more and more fragmented. As it becomes more fragmented, accessing any file on the disk takes longer. The process of eliminating *disk fragmentation* is called *disk optimization* or *disk compaction*. Utility programs that *optimize* a disk are referred to as disk optimizers, disk organizers, or defragmentation utilities.

Using the DEFRAG Command

The DEFRAG command is DOS's answer to disk fragmentation. The DEFRAG command looks at the specified drive and, in order to optimize disk performance, it rewrites all files on the disk in contiguous sectors. Once disk fragmentation is eliminated, files can be accessed faster.

However, fragmentation will continue to creep in as you use your computer. No matter what you do (unless you do nothing on your computer), fragmentation occurs. Your hard disk should be defragmented at least once a month, depending on usage—or even as often as once a week or more.

CAUTION *The DEFRAG command should never be run from within Windows or you may lose data. Further, it should not be used to optimize network drives or drives created with INTERLNK.*

The syntax of the command is

```
DEFRAG [drive:] [/F] [/Sorder] [/B] [/SKIPHIGH] [/LCD][/BW][/GO][/H]
```

In its simplest form, you would simply follow the DEFRAG command with a parameter indicating the drive to defragment, such as in the following example:

DEFRAG A:

Additional switches that can be used with the DEFRAG command are listed in Table 8.1.

TABLE 8.1 The DEFRAG command switches		
/B	Reboots your computer after defragmentation is complete.	
/BW	Starts the DEFRAG program using a black-and-white (monochrome) color scheme. Used on computers equipped only with a monochrome monitor.	
/F	Defragments files on the specified drive and does not leave empty spaces between files. Starts full defragmentation.	
/GO	Disables the graphic mouse and character set.	
/H	Moves hidden files to best optimize the disk.	
/LCD	Runs the DEFRAG program on a portable or notebook computer with an LCD (liquid crystal display) screen.	
/U	Defragments files on the specified drive and leaves empty spaces between files. Defragments files only, not directory listings.	
/Sorder	Establishes how files are defragmented and stored within each directory. If you use this switch, DEFRAG reorders your files on the disk in addition to defragmenting them. If you omit this switch, files are defragmented but left in their current order. You can use any one or more of the following options to specify the order desired in this switch. If you use more than one of these order options, be sure they do not negate each other, and do not separate them with spaces.	
	E	Orders by file name extension in alphabetical order.
	–E	Orders by file name extension in reverse alphabetical order.
	D	Orders by the file's creation date and time, earliest first.
	–D	Orders by the file's creation date and time, latest first.
	N	Orders by file name in alphabetical order.
	–N	Orders by file name in reverse alphabetical order.
	S	Orders by file size, smallest first.
	–S	Orders by file size, largest first.
/SKIPHIGH	Runs the DEFRAG program in conventional memory rather than upper memory. The default setting for DEFRAG (without adding this switch) is for DEFRAG to run in upper memory, if it is available.	
/V	Verifies the accuracy of the data after it is moved.	

If you want to optimize only files (not directories) on your hard drive (C:) and want the moved files to be verified, you would use the command form listed below:

```
DEFRAG C: /U /V
```

If you want to optimize only files (not directories) on your hard drive (C:) and have all the files written back to disk in alphabetical order (within each directory) and you also want the moved files verified, you would use the command form listed below:

```
DEFRAG C: /U /SN /V
```

On the other hand, to invoke a full optimization (files and directories) in alphabetical order by file name and verify each move, you would use the command:

```
DEFRAG C: /F /SN /V
```

The Menu Approach to Running the DEFRAG Program

In addition to running the DEFRAG program from the DOS prompt as described above (which assumes the use of the command switches listed in Table 8.1), you can also run the program without switches and select your options from the DEFRAG program menu bar. To use this latter method, you would type DEFRAG at the DOS prompt. The basic DEFRAG screen is shown in Figure 8.1.

Notice the Optimize menu and the options on it. It parallels the command line switches that you can use (which are listed in Table 8.1).

FIGURE 8.1
The DEFRAG command screen with the drop-down Optimize menu

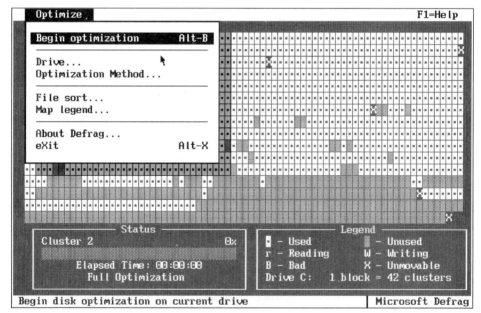

GUIDED ACTIVITY 8.1

Using the DEFRAG Command

In this Guided Activity, you will use the DEFRAG command on West Student Data Disk #3. It is not fragmented. Next, you will create a fragmented disk (West Student Data Disk #5) so that you can use the DEFRAG command to unfragment it. You will use the menu interface rather than issuing commands at the DOS prompt.

1. Insert West Student Data Disk #3 in drive A:.

2. At the DOS prompt, type DEFRAG and press [Enter].

   A dialog box appears and prompts you to "Select the drive you wish to optimize" as shown in Figure 8.2.

FIGURE 8.2
The DEFRAG command prompts you to select the drive to optimize

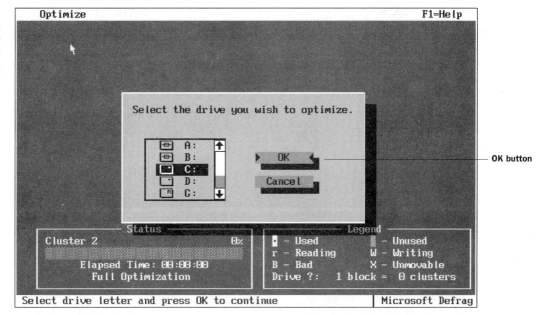

OK button

3. Press [↑] until you have selected the drive A: option or, if using a mouse, click on the A: drive option.

4. Click on the OK button or press [Enter].

   A screen message appears, indicating that the command is "Reading disk information...." More than likely, a screen will appear, as shown in Figure 8.3, indicating that optimization is not necessary. No fragmentation exists.

5. Press [Enter] to continue.

6. Select the Exit option from the Optimize menu.

   In the following steps, you will format a disk and then purposely fragment it. To fragment the disk files, you will first copy all files from the C:\WESTDATA.DS6 directory to a formatted disk in drive A:. This will be labeled as West Student Data Disk #5. The COPY command packs the files in contiguous sectors on a

FIGURE 8.3
*The
Recommendation
dialog box (not
suggesting
optimization)*

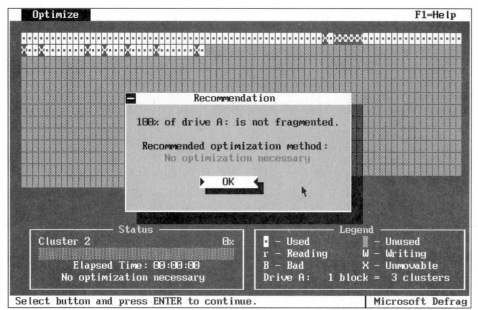

newly formatted disk. Then you will use the COPY command and redirection (explained in Unit 12) to enlarge some of the small files so that when they are stored on the disk, they must be spread over noncontiguous sectors by DOS.

7. Format a disk, attach a label indicating that the disk is West Student Data Disk #5, and insert the disk in drive A:.

8. Be sure you have logged onto drive C:, and change the directory to C:\WESTDATA.DS6.

9. Copy all files from the C:\WESTDATA.DS6 directory to the newly formatted disk in drive A:.

   44 files should be on the disk.

10. Log onto drive A:.

11. Type `COPY DIET.BAK+FLAGS.DOC DASHIT-1.DOC` and press .

NOTE *If using DOS 6.2, an "Overwrite (Yes/No/All)?" message will appear. Type Y to overwrite the target file.*

12. Type `COPY INDEFENS.DOC+MISC.ZIP MOM2.BAK` and press .

NOTE *If using DOS 6.2, an "Overwrite (Yes/No/All)?" message will appear. Type Y to overwrite the target file.*

13. Type `COPY STRATS1.DOC+STRATS2.DOC FAMOUS.DB` and press .

NOTE *If using DOS 6.2, an "Overwrite (Yes/No/All)?" message will appear. Type Y to overwrite the target file.*

14. Type `DIR *.* >>DINOSAUR.WP` and press .

15. Type `DEFRAG` and press .

FIGURE 8.4
The Recommendation dialog box (suggesting file optimization only)

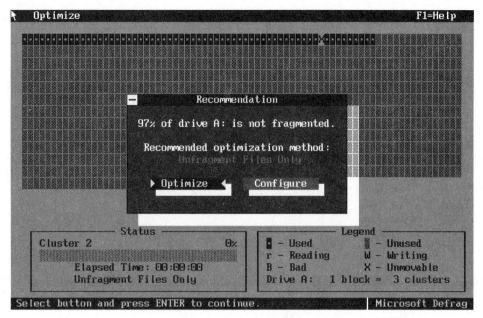

16. Select the drive A: option and click on the OK button or press [Enter].

A screen message appears, indicating that the command is "Reading disk information...." For West Student Data Disk #5, the screen will probably indicate that 97 percent of the disk is not fragmented. It suggests that you unfragment files only, as shown in Figure 8.4.

17. Click on the Optimize button or press [Enter].

18. Watch your monitor screen as the DEFRAG command moves files in order to store them in contiguous allocation units.

When done, DEFRAG displays the message "Finished condensing."

19. Click on the OK button or press [Enter].

20. When the dialog box appears, indicating that "Optimization of Drive A: Complete," click on the Exit DEFRAG button.

Protecting Your System from the Virus Invasion

Computer viruses are so named because their behavior mimics that of human viruses. A human virus attacks your system (body) and its results can range from a minor inconvenience to a potentially life-threatening illness. Likewise, computer viruses can cause anything from a minor inconvenience (such as displaying a harmless message on your screen) to a catastrophic reformatting of your hard drive, destroying all your data and the system files required to boot your computer.

Though computer viruses have been around for years, the public first became acutely aware of the problem just prior to March 6, 1992. The immediate threat at that time was the "Michelangelo virus." The virus was programmed to strike annually on

March 6 (the birthday of the famous artist who painted the Sistine Chapel and sculpted such works as the *Pietà* and *David*).

When activated, on March 6, the virus deletes files from the user's hard disk. Typically, once the virus is discovered, the damage is done. The Michelangelo virus is spread when an infected disk is used on a clean machine. Once the computer is infected, the virus is passed to other machines by sharing floppy disks.

What Is a Computer Virus?

A computer virus is a small block of code that contains instructions on how to reproduce itself, how to take control of your computer system, and how to cause your computer to do something you do not normally expect. The action performed by the virus may be displaying a humorous message on your computer screen, making a political statement in a text message, or damaging your system in some manner. The latter action is obviously the greatest concern to computer users.

Viruses tend to be classified by how they are transmitted. There are three broad categories of computer viruses:

- A *boot sector virus* replaces your disk's boot sector. Once your system is booted, the virus is in control and can infect any other disk that is connected to your system or inserted in one of its drives.

- A *file infector virus* is code added to an executable file (one that ends with the .COM, .EXE, or .SYS extension). Whenever the infected file is executed, the virus is activated and can be spread to other programs. This type of virus is often referred to as a *hacked program*, meaning that a *computer hacker* (a sometimes unprincipled computer enthusiast) tampered with the code of a legitimate program and added the virus to it.

- In the classic story of Helen of Troy, a Trojan horse was used to get within the city gates so that, after dark, the soldiers hidden within could do their "dirty work." A *Trojan horse virus* uses the same scenario. You willingly place the Trojan horse virus file on your system because you think it is something else—a utility program, a commercial application, or even an antivirus utility! The true nature of the program is disguised and you expect the program to perform a legitimate function.

The latter type of virus is often distributed to unsuspecting users on bootleg or pirated copies of commercial software that are illegally distributed. For instance, you may think you have received a "free" copy of a commercial word processing program from a "friend" or unreliable bulletin board system, when in fact you have received a Trojan horse virus. This type of virus can be extremely dangerous when you run it and find that it is deleting all files on your hard drive rather than creating new documents. Data destroyed by a Trojan horse virus is usually not recoverable.

Battling the Virus Invasion

There are several methods of battling the spread of computer viruses. Some of these methods include using the new DOS 6.0 commands, MSAV and VSAFE. Before exploring these new operating system utilities, let's first explore the other defenses that can help protect your computer system:

- Don't accept illegal, pirated, or bootleg software from friends, coworkers, or others. If the price you pay for a leading commercial application seems too good to be true—it is.

- If you download software from a bulletin board system (BBS), first scan it (using MSAV) before you use it. Further, only do business with those bulletin board systems that have a good reputation. If the system operator (SYSOP) appears to be careless about copyright infringement, fails to promptly remove commercial software placed on the BBS for free distribution, and does not keep a watchful eye out for obscene and prejudicial messages, the SYSOP is probably also careless about checking uploaded files for viruses. Many BBSs are run by responsible, hard-working operators who take great pride in running a professional BBS. Others have less concern about the quality and safety of the system they run. Always be cautious.

- Write-protect any executable files that should not change in size or are unlikely to be modified when running the program. A prime candidate is the COMMAND.COM file, which is often targeted by viruses because it appears on every bootable hard drive or disk.

- Write-protect your original application disks. Make a working copy, write-protect the working copy, and install from the backup rather than the original disk.

- Always inspect new files using MSAV before installing them on your system.

- If you can afford the system memory (RAM), constantly run a sentry program like VSAFE. It helps intercept viruses before they can attack your system.

Using the MSAV Command Program

The MSAV (Microsoft Anti-Virus) program scans your computer system for known viruses. Viruses are identified by their signature, that is, how they behave. One key indicator is a change in the size of executable files. The first time MSAV checks a directory for viruses, it creates a CHKLIST.MS file in the directory. The checksums of each program are stored in the file. A checksum is a value based on the program file size, the file's attributes, and its date and time stamp. Later, when MSAV is used to scan the directories again, the checksums of each program file are compared to the checksum value stored in CHKLIST.MS. When a difference occurs, it means you may have a virus infestation.

False MSAV Alarms

The MSAV command can return a false alarm when any of the following occur:

- The program file has been damaged by a non-virus-related problem.

- The presence of some memory-resident programs will cause the MSAV command to act as if a virus had attacked the system.

- Device driver conflicts can cause MSAV to think that a virus has attacked your system. Peripherals connected to your system (such as a CD-ROM drive, sound card, printer, monitor, or fax/modem) require device drivers, and sometimes these files reference the same computer port or the same interrupt, causing a conflict.

Executable Files Checked by MSAV

The Anti-Virus program checks files with the following extensions. These extensions are typically used on executable files that invoke or start application programs.

.386	.DLL	.OV*
.APP	.DRV	.PGM
.BIN	.EXE	.PIF
.CMD	.FON	.PRG
.DOM	.ICO	.SYS

Using the Microsoft Anti-Virus Program

The MSAV (Microsoft Anti-Virus program) operates in two modes. You can instruct it to search for viruses but not act upon them. This is called the Detect mode. Or you can instruct MSAV to find and remove the viruses it locates. This is the Detect and Clean mode.

From the command line, the MSAV program uses the following syntax:

```
MSAV [drive:] [/S][/C] [/R] [/A][/L] [/N] [/P] [/F] [/VIDEO]
```

The switches that are available for use with the MSAV program are listed in Table 8.2.

TABLE 8.2
MSAV command parameters

/S	Scans the specified drive but does not remove the virus.
/C	Scans the specified drive and removes the virus.
/R	Creates a report in the root directory that indicates the number of files checked, the number of viruses found (if any), and the number of viruses removed. You must specify this switch or no report is generated.
/A	Scans all drives except your floppy drives (A: and B:).
/L	When executed on a computer connected to a network, scans all local drives but not network drives or drives A: and B:.
/N	Displays the contents of the MSAV.TXT file, if it exists, and then scans the current drive or the drive you specify. When you use this switch, MSAV does not use the graphical interface. If it encounters a virus, an error code (86) is returned rather than an error message.
/P	Displays the MSAV command line interface rather than the graphical interface. In this unit, you will work exclusively with the graphical interface.
/F	This switch turns off the display of file names that have been scanned. This switch can only be used with the /N or /P switches.

TABLE 8.2 (Continued)	/video	Displays an additional list of switches that affect how the MSAV screen is displayed. Some of the more common of these options include:
	/25	This is the default setting of 25 lines per screen display.
	/28	Sets the screen display to 28 lines per inch. This switch should only be used with VGA display adapters.
	/BT	Enables the use of a graphics mouse in Windows.
	/BW	Runs MSAV, using a black-and-white color scheme.
	/LCD	Runs MSAV, using an LCD color scheme—as would be required when using a liquid crystal display on a notebook computer.
	/MONO	Runs MSAV, using a monochrome color scheme.
	/NGM	Runs MSAV, using the mouse character rather than the graphics character. "NGM" stands for "no graphics mouse."
	/PS2	Resets the mouse if the mouse cursor disappears or locks up.

If you want to run MSAV on only your hard drives (and skip your system's floppy disks), you would use this command form:

```
MSAV /A
```

If you only want to run MSAV on a new disk in drive A:, you would use this command form:

```
MSAV A:
```

The MSAV program can be run without specifying any switches or parameters. If you do so, it becomes a menu-driven program where you can select the actions you desire from the Main Menu screen shown in Figure 8.5.

FIGURE 8.5
THE MSAV Main Menu screen

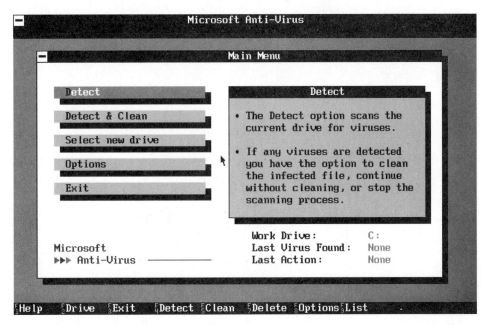

To see this interface, simply type the following command at the DOS prompt:

```
MSAV
```

In the remaining Guided Activities in this unit, you will use the MSAV user interface rather than the command line options.

The Second Virus Protection Feature

DOS 6.0 includes a second level of protection against computer viruses. That protection is offered by the VSAFE command, which invokes a memory-resident program that continuously monitors your computer system for activity that might represent the presence of a virus. The program consumes 22–44KB of working memory (RAM) and displays a warning message if it locates a virus.

NOTE *VSAFE should not be run when you are running Windows. Instead, use the MWAVTSR.EXE program. It enables VSAFE messages to be displayed within Windows. To use this program, you must load MWAVTSR from within Windows. You can do this by using the Program Manager's File Run command and selecting MWAVTSR.EXE or by adding the following command to your WIN.INI file:* LOAD=MWAVTSR.EXE. *"MWAVTSR" stands for "Microsoft Windows Anti-Virus Terminate-and-Stay-Resident" program.*

In this textbook, you will only use the MS-DOS versions of MSAV and VSAFE and not the Windows versions.

Using the VSAFE Command

The VSAFE program is started by executing the command at the DOS prompt. The command's syntax is indicated below:

```
VSAFE [/option[+ or -]...] [/NE] [/NX] [/Ax] or [/Cx] [/N] [/D] [/U]
```

The first parameter (/option) indicates how VSAFE will monitor your system for viruses. The options and default settings are indicated in Table 8.3. Keep in mind that these options are turned on by placing a plus sign (+) after the appropriate numeric code and turned off by following the appropriate numeric code with a minus sign (–).

By reviewing the default settings listed in Table 8.3, you will see that the default settings of the VSAFE command cause it to

- Warn you if a program tries to format your hard drive
- Check all executable program files for viruses
- Check all disks for boot sector viruses
- Warn you if a program tries to write to your hard disk's boot sector or partition table

  Using the default settings, VSAFE does *not*

- Warn of a program's attempt to stay in memory
- Prevent a program from writing to disk

TABLE 8.3 *Option codes for the VSAFE command*	1	Warns of a program or command issued that can completely erase your hard disk. The default setting is on.
	2	Warns of a program that attempts to stay resident in memory even after it is exited or closed. The default is off.
	3	Prevents programs from writing to your disk. The default is off.
	4	Checks executable files when opened by DOS. The default is on.
	5	Checks all disks for evidence of boot sector viruses. The default is on.
	6	Warns you of attempts to write to the boot sector or partition table of a hard disk. The option is on.
	7	Warns you of attempts to write to the boot sector of a floppy disk. The option is off.
	8	Warns you of attempts by a program to modify executable files. The default is off.

- Warn you if a program tries to write to a floppy disk's boot sector
- Warn you if a program tries to modify an executable program file

If you had to invoke this command (assuming there was no default setting), it would be entered at the command line as follows:

```
VSAFE /1+ /2- /3- /4+ /5+ /6+ /7- /8-
```

A few additional VSAFE command switches are listed in Table 8.4.

TABLE 8.4 *Additional VSAFE command switches*	/Ax	Establishes the quick key to display the VSAFE screen as the [Alt] key plus the key specified by the *x*; for example, /AV would establish the quick key as [Alt][V]. You would use either this switch or the /Cx switch, but not both.
	/Cx	Establishes the quick key to display the VSAFE screen as the [Ctrl] key plus the key specified by the *x*; for example, /CV would establish the quick key as [Ctrl][V]. You would use either this switch or the /Ax switch, but not both.
	/D	Disables the checksum feature.
	/N	Enables VSAFE to monitor for viruses on network drives.
	/NE	Does not allow the VSAFE program to be loaded into expanded memory.
	/NX	Does not allow the VSAFE program to be loaded into extended memory.
	/U	Removes the VSAFE program from memory.

As an example of how these switches can be combined, the following command form initially invokes (loads) the VSAFE command, enables it to check for programs that attempt to stay in memory after they are loaded, warns of any attempt to write to the boot sector of a floppy disk, and establishes the quick key to view the VSAFE screen as [Ctrl][V].

```
VSAFE /2+ /7+ /CV
```

If you have loaded VSAFE and want to remove it from memory, you would use the following command form:

```
VSAFE /U
```

Using MSAV and VSAFE to Protect Your System

In this Guided Activity, you will use both the MSAV and the VSAFE commands to check your West Student Data Disk for a virus infestation. Most likely, you will not find a virus—at least we hope you do not!

1. Insert West Student Data Disk #3 in drive A:.

2. At the DOS prompt, type MSAV and press [Enter].

NOTE *If you see the screen message "Bad command or file name," the DOS version of MSAV may not be installed on your workstation. Consult your instructor.*

Your screen will display the message "Reading disk information...."

3. When the Main Menu of the Microsoft Anti-Virus program appears, click on the Select new drive button.

4. When drive letters and symbols appear in the upper-left corner of the screen, click on the A: drive option.

    When done, the Work Drive: setting at the bottom-right corner of the dialog box will reflect the change to drive A:.

5. To have MSAV simply detect but not remove any viruses it finds, click on the Detect button.

    A screen message appears, indicating that MSAV is "Scanning memory for viruses."

    If MSAV finds a virus, you will see a dialog box displayed that gives you four options. They are:

Clean	Removes the virus from the disk.
Continue	Leaves the suspected virus and continues to search for any other potential viruses on the disk.
Stop	MSAV ceases looking for additional suspected viruses.
Delete	Removes the checksum files so that you can re-create them or eliminate them.

    When MSAV finishes scanning your disk without finding a virus, you will see a screen message similar to Figure 8.6.

6. Click on the OK button after you have read the screen or press [Enter].

7. When the Main Menu appears, click on the Exit button or press [F3].

FIGURE 8.6
*The Viruses
Detected and
Cleaned screen*

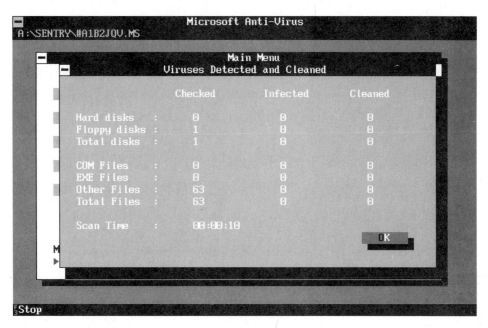

8. To finish closing the Microsoft Anti-Virus utility, click on the OK button or press Enter.

    In the following steps, you will load the VSAFE program and set it to warn of any program attempting to write to your disk. The following command form turns on the general write-protection feature (option 3 in Table 8.3).

9. Be sure that West Student Data Disk #3 is still in drive A:.

10. At the DOS prompt, type VSAFE /3+ and press Enter.

11. Type DIR A: and press Enter.

    The STRATS2.DOC file is toward the end of the list.

12. Type DEL A:STRATS2.DOC and press Enter.

    Your computer screen will display the message shown below:

    ```
    VSafe Warning
    Program is trying to write to Floppy disk
    Do you wish to continue?
    ```

    Deleting a file as well as saving one to disk is considered a write operation. Three buttons (Stop, Continue, Boot) appear on the screen. The Stop button will cease the delete operation. The Continue button causes the system to delete the file. The Boot button will reboot your system.

13. Type S to stop the delete operation.

    The VSAFE Warning screen may reappear a second time.

14. Type S again to stop the delete operation.

NOTE *If you cannot stop the operation and the error continues to appear, type B to boot the system.*

Your screen will display a write-protection error message.

15.   Type A to abort the deletion operation.

In the following steps, you will again issue the command to delete the STRATS2.DOC file—but this time you'll override the VSAFE warning and delete the file.

16.   Type DEL A:STRATS2.DOC and press ⏎Enter⏎.

17.   Type C to continue the delete operation.

NOTE *You may have to type C several times before the operating system will continue and delete the STRATS2.DOC file.*

18.   Type DIR A: and press ⏎Enter⏎.

The STRATS2.DOC file, formerly on the disk in drive A:, is now gone.

In the final step, you will unload the VSAFE program.

19.   Type VSAFE /U and press ⏎Enter⏎.

VSAFE is removed (unloaded) from memory when your screen records the occurrence of the message "VSafe removed from memory."

Using the DOS 6.0 On-Line Diagnosis Program

Beginning with DOS 6.0, Microsoft has added a new diagnostic program to the operating system. The MSD (Microsoft Diagnostic) program provides detailed technical information about your computer system. This can be very helpful if you are

- Wanting to know more about the components installed in your computer
- Solving a hardware or software problem, using a computer support hotline (technicians can often help solve your problem if they know more about your system)
- Solving potential causes of hardware or software problems or other conflicts you are encountering
- Determining if you have the appropriate hardware required for an application program you want to buy

The MSD program provides information on the following features of your computer system:

- Computer model and microprocessor
- Memory in your system unit
- Video adapter in use
- Version of DOS
- Type of mouse installed

- Other adapters in your system (network cards, video, and so on)

- Disk drives attached to the system

- Serial (COM) ports available

- Parallel (LPT) ports available

- Interrupts (IRQ) in use

- Terminate-and-stay-resident (TSR) programs in memory

- Device drivers (CD-ROM, printer, sound board, video board) in memory

Using the MSD Program

To start the MSD program, you simply enter the following command at the DOS prompt:

```
MSD
```

The MSD program has an easy-to-use interface, as demonstrated by the initial screen, as shown in Figure 8.7. Each button on the initial MSD screen provides access to the indicated category of technical data.

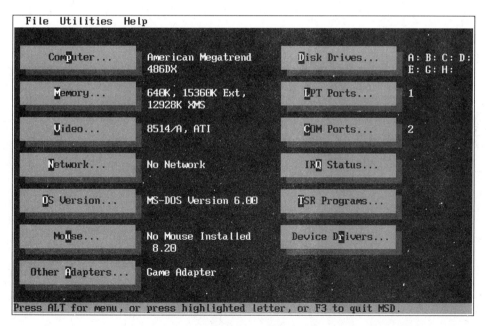

FIGURE 8.7
The initial MSD command screen

In addition to using the program's regular interface, you can use several switches to generate a report on your computer system. These options would be used when you do not want to use the menu interface and wish to create a report file with the information from the DOS prompt.

To generate a report, rather than use the menu interface, the syntax of the MSD command is

```
MSD [/I] [/F [drive:][path]filename] [/P [drive:][path]filename] [/S [drive:][path]filename]
```

The switches are listed in Table 8.5.

TABLE 8.5
MSD command switches

/F [drive:][path]filename	This switch prompts you for your name, company, address, country, phone number, and comments. Then it creates a complete MSD report. The report is saved, using the file name you specify.
/P [drive:][path]filename	This switch creates a complete MSD report without prompting you for any information. The report is saved, using the file name you specify. It does not include the identifying data that is included when you use the /F switch.
/S [drive:][path]filename	This switch creates a summary MSD report without prompting you for any information. The report is saved, using the file name you specify. It does not include the identifying data that is included when you use the /F switch.
/S	This switch creates a summary MSD report without prompting you for any information. The report is displayed on your monitor screen rather than saved to a disk file.

GUIDED ACTIVITY 8.3

Using the Microsoft Diagnostics Program

In this Guided Activity, you will issue the MSD command and gather information regarding the computer you are working on.

1. At the DOS prompt, type MSD and press [Enter].

   The MSD Menu screen will appear similar to Figure 8.7.

2. When the MSD Menu screen appears, click on the Computer button or type P (the highlighted letter).

   The screen should appear similar to Figure 8.8.

   Write down the following information from the Computer information screen:

   > BIOS Manufacturer:
   > Processor:
   > Bus Type:

3. Click on the OK button or press [Enter].

4. Click on the OS Version (operating system version) button or type O.

   Your screen should appear similar to Figure 8.9.

   NOTE *If you are using MS-DOS 6.2, the OS Version screen (shown in Figure 8.9) will reflect that version.*

FIGURE 8.8
The Computer information screen

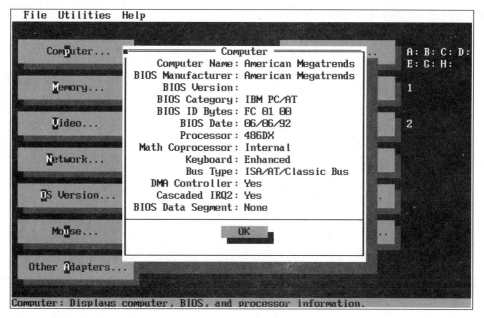

Write down the following information from the OS Version information screen:

Operating System:
Internal Revision:
DOS Located in:
Boot Drive:

5. When done, click on the OK button or press [Enter].

The MSD Menu screen includes additional buttons for Memory, Video, Network, Mouse, Other Adapters, Disk Drives, LPT Ports, COM Ports, IRQ Status, TSR Programs, and Device Drivers.

FIGURE 8.9
The OS Version screen

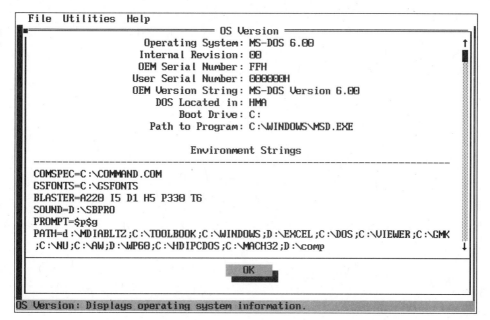

FIGURE 8.10
The TSR
Programs
information
screen

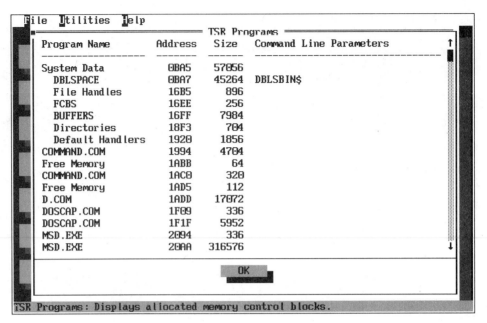

6. Look at the information provided, by selecting some of the other buttons. The final one you should select is the TSR Programs information. The TSR Programs screen should appear similar to Figure 8.10.

   Use the ⬇ key to review all listings. Somewhere on the list you should at least see the following entries:

   ```
   System Code
   COMMAND.COM
   MOUSE or MOUSE.COM
   MSD.EXE
   ```

   The last entry is the program code for the currently running program, MSD.

7. With the TSR Programs information screen visible, list any additional file names or program names that look familiar on the screen. List them below:

8. Click on the OK button or press [Enter].

9. Click on the File command on the menu bar and then select the Exit option, or press [F3], or press [Alt][F], [X] to quit.

10. At the DOS prompt, type VSAFE and press [Enter] to load the memory-resident program.

    VSAFE is a TSR program and it is now loaded.

11. At the DOS prompt, type MSD and press [Enter].

The MSD Menu screen will appear.

12. When the MSD Menu screen appears, click on the TSR Programs button or type T.

13. Look for any additional TSR programs listed on the screen. You should now see an additional entry for VSAFE.COM.

NOTE *You may need to scroll down the list to see VSAFE.COM.*

14. When done, click on the OK button or press [Enter].

15. Exit the MSD program.

16. Type VSAFE/U and press [Enter] to unload the VSAFE program from memory.

Summary

In this unit, you learned about disk fragmentation and how it can slow down disk access and thereby slow you down when using your computer. You discovered that the DEFRAG command can be used to optimize your disk. You also learned about computer viruses and how DOS 6.0 includes two new commands, MSAV and VSAFE, that assist in protecting your system from a virus attack. You also used the new Microsoft Diagnostics program to list technical details about your computer system.

Command Review

In this unit, you learned about several DOS commands. Most have optional switches. We have tried to cover both the common and the rarely used forms of each command. The following forms of this unit's commands are the most frequently used and should be reviewed carefully.

DEFRAG	Optimizes your hard drive or disk by eliminating disk fragmentation.
MSAV	Runs the Microsoft Anti-Virus program that will seek out potential viruses on your disk.
MSD	Runs the Microsoft Diagnostics program that provides technical information on your system, including the computer type, OS in use, and details on TSR programs, your mouse, LPT and COM ports, and more.
VSAFE	Loads a memory-resident virus protection utility that warns you of possible system activity caused by a computer virus.

Review Questions

1. What is disk fragmentation?

2. Why is disk fragmentation a problem?

3. What term is used to describe the process of eliminating disk fragmentation?

4. Name the DOS command that eliminates disk fragmentation.

5. What action occurs when you enter `DEFRAG B:` at the DOS prompt?

6. What action occurs when you enter `DEFRAG C: /SN /U` at the DOS prompt?

7. What happens if you run the DEFRAG command without using any switches or parameters?

8. Name three categories of computer viruses.

9. Name at least three methods of battling the spread of computer viruses.

10. What does the CHKLIST.MS file contain?

11. Name three types of files (based on file name extension) that are checked by MSAV for virus tampering.

12. What happens if you run the MSAV command without using any switches or parameters?

13. Name the command form to use if you want the MSAV command to check all drives except your floppy drives for viruses.

14. How is the VSAFE command different from MSAV?

15. What does the VSAFE /3+ command do?

16. How would you turn off the action created by the command in question 15?

17. Indicate the command form used to remove VSAFE from memory.

18. Which of the following are not technical data provided by the MSD program:

    Interrupts in use
    Installed version of DOS
    Version of WordPerfect installed on the system
    Viruses located on the computer's disk
    Computer model and processor in use

19. What does MSD stand for?

20. Which of the four commands covered in this unit were available in earlier versions of DOS (DEFRAG, MSAV, MSD, VSAFE)?

Exercises

Whenever instructed to format a disk, use your last name (first) and then your first name (such as BACON JON) as the volume label. If instructed to print data from the screen, be sure to write your full name, course number and section, course title, instructor's name, unit and exercise number, and today's date on the paper. Your instructor will indicate if the disk(s) created or printouts should be submitted for grading.

1. Use the appropriate DOS command to create a report (on disk) that lists technical details on your system. Be sure the report includes your name, company, address, country, phone number, and comments.

2. Use the steps in Guided Activity 8.1 to re-create a fragmented disk. Label it West Student Exercise Disk B. Use the appropriate DOS command to optimize West Student Exercise Disk B and to place the files in alphabetical order.

Key Terms

Boot sector virus	Disk compaction	Hacked program
Computer hacker	Disk fragmentation	Optimize
Computer virus	Disk optimization	Trojan horse virus
Disk access speed	File infector virus	

Documentation Research

Documentation Research questions are included at the end of most units to encourage you to explore and discover the additional features available with DOS 6.x. All Documentation Research questions within the text can be answered by using the on-line reference (accessed by using the HELP command). Review Guided Activity 2.8 if you are unsure how to use the HELP command.

1. How would you display a map of the upper memory area (UMA), the memory region from 640KB to 1,024KB?

2. How would you display the current communications parameters of all installed serial ports in your computer?

3. List the /video switches for the MSAV command that are not listed in the textbook.

4. Name the DEFRAG command exit code that indicates there was insufficient memory to defragment the disk.

5. Is disk information reported by the CHKDSK and DEFRAG commands different?

Text Editing Commands

Learning Objectives

At the completion of this unit, you should be able to

1. create a text file using the COPY CON: command,

2. create text files using the EDIT command,

3. select text and commands within the DOS Editor,

4. use the DOS Editor to copy, delete, move, and paste text from one location to another.

Important Commands

COPY CON:

EDIT

TYPE

Copying from the Console

Suppose you wish to create a small *text file* without loading your word processor. Can you do it from the DOS level? The answer is yes. There are three methods, two of which are covered in detail in this unit. Why would you want to create a text file? That issue will be addressed in Unit 11 when you discover the usefulness of batch files. For now, simply be concerned with how a text file can be created at the DOS level.

In an earlier unit, you learned to copy a file to the monitor (console) by using the reserved word CON: to represent the console. DOS also provides the capability of copying from the console (CON:) to a disk file. In essence, every keystroke appearing on the screen, after you invoke the COPY CON: command, will be redirected to a specified file. The syntax of the command is

```
COPY CON[:] [d:]filename.ext
```

If you wish the text to be stored in a file named SCREEN.TXT on drive A:, for example, the command would read

```
COPY CON: A:SCREEN.TXT
```

If your default drive is already A:, the command can be simplified to

```
COPY CON: SCREEN.TXT
```

The step-by-step process to create a file using the COPY CON: command would include:

- Type the command line and specify the file name.
- Press [Enter].
- Type each line of text to be stored in the file, and conclude each line by pressing the [Enter] key.
- After the last line, press [F6] or [Ctrl][Z] followed by the [Enter] key.

The last action generates the ^Z character, which is interpreted as the end-of-file (EOF) mark.

A few terms and conditions should be mentioned regarding the COPY CON: command:

- The colon on the end of CON: is optional.
- After pressing [Enter] at the end of each line of text in COPY CON:, you cannot go back to the previous line and edit it.
- Before pressing [Enter] at the end of each line, you can use the [Backspace] key or [←] arrow key to remove the character to the left of the cursor and can then retype it. The [Backspace] and [←] keys are the only editing keys available in COPY CON:.

The EOF mark looks like a ^Z on the screen, but is stored as the hexadecimal number 1A. The EOF mark is an important terminator to files created with COPY CON:, but not with many other types of files. Many software products use standard record sizes; that is, they store data in blocks of 128, 256, or 512 bytes. In this case, the EOF mark is unimportant, because the program knows that the end of the file is a multiple of the data block size. In other files, the EOF mark is important because it literally signals the end of the file. The software, or DOS, will continue reading data until the EOF mark is read.

GUIDED ACTIVITY 9.1

Creating a File Using the COPY Command

In this Guided Activity, you will create a file directly from your keyboard by using the COPY CON: command. You will use West Student Data Disk #6 throughout this unit.

NOTE *It is assumed that you will complete all Guided Activities in this unit one right after the other. Each one builds on the files created in the previous activity.*

1. Format a new disk.

2. Label it as West Student Data Disk #6.

3. Copy all files from the C:\WESTDATA.DS6 directory to the newly formatted disk and then change the default directory to the root directory.

4. When done creating West Student Data Disk #6, type DIR A: and press [Enter].

   The disk in drive A: should have 44 files on it.

5. Type CLS and press [Enter].

6. Type COPY CON: A:DIALECTS.TXT and press [Enter].

CHECKPOINT 9A What is the difference between the command in step 6 and entering COPY CON A:DIALECTS.TXT?

The DOS prompt will not reappear until you are done with the COPY CON: command. Instead, the cursor will drop down a line—ready for you to enter the text outlined in the next few steps.

7. Type the following text. Press [Enter] after each line.

   ```
   Linguistic geographers
   like to map the various dialects
   and their spread throughout
   a country--like the United States.
   ```

8. Press [Ctrl][Z].

TIP *You could press [F6] for this step rather than [Ctrl][Z].*

9. Press [Enter].

   The screen should appear similar to Figure 9.1 and include the message:

   ```
   1 file(s) copied
   ```

CHECKPOINT 9B What is the name of the file that was copied in this Guided Activity?

10. Type DIR A: and press [Enter].

    At the end of the directory listing you will see the DIALECTS.TXT file name.

FIGURE 9.1
*Screen text from
creating a text file
with COPY CON:*

```
C:\>COPY CON: A:DIALECTS.TXT
Linguistic geographers
like to map the various dialects
and their spread throughout
a country--like the United States.
^Z
        1 file(s) copied

C:\>
```

Limitations of COPY CON:

You may have noted that COPY CON: had some clear editing limitations when you were creating the text file. You could not return to the previous line to change it, nor could you insert a single missed character without deleting all characters to the right of it on the current line. After you press Ctrl Z, the limitations are even more drastic. Other than reentering the text for the entire file, you cannot edit a file with the COPY CON: command.

Recognizing these weaknesses, DOS provides another method of creating a text file—except this time there are commands to enable you to edit the file. The second method is the new EDIT command introduced with DOS 5.0.

NOTE *DOS actually provides a third method, which is the EDLIN command. EDLIN gives you access to a LINe EDitor that can be used to enter, copy, delete, insert, list, move, search, and replace lines of text in a text file (reverse the capital letters and you have the command name: EDLIN). The greatest advantage of the EDIT command over EDLIN is that it behaves more like a word processor, and less like a cryptic DOS utility. EDLIN uses very cryptic single-letter commands. EDLIN used to be distributed free with all versions of DOS. Beginning with DOS 6.0, you can still get EDLIN but it is not shipped with the standard DOS package or the MS-DOS upgrade kit. You must order the MS-DOS 6 Supplemental Disks (see the back inside cover of the* Microsoft MS-DOS 6 User's Guide) *to obtain EDLIN. Other command files available on the Supplemental Disks include ASSIGN.COM, BACKUP.EXE, COMP.EXE, CV.COM, EXE2BIN.EXE, GRAFTABL.COM, JOIN.EXE, MIRROR.COM, MSHERC.COM, PRINTFIX.COM, and DOSSHELL.EXE (beginning with DOS 6.2).*

The TYPE Command

Once you have created a file with COPY CON:, you may want to review and then modify it. The DOS TYPE command is used to display the contents of an *ASCII text file* to the monitor screen. ASCII text files are stored without formatting instructions, so the display you see will be unformatted. If the display from the TYPE command includes some strange hieroglyphics or graphic characters, then the file is not strictly a text file. The strange characters are referred to as *nonprinting characters* or *control characters*.

The syntax for the TYPE command is

```
TYPE [d:]filename.ext
```

If the file name has an extension, you must include it in the command line. For instance, the file NEWTEXT.TXT cannot be displayed to the screen using the command line

```
TYPE NEWTEXT
```

You must include the entire file name and extension:

```
TYPE NEWTEXT.TXT
```

If the file is not on the default drive, you would need to include the drive designation.

The control characters mentioned earlier refer to special characters incorporated into a word processing document file. These characters represent margin settings, boldface type, italics, tab settings, carriage returns, and line feeds, rather than printing characters (numbers and letters). If you forget the contents of a document file, a sneak peek is available by using the TYPE command at the DOS prompt. The TYPE command is not useful with program files, database files, and spreadsheet files. It is intended for use strictly with document files and text files (preferably unformatted).

GUIDED ACTIVITY 9.2

Using the TYPE Command

In this Guided Activity, you will display the contents of the DIALECTS.TXT file created in the last Guided Activity.

1. Type CLS and press Enter to clear your screen of data.

2. Type TYPE A:DIALECTS.TXT and press Enter.

    Figure 9.2 shows the screen results of using the TYPE command.

FIGURE 9.2
Results of using the TYPE command to view the DIALECTS.TXT file

```
C:\>TYPE A:DIALECTS.TXT
Linguistic geographers
like to map the various dialects
and their spread throughout
a country--like the United States.

C:\>
```

3. Type TYPE A:DIALECTS and press Enter.

    Your screen displays the message

    ```
    File not found - A:DIALECTS
    ```

    which confirms that the complete file name must be used with the TYPE command.

4. Type CLS and press Enter to clear the screen.

CHECKPOINT 9C Why is the CLS command used here?

Using the DOS Editor

Beginning with DOS 5.*x*, the operating system includes a new text file editor called the DOS Editor. It is invoked by typing EDIT at the DOS prompt or by selecting the EDITOR option from the Main group of the DOS Shell. The DOSSHELL command will be discussed in Unit 14. You can use either the point-and-click method (with a mouse) or the menu bar to select and execute DOS Editor commands.

Once loaded, the DOS Editor displays a screen similar to Figure 9.3.

FIGURE 9.3
The DOS Editor screen

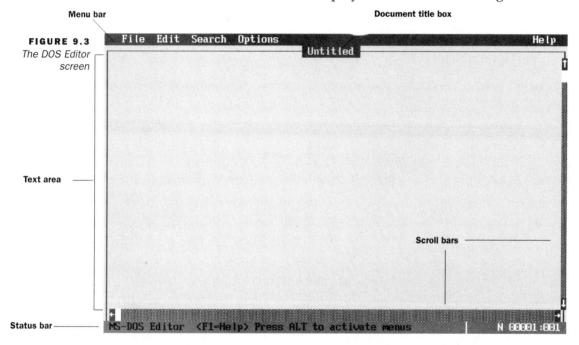

Notice that the screen is divided into five areas or parts:

MENU BAR Contains commands and options similar to the other DOS utility programs you have been exposed to (such as MSAV, MSD, and DEFRAG).

DOCUMENT TITLE BOX Displays the name of the currently loaded text file at the top center of the screen. If the text file is unnamed, the document title box displays the word "Untitled."

TEXT AREA Displays the text you enter and edit.

SCROLL BARS Used to move the cursor around the text area. The vertical scroll bar (right edge of the screen) scrolls toward the beginning or end of the document. The horizontal scroll bar (bottom of the screen) scrolls left or right to the beginning or end of a line of text. Scroll bars are only helpful when using a mouse. The ⬆, ⬇ ➡, ⬅, PgUp, PgDn, Home, and End keys can accomplish similar cursor movement actions; many people use a combination of these and the scroll bars.

STATUS BAR Located at the bottom of the screen, it displays information about commands or keys. It serves as an on-line help, indicating the purpose of specific keystrokes.

Additionally, you should know that the ⌈Tab⌉ key can be used to jump from one area of the DOS Editor screen to another.

Entering and Editing Text in the DOS Editor

Once the DOS Editor is loaded, you can begin typing text—just as you would in any word processor. The following are the basic editing keys used to delete text entered in the Editor. In the description of actions for each keystroke, you must understand the use of the following three terms:

DELETE Means the text is erased.

CUT Means the text is erased from its current location and stored in the Clipboard.

CLIPBOARD A temporary buffer area that stores the last block of text cut from a document.

Cut text may be pasted in a new location, whereas deleted text cannot be reinserted in a document.

Table 9.1 lists the edit keys used by the DOS Editor (invoked by typing EDIT at the DOS prompt). The most common editing keystrokes are explained in boldface type in Table 9.1.

TABLE 9.1 *EDIT command editing keystrokes*	
⌈Backspace⌉	**Deletes the character to the left of the cursor (⌈Ctrl⌉⌈H⌉ performs the same action).**
⌈Ctrl⌉⌈Ins⌉	**Cuts text and places it in the Clipboard.**
⌈Ctrl⌉⌈Q⌉, ⌈Y⌉	Cuts from the cursor location to the end of the line.
⌈Ctrl⌉⌈T⌉	Deletes the rest of a word
⌈Ctrl⌉⌈Y⌉	**Cuts the current line.**
⌈Del⌉	**Deletes the character above the cursor or selected (highlighted) text (⌈Ctrl⌉⌈G⌉ performs the same action).**
⌈End⌉⌈Enter⌉	Inserts a new blank line below the cursor location.
⌈Home⌉⌈Ctrl⌉⌈N⌉	Inserts a new blank line above the cursor location.
⌈Ins⌉	**Toggles between insert and typeover mode. In typeover mode, new text overwrites existing text at the cursor location.**
⌈Shift⌉⌈Del⌉	**Cuts the selected (highlighted) text.**
⌈Shift⌉⌈Ins⌉	**Inserts text from the Clipboard (text that was placed there using the ⌈Ctrl⌉⌈Ins⌉ keystroke).**
⌈Shift⌉⌈Tab⌉	Deletes leading spaces from selected lines.

If you need to move around a text file, the keys listed in Table 9.2 can be useful. The most common cursor movement keys used with the EDIT command are listed in boldface in Table 9.2.

TABLE 9.2
*EDIT
command
cursor
movement
keys*

Key	Description
Ctrl End	**Moves the cursor to the end of the document.**
Ctrl Home	**Moves the cursor to the beginning of the document.**
Ctrl Q, S	Moves the cursor to the beginning of the current line.
Ctrl Q, E	Moves the cursor to the top of the current window.
Ctrl Q, X	Moves the cursor to the bottom of the current window.
Ctrl Enter	Moves cursor to beginning of the next line.
Ctrl ←	Moves the cursor left one word.
Ctrl →	Moves the cursor right one word.
↓	**Moves the cursor down one line.**
End	**Moves the cursor to the end of the current line.**
F6	Moves to the next window.
Home	**Moves the cursor to the beginning of the current line (to the first indentation level).**
←	**Moves the cursor left one character.**
PgDn	**Moves the cursor down one page (screen).**
PgUp	**Moves the cursor up one page (screen).**
→	**Moves the cursor right one character.**
↑	**Moves the cursor up one line.**

Navigating with a Mouse and with Keystrokes in the DOS Editor

You will find it far easier to use a mouse with the DOS Editor, but if a mouse is not available, keystrokes can be used to accomplish the same tasks. In the Guided Activities that follow, you must understand the following guidelines:

- To select a menu item with a mouse, simply move the mouse pointer (a rectangle of color) to the appropriate command on the menu bar and click once. When the drop-down menu appears, click on the option you desire.

- To select a menu item using the keyboard, press the Alt key followed by typing the highlighted letter in the command name. To display options under the command names (File, Edit, and so on), simply press the ↓ key and the drop-down menu will unfold. To select one of the options, type the highlighted letter.

- To move from one field or box on the screen to another with the mouse, move the mouse pointer to the appropriate box or field and click once.

- To move from one field or box on the screen to another using the keyboard, press [Tab]. The [Tab] key cycles you through each box or field on the screen. For instance, on the File Open command dialog box, you may want to move the cursor from the File Name field to the Files box to the Dirs/Drives box and cycle through the three buttons at the bottom of the screen (OK, Cancel, and Help). If you accidentally go past the box or field you want, simply press [Shift][Tab] or continue pressing [Tab] until you recycle to the desired area of the screen.

- A single mouse click selects an item, while a double-click selects and executes it.

GUIDED ACTIVITY 9.3

Loading the EDIT Command

In this Guided Activity, you load the DOS Editor from the DOS prompt.

1. At the DOS prompt, type EDIT and press [Enter].

    Now your screen should appear similar to Figure 9.4.

FIGURE 9.4
The opening screen for the EDIT command

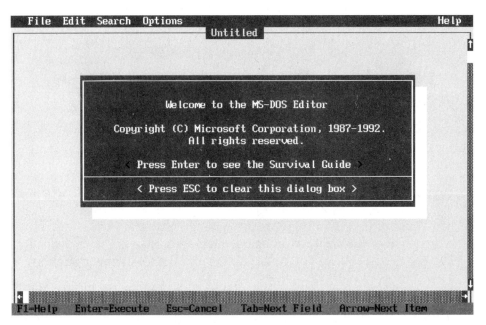

At this point you can press [Esc] to clear the dialog box or press [Enter] to see the Survival Guide (the EDIT command Help feature).

2. Press [Esc] to clear the dialog box.

3. To exit the EDIT command, select the File Exit command.

Opening an Existing File in the DOS Editor

To experiment with an existing file or create a new one, you must be able to open an existing file in the DOS Editor. The process includes these steps:

- Load the DOS Editor by typing EDIT at the DOS prompt and pressing Enter.

- Press Esc to bypass the Survival Guide (which is the Help feature for the EDIT command).

- Select the File Open command (see the last section if you are not sure how to select a command).

- Select the correct drive and directory where the file is stored.

- Select the specific file by file name.

By default, the File Open dialog box only displays files ending with the .TXT extension in the Files box on the screen. You can display all file names in the selected directory by changing the File Name text box to read *.* rather than *.TXT.

GUIDED ACTIVITY 9.4

Using the Cursor Movement Keys

In this Guided Activity, you experiment with the cursor movement keys listed in Tables 9.1 and 9.2. You use the STRATS2.TXT file from West Student Data Disk #6 in this Guided Activity.

1. Insert West Student Data Disk #6 in drive A:.

2. Load the DOS Editor.

    Your screen should appear similar to Figure 9.4.

3. Press Esc to clear the initial dialog box.

4. Select the File Open command from the menu bar.

    Your screen will appear similar to Figure 9.5.

5. When the Open dialog box appears, select the Dirs/Drives box (right side of the screen). You can do this by pressing the Tab key once or by moving the mouse pointer to that area of the screen and clicking once.

6. Use ↓ or PgDn or the scroll bar to move down the list of files until the drive A: designation appears in the box.

NOTE *Files in the current drive and directory are always listed alphabetically first in the Dirs/ Drives box, followed by drive designations for all drives attached to your system. The drive designators are listed in alphabetical order as shown below. Remember, they will appear after the list of file names.*

   [-A-]
   [-B-]

FIGURE 9.5

The Files listing screen after invoking the File Open command

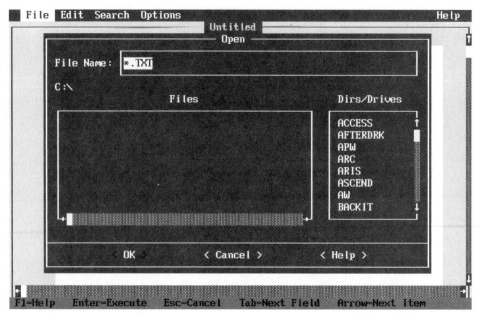

[-C-]
[-D-]
If you do not have a drive B: or a second hard drive (D:), your list will only include the following:
[-A-]
[-C-]

7. Highlight the [-A-] drive designation.

    Your screen should appear similar to Figure 9.6.

8. Click on the OK button, or press Enter.

    The screen now displays alphabetically the files with the default .TXT extension in the root directory of drive A: as shown in Figure 9.7.

    To load a specific file (in this case STRATS2.TXT), complete the following steps:

9. Double-click on the STRATS2.TXT file name, or if using the *keyboard* press Tab to switch to the File List area, use the arrow keys to highlight the STRATS2.TXT file name, and then press Enter.

    Your screen displays the STRATS2.TXT file as shown in Figure 9.8.

    Complete the following steps and observe how the cursor behaves after each step.

10. Press the PgDn key to move down one full screen of text.

11. Press the PgDn key to move down another full screen of text.

12. Press Ctrl Home to move to the beginning of the document.

13. Press Ctrl End to move to the end of the document.

FIGURE 9.6
*Drive A:
selected in the
Dirs/Drives box*

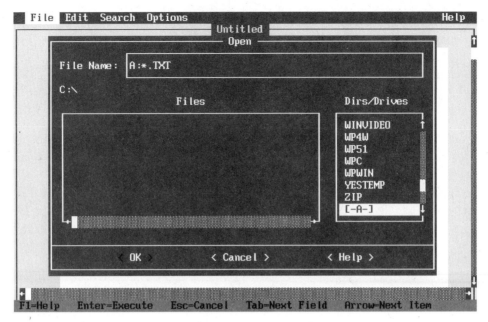

14. Press [PgUp] to move up one full screen of text.

15. Press [Ctrl][→] 5 times to move the cursor to the i in information.

16. Press [End] to move to the end of the current line.

17. Press [Home] to move to the beginning of the current line.

18. Press [Ctrl][←] to move to the beginning of the previous word.

19. Select the File Exit command to exit to the DOS prompt.

FIGURE 9.7
Files on drive A:

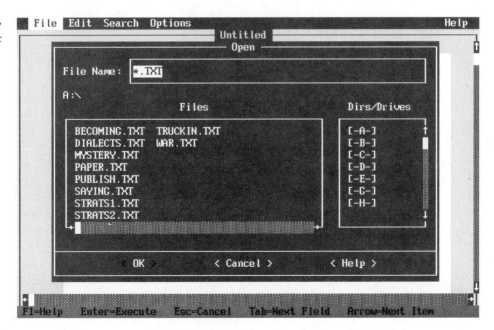

FIGURE 9.8
*Text of the
STRATS2.TXT file*

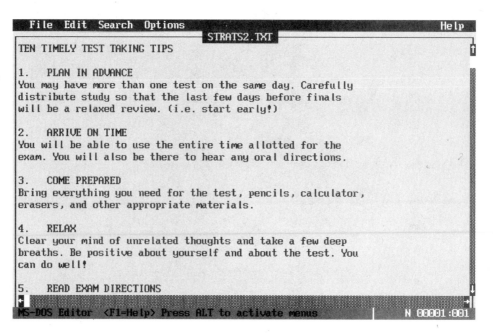

```
 File  Edit  Search  Options                              Help
                          ┌─ STRATS2.TXT ─┐
TEN TIMELY TEST TAKING TIPS                                        ↑

1.    PLAN IN ADVANCE
You may have more than one test on the same day. Carefully
distribute study so that the last few days before finals
will be a relaxed review. (i.e. start early!)

2.    ARRIVE ON TIME
You will be able to use the entire time allotted for the
exam. You will also be there to hear any oral directions.

3.    COME PREPARED
Bring everything you need for the test, pencils, calculator,
erasers, and other appropriate materials.

4.    RELAX
Clear your mind of unrelated thoughts and take a few deep
breaths. Be positive about yourself and about the test. You
can do well!

5.    READ EXAM DIRECTIONS                                         ↓
MS-DOS Editor  <F1=Help> Press ALT to activate menus    N 00001:001
```

Saving a Text File in the DOS Editor

To save a text file to disk (either a new file or a modified file), you would invoke the File Save command. Using the keyboard, you would

- Press ⌨Alt to select the menu bar.

- Type F to select the File command.

- Type S to select the Save option.

- Type the file name (and path if necessary) in the File Name text box on the Save dialog box screen and press ⏎Enter.

To save a file using a mouse:

- Click on the File command (on the menu bar).

- When the menu drops down, click on the Save option.

- Type the file name (and path if necessary) and press ⏎Enter or click on the OK button.

If the current file has already been saved once, you will not have to enter the file name the second (and every subsequent) time that you save it.

Once the file has been named, you can save it to another drive or save it using another file name, using the File Save As command.

GUIDED ACTIVITY 9.5

Creating and Saving a Text File with the DOS Editor

In this Guided Activity, you create a text file, using the DOS Editor. Next you save it, using the File Save command. After adding another paragraph, you save the text file again, using the File Save As command.

1. Insert West Student Data Disk #6 in drive A:.

2. Load the DOS Editor and clear the dialog box.

3. Type the following text. Press Enter after each line.

   "Symphony" is derived from the Greek and literally means "with sound." In its present form it is a composition for full orchestra, generally with four movements, but never less than three, first, an Allegro; second, an Andante or Adagio; third, a Scherzo, or Minuet and Trio; and fourth, an Allegro, finale. This is the conventional form as fixed by Haydn, though variations of the order frequently occur.

4. To save the text file, select the File Save command from the menu bar.

5. Type A:SYMPHONY.TXT and press Enter.

   Notice that the text file name appears in the File Name box at the top center of the EDIT command screen.

6. Press Ctrl End to move to the end of the text file.

7. If not already done, press Enter to add a blank line to the end of the document (to separate the existing paragraph from the next one you'll enter).

8. Type the following text. Press Enter after each line.

   In 1759, Count Morzin, a Bohemian nobleman, who passed his winters in Vienna and his summers at his country seat in Lukavec (where he kept his orchestra), appointed Joseph Haydn as his musical director and chamber composer. Haydn was 27 at the time. It was in Count Morzin's service that Haydn wrote his first symphony, in D major, a small work in three movements, for two violins, viola, bass, two oboes, and two horns.

9. Select the File Save As command from the menu bar.

CHECKPOINT 9D Why would you use the File Save As rather than the File Save command in the last step?

10. Type HAYDN1.TXT and press Enter.

Selecting and Moving Text

Before you can move text using the DOS Editor, you must understand how to select or highlight text. The keystrokes listed in Table 9.3 enable you to select text from the *keyboard*.

TABLE 9.3 *Text selection keys*		
	Shift ←	Selects the next character to the left of the cursor.
	Shift →	Selects the next character to the right of the cursor.
	Shift Ctrl ←	Selects the next word to the left of the cursor.
	Shift Ctrl →	Selects the next word to the right of the cursor.
	Shift ↓	If the cursor is at the beginning of a line, selects the current line of text.
	Shift ↑	If the cursor is at the beginning of a line, selects the line above the current cursor location.
	Shift PgDn	Selects from the cursor location to the bottom of the screen.
	Shift PgUp	Selects from the cursor location to the top of the screen.
	Shift Ctrl Home	Selects from the current cursor location to the beginning of the document.
	Shift Ctrl End	Selects from the current cursor location to the end of the document.

If you are using a *mouse*, you can select text as follows:

- Move the mouse pointer to the beginning of the desired block of text and press the left mouse button.

- Hold down the left mouse button while you drag the mouse pointer to the end of the desired block before releasing the mouse button.

You can also quickly select a single word by double-clicking on any character within the word.

Moving Text in the DOS Editor

Once you select the text, you can move it to a new location using the following method:

- Select the text to be moved.

- Select the Edit Cut command or press Shift Del.

- Move the cursor to the desired location.

- Select the Edit Paste command or press Shift Ins.

Keep in mind that only one block of text at a time may be stored in the Clipboard. When you delete a block of text to the Clipboard—whether a word or a page—any text stored in that special buffer is overwritten.

GUIDED ACTIVITY 9.6

Moving Text in the DOS Editor

In this Guided Activity, you move a block of text by first deleting the text to the Clipboard and then inserting the text from the Clipboard back into the document at the cursor location. The HAYDN1.TXT file should still be loaded from the last activity.

1. Move the cursor under the letter I in the phrase In 1759.

2. To select the remainder of the document, press Shift Ctrl End.

   Your screen should appear similar to Figure 9.9.

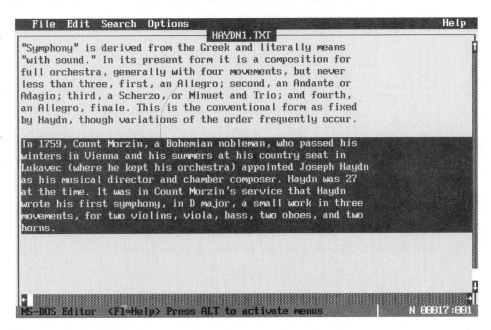

FIGURE 9.9
Selected text

3. Press Shift Del to delete the selected text into the Clipboard.

4. Press Ctrl Home to move to the beginning of the document.

5. Press Shift Ins to insert text from the Clipboard at the current cursor location.

6. Move the cursor to the end of the first paragraph and press Enter to add a blank line between paragraphs.

7. Select the File Save As command.

8. Type HAYDN2.TXT and press Enter.

Copying and Pasting Text in the DOS Editor

Copying text (as opposed to moving it) leaves the original text in its original location. Both the copy and move operations in the DOS Editor use the Clipboard (a buffer or temporary storage area). Copying text requires these steps:

- Select the text to duplicate.
- Select the Edit Copy command or press Ctrl Ins.
- Move the cursor to the desired location for the text.
- Select the Edit Paste command or press Shift Ins.

Remember that only one block of text at a time may be stored in the Clipboard. When you copy a block of text to the Clipboard, any text stored in that special buffer is overwritten.

NOTE *You can copy from one file to another by selecting the desired text in the first file, using Edit Copy, loading the target file, moving the cursor to the desired location, and executing the Edit Paste command.*

GUIDED ACTIVITY 9.7

Copying and Pasting Text in the DOS Editor

In this Guided Activity, you copy text from a text file to the Clipboard and then paste the same text into the current document at the cursor location.

1. Move the cursor under the double quotation mark (just prior to the word Symphony) at the beginning of the second paragraph.
2. Press Shift ↓ 7 times to select the second paragraph.
3. Select the Edit Copy command from the menu bar.
4. Press Ctrl End to move to the end of the document.
5. Select the Edit Paste command from the menu bar.
6. Continue on to the next Guided Activity without saving the file or exiting the DOS Editor.

Deleting Blocks of Text

Though you can delete a character at a time (using the Backspace and Del keys), you will find many occasions where it is faster and more efficient to delete a word, line, or block of text with a couple of keystrokes rather than one keystroke per character. To delete blocks of text (a word, a line, a paragraph, and so on), you must first select it and then press Del.

The selection keys listed in Table 9.3 can be very helpful in selecting large and small blocks of text for deletion. Review those keystrokes now.

GUIDED ACTIVITY 9.8

Deleting a Block of Text

In this Guided Activity, you select and then delete a block of text.

1. Move the cursor under the double quotation mark (just prior to the word Symphony) at the beginning of the third paragraph.

2. Press 7 times to select the second paragraph.

3. Press the ⌨Del key once.

4. Continue on to the next Guided Activity without saving the file or exiting the DOS Editor.

GUIDED ACTIVITY 9.9

Exiting Without Saving Changes

In this Guided Activity, you will exit the DOS Editor but not save the changes made during the last two Guided Activities.

1. Select the File Exit command from the menu bar.

2. When prompted "Loaded file is not saved. Save it now?" (as shown in Figure 9.10), type N to not save the changes.

FIGURE 9.10
Warning message

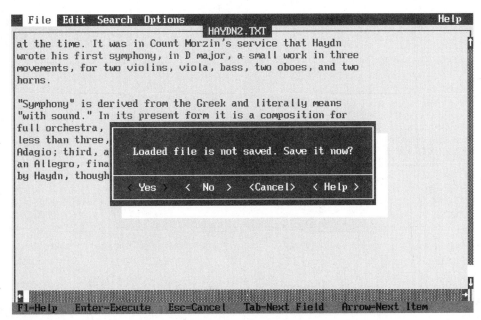

GUIDED ACTIVITY 9.10

Creating a Text File and Indicating the File Name from the DOS Prompt

In this Guided Activity, you will create a new file on the disk in drive A:. After entering some text, you will edit the file and save it.

1. Insert West Student Data Disk #6 in drive A:.

2. Type EDIT A:SPEECH.TXT and press [Enter].

✓ CHECKPOINT 9E Will the file created in step 2 have a file name extension?

The screen will show the EDIT screen but the A:SPEECH.TXT file name is already on the title bar.

3. Type the following text. Press [Enter] after each line of text.

    ```
    The major dialects include:
         Northern speech,
         Midland,
         MishMouth,
         Highland South, and
         Coastal Southern.
    ```

4. Save the file and exit the DOS Editor.

    You should now be back at the DOS prompt.

    The following steps will prove that the file was saved:

5. Type CLS and press [Enter].

6. Type TYPE A:SPEECH.TXT and press [Enter].

    The screen will display the text you just entered as shown in Figure 9.11.

FIGURE 9.11
The
A:SPEECH.TXT
text file

```
C:\>TYPE A:SPEECH.TXT
The major dialects include:
Northern speech,
Midland,
MishMouth,
Highland South, and
Coastal Southern.


C:\>
```

7. Type CLS and press [Enter].

8. Type EDIT A:SPEECH.TXT and press [Enter] to reopen the document.

9. Move the mouse pointer to the fourth line of the text and press [Ctrl][Y] to delete it.

10. Move the insertion point (cursor) to the end of the document by pressing [Ctrl][End], then type the following text. Press [Enter] after each line of text, including the last line.

```
Other minor dialects can be
identified including those
found in the NYC area.
```

11. Press [Enter] to enter a blank line.

12. Type the following text. Press [Enter] after each line of text.

```
Numerous Non-English
languages are also mapped
by geographic linguists.
```

13. Save the modified file as SPEECH2.TXT.

Your screen should now appear similar to Figure 9.12.

FIGURE 9.12
Listing of the modified A:SPEECH2.TXT file

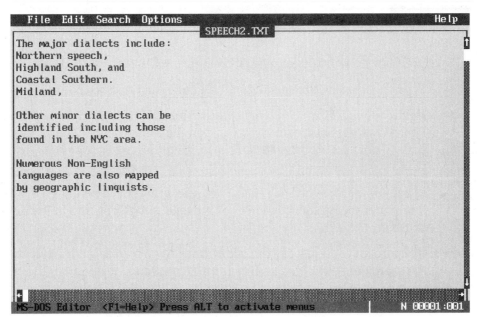

14. Exit from the DOS Editor and return to the DOS prompt.

Search Operations in the DOS Editor

The Search command can be used to find occurrences of a specific *text string* or word. For instance, if you think you may have misspelled a word, you can do a search for the *incorrect* spelling.

The process includes the following steps:

- Select the Search command from the menu bar.

- Select the Find option on the Search menu.

FIGURE 9.13
The Find dialog box

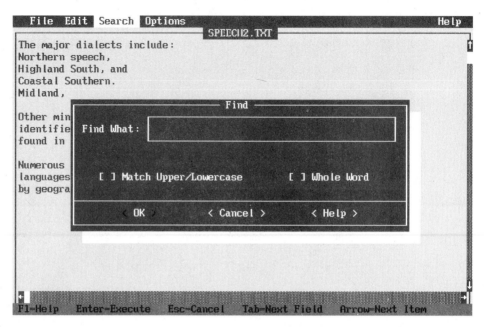

Your screen will appear similar to Figure 9.13.

- Type the text you are seeking in the Find What: text box.

- If you want to only search for text that matches the case of what is entered in the Find What: text box, you must click on the Match Upper/Lowercase check box. If you do not care about matching case, leave the check box empty (deselected).

- Click on the Whole Word check box if you only want to find the designated text as a stand-alone word. If you do not select this check box, the DOS Editor will look for embedded occurrences of the text string specified in the Find What: text box.

- When ready, you have two basic options—you can select the OK button to begin the search or select the Cancel button if you have decided not to conduct the search.

NOTE *Keyboard users must use* Tab *to move the cursor to either the Match Upper/Lowercase or the Whole Word check box, and then press* Spacebar *to select or deselect the option.*

You can repeat a search operation using any one of the following methods:

- Press F3.

- Press Ctrl L.

- Select the Search Repeat Last Find command from the menu bar.

Embedded Occurrences of the Text String

If the text string entered in the Find What: text box is the word in, EDIT looks for the first occurrence—whether it is the word in itself or the letters in embedded in a word, such as the words in the following list:

```
sing
tin
jumping
tapping
lines
```

If you wish to find only the word in (presumably in the middle of a sentence), you must include the space before and after the word in the Find What: text box—or select the Whole Word check box on the Find dialog box. When the check box is selected, it appears as shown in Figure 9.14—here with a text string of the.

FIGURE 9.14
The Whole Word check box selected on the Find dialog box

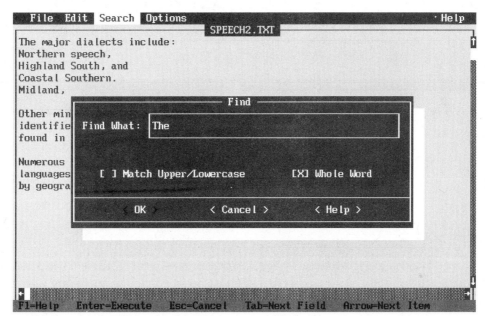

Using the Search and Replace Operation in the DOS Editor

In addition to the Search Find command, EDIT also includes a Search Change command. It seeks the text you specify and replaces it with new text that you also specify.

The process includes the following steps:

- Select the Search command from the menu bar.

- Select the Change option on the Search menu.

  Your screen will appear similar to Figure 9.15.

- Type the text you are seeking in the Find What: text box.

- Type the replacement text in the Change To: text box.

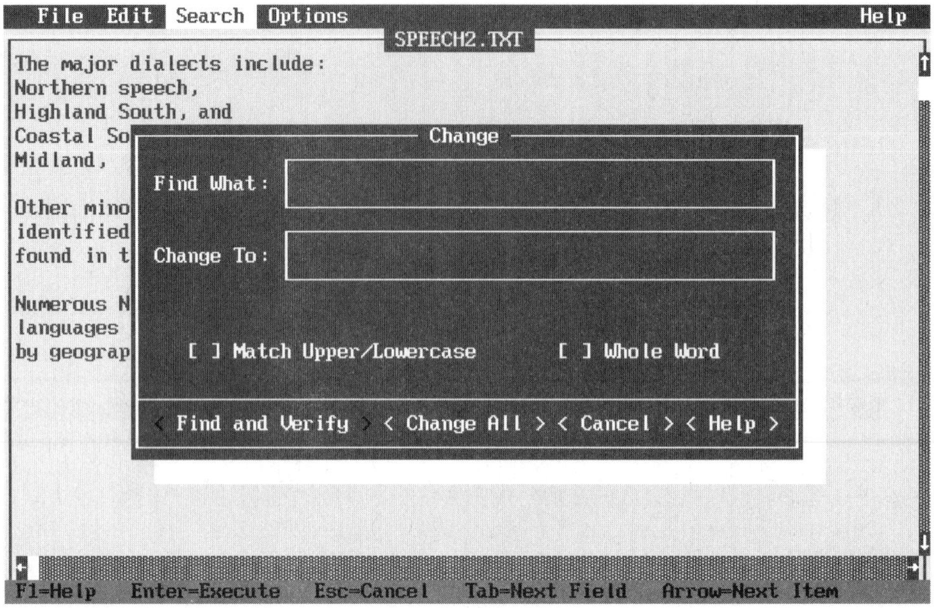

FIGURE 9.15
*The Change
dialog box*

```
  File  Edit  Search  Options                                    Help
                          SPEECH2.TXT
The major dialects include:
Northern speech,
Highland South, and
Coastal So┌───────────────────── Change ──────────────────────┐
Midland, │                                                      │
         │   Find What: ┌─────────────────────────────────┐    │
Other mino│             └─────────────────────────────────┘    │
identified│                                                     │
found in t│   Change To: ┌─────────────────────────────────┐    │
          │             └─────────────────────────────────┘    │
Numerous N│                                                     │
languages │                                                     │
by geograp│   [ ] Match Upper/Lowercase        [ ] Whole Word   │
          │                                                     │
          ├─────────────────────────────────────────────────────┤
          │ < Find and Verify > < Change All > < Cancel > < Help > │
          └───────────────────────────────────────────────────────┘


F1=Help    Enter=Execute    Esc=Cancel    Tab=Next Field    Arrow=Next Item
```

- If you want to only locate text that matches the case of what is entered in the Find What: text box, you must click on the Match Upper/Lowercase check box. If you do not care about matching case, leave the check box empty (deselected).

- Select the Whole Word check box if you only want to find the designated text as a stand-alone word. If you do *not* select this check box, the DOS Editor will look for embedded occurrences of the text string specified in the Find What: text box.

- When ready, you have three basic options— you can select the Find and Verify button to begin the search (which locates each occurrence and asks you to verify that you want it changed), you can select the Change All button (which automatically changes all occurrences of the first text string with the Change To: text box text), or you can select the Cancel button (if you have decided not to conduct the search and replace operation).

GUIDED ACTIVITY 9.11

Modifying an Existing Text File with EDIT

In this Guided Activity, you will again edit the SPEECH2.TXT file on West Student Data Disk #6 in drive A:. First you will make some minor changes and then you will use the Search Find and Search Change commands to modify the text file.

1. Type EDIT A:SPEECH2.TXT and press [Enter].

2. Change the first line to read: The major US dialects include:.

3. Press [Ctrl][Home] to move to the beginning of the text file.

4. Select the Search Find command from the menu bar.

5. In the Find What: text box, type `South`.

6. Select the OK button.

7. Press `F3` to repeat the last search operation.

8. Select the Search Change command from the menu bar.

9. Type `US` in the Find What: text box.

10. Type `United States` in the Change To: text box.

11. Select the Whole Word check box.

TIP *If using the keyboard, you can place an X in a check box by pressing the* `Spacebar`.

12. Select the Find and Verify button.

13. Select the Change button to make the replacement.

14. When the "Change Complete" message appears, click on the OK button or press `Enter`.

15. Select the Search Change command from the menu bar.

16. Type `NYC` in the Find What: text box.

17. Type `New York City` in the Change To: text box.

18. Deselect the Whole Word check box.

19. Select the Change All button.

20. When the "Change Complete" message appears, click on the OK button or press `Enter`.

21. Select the File Save As command and save the document as SPEECH3.TXT.

22. Do not exit the DOS Editor.

Printing Text Files with the DOS Editor

You can also print text files using the DOS Editor. The Print option is located under the File command on the menu bar.

The File Print command has two options:

- Selected Text Only

- Complete Document

Printing the complete (entire) document is self-explanatory. To print selected text, you must select (highlight) the desired text before you select the File Print command—which then defaults to the Selected Text option. If you do not select text prior to executing the File Print command, it defaults to printing the complete document.

GUIDED ACTIVITY 9.12

Printing a Text File Using the DOS Editor

In this Guided Activity, you will print the SPEECH3.TXT document, which should still be open from the last Guided Activity.

1. With the DOS Editor loaded and the SPEECH3.TXT text file open, select the File command.

2. Select the Print option.

3. Be sure your printer is turned on, on-line, and loaded with paper.

4. When the Print dialog box appears, as shown in Figure 9.16, select the OK button.

FIGURE 9.16
The Print dialog
box

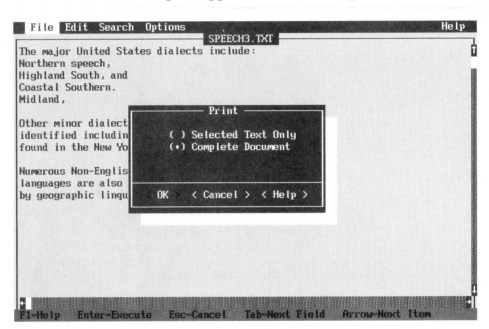

5. Because your text file has no form feed character at the end, you will need to put the printer off-line (press the on-line button), press the form feed button to advance the paper, and then put the printer back on-line (press the on-line button again).

6. Close the SPEECH3.TXT text file and exit from the DOS Editor.

Summary

In this unit, you learned how to create a text file using either the COPY CON: command or the EDIT command. You also learned how to navigate around the DOS Editor screen, how to select text and commands, and how to use the DOS Editor (EDIT command) to copy, delete, move, and paste text from one location to another.

Command Review

In this unit, you learned several DOS commands. Most have optional parameters or switches. We have tried to cover both the common and the rarely used forms of each command. The following forms of this unit's commands are the most frequently used and should be reviewed carefully.

COPY CON: A:NEWFILE	Creates a new text file named NEWFILE on drive A:.
EDIT	Loads or opens the DOS Editor, which enables you to create or edit text files.
EDIT A:TESTFILE.TXT	Loads or opens a text file in the DOS Editor called TESTFILE.TXT on drive A:.

Review Questions

1. Name the command that starts the DOS Editor.

2. What advantages does EDIT have over COPY CON:?

3. What function does the TYPE command perform?

4. How would you load the DOS Editor from the DOS prompt?

5. Name the part of the DOS Editor screen that lists commands and options.

6. What are the bars called (on the DOS Editor screen) that enable you to move the cursor around the text area?

7. In the DOS Editor, which key deletes the character above the cursor?

8. In the DOS Editor, which key deletes the character to the left of the cursor?

9. In the DOS Editor, which keystroke moves the cursor to the end of the document?

10. In the DOS Editor, which key moves the cursor to the beginning of the document?

11. In the DOS Editor, which command saves a document?

12. In the DOS Editor, why would you use the File Save As command?

13. In the DOS Editor, which keystrokes would you use to select all text from the current cursor location to the end of the document?

14. Which two menu bar DOS Editor commands are used to move text?

15. What is the difference between copying and moving text?

Exercises

Whenever instructed to format a disk, use your last name (first) and then your first name (such as BACON JON) as the volume label. If instructed to print data from the screen, be sure to write your full name, course number and section, course title, instructor's name, unit and exercise number, and today's date on the paper. Your instructor will indicate if the disk(s) created or printouts should be submitted for grading.

1. Use EDIT to create a file named THISTERM.TXT. In the file, on separate lines, include your name, address, and each course in which you are currently enrolled.

2. Use EDIT to create a text file named ANSWERS.TXT. In the file answer the Review Questions assigned by your instructor. Be sure to number each answer to correspond with the appropriate Review Question. The last four lines in the text file should be your name, the course title and number, instructor's name, and meeting times of the course.

3. Use EDIT to create a text file named POETRY.TXT. The file should consist of the text of any poem you choose. The last four lines in the text file should be your name, the course title, instructor's name, and meeting times of the course.

4. Use EDIT to create a text file that includes the full names of at least half of the students in the class. Names must be correctly spelled. Each name should be on a separate line in the file. Save the file, using the name CLASSMAT.ES.

5. Use the TYPE command to display the contents of CLASSMAT.ES to the screen. Make a screen dump of the file on the screen and hand in the results.

6. Format a disk and then use the DOS EDIT command to create the following text file. The file should be named NET_SINS.TXT. Each line of text should flow as shown below.

```
In the March 1991 issue of PC WORLD, a column titled "The
Ten Deadly Network Sins" detailed the most common problems
and misconceptions related to setting up a network. In
summary, the ten deadly sins include the following:

Taking a home handy-man approach to setting up a network.
Networks are complicated and require the services of
trained professionals.

Using the "bargain basement" approach. Low cost hardware and
software may cost you more in the long run.

Using an untested reseller or system integrator. Look for
credentials and experience.

Letting your network "just happen" due to poor planning and
design.
```

Buying into unrealistic expectations of how soon the network will be up and running. Implementation is never quick and easy.

Assuming that everything will work properly when the last wire is connected. Allow for a testing and debugging period when problems are addressed before you move strategic applications onto the new network.

Assuming that networks maintain themselves. Network administration is not a job for just anyone. It takes skill and training.

Assuming that giving users a password and logon procedure is sufficient. Lack of user training is a serious problem.

Assuming that regular, periodic backups are unnecessary. Improper backup procedures always lead to disaster.

Thinking about disaster recovery, tomorrow. If the activities on the network are crucial to your business, be sure to plan ahead for the possibility of the system going down. It will happen.

Key Terms

ASCII text file   Nonprinting character   Text string
Control character   Text file

Documentation Research

Documentation Research questions are included at the end of most units to encourage you to explore and discover the additional features available with DOS 6.x. The first two Documentation Research questions below can be answered by using the on-line reference (accessed by using the HELP command). Review Guided Activity 2.8 if you are unsure how to use the HELP command. The other questions require you to use the Help command within the DOS Editor.

1. Name the .EXE file that is required to run EDIT.COM.

2. The EDIT command can only print one type of file. Name it.

3. Name the quick key that enables you to set a bookmark within a document.

4. Name the quick key that enables you to jump to a bookmark within a document.

5. Name the quick key that increases the size of the EDIT command text window.

6. Name the quick key that decreases the size of the EDIT command text window.

APPLICATION

Creating Text Files

Creating a Text File with COPY CON:

In Unit 9, you learned about the COPY CON: command. In this application, you will build a text file using that command, save it to disk, and turn the disk in to your instructor.

1. Create a file called WISEONES.TXT.

2. Enter the following text into the file. Remember to proofread carefully before pressing ⏎Enter at the end of each line. The text file must match the following text perfectly, including correct spelling, spacing, and punctuation.

```
Once upon a time
opportunity failed to knock
at the wise person's door.
But the wise person advertised
and opportunity came to stay.

It is always too hot or too cold
for the man or woman
who wants to quit.
```

3. Submit the file to your instructor on a disk. Be sure to write your name, course and section number, instructor's name, and today's date on the disk label.

Creating a File with the EDIT Command

In Unit 9, you learned about the EDIT command. In this application, you use the EDIT command without the aid of step-by-step instructions.

1. Create a file called POORRICH.ALM.

2. Enter the following text into the file exactly as it appears. Remember to proofread carefully and correct any errors before turning in the file.

```
Poor Richard Jr's Almanac
was published in the first
decade of this century. The
book includes many amusing and
thought provoking comments
for today's students.

"The hard part is not to work
for success but to wait for it
to ripen".

"If the rich man could get
through the eye of the needle
as easily as he squeezes
through the loopholes of the law,
his future would be safe".

"The man who is his own
worst enemy generally loves
his enemy".

"A presidential candidate is known
by the opinions he tries to keep
to himself".

"He who takes his own time generally
takes other people's, too".

If there is any criticism of Poor
Richard Jr's Almanac, it is the
consistent use of sexist language.
Many of the "pearls of wisdom" could
be rewritten to avoid male-oriented
terms. Two examples are:
```

3. Without retyping the text in WISEONES.TXT, add it to the end of POORRICH.ALM.

4. Separate the original text in POORRICH.ALM from the new text added from WISEONES.TXT by a blank line.

5. Add quotation marks around the two paragraphs added from WISEONES.TXT.

6. Be sure the punctuation (periods at end of quotes) are inside the quotation marks. The original text in the book is incorrectly punctuated. Use EDIT to correct it.

7. Save your file to disk, using the POORRICH.ALM file name. Submit the file to your instructor on a disk. Be sure to write your name, course and section number, instructor's name, and today's date on the disk label.

Disaster Prevention Commands

10

Learning Objectives

At the completion of this unit, you should be able to

1. define the key component in any disaster recovery plan,

2. understand when to use the MSBACKUP command rather than the COPY or DISKCOPY commands,

3. list the two primary copy-protection methods used by software manufacturers and comment on how they affect the use of the MSBACKUP command,

4. list the three DOS commands that interfere with the MSBACKUP command,

5. discuss the need for a periodic system backup,

6. define the four uses of the ATTRIB command,

7. list at least two uses of a write-protected file,

8. use the XCOPY and REPLACE commands.

Important Commands

ATTRIB

MSBACKUP

REPLACE

XCOPY

How to Smile When Disaster Strikes

Disaster recovery planning is a basic part of the planning process for any data processing center. Yet personal computer users tend to ignore this aspect of planning and implementation until disaster strikes.

The most common function in a disaster recovery plan is scheduling regular system and data backups. A complete disaster recovery plan must also consider *alternative processing strategies* (ways of getting work done when your computer is out of commission), testing, security, *manual backup systems*, cost-effectiveness, and impact on the *enterprise* (business or department). Our scope of concern in this unit centers on backup systems as provided by MS-DOS.

Three considerations enter into any backup strategy:

- The kind of medium to be used as *backup disks*

- The type of backup

- The frequency of the backup (called the *backup cycle*)

Backup Medium

Personal computer systems use several types of media for backups, including tape, disk, and cartridge. Not until the advent of version 6.0 did DOS support disk-to-tape backups, or backups to any medium other than floppy disks and hard drives. The MSBACKUP command (introduced with DOS 6.0) can back up to any device that can be specified with a drive letter. This can include a second hard drive in your system, a floppy disk, a tape drive, a Bernoulli drive (removable cartridge), or an optical cartridge (or floptical).

NOTE *Historically, with DOS 2.0, the backup process permitted the backing up of files from a hard disk to floppy disks only. DOS 3.1 added the capability of backing up from one floppy disk to another, from a floppy disk to a hard disk, and from one hard disk to another hard disk.*

Backup Types

The MSBACKUP command supports three types of system backups: Full (a complete backup of all specified files), incremental (backs up only files that have been modified or created during a time period you specify), and differential (backs up all files modified or created since the last full backup).

The Backup Cycle

There appears to be a direct correlation between users who have lost data and users who make periodic backups of their system data. The more work they have lost, the more frequently they seem to back up their systems.

There is no such thing as a typical backup schedule. Many factors contribute to determining how frequently you should perform a full, incremental, or differential backup. Some of those considerations include:

- How often do you create and modify files?

- How crucial are the files to the continued financial success and operation of your home or business?

- Is the data available in some other format from another source?

- How much time can you devote to recreating or rebuilding the information stored in the files?

- Can the information be recreated or rebuilt from scratch?

Keep in mind that periodic backups do not necessarily need to include the directories storing your application programs. Those files should be available on the original program disks received when you purchased the software. The only exception to this rule would be that you might want to back up an application program that required extensive setup and configuration; an example of this type of directory would be your Windows directory. If you have installed numerous Windows applications, created groups, and installed PIF files that would take a significant period of time to rebuild, you might want to back up the Windows directory in addition to all directories storing data.

Your backup cycle might include the following:

- A full backup at least once a week

- A differential backup at the end of each day (this assumes that you work with the same files each day)

- An incremental backup when you continue to modify a group of files for which you may want to retain earlier versions (do an incremental backup of the specified group of files at the end of each work session where you have modified any of the files)

The above backups would be done once or more often each week. In addition, most businesses would expect to perform separate monthly and year-end backups. These are completely separate from the weekly backup sets. With financial applications it is even more critical to create backups for regular accounting periods. You should create an end-of-the-week backup (one per week in the month), a monthly backup (one per month in the year), and a year-end backup (could be a fiscal or calendar year backup—though the former is more usual).

Special-Case Backups

In addition to the above *opportunities* for backing up your data, five other special occurrences should be a signal to back up your data. Each of these cases places data at risk.

You should back up your data prior to embarking on the following activities:

- *Moving your computer.* Whether the move is across the hall or across the country, your data is vulnerable when you move your system unit.

- *Cleaning up your hard disk* to free up disk space. Periodically, you must trim the branches on your directory tree and eliminate files and directories that are no longer needed. Without fail, you will delete one or more files that you later realize are still important (or needed by your coworkers). A good backup protects you from your own housekeeping efforts.

- *Compressing your hard disk.* With DOS 6.0, disk compression has moved into the mainstream of computing. Unfortunately, problems do occur. Using the DOS 6 DBLSPACE command, you can increase disk space in the range of 70–100 percent, but with that comes a risk—especially if the power fails or someone accidentally tampers with your computer while the disk is being compressed (since the process can take 2–8 hours, depending on the size of your hard drive and the number and type of files stored). Save yourself a big headache and back up before running DBLSPACE on your PC.

- *Running utilities to defragment your hard disk,* such as the DOS 6 DEFRAG command. The chances for problems are typically small, but any utility that alters the surface of your hard disk should be run only after completing a full backup.

- *Adding new hardware components* to your system. Installing new hardware typically requires opening your system unit, reconfiguring your system, and installing new device drivers. It can be a blessing to have a backup so that you can return your system to its former state—should anything go wrong.

Why Disaster May Strike

In Unit 1, we discussed the care and handling of disks. From that discussion, it should be clear that floppy disks may become damaged. Even expert care can sometimes be voided when family or friends accidentally stack books on a disk, spill liquid on a disk, or handle the exposed surface of the disk. A hard disk appears more protected. It is encased in a metal enclosure inside the PC's system unit. Unfortunately, anything mechanical eventually wears out. A hard disk is no exception.

A *hard disk crash* is every user's greatest fear—yet every hard disk will crash. It is only a matter of when. The term "hard disk crash" means that the read-write head in the hard disk unit comes in destructive contact with the disk platters. A hard disk is composed of several rigid platters, not unlike a series of rigid disks. When the head gouges or scratches the recording surface of a platter, data is lost and that area can no longer store data. If the damage occurs on the area reserved for track 0 (where the directory and file allocation tables reside), the hard disk becomes unusable.

What causes a hard disk crash or head crash? The two primary causes are:

- The read-write head mechanically fails and bumps into the recording surface.

- The system unit is jarred or moved while the read-write head is in motion, which causes the head to damage the recording surface.

In normal operation, the read-write head floats over the recording surface. If the head physically comes in contact with the platter, damage occurs. With the original IBM PC, the IBM Diagnostic disk (provided with each new system unit) included a program to park the head of the hard disk drive. Before a hard disk system unit was moved, the read-write head had to be parked. The software would move the head to a position above the platters and beyond the last track or cylinder. In that position, vibrations from moving the system unit were less likely to cause damage.

That procedure is now obsolete because the majority of hard drives manufactured today automatically park the read-write heads when the power is turned off.

Not all hard disk failures are the result of a read-write head crash. Additional problems include:

- Damage from power surges such as during an electrical storm
- Damage from radio frequency interference (RFI)
- Damage from static electricity

Using the MSBACKUP Command Versus COPY and DISKCOPY

Both the COPY and DISKCOPY commands may be used if a backup is limited in scope. For instance, if all data is on a disk or two, either COPY or DISKCOPY will work. Because the DISKCOPY command is intended for floppy disk copying only, however, it cannot be used to back up files on a hard disk.

The COPY command, on the other hand, can be used to back up data from a hard disk. Two limitations exist for this type of backup:

- Any disk is limited in the number of files it can store in its directory. To be specific, the limitation is on the number of files that may be stored in the root directory. That number may be increased by creating subdirectories under the root directory to store additional data files. Each file on the disk, the disk volume label, each subdirectory, and each hidden file count toward the root directory limit indicated in the Directory Listings column of Table 10.1.
- Any disk is limited in the amount of bytes it can store. A disk's storage capacity is further reduced by the space occupied by the boot record, the FAT, and the directory table. For example, a 360KB floppy can really only store 354KB in data.

Table 10.1 shows the various disk types, sectors per track, number of directory entries, and other disk data. When any of these limits is exceeded during a backup operation, the copying process terminates with the error message "insufficient disk space" and results in an incomplete backup of the designated files. The MSBACKUP command does not suffer from this restriction. If a single file or group of files cannot fit on a single disk, MSBACKUP will split it over two or more disks (it prompts you to insert any additional disks needed to complete the backup).

When backing up a hard disk or subdirectory requires more than two to three disks, the COPY command becomes an awkward substitute for the MSBACKUP command.

TABLE 10.1	DISK TYPE	STORAGE	SIZE	SECTORS	FAT SECTORS	DIR SECTORS	DIRECTORY LISTINGS
Data on various disk types	SS2D	160KB	5.25	8	2	4	64
	SS2D	180KB	5.25	9	4	4	64
	2S2D	320KB	5.25	8	2	7	112
	2S2D	360KB	5.25	9	4	7	112
	2S2D	720KB	3.5	9	6	7	112
	2S4D	1.2MB	5.25	15	14	14	224
	2S4D	1.44MB	3.5	18	18	14	224
	Hard disk	10MB		17	16	32	512
	Hard disk	20MB		17	80	32	512
	Hard disk	30MB		17	120	32	512

NOTE *One distinct advantage of the MSBACKUP command is its ability to divide a large file over two or more disks. The COPY command cannot copy a 2MB file to a 1.44MB target disk. The MSBACKUP command will back up that file to two disks. Of course, the file cannot be accessed or used until it is restored to a single disk, using the MSBACKUP command.*

Introduced with DOS 6.0, MSBACKUP is an external DOS command created specifically to handle the following tasks:

- Backing up all files on a disk

- Backing up only files that have changed since the last backup

- Running scheduled backups automatically on a regular basis

- Restoring files that are backed up with MSBACKUP

The syntax of the command is

```
MSBACKUP [setup_filename][/BW or /LCD or /MDA]
```

NOTE *Prior to DOS 6.0, the BACKUP and RESTORE commands were used for this function. BACKUP is no longer shipped with DOS unless you order the Supplemental Disks (see the back inside cover of the* Microsoft MS-DOS 6 User's Guide). *The RESTORE command is still shipped with DOS because users will need it to restore files and disks backed up using the old DOS BACKUP command. The old commands were entered on the command line and did not offer a menu interface such as MSBACKUP does. Only the MSBACKUP command is covered in this textbook.*

If you use the Setup_Filename parameter, it tells MSBACKUP to use that setup file to determine which files to back up and the type of backup to make (full, incremental, or differential). Setup files must have a .SET extension and are created when you save file selections and MSBACKUP program settings. If you do not specify a setup file, MSBACKUP uses the DEFAULT.SET setup file (it is shipped with DOS).

Other MSBACKUP Command Switches

The MSBACKUP command has three other switches—each dealing with the type of monitor attached to your computer system. The switches are listed below.

/BW Causes the MSBACKUP screen to use a black-and-white scheme.

/LCD Causes MSBACKUP to display video compatible with an LCD (liquid crystal display) screen such as is used on a notebook or laptop computer.

/MDA Causes MSBACKUP to display video compatible with a monochrome display adapter.

What to Do After the Crash

After a hard disk failure or any other disaster, the MSBACKUP command is used to transfer files from the sets of backup disks to a new hard disk or a reformatted disk.

Guidelines on Using the MSBACKUP Command

The MSBACKUP command is not the same as the COPY command. The commands and the files they create are not interchangeable. Files created by the MSBACKUP command cannot be accessed or used until they have been restored. In fact, the MSBACKUP command only creates a single file on the backup disk. The file is given a file name such as

```
CC30626A.001
```

The meaning of the file name is explained in Table 10.2.

TABLE 10.2 *Interpretation of MSBACKUP file name characters*	CHARACTER PLACE IN FILE NAME	MEANING
	1st	The first drive backed up on this set of disks.
	2nd	The last drive backed up on this set of disks.
	3rd	The last digit of the year based on the system clock.
	4–5	The month the backup was made, based on the system clock.
	6–7	The day of the month the backup was made, based on the system clock.
	8th	If more than one backup is made on the same day on the same drive(s), this character indicates the order of the backup (A is the first, B the second, and so on).

The extension indicates the disk number in the sequence of disks required to complete the backup. For example, if the second backup of selected files on drives C: and D: on March 26, 1994 required three disks, those disks would each have one of the following files stored on it as a result of the backup.

```
CD40326B.001
CD40326B.002
CD40326B.003
```

Though the file name numbers each disk, it is wise to also number each disk on its label. The MSBACKUP command requires (when restoring files) that the disks be fed into your disk drive in the same order in which they were created.

NOTE *The MSBACKUP command creates a catalog for each backup session. The catalog stores information on the files backed up and indicates whether the backup was full, incremental, or differential. You can also tell which type of backup was performed by looking at the volume label of any one of the backup disks. The label will include an extension that indicates a full backup (FUL), incremental backup (INC), or differential backup (DIF).*

Before beginning a backup, be sure to have sufficient disks available to complete the backup. MSBACKUP displays on your monitor screen the estimated number of disks required to back up the files you have selected. It will take around twenty-eight 360KB disks or seven 1.44MB floppy disks to back up each 10MB of hard disk storage.

The BACKUP command will erase all files off a disk unless the /A switch is used. *This is cause for caution.* Backup disks should be clearly labeled as such. Data on any disk mistakenly used as a backup disk will be lost. Further, it is wise to have a minimum of two completely separate sets of backup disks—one of which is stored off the premises (in case of fire). Most seasoned computer users have been through the horrendous experience of having a read error on a hard disk, having only a single set of backup disks, and finding the set flawed. The greater the number of backups, the greater the safety in case of disaster.

To maximize the chances of having a recent, usable set of backup disks available when necessary requires greater redundancy. Redundancy requires that hardware, software, and data be duplicated. True *redundancy* in a microcomputer business setting would require:

- A backup microcomputer available for each user if the user's original machine malfunctioned

- An archival set of program disks available to reinstall

- A recent, complete backup of all data created by the user

MSBACKUP Antagonists

Three DOS commands exist that can play havoc with the backup-and-restore process. The first two are JOIN and SUBST, DOS commands born with the advent of DOS version 3.1. They should never be invoked while the MSBACKUP command is to be used. The third is ASSIGN. Both ASSIGN and SUBST may confuse either DOS or the user as to the true drive designation to be used in a backup-and-restore process. The JOIN command can confuse the tree structure, thus making the structure invalid after a backup-and-restore procedure.

There is one additional class of problem software that loves to play havoc with carefully planned and executed backups. It is the group of handy little memory-resident programs such as clock display software, background communications programs, print spoolers, note pads, telephone dialers, screen savers, and much more. These programs increase productivity, but may cause untold grief when running concurrently with DOS's MSBACKUP command. If you are getting ready to back up or restore your files, first reboot the system without reloading any memory-resident programs!

Copy Protection and the Backup Process

One final caveat for the user. Although most major manufacturers have removed *copy protection* from their software, the nuisance remains on some software. To understand the impact on backup procedures, it is important to understand how copy protection works. On a non-copy-protected disk, the DOS DISKCOPY command creates a duplicate disk by reading each track in sequence and copying the data to the corresponding track on the source disk. The COPY command copies a file sector by sector (or allocation unit by allocation unit) from one disk to another. With the COPY command, there is no guarantee that the file will be stored on the target disk at the same physical location—that is, in the same track or sector as the file occupied on the source disk.

Copy protection thwarts copying by any one of a number of methods, including rearranging the order in which the tracks are recorded, recording between tracks, recording tracks backward, using spiral rather than concentric tracks, and deliberately writing or creating bad sectors that must exist in specific locations before the disk is readable.

Typically, two methods of copy protection persist:

- Use of a key disk

- Use of an install procedure that permits a limited number of installs of the copy-protected program

Manufacturers using the first copy-protection method keep all the "protected" files on the key disk. The key disk must be in one of the floppy disk drives for the copy-protected software to work. With this scheme, the files to be placed on a hard disk are typically not copy-protected. This method does not affect the use of the MSBACKUP command, unless you attempt to back up and restore the key disk.

The latter method installs *protected* files on the hard disk. These files cannot be copied using the DOS COPY, DISKCOPY, or MSBACKUP command. Some copy-protection schemes create hidden or system files in a hidden directory. In essence, if you have backed up your files and the hard disk crashes, there is no way to restore the copy-protected files from the backup disks. Because a limited number of installs are allowed—usually one or two—a hard disk crash means you have lost one install. After a hard disk failure, only two options exist: try to uninstall the copy-protected programs (often not a real possibility), or contact the software manufacturer and appeal for mercy. Some software manufacturers will swap new disks for the defective ones while others will want payment for new disks.

The point of this discussion? Do not expect the MSBACKUP command to provide a usable disaster recovery system for copy-protected software. In fact, you can anticipate an 80 percent chance that trying to back up or restore copy-protected software will fail.

Backing Up—A Wearisome Exercise

One of the dreariest tasks for most computer users is backing up files. It is tedious to use the MSBACKUP command. However, it is even more tedious—even nightmarish—to have to rebuild files that required hundreds of hours to build. Just remember that periodic backups are essential. Backups should occur as often as dictated by the maxim "Back up everything you cannot afford to lose!" If you cannot afford to lose a day's work, then your backup should be done at least daily. Don't let a tedious task deter you from having the security of a complete system backup.

The MSBACKUP Command Screen

When you first load MSBACKUP at the DOS prompt, using the command MSBACKUP, the opening screen will appear similar to Figure 10.1.

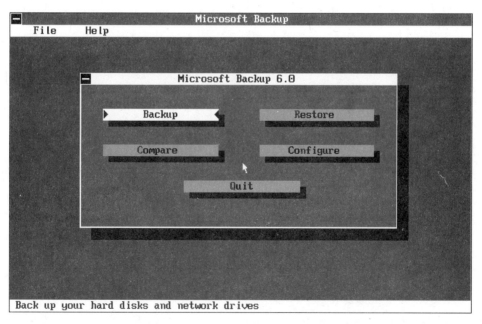

FIGURE 10.1
The Opening MSBACKUP command screen

From the MSBACKUP opening screen, you can click on one of the five buttons or type the highlighted letter to activate the appropriate command. Your options include

BACKUP To back up one or more files or directories.

COMPARE To verify that the source files were accurately backed up.

CONFIGURE   To configure MSBACKUP to work with your system. Include specifying both the type of disk drive to back up to and the mouse and screen settings, and enables you to test your system for accurate backups.

RESTORE   To restore files backed up with MSBACKUP to the original source disk or another disk of your choosing.

QUIT   To exit from MSBACKUP to the DOS prompt.

GUIDED ACTIVITY 10.1

Using the MSBACKUP Command

In this Guided Activity, you will copy files from the \WESTDATA.DS6 directory to a new directory named \WEST on your hard disk. Then you will use the MSBACKUP command to create a backup of files from the \WEST directory. Then you will back up the files onto a disk labeled BACKUP 001, delete them from the \WEST directory, and subsequently restore the files.

1. Log on to the root directory of your hard disk.

2. You will need a formatted blank disk for this Guided Activity. Do not use one of your West Student Data Disks. Instead take any other disk (it can have files on it—so long as you will no longer need them) and label it as the DOS BACKUP DISK 001.

3. Type MD\WEST and press [Enter] to create a new directory on your hard disk.

NOTE   *You will remove this directory at the end of this unit in Guided Activity 10.7.*

4. Type CD\WEST and press [Enter] to change the default directory to the newly created \WEST subdirectory. This step confirms that the directory was created.

5. Type CD\WESTDATA.DS6 and press [Enter] to switch to the directory where all your student data files are stored.

NOTE   *If these files are located elsewhere, your instructor will inform you.*

6. Type COPY *.* C:\WEST/V and press [Enter] to copy all 44 files from the \WESTDATA.DS6 directory to the newly created \WEST subdirectory.

7. Change the default directory to \WEST. The DOS prompt should read "C:\WEST>."

8. Type COPY BECOMING.TXT DREAMIT and press [Enter].

9. Type COPY SAYING.TXT+BECOMING.TXT NEWFILE and press [Enter]

CHECKPOINT 10A   What is the result of the command in the last step?

10. While still logged on to the C:\WEST directory, type DIR/W and press [Enter].

Of the 48 files listed by the DIR command, 2 are really directory listings. They are represented by the ..<DIR> and .<DIR> listings. The former represents the parent directory (the directory immediately above the current one) and the latter notation represents the current directory.

FIGURE 10.2
*MSBACKUP
reading
directory
information*

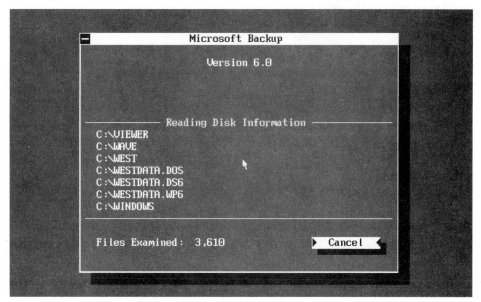

11. Type MSBACKUP and press Enter.

After reading the disk information (shown in Figure 10.2), MSBACKUP again displays the opening screen (labeled Microsoft Backup 6.0) as shown in Figure 10.1.

12. Type B or click on the Backup button to select that option.

The Setup File box on the screen should indicate that DEFAULT.SET file will be used for the backup (unless you indicate otherwise), as shown in Figure 10.3.

You will create your own setup file shortly.

FIGURE 10.3
*Backup Screen
with Setup
File box*

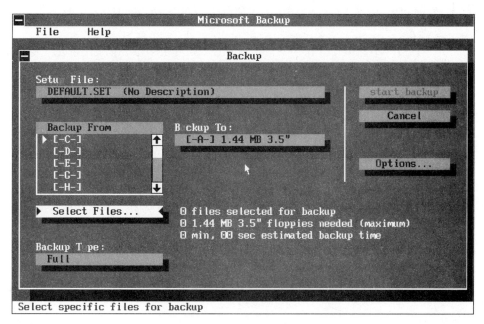

13. Be sure that the Backup To box indicates the target drive you will use when backing up your files (probably [-A-]) followed by the appropriate disk drive size (360K 5.25", 720K 3.5", 1.2MB 5.25", or 1.44MB 3.5").

14. Be sure that the Backup From box indicates the source drive you will use when backing up your files (probably [-C-]).

15. Press L or click on the Select Files button to designate which files you want backed up.

    The bottom of the screen should indicate

    ```
    Selected Files: 0 [        0 K]
    ```

    The Directory Tree box is located on the left side of the screen.

16. In the Directory Tree box, use the scroll bars or `PgDn` and `↑` or `↓` to highlight the \WEST directory you created earlier in this Guided Activity.

17. Once the \WEST directory is highlighted, double-click on it or press the `Spacebar` to select it. This step selects all files in the \WEST directory and means that they'll all be backed up.

    Notice that once a directory of files is selected in the Directory Tree box, a triangular marker appears in front of it. When a file is selected in the Files box, a check mark appears in front of it.

    The bottom of the screen should now indicate the number of files to back up with this message:

    ```
    Selected Files: 46 [        64 K]
    ```

18. Click on the OK button or press `Enter`.

19. Be sure that the Backup Type box indicates a Full backup (not Differential or Incremental).

    You have now completed setting up the backup and ordered the following conditions:

    - All files in \WEST will be backed up.

    - It will be a full backup, not incremental or differential.

    - Files will be backed up from drive C: to drive A: (those are probably your settings).

    This is information that is stored in an MSBACKUP setup file. In the next few steps, you will save this setup in a .SET file, so that it can be used again.

20. From the Backup screen, select the File Save Setup As command (from the menu bar).

NOTE *Do* not *select the File Save Setup command.*

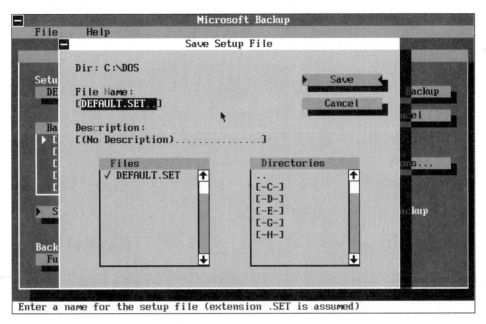

FIGURE 10.4
The Save Setup File screen

21. On the Save Setup File screen, shown in Figure 10.4, the File Name box should be selected. Type CLASS (DOS will automatically add the .SET extension, which is required of all setup files).

CHECKPOINT 10B What extension do you think the DEFAULT setup file name has?

22. Press [Tab] to move to the Description field and type DOS CLASS FILES.

23. Press [Tab] until the Save button is highlighted and then type S or click on the Save button or press [Enter].

24. Once the Backup screen reappears, type S or click on the Start Backup button.

    Notice the information on the screen. The bottom-right screen includes two columns of data. The first estimates the number of disks, files, bytes, and time involved in the backup. The second column, after completing the backup, will include the actual number of disks used, files copied, bytes copied, and the actual time required for the backup.

25. When prompted to "Insert diskette # 1 into drive A:," place the DOS BACKUP DISK 001 in drive A:.

26. Type C or click on the Continue button or press [Enter].

    If the target disk has any files on it at all, you will see the following message (as shown in Figure 10.5):

    ```
    You have inserted a disk which
    contains existing directories and files.

    Do you want to Overwrite this disk,
    or Retry using another disk?
    ```

FIGURE 10.5
A warning message displayed when the target disk has files on it

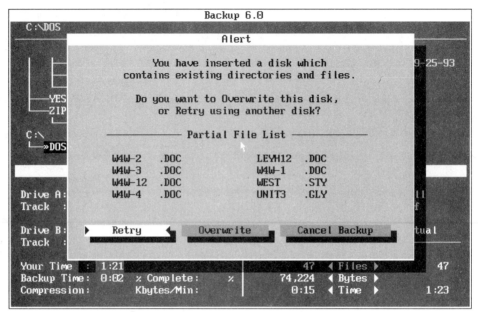

If the disk has previously been used for an MSBACKUP backup, the message will be slightly different and appear similar to the one listed below:

```
You have inserted Backup diskette
#1 from backup set CC30710A.FUL.

This diskette was created using the
WEEKLY setup on 7-10-93.

Do you want to overwrite this diskette
or retry using another diskette?
```

In either case, three buttons appear that enable you to Retry, Overwrite, or Cancel Backup.

NOTE *The Retry button is useful if you want to switch disks and retry the backup using a new disk (rather than overwriting files on the current target disk). The Cancel Backup button enables you to cancel the entire process rather than continuing. If you select the Overwrite button, DOS assumes it is okay to overwrite all files on the target disk.*

27.   If you are sure that the files on the target disk are no longer needed, type O or click on the Overwrite button.

CHECKPOINT 10C If the disk in drive A: has files you want to keep and not overwrite, what should you do?

When the backup is complete, the Backup Complete dialog box, as shown in Figure 10.6, will appear. Notice the Actual column (behind the Backup Complete dialog box—bottom-right corner of your screen), which shows the actual number of disks, files, bytes, and time used for the backup.

NOTE *The KBytes Per Min, Compression, and Bytes listed on the Backup Complete screen may vary from Figure 10.6.*

FIGURE 10.6
The Backup Complete dialog box

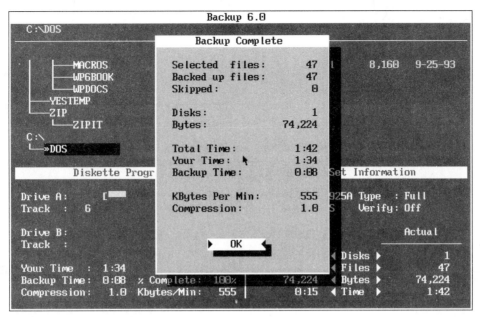

```
                              Backup 6.0
 C:\DOS
                          Backup Complete
        ┌──MACROS        Selected  files:        47   │    8,160   9-25-93
        ├──WP6BOOK       Backed up files:        47
        └──WPDOCS        Skipped:                 0
       ─YESTEMP
       ─ZIP             Disks:                   1
         └──ZIPIT        Bytes:              74,224
 C:\
    └──»DOS              Total Time:           1:42
                         Your Time:     ▶      1:34
         Diskette Progr  Backup Time:          0:08   Set Information

 Drive A:      [▬▬▬]     KBytes Per Min:        555   925A  Type  : Full
 Track  :   6            Compression:           1.0   S     Verify: Off

 Drive B:                                                          Actual
 Track  :                   ▶    OK    ◀
                                                      ◀ Disks ▶         1
 Your Time  :  1:34                                   ◀ Files ▶        47
 Backup Time:  0:08   % Complete:  100%      74,224   ◀ Bytes ▶    74,224
 Compression:  1.0   Kbytes/Min:   555        0:15   ◀ Time  ▶      1:42
```

28. Click on the OK button or press [Enter] to continue.

     The opening MSBACKUP screen should appear.

29. Click on the Quit button or type Q to exit the program.

GUIDED ACTIVITY 10.2

Checking the Backup for Accuracy

This Guided Activity is a follow-up to the preceding one. You will use the Compare feature of the MSBACKUP command to ensure that the backup disk made in the last Guided Activity is accurate.

1. At the DOS prompt, type MSBACKUP and press [Enter].

    After reading the disk information, MSBACKUP displays the opening screen as shown in Figure 10.1.

 CHECKPOINT 10D What other options are available on the MSBACKUP opening screen besides the Backup and Compare options?

2. Type C or click on the Compare button to select that option.

3. Type G or click on the Catalog button to select that option.

4. In the Files box, scroll down until you locate the CLASS.CAT file. Highlight the CLASS.CAT catalog name.

5. Double-click on CLASS.CAT or press [Spacebar] and then press [Enter] to load the setup file you created in Guided Activity 10.1.

6. Press [Tab] until the Compare Files box is highlighted or click on the Compare Files box.

7. Double-click on the [-C-] option or press the [Spacebar] to change the setting to "[-C-] All files."

8. Once the Compare Files box is set to compare all files, press [Tab] until the Start Compare button is selected and type S or click on the Start Compare button or press [Enter].

    The MSBACKUP command will display the message "Insert diskette # 1 of backup set...into drive A."

9. The DOS BACKUP DISK 001 should still be in drive A:. If it is, type C or click on the Continue button or press [Enter]. If not, insert the disk and then type C or click on the Continue button or press [Enter].

    After the comparison is made, the Compare Complete dialog box should appear on your screen as shown in Figure 10.7. Notice that the fourth line provides a report on the success of the comparison. If the comparison found no errors, it should read

    `Did Not Match: 0`

FIGURE 10.7
The Compare Complete dialog box

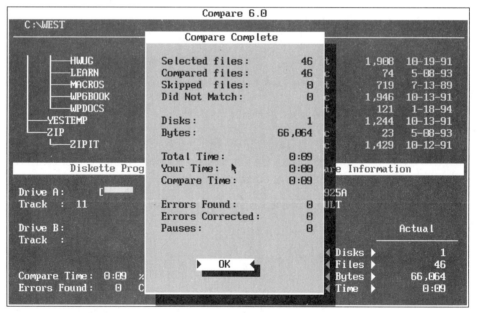

10. Click on the OK button or press [Enter] when you are done reviewing the Compare Complete dialog box.

11. Type Q or click on the Quit button to exit the MSBACKUP command.

12. To view the file name on the backup disk, type DIR A: and press [Enter].

    Your screen should display a file name that represents a backup made on a single drive (probably drive C:) on today's date. Check Table 10.2 to interpret the name.

GUIDED ACTIVITY 10.3

Restoring Files Using MSBACKUP

This Guided Activity is a follow-up to the preceding two. During this activity, you will first delete all files from the C:\WEST directory and then restore them from the DOS BACKUP DISK 001 to the C:\WEST directory.

1. This activity is meant as a follow-up to the last Guided Activity. The DOS BACKUP DISK 001 should still be in drive A:.

2. You should still be logged on to drive C: with the default path being C:\WEST. If this is not the case, use the CD command to change to the C:\WEST subdirectory.

3. Type DIR and press ⏎Enter. The 44 files copied earlier from the \WESTDATA.DS6 directory, 2 files created, and 2 directory listings should be in this directory; if not, you may be logged on to the wrong directory.

4. Type DEL *.* and press ⏎Enter.

CHECKPOINT 10E Name the drive and path where files will be deleted in step 4.

5. The screen will display the message "All files in directory will be deleted! Are you sure (Y/N)?" Type Y and then press ⏎Enter. This command will delete all files in the C:\WEST subdirectory.

6. Type DIR and press ⏎Enter.

    The subdirectory C:\WEST should not include any files. The screen should only list the two directory listings.

7. Type MSBACKUP and press ⏎Enter.

8. On the opening screen, type R or click on the Restore button to select the Restore option.

9. To use the same catalog that you created earlier in this unit, type G or click on the Catalog button.

10. Scroll down in the Files box until you locate the CLASS.CAT file and then highlight it.

11. To select the CLASS.CAT file, press the ⎵Spacebar or double-click on the catalog file name (CLASS.CAT) and then press ⏎Enter.

    The Backup Set Catalog box should read "CLASS.CAT DOS CLASS FILES."

12. Press ⭾Tab 3 times or click on the Restore Files box to select it.

    At this point, the bottom of the screen indicates that "0 files are selected for restore."

13. With [-C-] highlighted, press the ⎵Spacebar or double-click on the [-C-] option.

    The bottom of the screen should now indicate "46 files selected for restore."

NOTE *If the Restore To: option (center of the screen) is not set to Other Directories, select the option and change it to read Other Directories (the default setting).*

FIGURE 10.8
*The MSBACKUP
Restore option
Alert box*

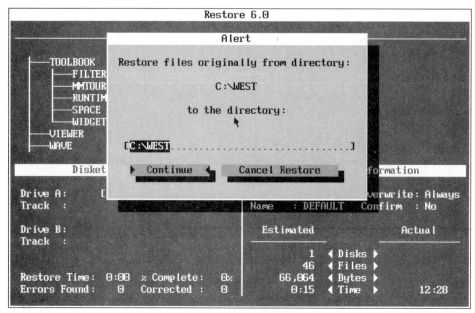

14. Tab to the Start Restore button and type S or click on the Start Restore button to continue with the restore process.

15. When prompted to "Insert diskette # 1 of backup set...into drive A.," be sure that DOS BACKUP DISK 001 is still in the drive, and then press Enter to continue.

   An Alert box, similar to Figure 10.8, will appear. This gives you the option to restore files to a directory other than the one from which they were initially backed up.

   The Alert box instructions advise you that MSBACKUP will

   ```
   Restore files originally from directory:
   C:\WEST
   to the directory:
   C:\WEST
   ```

   You can overwrite the last line of the alert by simply typing in a new target directory.

   In the remainder of this Guided Activity, you will restore the files to the original directory (C:\WEST) where you originally backed them up.

16. Press Tab and then type C or click on the Continue button or press Enter to continue.

17. After the files are all restored, the Restore Complete dialog box appears, as shown in Figure 10.9.

   If the restoration was successful, the top three lines of the Restore Complete dialog box should read

   ```
   Selected files:   46
   Restored files:   46
   Skipped files:     0
   ```

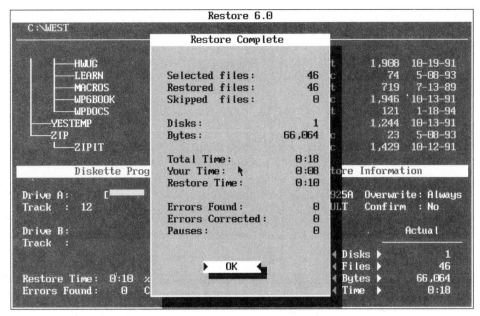

18. Click on the OK button or press .

19. When the Microsoft Backup 6.0 screen appears, type Q or click on the Quit button to exit the MSBACKUP command.

20. To view the file names restored to the C:\WEST directory, type DIR and press Enter.

   The directory should include 48 files, including the 2 directories.

21. Be sure that the default drive and path is C:\WEST, and then on your own *delete* all files in the directory, before proceeding to the next Guided Activity.

GUIDED ACTIVITY 10.4

Completing a Partial Restore Operation

In this Guided Activity, you will restore only selected files to the C:\WEST directory from the DOS BACKUP DISK 001.

1. This activity is meant as a follow-up to the last Guided Activity. The DOS BACKUP DISK 001 should still be in drive A:.

2. You should still be logged on to drive C: with the default path being C:\WEST. If this is not the case, use the CD command to change to the C:\WEST subdirectory.

3. Type DIR and press Enter.

   All files should have been deleted from this directory during the last step of Guided Activity 10.3. The screen should only list the two directory listings.

4. Type MSBACKUP and press Enter.

5. On the Microsoft Backup 6.0 screen, type R or click on the Restore button to select the Restore option.

6. To use the same catalog that you created earlier in this unit, type G or click on the Catalog button.

7. Scroll down in the Files box until you locate the CLASS.CAT file and then highlight it.

8. To select the CLASS.CAT file, press the [Spacebar] or double-click on the catalog file name (CLASS.CAT) and then press [Enter].

    The Backup Set Catalog box should read "CLASS.CAT DOS CLASS FILES."

9. Press [Tab] 4 times and press [Enter] or click on the Select Files button to select it.

    At this point, the bottom of the screen indicates

    ```
    Selected Files: 0 [        0 K]
    ```

10. Use [PgDn], [↑], [↓], or the scroll bar to locate the \WEST directory in the Directory Tree box.

11. Press [Tab] to move the highlighter to the Files box.

12. Select all files in the \WEST directory that end with the .DOC extension.

    TIP *You can select files by double-clicking on the file name, or highlighting each file name and then pressing* [Spacebar] *. Remember to use the scroll bar or* [↓] *to view the entire list of files.*

CHECKPOINT 10F Why would you choose to restore only a single file or select group of files?

    Fifteen files that equal 20KB should be selected when you are done.

13. Click on the OK button or press [Enter].

    The bottom of the screen should now indicate "15 files selected for restore."

14. Tab to the Start Restore button and type S or click on the Start Restore button to continue with the restore process.

15. When prompted to "Insert diskette # 1 of backup set...into drive A.," be sure that DOS BACKUP DISK 001 is still in the drive, and then press [Enter] to continue.

16. When the Alert box appears, press [Tab] and type C or click on the Continue button to continue.

    After the files are all restored, the Restore Complete dialog box appears. If the restoration was successful, the top three lines of the Restore Complete dialog box should read

    ```
    Selected files:   15
    Restored files:   15
    Skipped files:     0
    ```

17. Click on the OK button or press [Enter].

18. When the Microsoft Backup 6.0 screen appears, type Q or click on the Quit button to exit the MSBACKUP command.

19. To view the file names restored to the C:\WEST directory, type DIR and press ⌨Enter.

The directory should include 17 files, including the 2 directories.

Another Safety Command—ATTRIB

In addition to the ability to perform periodic backups of data files, DOS provides another safety feature—setting the *attribute byte* to prevent accidental erasure of one or more files. Each time a file is created on a disk, a directory entry is also created. The eleventh byte of each directory entry is the attribute byte.

Some of the eight bits that comprise the eleventh byte are used to indicate the following conditions for the file:

READ-ONLY   Determines if you can only read the file or can also modify it. A file with this attribute cannot be deleted using the DEL command.

ARCHIVE FILE   Determines if the file has been backed up (using MSBACKUP or similar utility) after the last modification of the file.

SYSTEM FILE   Determines if the file is a system file (required by the operating system).

HIDDEN FILE   Determines if the file is displayed by the DIR command (normal file) or is not displayed (hidden file).

The DOS ATTRIB command is used to set the attribute byte, which determines whether a file is a read-only file, an archive file, a system file, a hidden file, or is marked for a combination of these attributes.

The ATTRIB command can use any of the switches listed in Table 10.3.

TABLE 10.3
ATTRIB command switches

+A	turns on the archive file attribute.
–A	turns off the archive file attribute.
+H	turns on the hidden file attribute.
–H	turns off the hidden file attribute.
+R	turns on the read-only file attribute.
–R	turns off the read-only file attribute.
+S	turns on the system file attribute.
–S	turns off the system file attribute.

Using the switches indicated in Table 10.3, you can change any of a file's attributes with the following command syntax:

```
ATTRIB [+switch or -switch][d:][path][filename.ext]
```

For example, to *write-protect* (that is, make *read-only*) a file on drive A: named FISCAL.RPT, the attribute bit must be set to a value of 1. Therefore, the command takes the form of

    ATTRIB +R A:FISCAL.RPT

You can also use the ATTRIB command to determine the attribute byte's settings for a specified file. For instance, to determine that the FISCAL.RPT file was successfully set to read-only, you can enter the command

    ATTRIB A:FISCAL.RPT

Assuming the file is marked read-only, DOS will respond with the message

    R A:\FISCAL.RPT

If the file's attribute were set to a *read-and-write* state, then the message would appear as

    A:\FISCAL.RPT

The "R" appearing at the left margin indicates that the file is read-only or write-protected. If you subsequently determine that the file is not important, and you want to delete it or modify it, you would need to set the attribute back to read-and-write enabled. The read-only attribute may be reset to 0, which enables the file to be modified or deleted, by using the following command form:

    ATTRIB -R A:FISCAL.RPT

Global wild card characters may be used with the ATTRIB command; so an entire group of files may be write-protected by using a single command line.

NOTE *The purpose of using the ATTRIB command to write-protect a file in this scenario is to set up the file so that it may be accessed and viewed but not modified without changing the attribute bit back to 0, that is, not write-protected. The ATTRIB command is useful primarily with files saved for archival purposes. Files that are modified daily are not good candidates for the ATTRIB command. Another use of ATTRIB would be to write-protect files that should not be altered by casual users, hackers, or computer viruses. Examples of this type of file would include COMMAND.COM, as well as all .EXE and .COM files.*

The ATTRIB command can also be useful in storing *boilerplate documents* used as templates for documents created in your word processor. Whether at home or work, you may find that certain form letters, with minor modifications, are frequently sent out to friends or clients. The standard text of the document can be created and stored as a separate file. When needed, the file is opened (loaded) and minor changes made (to personalize the document for the specific situation), then the file is saved to a new name (not write-protected). Using this scenario, you might want to set the template file's attribute byte to read-only so that no one accidentally modifies the original. Once any file (with the attribute set to read-only) is copied, the duplicate copy is not write-protected. Modifications and additions may be made to the new file, yet the boilerplate file remains intact and write-protected.

The same process could be used with generic worksheets created by a spreadsheet program. For instance, a standard worksheet can be created to store monthly telephone traffic in a department. The file, PHONELOG.WS, is then write-protected, using the ATTRIB command. Each month a new copy of the master file is created by using the command

```
COPY PHONELOG.WS PHONEJUL.WS
```

Our example shows the command format for the month of July. Subsequent files created for subsequent months might be named PHONEAUG.WS, PHONESEP.WS, PHONEOCT.WS, and so on. Because the new files are copied, they lack the read-only attribute of the PHONELOG.WS file.

An added feature of the ATTRIB command relates to the erasing of files. A file marked as read-only by the ATTRIB command cannot be erased using either the DEL or ERASE commands. However, the FORMAT command will eliminate read-only files.

NOTE *You will find that the EDIT command will load a write-protected file. However, when you make changes to the file and try to save it, you'll see an error message that reads "Path/File Access Error." You actually have two methods within DOS of viewing the contents of a read-only file. You can use the EDIT command, or view the file using the TYPE command.*

Setting the Archive Bit

Another use of the ATTRIB command, mentioned in Table 10.3, is to set the archive bit (one of the 8 bits that comprise the attribute byte) that determines whether MSBACKUP considers the file modified since the last backup. Whenever a file is backed up, the archive bit is turned off. Once you modify the file, the archive bit is reset to indicate that the file has not been archived (backed up) since it was modified. The ATTRIB command can be used to reset this flag. There may be occasions when you want to reset the archive bit, thus forcing MSBACKUP to archive the file even though it has not been modified.

To turn on the archive bit for a file named NOMODIFY.TXT, you would use the command

```
ATTRIB +A NOMODIFY.TXT
```

This would cause the MSBACKUP command to assume that the file was modified and cause it to be backed up even if it had not changed since the last backup.

The following command would turn off the archive bit and cause the file not to be backed up:

```
ATTRIB -A NOMODIFY.TXT
```

Once again, you can view the status of a file's archive bit by entering the ATTRIB command followed by the file name:

```
ATTRIB NOMODIFY.TXT
```

If the archive attribute is turned on, the screen will respond with the message

```
A   NOMODIFY.TXT
```

If the "A" does not appear, the archive bit is turned off. Global wild card characters may also be used with this version of the ATTRIB command; so a group of files may have their archive bit turned on (or off) by a single command line.

NOTE *You can set two or more attributes with a single command. For example, the following command would set the read-only attribute to 1 and turn on the archive bit.*

```
ATTRIB R+ A+ NOMODIFY.TXT
```

Using the ATTRIB Command with Directories

The ATTRIB command can be used to modify the attributes (hidden, system, archive, and read-only) of an entire directory as well as the files in the directory. For instance, if you want to hide a specific directory (named C:\MYNOTES), you must specify the directory name. Wild card characters cannot be used in this case. The command would be entered as

```
ATTRIB +H C:\MYNOTES
```

Once the directory is hidden, the DIR command will not list it. In all other regards, you can use the directory. You can change to it (CD \MYNOTES), do a directory listing of the files in it (DIR C:\MYNOTES), plus delete, copy, and modify files within the directory.

Another ATTRIB feature, added with DOS 6.0, is the ability to set the attributes of all files in a specified directory (using the wild card characters) and all files in the subdirectories of that directory (using the new /S switch). For example, assume that you want to make read-only all files that are stored in the C:\TEMPLATE directory and its two subdirectories (C:\TEMPLATE\LETTERS and C:\TEMPLATE\FORMS). You could accomplish that task with one command as shown below.

```
ATTRIB +R C:\TEMPLATE\*.* /S
```

GUIDED ACTIVITY 10.5

Marking Files Read-Only with the ATTRIB Command

In this Guided Activity, you will create a small file using EDIT, mark that file as read-only, copy it several times, and then delete all but the file marked by the attribute byte as read-only. This will demonstrate that when a file marked as read-only is copied, the copy is not write-protected, and that a file marked as read-only cannot be deleted.

1. Insert West Student Data Disk #3 in drive A:, type FORMAT A:/Q/U, and press Enter. This formats the disk so that it is blank.

2. Log on to drive A:.

3. Type MD UNIT-10 to create a new directory on A:.

4. Type CD UNIT-10 to change to the new directory.

5. Type CLS and press Enter.

6. Type DIR and press [Enter]. There should be no files in the new directory.

7. Type EDIT MASTER.WS and press [Enter].

8. Type the following text. Press [Enter] after each line of text.

   Let's pretend this is a master copy
   of a budget worksheet
   created by your favorite electronic
   spreadsheet program.

   Your screen should look like Figure 10.10. If the text is incorrect, modify your file.

FIGURE 10.10
*Text of
MASTER.WS file*

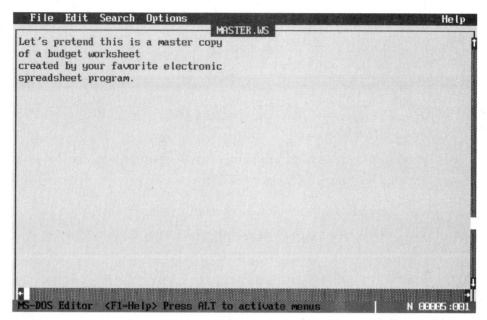

9. Select the File Save command to save the file.

10. Select the File Exit command to exit the DOS Editor.

11. Type DIR and press [Enter].

    A single file, MASTER.WS, is listed in this directory.

12. Type ATTRIB +R MASTER.WS and press [Enter].

CHECKPOINT 10G Why would you set the attribute byte of a document to read-only?

   The file is now write-protected and marked as read-only by the ATTRIB command. The second step following will verify that MASTER.WS is write-protected.

13. Type CLS and press [Enter].

14. Type ATTRIB *.* and press [Enter].

FIGURE 10.11

Response to
ATTRIB A:*.*
command

```
A:\UNIT-10>ATTRIB *.*
    A    R     A:\UNIT-10\MASTER.WS

A:\UNIT-10>
```

The screen message should look like Figure 10.11. The R to the left of the MASTER.WS file name indicates that the attribute byte is set to read-only. Further, the A or archive bit (left-hand margin) is set on; that is, it indicates that the file has been created or modified since the last backup. To reconfirm that MASTER.WS is protected from modification, you will try to edit it using EDIT.

15. Type EDIT MASTER.WS and press [Enter].

16. When the EDIT screen appears, press [Ctrl][Y] to delete the first line of the text file.

17. Select the File Save command.

    An error message will appear (because the file is marked read-only) saying, "Path/File access error."

18. When the error message appears, press [Enter] or click on the OK button.

19. Select the File Exit command.

20. Type N to indicate that you do not want to save the modified file.

    The next few steps will create duplicates of the MASTER.WS file under four different file names.

21. Type COPY MASTER.WS JUNE93$$.WS and press [Enter]. The screen will respond with the message "1 file(s) copied."

22. Use the COPY command to create three additional files named JULY93$$.WS, AUG93$$.WS, and SEPT93$$.WS.

    In the next step you will check to be sure that the newly created files are on the disk in drive A: in the \UNIT-10 directory.

23. Type DIR and press [Enter].

    The following files should be listed in the directory listing:

    ```
    MASTER.WS
    JUNE93$$.WS
    JULY93$$.WS
    AUG93$$.WS
    SEPT93$$.WS
    ```

    The MASTER.WS file is read-only, but what about the files copied from it?

24. Type CLS and press [Enter].

25. Type EDIT JUNE93$$.WS and press [Enter].

In the next few steps, you will slightly modify the file.

26. Move the cursor under the m in the word master on the first line of the text file.

27. Press [Ctrl][T] to delete the word and then press [Del] to delete the extra space *or* move the mouse pointer to any character in the word master and double-click to select it and then press [Del] twice (once for the word and once for the extra space).

The text file should now appear as shown in Figure 10.12. Notice that the word "master" from the first line is gone.

FIGURE 10.12
Screen display of text from this activity

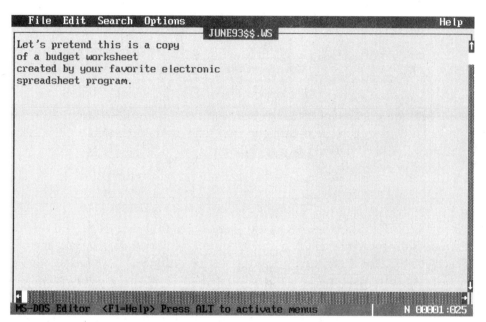

28. Select the File Exit command.

29. When prompted "Loaded file is not saved. Save it now?," type Y or press [Enter].

30. Type DIR and press [Enter].

Notice that the file JUNE93$$.WS is now only 114 bytes long rather than 121 bytes long, that is, the length of MASTER.WS. You were definitely able to modify the copy of a read-only file—even though the original was write-protected.

NOTE *If you did not press [Enter] after entering the last line of the MASTER.WS file, that file will be only 119 bytes long and JUNE93$$.WS will be only 112 bytes long.*

31. Type ATTRIB *.* and press [Enter].

The newly created files have the archive attribute bit set on (A is in the left margin).

Finally, the next few steps attempt to assure you that read-only files cannot be deleted. Only the MASTER.WS file is marked (using the ATTRIB command) as a read-only file.

32. Type DEL *.* and press [Enter]. This command will delete all files on drive A: in the \UNIT-10 directory.

33. When prompted, type Y and press ⏎ to delete all the files.

34. Type DIR and press ⏎.

Of the files created in this Guided Activity, only one remains—MASTER.WS. Clearly, the file marked as read-only withstood the DEL command and is still safely available to you.

Copying Groups of Files with XCOPY

The MSBACKUP command has several distinct disadvantages:

- You cannot access or modify files backed up with MSBACKUP until they are restored.

- The MSBACKUP command copies files one at a time. The first file must be read into memory from the source disk, then copied to the target disk. This process is slow since each file must be found, read, and copied before the next file is found, read, and copied to the target disk.

The XCOPY command provides an alternative to each of these problems. It can also be used to back up files. It cures the above shortcomings of the MSBACKUP command, but has one outstanding weakness itself. We will discuss the weakness first.

XCOPY can only copy the number of files that may be stored on one disk at a time. Suppose you use the XCOPY command with a global wild card that would select 800KB of files; however, your system only uses 720KB disks. XCOPY will begin copying until the target disk is full and then abort the copying process—just as the COPY command (outside the DOS Shell) would do. This also means that you cannot use XCOPY to back up or make a duplicate of a single file that exceeds the size of your target disk. In such a case, you must use the MSBACKUP command.

In the areas where disadvantages are listed for the MSBACKUP command, the XCOPY wins hands-down because of the following:

- Files copied with XCOPY may be read and modified immediately.

- The final advantage is speed. XCOPY copies as many files into memory as RAM will hold and then begins writing those files out to the target disk. With fewer reads of the source disk and fewer writes to the target disk, the speed of the copying is increased.

There is one other minor annoyance with XCOPY—you cannot use this command to copy hidden or system files. If you want to copy these types of files, you must first use the ATTRIB command to turn off these attributes.

CAUTION *While the DISKCOPY command will copy hidden and system files, it can only copy from floppy disk to floppy disk. It is not wise to turn off the system or hidden attributes on the system files created on a bootable disk.*

The XCOPY command is an external command that uses the following syntax:

```
[d:][path]XCOPY s:[path][filename.ext] t:[path][filename.ext]
```

To copy all files from the current directory on drive A: to drive B:, the command form would be

```
XCOPY A: B:
```

or

```
XCOPY A:*.* B:
```

You can use file names and global wild card characters to restrict the files to be copied. The XCOPY command also has ten switches available. They are listed in Table 10.4.

TABLE 10.4 *The XCOPY command switches*	

Switch	Description
/A	Only copies files with the archive bit set on, but does not change the source file archive bit.
/D:Date	Only copies to the target disk any files created on or after the date specified. The date must be specified using the COUNTRY format you are using. In the United States, this format is usually MM/DD/YY. For instance, to copy only files created since June 1, 1994, you would use the switch /D:06/01/94.
/E	Copies empty subdirectories to the target disk. This switch must be used in conjunction with the /S switch.
/M	Only copies files with the archive bit set on and then turns the source file archive bit off.
/P	Prompts you with a (Y/N?) before copying each file.
/S	Copies all files from the current directory and its subdirectories, unless the subdirectories are empty.
/V	Verifies that sectors written from the source to the target disk are written correctly.
/W	Prompts you to press a key before the XCOPY command will proceed to make the copies. This enables you to insert a disk in the source drive before XCOPY begins its work.

The following two new switches were introduced with MS-DOS version 6.2:

Switch	Description
/Y	Turns off the "Overwrite (Yes/No/All)?" prompt that warns you when you are about to overwrite a file on the target disk. The /Y switch can be preset using the COPYCMD environment variable.
/–Y	Turns on the "Overwrite (Yes/No/All)?" prompt that warns you when you are about to overwrite a file on the target disk. This is the default setting with DOS 6.2.

If you were to use the COPY command, DOS must read the first file from drive A:, copy it to drive C:, read the second file from A:, and copy again to drive C:. The process continues until all files are copied—one at a time. You could grow old waiting.

On the other hand, when the XCOPY command is executed DOS first reads the command into memory (it is an external DOS command). Next, XCOPY reads as many files from the source drive into memory as it can hold in RAM and then transfers the files to the target drive. Only if the size of source files exceeds the amount of available RAM does XCOPY return to the source drive to read again.

Before you press ⏎Enter, be prepared to watch the drive C: and A: lights. First DOS reads the external XCOPY command into memory. Then, after XCOPY reads the files on drive C: into memory, the C: drive light does not show activity again. If you use the COPY command, DOS reads the first file from drive C:, copies it to drive A:, reads the next file from C:, and copies again to drive A:. This process continues until all files on the source disk are copied, one by one to the target disk.

The more efficient XCOPY command reads as many files from drive C: into memory as it can hold in RAM, and then copies them to drive A:. Once you press ⏎Enter, the XCOPY command is read into memory, then DOS accesses drive C: again to read all files into memory and does not return to drive C: until the process is complete. Watch the drive lights.

NOTE *Beginning with DOS 6.2, if executing the XCOPY command will overwrite a file on the target drive with a file using the same name from the source drive, DOS displays the "Overwrite (Yes/No/All)?" message. When this message appears, you can type Y and press ⏎Enter to overwrite the file on the target drive, type N and press ⏎Enter to not overwrite it and not copy the file, or type A and press ⏎Enter to overwrite all duplicate files that may be encountered during the current execution of the XCOPY command. You can avoid this prompt entirely by adding the /–Y switch to the XCOPY command. For example, you can enter the command as* `XCOPY *.* A:/-Y`*.*

GUIDED ACTIVITY 10.6

Using the XCOPY Command

In this Guided Activity, you will use the XCOPY command to transfer all files created in the last Guided Activity to a subdirectory under the \WEST directory on your hard disk.

1. Insert West Student Data Disk #3 in drive A:. Be sure the default drive and path is A:\UNIT-10 (the directory created in Guided Activity 10.5).

2. Type `DIR` and press ⏎Enter.

    Only one file, MASTER.WS, remains in the directory because you deleted the other files in Guided Activity 10.5. In the following steps, you will undelete those files.

3. Type `UNDELETE *.*` and press ⏎Enter.

NOTE *If you do not have Sentry Delete installed, you will be prompted to type the first character of the file name of the deleted files. You must supply the missing character when prompted.*

4. Each time you are prompted with the message "Undelete (Y/N)?," type Y.

5. If you see the message "The filename already exists. Type a different filename. Press F5 to bypass this file," press F5 to skip the file.

6. Type DIR and press Enter.

   The \UNIT-10 directory should now include five files with the .WS extension.

7. Log on to the hard disk directory named \WEST.

8. Type DIR and press Enter. This directory should have 15 files with the .DOC extension and 2 directory listings.

9. Type CLS and press Enter.

10. Type MD WKSHEETS and press Enter.

11. Type CD WKSHEETS and press Enter to change to the new directory.

12. Type XCOPY A:*.* C: and press Enter.

CHECKPOINT 10H What is the primary reason for using the XCOPY command in the last step (rather than the COPY command)?

> Figure 10.13 displays the screen messages generated by executing the XCOPY command. Once XCOPY is executed, the "Reading source file(s)..." message is displayed. All files are transferred in one "read" from drive C:.

FIGURE 10.13
Screen messages from the XCOPY command transferring files to drive C:

```
C:\WEST>MD WKSHEETS

C:\WEST>CD WKSHEETS

C:\WEST\WKSHEETS>XCOPY A:*.* C:
Reading source file(s)...
A:MASTER.WS
A:JUNE93$$.WS
A:JULY93$$.WS
A:AUG93$$.WS
A:SEPT93$$.WS
        5 File(s) copied

C:\WEST\WKSHEETS>
```

13. Type DIR and press Enter.

   All the .WS files are now in the \WEST\WKSHEETS directory.

   In the next few steps, you will delete the files from drive A: and then use the XCOPY command (with the /S switch) to copy files from the \WEST and \WEST\WKSHEETS directories to the A: drive. This demonstrates that XCOPY can back up more than one directory at a time.

14. Log on to drive A:.

15. Type CD\ to switch to the root directory.

16. Type DIR and press Enter. There should be no files except for the UNIT-10 directory.

17. Type DELTREE UNIT-10 and press Enter.

18. When prompted, type Y and press [Enter].

19. Type DIR and press [Enter]. The disk now contains no files. Even the MASTER.WS file (which had its attribute byte set to read-only) was deleted, using the DELTREE command.

20. Log on to drive C:.

21. Type CD\WEST and press [Enter]. Your default drive and path should now be C:\WEST.

22. Type CLS and press [Enter].

23. Type DIR and press [Enter]. Only 15 files should be in this directory, plus 3 subdirectory listings. Figure 10.14 shows the DIR command listing, including the subdirectory named WKSHEETS <DIR>.

FIGURE 10.14
*DIR listing of
files in C:\WEST
directory*

```
Volume Serial Number is 1CC9-3931
Directory of C:\WEST

.               <DIR>         09-25-93     8:11a
..              <DIR>         09-25-93     8:11a
ALIGN    DOC        1792 09-19-87     9:15p
DASHIT-1 DOC          18 05-12-93     8:12a
DIET     DOC        1310 08-15-91     8:15a
DINOSAUR DOC          26 05-08-93     7:51p
FLAGS    DOC        2048 01-09-88     5:17p
INDEFENS DOC        1536 01-31-88     7:25a
MOM1     DOC         419 10-04-88     7:28p
MOM2     DOC         667 10-04-88     7:44p
MOM3     DOC        1536 10-04-88     7:43p
STRATS1  DOC        4074 10-13-91     8:04p
STRATS2  DOC        4019 10-13-91     8:02p
TODOLIST DOC          74 05-08-93     7:59p
WAR      DOC        1946 10-13-91     8:24p
WINNEWS1 DOC          23 05-08-93     7:56p
WIN_MODE DOC        1429 10-12-91     9:18p
WKSHEETS      <DIR>         09-25-93     9:34a
        18 file(s)        20917 bytes
                       58343424 bytes free

C:\WEST>
```

24. Type CLS and press [Enter].

25. Type XCOPY *.* A:/S and press [Enter].

Figure 10.15 displays the screen activity from executing the XCOPY command.

26. Type DIR A: and press [Enter].

The disk in drive A: contains the 15 files originally in the \WEST directory plus a new subdirectory that was not originally on drive A:. This new directory, A:\WKSHEETS, is drawn from the directory of the same name on drive C:.

FIGURE 10.15
*XCOPY screen
activity*

```
C:\WEST>XCOPY *.* A:/S
Reading source file(s)...
ALIGN.DOC
DASHIT-1.DOC
DIET.DOC
DINOSAUR.DOC
FLAGS.DOC
INDEFENS.DOC
MOM1.DOC
MOM2.DOC
MOM3.DOC
STRATS1.DOC
STRATS2.DOC
TODOLIST.DOC
WAR.DOC
WINNEWS1.DOC
WIN_MODE.DOC
WKSHEETS\MASTER.WS
WKSHEETS\JUNE93$$.WS
WKSHEETS\JULY93$$.WS
WKSHEETS\AUG93$$.WS
WKSHEETS\SEPT93$$.WS
        20 File(s) copied

C:\WEST>
```

Let's check the A:\WKSHEETS subdirectory to be sure the .WS files (plus two directories) on drive C: were properly copied to the target disk in drive A:.

27. Type A: and press [Enter] to change the default drive to A:.

28. Type CD WKSHEETS and press [Enter]. Your default directory is now A:\WKSHEETS.

29. Type DIR and press [Enter].

The five .WS files are in the subdirectory.

The next two steps return you first to the root directory on drive A: and then to the \WEST directory on drive C:.

30. Type CD\ and press [Enter].

31. Type C: and press [Enter].

The REPLACE Command—A Handy Option

When using the XCOPY command to back up important files, the REPLACE command is a useful companion to it. REPLACE is an external DOS command. The syntax of the command is

```
[d:][path]REPLACE [s:][path]filename.ext [t:]
```

If you had used the XCOPY command to back up chapters of a manuscript (files named UNIT1.DOC, UNIT2.DOC, UNIT3.DOC, and UNIT4.DOC), you could periodically "replace" the backed-up versions with the newer versions (presumably from your hard disk) by entering the command

```
REPLACE UNIT?.DOC A:
```

This command form assumes

- You are logged on to the hard disk directory that contains the four unit files.

- Only four files (UNIT1.DOC through UNIT4.DOC) exist on the target and source disk.

- You wish to update the backup disk in drive A:.

If UNIT5.DOC exists on the default drive but not on drive A:, it will not be copied to the disk in drive A:. The REPLACE command does just as its name implies—without a special switch, it replaces files. If a file does not exist on the target disk, it does not copy it.

NOTE *If you type either* `XCOPY *.DOC A:` *or* `COPY *.DOC A:`, *all files with the .DOC extension are copied from the default drive to the disk in drive A:. If you want to copy all files, use COPY or XCOPY. Suppose, however, that you have created several document files and already created backup copies of all the files on drive A:. Then you modify a few of the files, but not all of them. Using the* `REPLACE *.DOC A:` *command is more efficient than using COPY or XCOPY, because it will only replace older versions of the files already existing on drive A: with the new versions from the default drive.*

There are six REPLACE command switches that provide greater flexibility. They are listed in Table 10.5.

TABLE 10.5 *The REPLACE* *command* *switches*	/A	Adds all files from the source to the target disk that do not already exist on the target drive. Cannot combine with /S or /U switches.
	/P	Prompts you to respond Y/N to each proposed replacement. If you press Y, the file is copied to the target. If you press N, it is not copied.
	/R	Copies read-only files and unprotected (write-enabled) files to the target disk. Though the on-line Help indicates the need to use this switch when copying read-only files, in actual practice the REPLACE command copies read-only files without using this switch.
	/S	Replaces files after searching all directories and subdirectories of the target for the specified file(s). Cannot combine with /A switch.
	/U	Replaces files on the target disk with files by the same name on the source disk—if the target disk files have an older creation date. Cannot combine with /A switch.
	/W	Waits until you insert a disk in the source drive before proceeding.

Most of these switches may be combined, except as noted in Table 10.5.

In the earlier example with the four unit files, let's assume that the UNIT1.DOC file did not exist on the target drive but did on the source. It can be copied to the target by using the following command line:

```
REPLACE UNIT?.DOC A:/A
```

After all four files are on the target disk, you can update each file to the most recent version by simply entering

```
REPLACE UNIT?.DOC A:/U
```

This command form determines if the file on the source is more recent than the same file on the target. If the source file is newer (based on creation date and time), REPLACE will copy it onto the target disk—in effect, updating the target with the most recent version.

NOTE *If using the REPLACE command, you should note that it is very important that your system clock be accurate. The time and date stamp on each file is used to determine the most recent version. Don't forget to reset your system clock in the spring and fall if your geographic area is affected by the daylight savings time change.*

GUIDED ACTIVITY 10.7

Using the REPLACE Command

In this Guided Activity, you will create a small file with EDIT and then use the REPLACE command to copy and later update the file on a backup disk.

1. Be sure that West Student Data Disk #3 from Guided Activity 10.6 is still in drive A:.

2. Log on to the \WEST directory on your hard disk.

3. Type CLS and press Enter.

FIGURE 10.16
Results of ATTRIB command

```
C:\WEST>ATTRIB *.*
            C:\WEST\ALIGN.DOC
            C:\WEST\DASHIT-1.DOC
            C:\WEST\DIET.DOC
            C:\WEST\DINOSAUR.DOC
            C:\WEST\FLAGS.DOC
            C:\WEST\INDEFENS.DOC
            C:\WEST\MOM1.DOC
            C:\WEST\MOM2.DOC
            C:\WEST\MOM3.DOC
            C:\WEST\STRATS1.DOC
            C:\WEST\STRATS2.DOC
            C:\WEST\TODOLIST.DOC
            C:\WEST\WAR.DOC
            C:\WEST\WINNEWS1.DOC
            C:\WEST\WIN_MODE.DOC

C:\WEST>
```

4. Type ATTRIB *.* and press [Enter] to display the attribute byte settings for all files on the current path and directory.

   Figure 10.16 shows the results of this command. All files have the archive bit set off; that is because they are restored files and therefore DOS assumes that a backup exists—and because the files have not been modified since their restoration.

5. Type CLS and press [Enter].

6. Type REPLACE *.* A: and press [Enter].

   The command causes all 15 files to be replaced on drive A: with the versions from drive C:.

   Figure 10.17 displays the results of executing the REPLACE command.

FIGURE 10.17
The results of the REPLACE command

```
Replacing A:\FLAGS.DOC

Replacing A:\INDEFENS.DOC

Replacing A:\MOM1.DOC

Replacing A:\MOM2.DOC

Replacing A:\MOM3.DOC

Replacing A:\STRATS1.DOC

Replacing A:\STRATS2.DOC

Replacing A:\TODOLIST.DOC

Replacing A:\WAR.DOC

Replacing A:\WINNEWS1.DOC

Replacing A:\WIN_MODE.DOC

15 file(s) replaced

C:\WEST>
```

7. Type CLS and press [Enter].

   In the next few steps, you will create a new file and then use a new switch with the REPLACE command. The /A switch appends files from the source disk onto the target disk—if they do not already exist on the target disk.

8. Type REPLACE *.* A:/A and press [Enter].

   You will see a "No files added" message on the screen. This form of the REPLACE command only adds files to the target disk if the file does not already exists on the target disk.

9. Type CLS and press [Enter].

10. Type EDIT 1CORNER and press [Enter].

11. Type the following text. Press 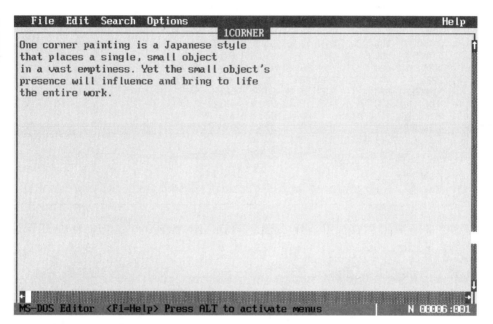 after each line of text.

```
One corner painting is a Japanese style
that places a single, small object
in a vast emptiness. Yet the small object's
presence will influence and bring to life
the entire work.
```

Your screen should look like Figure 10.18.

FIGURE 10.18
The 1CORNER file created using EDIT

```
 File  Edit  Search  Options                              Help
                          ┌ 1CORNER ┐
One corner painting is a Japanese style
that places a single, small object
in a vast emptiness. Yet the small object's
presence will influence and bring to life
the entire work.






MS-DOS Editor  <F1=Help> Press ALT to activate menus        N 00006:001
```

12. Select the File Save command.

13. Select the File Exit command.

14. Type CLS and press Enter.

15. Type REPLACE *.* A:/A and press Enter.

The screen will display the messages shown in Figure 10.19. This form of the REPLACE command appended one file from the source drive to the target disk in drive A:.

16. Type DIR A: and press Enter.

FIGURE 10.19
Screen messages generated by using the REPLACE /A command

```
C:\WEST>REPLACE *.* A:/A

Adding A:\1CORNER

1 file(s) added

C:\WEST>
```

FIGURE 10.20

The 1CORNER file appears in the DIR listing

```
Volume in drive A has no label
Volume Serial Number is 2048-10DA
Directory of A:\

ALIGN    DOC      1792 09-19-87   9:15p
DASHIT-1 DOC        18 05-12-93   8:12a
DIET     DOC      1310 08-15-91   8:15a
DINOSAUR DOC        26 05-08-93   7:51p
FLAGS    DOC      2048 01-09-88   5:17p
INDEFENS DOC      1536 01-31-88   7:25a
MOM1     DOC       419 10-04-88   7:28p
MOM2     DOC       667 10-04-88   7:44p
MOM3     DOC      1536 10-04-88   7:43p
STRATS1  DOC      4074 10-13-91   8:04p
STRATS2  DOC      4019 10-13-91   8:02p
TODOLIST DOC        74 05-08-93   7:59p
WAR      DOC      1946 10-13-91   8:24p
WINNEWS1 DOC        23 05-08-93   7:56p
WIN_MODE DOC      1429 10-12-91   9:18p
WKSHEETS     <DIR>      09-25-93   9:37a
1CORNER           185 09-25-93   9:47a
       17 file(s)      21102 bytes
                     1426432 bytes free

C:\WEST>
```

The 1CORNER file now appears on the directory listing for drive A: as shown in Figure 10.20.

17. Type CLS and press [Enter].

18. Type REPLACE *.* A:/P and press [Enter].

This command form causes REPLACE to prompt you whether to copy each file meeting the command specifications (in this case, *.* means all files).

19. The first message will read "Replace A:\ALIGN.DOC (Y/N)?" Each time you receive a prompt, type Y to instruct DOS to copy the listed file.

20. Type REPLACE *.* A:/U and press [Enter].

The message "No files replaced" appears because no files in the C:\WEST directory have been modified more recently then the copies on the disk in drive A:. In the following steps, you will modify STRATS1.DOC and then try the REPLACE command with the /U switch again.

21. Type EDIT STRATS1.DOC and press [Enter].

22. Change the word attends to attend in the first numbered line by deleting the s.

23. When done, select the File Save command.

24. Select the File Exit command.

25. Type REPLACE *.* A:/U and press [Enter].

Only the STRATS1.DOC file is replaced on drive A:.

To clean up the hard disk on your workstation, complete these steps:

26. Change to the root directory of your hard disk.

27. Type `DELTREE \WEST` and press [Enter].

28. When prompted, type `Y` and then press [Enter].

The \WEST directory and its \WKSHEETS subdirectory should now be erased.

Summary

In this unit, you discovered that you can safely protect your work by making periodic backups using the MSBACKUP command, and make specific files read-only or hidden using the ATTRIB command. For smaller backup jobs, you learned how to use the XCOPY and REPLACE commands.

Command Review

In this unit you learned several DOS commands. Most commands have optional switches. We have tried to cover both the common and the rarely used forms of each command. The following forms of this unit's commands are the most frequently used and should be reviewed carefully.

ATTRIB +A MYFILE	Turns the specified file's archive bit on.
ATTRIB –A MYFILE	Turns the specified file's archive bit off.
ATTRIB +R MYFILE	Marks the specified file as read-only.
ATTRIB –R MYFILE	Marks the specified file as read-and-write accessible.
ATTRIB +H MYFILE	Marks the specified file as a hidden file.
ATTRIB –H MYFILE	Marks the specified file as a normal (nonhidden) file.
MSBACKUP	Runs the Microsoft Backup 6.0 program, a menu-driven utility used to back up and restore files.
REPLACE *.* A:/U	Replaces any files on drive A: that are older than the corresponding files on the default drive. In essence, it updates files when the source disk files are newer than the files on the target disk.
REPLACE A:*.* B:	Copies all files from drive A: to B: if the files already exist on drive B:.
REPLACE A:*.* B:/A	Copies all files from drive A: to B: if the files do not already exist on drive B:.

XCOPY A: B:	Copies all files from drive A: to B:.
XCOPY A:*.DOC B:	Copies all document files (with the .DOC extension) from drive A: to B:.

Review Questions

1. How are the uses of the COPY and DISKCOPY commands different from the uses of the MSBACKUP command?

2. Name at least three considerations related to any backup strategy.

3. What is meant by "backup cycle"?

4. Which DOS commands should never be in effect when using the MSBACKUP command?

5. What are the two primary methods used for copy-protecting application software? What impact does each have on the backup and restore process?

6. What four purposes does the ATTRIB command serve?

7. Why would globally changing all files to read-only not be wise?

8. Give an example in which it would be useful to write-protect a file with the ATTRIB command.

9. When you back up files to a disk using the MSBACKUP command, how many files are located on the target disk?

10. How would you find out the archive and read-only status of a file?

11. If you select (using wild card characters) more than 3MB of files, what happens when you try to execute the XCOPY command (assuming the target is a disk drive)?

12. Which two types of files cannot be copied using the XCOPY command?

13. What is the effect of using the /U REPLACE command switch?

14. What is the effect of using the /A REPLACE command switch?

15. What is the effect of not using any switches with the REPLACE command?

Exercises

Whenever instructed to format a disk, use your last name (first) and then your first name (such as BACON JON) as the volume label. If instructed to print data from the screen, be sure to write your full name, course number and section, course title, instructor's name, unit and exercise number, and today's date on the paper. Your instructor will indicate if the disk(s) created or printouts should be submitted for grading.

1. Create a text file with the following text and then change it to a read-only file. Its file name should be HOW2CRAM.TXT.

    ```
    If you're going to pull an all-night cram session
    stay up all night two nights before the test.
    The night before, briefly review your notes
    and then go to bed early.
    ```

2. Create a text file with the following text and then change it to a read-only file with the archive bit turned *off*. Its file name should be DROWNED.TXT.

    ```
    John Cormick, a young man, while paddling
    about on a plank in the canal, near St. Catherines,
    slipped from it and was drowned - Aug. 8, 1855.
    from the Canada Christian Advocate
    ```

Key Terms

Alternative processing strategy	Copy protection	Read-and-write
Attribute byte	Disaster recovery planning	Read-only
Backup cycle	Enterprise	Redundancy
Backup disk	Hard disk crash	Write-protect
Boilerplate document	Manual backup system	

Documentation Research

Documentation Research questions are included at the end of most units to encourage you to explore and discover the additional features available with DOS 6.*x*. All Documentation Research questions within the text can be answered by using the on-line reference (accessed by using the HELP command). Review Guided Activity 2.8 if you are unsure how to use the HELP command.

1. MSBACKUP creates two backup catalogs each time you back up your hard disk. One is stored on your hard disk. Where is the other stored?

2. Can you start MSBACKUP from a floppy disk?

3. How much memory (RAM) is required to run MSBACKUP?

4. If your system displays an insufficient memory message when you try to run MSBACKUP, what should you do?

Using Disaster Prevention Commands

Restoring an ASCII Text File

In Unit 10, we discussed the DOS command used to back up and restore both program and data files. In this application, you restore a file that was created using MSBACKUP.

1. Obtain a copy of the backup disk from your instructor.

2. Create a \WESTBKUP directory on your workstation's hard drive.

3. Restore all files on the disk from your instructor in the \WESTBKUP directory.

4. Once files are restored, redirect the text of any file(s) in \WESTBKUP to a printer.

5. Copy the file(s) in \WESTBKUP to a disk and label it WESTBKUP.

6. Delete the \WESTBKUP directory and any files it contains from your hard drive.

7. Submit a printed copy of the text of any file(s) to your instructor with the WESTBKUP disk. Be sure to write your name, course and section number, instructor's name, and today's date on the disk label.

Safeguarding Files with the ATTRIB Command

In this application, you create an ASCII text file using EDIT and then mark it as a read-only file.

1. Create a text file using EDIT. Use the following text as the contents of the file. Each line below should be on a separate line in your file (created with EDIT). The file name for the text file should be composed of the first eight characters of your first name. The text is:

```
I am a firm believer in procrastination.
Last year I even thought about forming a club of
procrastinators—but never got around to it.
I'm not sure it was a wise idea anyway.
I was going to talk to some friends about serving as
officers—but figured I could do it tomorrow.
Finding officers might be difficult though.
What true procrastinator would want to start
a meeting on time?
In fact, who would chair the meetings?
We'd never get around to elections.
Can you imagine being the treasurer?
Everyone would defer paying dues until December 31st.
Committees would never meet—until tomorrow.
Our creed could be:
"Never do today what you can postpone until tomorrow."
Most of our members would prefer to do nine stitches
rather than a single one in time.
Well, maybe it is just an idea "before its time."
I guess I'll think it over some more—tomorrow.
```

2. Use the appropriate DOS command to mark the file as read-only.

3. Double-check your work. Try to delete the file. If it cannot be deleted, you have correctly given the file the read-only attribute.

4. Submit the file to your instructor on a disk. Be sure to write your name, course and section number, instructor's name, and today's date on the disk label.

Additional DOS Commands

IV

■ **PART FOUR** of this text covers several additional, crucial DOS concepts. Primary among these is the use of special batch files (CONFIG.SYS and AUTOEXEC.BAT) and the use of other BATCH subcommands (CALL, ECHO, GOTO, PAUSE, and SHIFT).

Additionally, Part IV covers pipes, filters, and redirection of input and output in Unit 12, as well as uses of the MODE command, screen control using ANSI.SYS and PROMPT, and creating virtual drives in Unit 13. The final unit, Unit 14, examines the need for and use of the DOS Shell available with DOS 4.*x*, 5.*x*, and 6.*x*.

Batch Commands

11

Learning Objectives

At the completion of this unit, you should be able to

1. use EDIT to create or modify a batch file,

2. use EDIT to create or modify your AUTOEXEC.BAT file,

3. understand the purpose of the CONFIG.SYS file and the BREAK, BUFFERS, DEVICE, and FILES commands,

4. use the BATCH subcommands including CALL, ECHO, FOR, GOTO, IF, PAUSE, REM, and SHIFT.

Important Commands

BATCH

BUFFERS

CALL

ECHO

FILES

FOR

GOTO

IF

PAUSE

REM

SHIFT

The Invisible, Never-Typed, Hidden DOS Command

In Unit 9, you learned how to create text files with the COPY CON: and EDIT commands. That unit explained *how* small text files could be created; this unit will explain *why*. DOS has a BATCH command, but it is not invoked by typing BATCH. For that reason, it is considered an invisible or hidden DOS command. To use the BATCH command, you execute a **batch file**. By definition, batch files end with the extension .BAT. A few common batch file names are:

```
AUTOEXEC.BAT
INSTALL.BAT
SETUP.BAT
MENU.BAT
```

To execute a batch file, you simply enter the file specification (without the extension) and press [Enter]. For instance, to run the INSTALL.BAT batch file, you would enter

```
INSTALL
```

A batch file may be created using the COPY CON: or the EDIT command. EDIT is the easier method because it offers better editing capabilities. You can also use your word processor to create a batch file—if it is saved as an ASCII text file. For instance, Microsoft Word allows you to save a file (Transfer Save command) as unformatted, which is its equivalent of an ASCII text file. WordPerfect uses the Text In/Text Out command ([Ctrl][F5]) to let you save a document as a DOS text file. Windows applications such as WordPerfect for Windows and Word for Windows enable you to save text files using the File Save As command.

What is inside a batch file? Batch files may contain any of the DOS commands provided with DOS 6.*x*, plus any of a group of special BATCH subcommands.

The BATCH Subcommands

There are eight special BATCH mode subcommands available through DOS 6.*x*. These commands provide flexibility and enable you to do limited programming in a batch file. A brief listing and description of the commands follow.

CALL Transfers control from the current batch file to another. When the other batch file finishes execution, control is returned to the remaining commands in the first batch file.

ECHO Allows or disallows the display of the commands invoked by the batch file. To eliminate screen clutter, it is often helpful to turn off the display to the monitor screen.

FOR Allows repetitious execution of DOS commands.

GOTO Sends control of the batch file to a specified point in the program. The point in the program is identified by a label.

IF Used for decision making in batch files. If one condition exists, the program executes one series of commands, whereas if that condition does not exist, another series of commands is executed.

PAUSE Stops execution of the batch file until you press a key. The PAUSE command displays the message "Press any key to continue..." on the monitor screen.

REM Enables you to incorporate comments or REMarks in your batch file. The REM statements display to the monitor screen unless you set ECHO OFF.

SHIFT Allows the ten replaceable parameters (%0 through %9) to be reused for additional values in a single batch file.

Before considering these new commands individually, let's discuss the DOS commands you already know and how they can be used in your batch files. When you execute a batch file, the commands within the file are executed as if they were typed on the computer keyboard at the DOS prompt. Each DOS command requires the same parameters you would enter at the DOS prompt. In previous units, you learned to use the CHKDSK, CLS, COMP, COPY, DATE, DEL, DIR, DISKCOMP, DISKCOPY, FORMAT, PROMPT, REN, SYS, and TIME commands. Each of these commands can be used in a batch file along with all of the DOS commands you have yet to learn.

A good example might be an INSTALL.BAT file. Commercial and public domain software packages often come with an installation program. A simple INSTALL.BAT file is shown below.

```
 1:    @ECHO OFF
 2:    CLS
 3:    ECHO Insert Program disk in drive A:
 4:    PAUSE
 5:    IF EXIST C:\SMART\DATA GOTO JUMP1
 6:    ECHO Creating C:\SMART\DATA subdirectory...
 7:    MD C:\SMART\DATA
 8:    :JUMP1
 9:    IF EXIST C:\SMART\NEW GOTO JUMP2
10:    ECHO Creating C:\SMART\NEW subdirectory...
11:    MD C:\SMART\NEW
12:    :JUMP2
13:    COPY A:\DATA\*.* C:\SMART\DATA
14:    COPY A:\NEW\*.* C:\SMART\NEW
15:    IF EXIST C:\SMART\NEW\NEWCLASS.DB GOTO END
16:    COPY A:\NEW\NEWCLASS.* C:\SMART\NEW
17:    :END
18:    ECHO INSTALLATION COMPLETE.
```

This file may look like a jumble, but by the time you complete this unit, you will understand every command in the file. For now, examine lines 13, 14, and 16. In their most basic form, these lines tell the computer to copy files from drive A: to drive C:. These particular lines of the batch file are slightly more complicated because they include path names. If you ignore the path names, lines 13 and 14 copy all files (using the wild card character) from drive A: to C:. Line 16 copies any NEWCLASS file, no matter what the extension, to drive C:.

The strength of the batch file is that it can automate repetitious tasks. In data processing, *batch processing* is a technique in which computing tasks are coded and collected into groups for processing. Typically these tasks are routine, regularly scheduled manipulation of data by the computer. Regular batch processing tasks include

- Generating grade report cards

- Generating payroll and accounts payable checks

- Generating inventory lists based on transactions over a given period of time

- Generating mailing labels for clients and prospective clients

In each case, the task is repetitious and requires limited human intervention (paper must be loaded or changed). The BATCH command is the personal computer version of the mainframe job control language. Each batch file can contain DOS and BATCH subcommands to accomplish routine tasks.

The AUTOEXEC.BAT File: The Start 'em Up File

The most common batch file is the AUTOEXEC.BAT file. It is a special purpose batch file activated each time your system is booted. In other words, DOS looks for an AUTOEXEC.BAT file in the root directory of your disk each time you start up the computer. If an AUTOEXEC.BAT file is found, the commands contained in it are executed automatically. The contents of an AUTOEXEC.BAT file may activate an internal clock (on older model PCs), change the DOS prompt, load memory-resident programs like SideKick or PC Tools, establish a path to the DOS files, or load a DOS shell/menu system. The following AUTOEXEC.BAT file turns off the display of executed commands to the screen, sets the DOS prompt, executes four DOS commands, loads a software package called WordPerfect, and then returns control to the root directory (when you exit WordPerfect).

```
1:    @ECHO OFF
2:    PROMPT $P$G
3:    CLS
4:    DATE
5:    TIME
6:    CD\WP60
7:    WP
8:    CD\
```

Line 2 modifies the DOS prompt, line 3 clears the screen, lines 4 and 5 prompt you to enter the current date and time, and then in line 6 the DOS CD command changes the current directory to the one containing the WordPerfect program. Line 7 simply loads WordPerfect. Line 8 changes to the root directory after quitting WordPerfect.

This is a rather simple AUTOEXEC.BAT file. This special file could be far more complex. In fact, the following is a fairly standard AUTOEXEC.BAT file created when installing DOS:

```
 1:    @ECHO OFF
 2:    SET COMSPEC=C:\DOS\COMMAND.COM
 3:    VERIFY ON
 4:    PATH C:\DOS;C:\QDOS;C:\PCL;C:\PCTOOLS;
 5:    APPEND /E
 6:    APPEND C:\DOS
 7:    PROMPT $P$G
 8:    C:\DOS\GRAPHICS
 9:    VER
10:    PRINT /D:LPT1
11:    CD\PAINTLIB
12:    PRTDRV
13:    CD\
14:    DATE
15:    TIME
16:    DOSSHELL
```

Some of these commands have not yet been explained in the text, but will be in future units. You should recognize the commands in lines 4, 7, 11, 13, 14, and 15. The command in line 3 turns on automatic verification so that you do not need to use the /V parameter when using the DOS COPY command. Line 8 executes a DOS command located in the C:\DOS directory. Line 9 simply displays the current version of DOS on the screen. The important point is that each of these commands is executed every time you turn on (boot or warm boot) your system.

GUIDED ACTIVITY 11.1

Creating Your First AUTOEXEC.BAT File

In this Guided Activity, you will create West Student Data Disk #7 and use the SYS command to make it bootable. You will add also an AUTOEXEC.BAT file to the disk.

1. You should be logged on to drive C:.

2. Label a formatted blank disk as West Student Data Disk #7 and place it in drive A:.

3. Type SYS A: and press [Enter].

   You will see the DOS message "System transferred" if the command is successful.

4. Type EDIT A:AUTOEXEC.BAT and press [Enter].

5. Type the following text. Press <kbd>Enter</kbd> at the end of each line.

```
CLS
VER
PROMPT $P$G
DATE
TIME
```

Your screen should display the text shown in Figure 11.1.

FIGURE 11.1
AUTOEXEC.BAT file created with the EDIT command

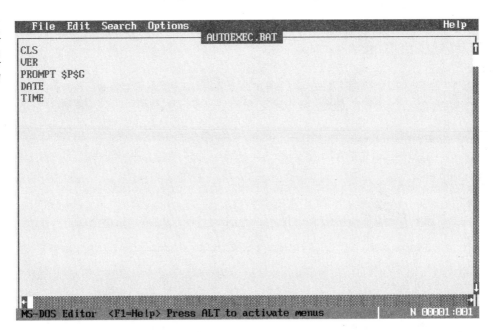

6. Select the File Save command.

7. Select the File Exit command.

8. Press <kbd>Ctrl</kbd><kbd>Alt</kbd><kbd>Del</kbd> to warm boot your system. The system disk you just created should still be in drive A:.

✓ **CHECKPOINT 11A** Why is it better to warm boot your system rather than use the On/Off switch?

9. When the computer prompts you for date and time, enter the current date and time or press <kbd>Enter</kbd> twice if the date and time are correct.

   If the AUTOEXEC.BAT file worked successfully, your screen will look like Figure 11.2.

10. Type CLS and press <kbd>Enter</kbd>.

11. Type DIR and press <kbd>Enter</kbd>.

NOTE *If you are using MS-DOS 6.2, the COMMAND.COM file shown in Figure 11.3 will be slightly larger (54,619 bytes in size).*

```
A:\>VER

MS-DOS Version 6.00


A:\>PROMPT $P$G

A:\>DATE
Current date is Sat 09-25-1993
Enter new date (mm-dd-yy):

A:\>TIME
Current time is  1:28:04.21p
Enter new time:

A:\>
A:\>
```

Your screen should display the two files shown in Figure 11.3, including the AUTOEXEC.BAT file you just created.

NOTE   *If you did not press* ⏎Enter *after entering the TIME command in the AUTOEXEC.BAT file, that file will only be 35 bytes in size.*

12. Remove the disk from drive A: and reboot your computer.

```
A:\>DIR

 Volume in drive A has no label
 Volume Serial Number is 1E4F-1BE2
 Directory of A:\

COMMAND  COM     52925 03-10-93   6:00a
AUTOEXEC BAT        37 10-11-93   8:28p
        2 file(s)      52962 bytes
                     1272832 bytes free

A:\>
```

A Little Programming with the BATCH Mode Subcommands

It is time to examine the special *BATCH mode* subcommands further. These commands provide flexibility and enable you to do limited programming in a batch file. The following sections go into additional detail on each of the eight subcommands.

Do You See an ECHO?

The first command examined in this unit is the ECHO command. It has six forms and serves several similar but different functions:

ECHO OFF Turns off the display of commands to the screen. With the ECHO OFF, screen mssages are cut to a minimum. You will not see each DOS command echoed on the screen when it is invoked by the batch file.

ECHO ON Turns on the display of executed commands to the screen. Every line of your batch file will be echoed to the screen.

ECHO *message* Displays the *message* following the ECHO command to the screen.

ECHO: Displays a blank line to the screen. A series of ECHO: commands can be used to move the prompt to the middle or bottom of the screen. ECHO. can be used to accomplish this same function.

ECHO Causes DOS to respond with a message indicating that either "Echo is on" or "Echo is off."

@ECHO The @ symbol can be used to begin any line in a batch file. When used, that line of the file will be executed but the command is not displayed to the screen. It has the effect of turning ECHO OFF for one line of a batch file. Typically, this form of the ECHO command is used as the first line of a batch file. In the earlier examples of batch files, both began with the line @ECHO OFF. Without the @ sign, the screen would have displayed the message "ECHO OFF" and then turned off the echo.

PAUSE then Press

The PAUSE command is best described by its name. It temporarily halts or pauses the execution of a batch file and displays the message "Press any key to continue…" on the screen. When ready for batch file execution to continue, just press any key.

Often the PAUSE command will be followed by the CLS command. A common example would be a series of "help" screens included with a software program. Instructions for the program are displayed by executing a batch file. One page of text is written to the screen using the TYPE command, then the PAUSE command stops execution of the file. When you press any key, the CLS command is invoked, followed by another TYPE command, which shows the next page of text. In this case, each page of text is stored in a text file and displayed by using the TYPE command.

A segment of this variety of batch file is listed below:

```
11:   TYPE A:PAGE0001.TXT
12:   PAUSE
13:   CLS
14:   TYPE A:PAGE0002.TXT
15:   PAUSE
16:   CLS
```

Document with the REM Command

The REM (remark) command is used for documentation purposes. Whenever you create a batch file, you should document the code you have written. Even if you have only created a simple little batch file, use at least a single REM statement to record the file's purpose. REM commands are not displayed if you precede them in the batch file with the ECHO OFF command.

The syntax of the command is

```
REM message
```

The *message* may be up to 123 characters long. A typical REM statement describes the use of the batch file or provides other documentation; for example:

```
1:   REM This batch file is used to install a program from the source
2:   REM disk in drive A: to the \PROGRAM directory on drive C:.
3:   PAUSE
4:   COPY A:*.* C:\PROGRAM/V
```

REM commands without a message may be used to add blank lines within the program. This helps make a file more readable, especially if the batch file is long and complex. In this case, we are talking about the readability of the batch file text, not the readability of text displayed to the screen. For the latter purpose, use the ECHO: command.

Breaking Out

To break out of a batch file while it is executing, press [Ctrl][C]. When you press these keystrokes, DOS responds with the message

```
Terminate batch job (Y/N)?
```

If you press Y, the batch job will end. If you press N, execution returns to the command that would have been executed next if you had not pressed [Ctrl][C]. There may be times when you wish to break out of a batch file. You may have inadvertently created a file that goes into a **continuous loop**. Or there may be times when you begin executing a batch file and wish to halt it before completion. Even the AUTOEXEC.BAT file may be interrupted using the [Ctrl][C] keys.

GUIDED ACTIVITY 11.2

Creating a Batch File Using ECHO and PAUSE

In this Guided Activity, you will use the BATCH commands ECHO and PAUSE. Once you feel comfortable with these basic commands, you can proceed to the more "programmable" type commands.

For the remaining Guided Activities in this unit, you should be logged on to drive C:.

1. Place West Student Data Disk #7 in drive A:.

2. Type EDIT A:MESSAGES.BAT and press ⏎Enter.

3. Type the following text. Press ⏎Enter after each line.

```
ECHO Ralph Waldo Emerson was born May 25, 1803 in Boston.
PAUSE
ECHO He was the second of five sons born to the Rev. William
ECHO Emerson and Ruth Haskins-Emerson.
PAUSE
ECHO The young Emerson entered Harvard in 1817 and graduated
ECHO in 1821.
PAUSE
ECHO Among his writings, Emerson stated:
ECHO:
ECHO:
ECHO "Fear always springs from ignorance."
PAUSE
ECHO In the essay "Self Reliance," Emerson writes:
ECHO:
ECHO:
ECHO "Nothing is at last sacred but the integrity
ECHO of your own mind."
ECHO:
ECHO:
PAUSE
```

CHECKPOINT 11B What does the PAUSE command do?

CHECKPOINT 11C Why would you use the ECHO: command form?

Your file should now appear similar to Figure 11.4.

4. Select the File Save command.

5. Select the File Exit command.

6. Type CLS and press ⏎Enter.

The next two steps will execute the batch file. Note that you do not need to type the extension, only the file specification.

7. Type A:MESSAGES and press ⏎Enter.

Notice the screen prompt to "Press any key to continue…". Also be aware that all the ECHO commands and their messages are displayed twice. The screen is very confusing because it is cluttered with the commands and the results of the commands.

8. Press any key each time you are prompted, until the DOS prompt returns.

Now you will reedit the MESSAGES.BAT file and add the ECHO OFF statement. This will simplify the screen displays.

FIGURE 11.4
*MESSAGES.BAT
batch file listing*

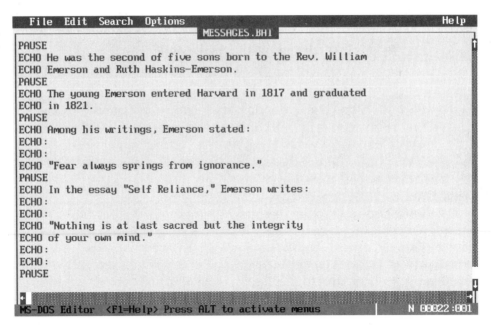

```
 File   Edit   Search   Options                                    Help
┌──────────────────── MESSAGES.BAT ────────────────────┐
│PAUSE                                                               ↑│
│ECHO He was the second of five sons born to the Rev. William        │
│ECHO Emerson and Ruth Haskins-Emerson.                              │
│PAUSE                                                               │
│ECHO The young Emerson entered Harvard in 1817 and graduated        │
│ECHO in 1821.                                                       │
│PAUSE                                                               │
│ECHO Among his writings, Emerson stated:                            │
│ECHO :                                                              │
│ECHO :                                                              │
│ECHO "Fear always springs from ignorance."                         │
│PAUSE                                                               │
│ECHO In the essay "Self Reliance," Emerson writes:                  │
│ECHO :                                                              │
│ECHO :                                                              │
│ECHO "Nothing is at last sacred but the integrity                   │
│ECHO of your own mind."                                             │
│ECHO :                                                              │
│ECHO :                                                              │
│PAUSE                                                               ↓│
│←┤                                                                 ├→│
└────────────────────────────────────────────────────────────────────┘
 MS-DOS Editor  <F1=Help> Press ALT to activate menus      N 00022:001
```

9. Type EDIT A:MESSAGES.BAT and press [Enter].

10. At the beginning of the file, type @ECHO OFF and then press [Enter].

CHECKPOINT 11D Describe the effect of using the @ECHO OFF command.

11. Type CLS and press [Enter].

12. Save the file and exit from the DOS Editor.

13. Type A:MESSAGES and press [Enter] to invoke the batch file.

14. Press any key each time you are prompted, until the DOS prompt reappears.

    The screen should appear similar to the illustration in Figure 11.5.

    The double listing of text and commands is eliminated. In the next few steps, you will add some finesse to the batch file by clearing the screen after each pause.

15. Type EDIT A:MESSAGES.BAT and press [Enter].

16. Move the insertion point to the beginning of line 5.

    Check the right end of the status bar. If it reads "00005," the cursor is on line 5.

17. Type CLS and press [Enter].

18. Move the insertion point to the beginning of line 9.

19. Type CLS and press [Enter].

20. Move the insertion point to the beginning of line 13.

FIGURE 11.5
*Edited
MESSAGES.BAT
batch file*

```
He was the second of five sons born to the Rev. William
Emerson and Ruth Haskins-Emerson.
Press any key to continue . . .

The young Emerson entered Harvard in 1817 and graduated
in 1821.
Press any key to continue . . .

Among his writings, Emerson stated:


"Fear always springs from ignorance."
Press any key to continue . . .

In the essay "Self Reliance," Emerson writes:


"Nothing is at last sacred but the integrity
of your own mind."


Press any key to continue . . .

C:\>
```

21. Type CLS and press [Enter].

22. Move the insertion point to the beginning of line 19.

23. Type CLS and press [Enter].

    The screen should appear similar to Figure 11.6.

24. Save the file and exit the DOS Editor.

25. Type A:MESSAGES and press [Enter] to invoke the batch file.

FIGURE 11.6
*MESSAGES.BAT
after inserting
three lines*

```
 File  Edit  Search  Options                              Help
┌──────────────────── MESSAGES.BAT ────────────────────┐
@ECHO OFF
CLS
ECHO Ralph Waldo Emerson was born May 25, 1803 in Boston.
PAUSE
CLS
ECHO He was the second of five sons born to the Rev. William
ECHO Emerson and Ruth Haskins-Emerson.
PAUSE
CLS
ECHO The young Emerson entered Harvard in 1817 and graduated
ECHO in 1821.
PAUSE
CLS
ECHO Among his writings, Emerson stated:
ECHO :
ECHO :
ECHO "Fear always springs from ignorance."
PAUSE
CLS
ECHO In the essay "Self Reliance," Emerson writes:
ECHO :
MS-DOS Editor  <F1=Help> Press ALT to activate menus        N  00020:001
```

CHECKPOINT 11E Why doesn't the previous step ask you to type A:MESSAGES.BAT?

26. Press any key when prompted until the DOS prompt returns.

Programming with BATCH Commands

Programmers have an arsenal of structures available to them when they write code. These *programming structures* include the availability of *variables, decision-making structures,* and *subroutines*. Though the BATCH command is not as powerful as programming languages like Pascal, C, COBOL, or even BASIC, a rudimentary form of each of these structures is present in BATCH.

In the remainder of this unit, you will be exposed to a brief discussion of these programming structures. This text is not intended to make you an expert programmer, only to expose you to the basic concepts as illustrated by the BATCH commands.

Decision Making

The most basic programming structure is the IF...THEN statement. It permits decision making within a batch file. Decision making with the IF statement is similar to driving down a road that branches in two directions. You must decide to continue going straight or branch to the right. How do you decide? It depends on your current *condition* or options. If on your way home, that is one condition—and you continue on the main road. If you are going to shop, that is another condition—and you branch to the right.

In a batch file, if one condition exists, the execution of the program continues in one direction. If any other condition exists, program execution branches off in a different direction. The syntax of the command is

```
IF [condition][action]
```

There is no THEN keyword (as there is in BASIC and other languages). If the condition exists, then the specified action is taken. The BATCH IF command has four conditions it can evaluate:

string(1) == string(2)   This condition checks to see if the first text string is equal to the second text string. The strings must match exactly, including punctuation, spacing, spelling, and capitalization. If the strings match, then the specified action occurs.

EXIST [d:][path]filename   This condition checks to see if the named file exists. If it does exist, the specified action occurs.

NOT EXIST [d:][path]filename   This condition checks to see if the named file does not exist. If it does not exist, the specified action occurs.

ERRORLEVEL n   DOS returns specific error messages based on the type of event that has occurred. For instance, if an ERRORLEVEL or exit code of 2 is returned when executing the XCOPY command, it indicates that the user interrupted the command by pressing Ctrl C. An ERRORLEVEL of 0 means the command was successful.

Exit Codes

Some of the DOS commands that return exit or error codes include DISKCOMP, DISKCOPY, FORMAT, GRAFTABL, KEYB, REPLACE, and XCOPY. To this point in the text, we have discussed several of these commands. The exit codes for some of these commands are listed in Table 11.1. Exit codes for the other commands can be determined using the on-line Help feature.

TABLE 11.1
DOS Command Exit Codes

CHKDSK COMMAND EXIT CODES

0	No error occurred.
255	One or more errors occurred.

DISKCOMP COMMAND EXIT CODES

0	The source and target disks compared OK and are identical.
1	The source and target disks did not compare OK—they are not identical.
2	The DISKCOMP command was terminated by the user's pressing [Ctrl][C].
3	An unrecoverable hard error occurred—such as a read or write error.
4	An initialization error occurred—insufficient memory, invalid drive(s), or incorrect syntax.

DISKCOPY COMMAND EXIT CODES

0	DISKCOPY command was successful.
1	An unrecoverable but nonfatal read or write error occurred—disk may or may not be usable.
2	The DISKCOPY command was terminated by the user's pressing [Ctrl][C].
3	The DISKCOPY command was unable to read the source disk or format the target disk.
4	An initialization error occurred—insufficient memory, invalid drive(s), or incorrect syntax.

FORMAT COMMAND EXIT CODES

0	FORMAT command was successful.
3	The FORMAT command was terminated by the user's pressing [Ctrl][C] or [Ctrl][Break].
4	A fatal formatting error occurred (other than 0, 3, or 5).
5	User indicated N when prompted "Proceed with format (Y/N)?"

MOVE COMMAND EXIT CODES

0	MOVE command was successful.
1	An error was encountered moving one or more of the specified files.

XCOPY COMMAND EXIT CODES

0	XCOPY command was successful.
1	No files were found to copy.
3	The XCOPY command was terminated by the user's pressing [Ctrl][C].
4	Insufficient memory or disk space to complete command, or user entered an invalid drive or invalid syntax on the command line.
5	A disk write error occurred.

Further Clarification on Decision-Making Conditions

A few examples might help clarify these conditions that may be tested by the IF command. In the following example, you have logged on to drive A: and the batch file installs specific files on drive C:. Suppose you wish to check if a given file exists on drive C: before copying it from drive A: to C:. The file in question is named CONFIGUR.001. In the following example, the EXIST condition is tested.

```
12:    IF EXIST C:CONFIGUR.001 GOTO :DONTCOPY
13:    COPY A:CONFIGUR.001 C:/V
14:    :DONTCOPY
```

Telling the Program Where to GOTO

The GOTO command, used in the preceding example, redirects control of the batch file to another location in the program. The BATCH GOTO command can only redirect to a label. In the above example, the label is called :DONTCOPY. If the file CONFIGUR.001 is found on drive C: (which means the EXIST condition is true), then batch file control is transferred to line 14. Line 13 is not executed and the file is not copied to C:. If the file is not found, which makes the EXIST condition false, then the GOTO action is not executed. In this latter situation, batch file control passes to the next sequentially numbered line—line 13. The file is then copied to drive C:.

All labels in batch files must begin with the colon and exist on a line by themselves. The label is not executed. It is simply a marker for use with the GOTO command. Technically, batch file execution is transferred to the line *after* the label.

A label can be as long as you care to make it, but only the first eight characters are used by DOS. For instance, you will confuse DOS if your batch file has two labels with the same first eight characters. In the following example, DOS would not know which label to use (lines 14 and 16):

```
12:    IF EXIST C:CONFIGUR.001 GOTO :DONTCOPYTHISFILE
13:    COPY A:CONFIGUR.001 C:/V
14:    :DONTCOPYIT
15:    ECHO This is not the correct label
16:    :DONTCOPYTHISFILE
```

In this segment of code, the confusion created by both labels' having the same first eight characters is inconsequential. In most cases, the confusion would not be acceptable. Just be sure the first eight characters of each batch label are distinctive.

The Negative EXIST Condition

There is a more efficient way to program the above example. The code could be entered on a single line by using the NOT EXIST condition. It could be entered as

```
IF NOT EXIST C:CONFIGUR.001 COPY A:CONFIGUR.001 C:CONFIGUR.001/V
```

In this case, if the file CONFIGUR.001 does not exist on drive C:, then it will be copied from drive A: to C:.

GUIDED ACTIVITY 11.3

Using the EXIST Condition in a Batch File

In this Guided Activity, you will use both the EXIST condition and the GOTO BATCH command. These new commands will be combined with the BATCH commands you learned earlier in the unit. You will need West Student Data Disk #7 and will use two files (MONSTERS and MYSTERY.TXT) from the C:\WESTDATA.DS6 subdirectory on your hard drive.

NOTE *Confirm with your instructor that the West Student Data Disk files are on drive C: in the \WESTDATA.DS6 directory. If they are stored elsewhere, you will need to modify the batch files accordingly.*

1. Place West Student Data Disk #7 in drive A:.

2. Type CLS and press [Enter].

3. Type DIR A: and press [Enter].

   Notice that only three files exist on West Student Data Disk #7: COMMAND.COM, AUTOEXEC.BAT, and MESSAGE.BAT.

4. Type EDIT A:JOKES.BAT and press [Enter].

5. Type the following text. Press [Enter] after each line.

```
@ECHO OFF
CLS
IF EXIST A:MONSTERS GOTO :DONTCOPY
COPY C:\WESTDATA.DS6\MONSTERS A:/V
:DONTCOPY
IF EXIST A:MYSTERY.TXT GOTO :COPYDONE
COPY C:\WESTDATA.DS6\MYSTERY.TXT A:/V
:COPYDONE
TYPE A:MONSTERS
PAUSE
CLS
TYPE A:MYSTERY.TXT
PAUSE
CLS
```

CHECKPOINT 11F What is the text ":DONTCOPY" called within a batch file?

Your screen should appear similar to Figure 11.7.

6. Save the document and then exit the DOS Editor.

7. Type A:JOKES and press [Enter] to invoke the JOKES.BAT batch file.

   The top of your screen will display the messages

```
1 file(s) copied
1 file(s) copied
```

FIGURE 11.7
*JOKES.BAT
batch file listing*

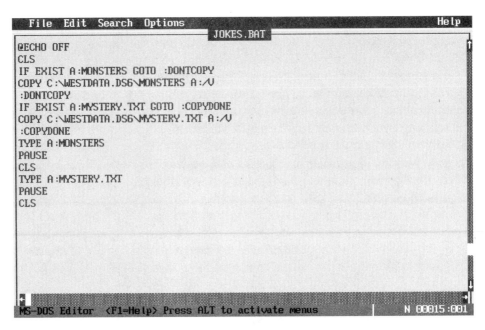

```
  File   Edit   Search   Options                              Help
                          JOKES.BAT
@ECHO OFF
CLS
IF EXIST A:MONSTERS GOTO :DONTCOPY
COPY C:\WESTDATA.DS6\MONSTERS A:/V
:DONTCOPY
IF EXIST A:MYSTERY.TXT GOTO :COPYDONE
COPY C:\WESTDATA.DS6\MYSTERY.TXT A:/V
:COPYDONE
TYPE A:MONSTERS
PAUSE
CLS
TYPE A:MYSTERY.TXT
PAUSE
CLS




MS-DOS Editor   <F1=Help> Press ALT to activate menus      N 00015:001
```

The two files MONSTER and MYSTERY.TXT were not found on the disk in drive A:, so the batch file copied them to that drive. Since @ECHO OFF began the batch file, the commands in the batch file were not echoed to the monitor screen. However, regular DOS messages, such as the "file(s) copied" message, are sent to the screen.

8. Press a key each time you are prompted.

9. Type A:JOKES again and press Enter.

    This time, since the two files have already been copied to drive A:, the files are not recopied. The "file(s) copied" message does not appear.

10. Press any key until the DOS prompt returns to the screen.

Using Replaceable Parameters in Batch Files

The BATCH command provides a set of variables for you to use in batch file programming. A variable is a programming device used to represent something else. Its value or what it represents may vary each time the variable is used. In earlier units, we discussed parameters, which modify a command. The DOS replaceable parameter is both a variable that represents something else, and also a parameter because it follows the batch file name just like a parameter follows a DOS command.

DOS provides ten replaceable parameters. Each begins with the percent sign and is numbered between 0 and 9, as follows:

%0	%5
%1	%6
%2	%7
%3	%8
%4	%9

The %0 parameter is limited; it can only represent the batch file's name and path. The others can represent any text you wish. In the following batch file, %1 and %2 are meant to represent file names. This batch file is called C.BAT and is used to save a few keystrokes when copying and then comparing files.

```
1:    COPY %1 %2/V
2:    PAUSE
3:    COMP %1 %2
```

To copy using the verify parameter and then compare the files, you would type the following.

```
C A:TESTFILE.DOC B:
```

The batch file would assume that the first text string following the batch file name was to be substituted for %1 and the second text string would substitute for %2. The batch file would then complete these commands, as follows:

```
COPY A:TESTFILE.DOC B:/V
PAUSE
COMP A:TESTFILE.DOC B:
```

In a simple INSTALL.BAT file, the replaceable parameters could be used to designate the drive containing the installation disk and the target disk. The following example uses %1 as the source drive and %2 as the target:

```
1:    @ECHO OFF
2:    CLS
3:    COPY %1*.* %2/V
```

If the batch file name is INSTALL.BAT, to copy the files from drive A: to the hard disk (C:), you would type

```
INSTALL A: C:
```

The Shifty BATCH Command

In most cases, ten replaceable parameters are more than enough in a batch file. However, anytime a limitation is imposed, someone finds a need to exceed that limitation. The SHIFT command is the DOS answer to the limitation. Each time the SHIFT command is used, the values of the ten variables "shift." For example, suppose you had a batch file called NUMBERS.BAT and entered the following command line:

```
NUMBERS 1 2 3 4 5 6 7 8 9 10 11 12 13
```

Without using the SHIFT command, the values of all the replaceable parameters would be

```
%0    NUMBERS.BAT
%1    1
%2    2
%3    3
```

```
%4      4
%5      5
%6      6
%7      7
%8      8
%9      9
```

The values 10 through 13 are lost. Here is the text of the NUMBERS.BAT file.

```
1:    @ECHO OFF
2:    CLS
3:    ECHO Variables equal %1 Through %9
4:    SHIFT
5:    ECHO Variables equal %1 Through %9
6:    SHIFT
7:    ECHO Variables equal %1 Through %9
8:    SHIFT
9:    ECHO Variables equal %1 Through %9
10:   SHIFT
```

The results of running this batch file would be the screen display shown in Figure 11.8. The SHIFT command on lines 4, 6, 8 and 10 causes the values stored by the replaceable parameters (%1 and %9) to change. The %1 parameter initially equals 1. The SHIFT command then causes it to take the second value entered (2). The next occurrence of the SHIFT command causes it to take the third value entered on the command line (3). The same process occurs for %9. It initially holds the value 9. After four shifts, it becomes equal to 12.

In the next Guided Activity, you will create this batch file and execute it.

FIGURE 11.8
The NUMBERS.BAT screen display using the SHIFT command

```
Variables equal 1 through 9
Variables equal 2 through 10
Variables equal 3 through 11
Variables equal 4 through 12
C:\>
```

GUIDED ACTIVITY 11.4

Shifting Variables

In this Guided Activity, you will create the batch file described in the previous section. It will accept more than nine values for the replaceable parameters and display their values to the screen.

1. West Student Data Disk #7 should still be in drive A: from the last activity.

2. Type EDIT A:NUMBERS.BAT and press [Enter].

3. Type the following text. Press [Enter] after each line.

```
@ECHO OFF
CLS
ECHO Variables equal %1 through %9
SHIFT
ECHO Variables equal %1 through %9
SHIFT
```

 CHECKPOINT 11G What kind of variable is %1?

4. Move the cursor under the E in the word ECHO on line 3.

5. Hold down Shift and press ⬇ 4 times to highlight the last four lines of the text file.

6. Select the Edit Copy command from the menu bar.

7. Press ⬇ once to deselect the highlighted block of text.

8. Select the Edit Paste command from the menu bar.

   The Edit Paste command copies lines 3 through 6 to the end of the file. The screen display should look like Figure 11.9.

FIGURE 11.9
Screen listing of NUMBERS.BAT file

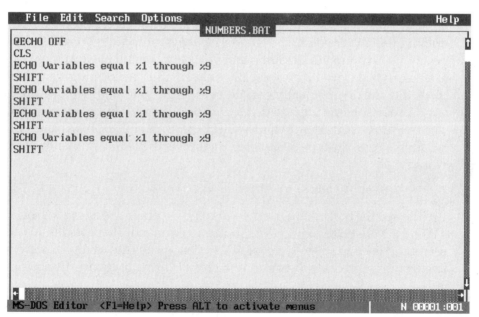

9. Save the file and then exit the DOS Editor.

10. Type CLS and press Enter.

NOTE *In the next step, be sure to include a space between each number.*

11. Type A:NUMBERS 1 2 3 4 5 6 7 8 9 10 11 12 13 and press Enter.

   The screen should look like Figure 11.8, earlier. The value 13 was not used in the batch file. One more SHIFT command would have been required.

Looping It Up in Batch Mode

The FOR command allows *iteration* or repetitive processing within a batch file. FOR is a powerful and complex BATCH command. It uses a set of variables, but not the ten replaceable parameters. Instead, the variables are preceded (in a batch file) by two percent signs and then a letter. For instance, any of the following are variables that may be used in a FOR statement.

```
%%A
%%B
%%C
%%D
...
%%X
%%Y
%%Z
```

The actual syntax of the FOR command is

```
FOR %%A IN (set) DO command
```

The %%A may be replaced by any variable between %%A and %%Z. The *set* is nothing more than a list. The IN and DO keywords are required. The *command* may be any DOS command. Assume that you have several backup files (with the .BAK extension) that must be periodically deleted after performing system backups. The .BAK files are automatically created every time you modify a document file in your word processor. You wish to delete the .BAK files for only five files, not all .BAK files. The five are ONE.BAK, TWO.BAK, THREE.BAK, FOUR.BAK, and FIVE.BAK.

In this case, the *command* to be executed is the DEL command. The command line would read

```
FOR %%A IN (ONE TWO THREE FOUR FIVE) DO DEL %%A.BAK
```

The set (the names in parentheses) is the list of file specifications including ONE, TWO, THREE, FOUR, and FIVE. The DEL command is repeated until each item in the set is used once as a substitute for %%A. That means the results of this one command line would be precisely the same as the results of the following five command lines.

```
DEL ONE.BAK
DEL TWO.BAK
DEL THREE.BAK
DEL FOUR.BAK
DEL FIVE.BAK
```

The complex FOR command line above is not just a more confusing version of

```
DEL *.BAK
```

Remember, our assumption is that other .BAK files exist on the target drive—files that are not to be deleted.

Let us examine one more example. Assume that each year, you create 12 new worksheet files for use as a series of budget worksheets. You have created a BUDGETMS.WS (budget master) worksheet. Now you want to create 12 identical worksheets, each with a different name. The following command in a batch file called NUMONTHS.BAT would accomplish the task.

```
FOR %%M IN (JAN FEB MAR APR MAY JUN JUL AUG SEP OCT NOV
DEC) DO COPY BUDGETMS.WS %%M.WS
```

Although this is not displayed above as a single line, it should be in the batch file. Can you figure out the results of executing this line? It will create 12 new files, each identical to BUDGETMS.WS except for their file names. The file names would be JAN.WS, FEB.WS, MAR.WS, APR.WS, MAY.WS, JUN.WS, JUL.WS, AUG.WS, SEP.WS, OCT.WS, NOV.WS, and DEC.WS.

To take the example one step further, this batch file could be used each year if the files were given distinctive names; that is, if the year could be incorporated into the file name. That could be accomplished by using a replaceable parameter. Here is a modified NUMONTHS.BAT file:

```
FOR %%M IN (JAN FEB MAR APR MAY JUN JUL AUG SEP OCT NOV
DEC) DO COPY BUDGETMS.WS %%M%1.WS
```

Although this is not displayed above as a single line, it should be in the batch file. The addition of the %1 variable allows you to enter the following command line:

```
NUMONTHS 94
```

The result is the creation of 12 files named JAN94.WS, FEB94.WS, MAR94.WS, APR94.WS, MAY94.WS, JUN94.WS, JUL94.WS, AUG94.WS, SEP94.WS, OCT94.WS, NOV94.WS, and DEC94.WS.

Notice that the replaceable parameter in a batch file is preceded by a single % while the FOR variable is preceded by a double %. If you place only a single % before the FOR variable in a batch file, DOS thinks it is a replaceable parameter—but when it cannot find the number 0 through 9 following the percent sign, DOS gets confused and gives you a "bad parameter reference" error.

A replaceable parameter cannot be used at the DOS prompt. It must be used within a batch file. The FOR command can be used in *immediate mode* (that is, when commands are executed immediately rather than in batch mode). However, when using the FOR variables in immediate mode, you must drop off one % sign. The earlier FOR command line listed in this unit could be entered at the DOS prompt as

```
FOR %M IN (JAN FEB MAR APR MAY JUN JUL AUG SEP OCT NOV DEC) DO COPY BUDGETMS.WS %M.WS
```

To give you some hands-on experience, you will execute a FOR command in batch mode as well as immediate mode in the next Guided Activity.

GUIDED ACTIVITY 11.5

Using the FOR Command in a Batch File

In this Guided Activity, you will create a batch file using the FOR command. First it will be used in batch mode to create seven duplicate files. Subsequently, you will use the FOR command in immediate mode to delete five of the seven files.

1. West Student Data Disk #7 should still be in drive A:.

2. Type CLS and press ⏎Enter.

3. Type EDIT A:FASTCOPY.BAT and press ⏎Enter.

CHECKPOINT 11H Must the FASTCOPY batch file end with a .BAT extension?

4. On the first line, type DIR A:*.DB and press ⏎Enter.

   When executed by the batch file, the DIR command will verify that no files with a .DB extension exist on the disk in drive A:.

5. Type PAUSE and press ⏎Enter.

6. Type FOR %%F IN (1 2 3 4 5 6 7) DO COPY C:\WESTDATA.DS6\FAMOUS.DB A:%%F.DB and press ⏎Enter.

NOTE *Be sure that both occurrences of %%F are either in uppercase or lowercase. They must match.*

   This FOR command will create seven duplicate copies of the FAMOUS.DB file (located in the C:\WESTDATA.DS6 subdirectory on your hard disk), but each will be given a numeric file name (1 through 7) with a .DB extension.

7. Type PAUSE and press ⏎Enter.

8. Type CLS and press ⏎Enter.

9. Type DIR A:*.DB and press ⏎Enter.

   When executed in the batch file, this DIR command will demonstrate that seven files now exist with a .DB extension on the disk in drive A:.

   Double-check each line of the batch file and correct any errors. Your screen should look like Figure 11.10.

10. Save the file and exit the DOS Editor.

11. Type A:FASTCOPY and press ⏎Enter.

    Notice that no files are found when the first DIR command is executed.

12. When prompted, press any key.

    The screen will show the COPY command activity invoked by the FOR command.

13. When prompted, press any key to continue.

    The second DIR command is executed, showing the newly created files. Seven files appear, 1.DB, 2.DB, 3.DB, 4.DB, 5.DB, 6.DB, and 7.DB.

FIGURE 11.10
Listing of FASTCOPY.BAT file

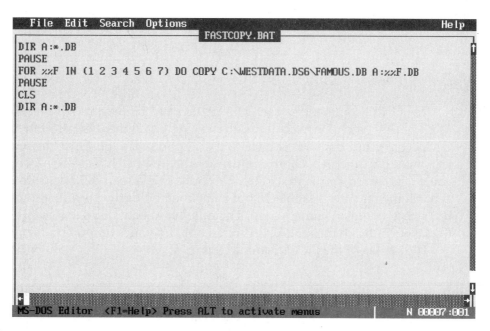

Now you can erase five of these seven files by using the FOR command in the immediate mode.

NOTE *Before pressing* [Enter] *in the next step, proofread the text entered to be sure it is correct.*

14. Type `FOR %F IN (1 2 3 5 7) DO DEL A:%F.DB` and press [Enter].

While this command is executing, the screen shows the deletion activity.

15. Type `DIR A:*.DB` and press [Enter].

FIGURE 11.11
DIR listing after using the FOR command to delete files

```
C:\>
C:\>FOR %F IN (1 2 3 5 7) DO DEL A:%F.DB

C:\>DEL A:1.DB

C:\>DEL A:2.DB

C:\>DEL A:3.DB

C:\>DEL A:5.DB

C:\>DEL A:7.DB

C:\>DIR A:*.DB

 Volume in drive A has no label
 Volume Serial Number is 183C-14DE
 Directory of A:\

4        DB        26 05-08-93    7:45p
6        DB        26 05-08-93    7:45p
        2 file(s)         52 bytes
                     1266688 bytes free

C:\>
```

Only two files remain, 4.DB and 6.DB. Your screen should look like Figure 11.11.

CALLing All Batch Files

The CALL command is used to execute a batch file from within another batch file. The first batch file executes until the CALL statement is encountered, then the CALL command transfers control to the second batch file. Once the second batch file is completely executed, control returns to the first batch file. The second batch file could call a third, or the first batch file could be made to call two different batch files. A batch file may even call itself, but some method of final termination should be built in, to avoid an endless loop. The number of batch files that may be called and the layers of batch files called is limited only by your computer's memory.

The syntax of the CALL command is

```
CALL [d:][path]filename
```

If the batch file called is not on the default drive, indicated by the DOS prompt, you must indicate the drive designation and path to the file. For instance, if the default drive is A: and the file TRYAGAIN.BAT is on drive C: in the \DOS directory, you would use the following CALL statement.

```
CALL C:\DOS\TRYAGAIN
```

In the following example, two batch files are used. The first, called FILE1.BAT, includes the following text:

```
1:    @ECHO OFF
2:    CLS
3:    ECHO This is FILE1.BAT
4:    ECHO:
5:    ECHO:
6:    CALL FILE2
7:    ECHO You're back in FILE1.BAT now.
```

The text in FILE2.BAT is

```
1:    @ECHO OFF
3:    ECHO This is FILE2.BAT
4:    ECHO:
5:    ECHO:
```

If the first batch file (FILE1.BAT) is executed, the screen would look like Figure 11.12.

FIGURE 11.12
Screen messages from executing FILE1.BAT, which calls FILE2.BAT

```
This is FILE1.BAT


This is FILE2.BAT


You're back in FILE1.BAT now.
A:\>
```

GUIDED ACTIVITY 11.6

The CALL Command

In this Guided Activity, you will create the two batch files described in the previous section.

NOTE *Occasionally, within this text we do not give you step-by-step instructions. Up to this point, you have used the EDIT command and should know how to create and edit a batch file. Without the step-by-step directions, create the following batch files.*

1. Be sure that West Student Data Disk #7 is still in drive A: from the last activity.

2. Both of the batch files created in the following steps should be saved on the disk in drive A:.

3. Log on to drive C:.

4. Create the batch file listed below. It should be given the file name A:FILE1.BAT.

```
@ECHO OFF
CLS
ECHO This is FILE1.BAT
ECHO:
ECHO:
CALL FILE2
ECHO You're back in FILE1.BAT now.
```

5. Create the batch file listed below. It should be given the file name A:FILE2.BAT.

TIP *Without quitting the DOS Editor, you can clear the screen and create a new text file, using the File New command.*

```
@ECHO OFF
ECHO This is FILE2.BAT
ECHO:
ECHO:
```

6. After creating and saving FILE1.BAT and FILE2.BAT, do a DIR listing to be sure they are on the disk in drive A:.

7. Clear the screen.

8. Type A:FILE1 and press [Enter] to invoke the first batch file.

Your screen should look like the display in Figure 11.13. Notice the "Bad command or file name" message. The first batch file is looking for FILE2.BAT on the default drive, or drive C:. However, the file is located on drive A: and is not found by DOS. To execute the batch files properly, you can either change the first batch file by including the drive and path in the CALL command, or change your default drive to A:.

9. Change your default drive to A:.

FIGURE 11.13
*Error message
when executing
FILE1.BAT*

```
This is FILE1.BAT


Bad command or file name
You're back in FILE1.BAT now.
C:\>
```

10. Clear the screen.

11. Type FILE1 and press [Enter].

The results are displayed in the earlier Figure 11.12. Go back and review the results in that illustration.

Configuration System File

The CONFIG.SYS file is read and executed even before the AUTOEXEC.BAT file. It is similar to a batch file. The text in the CONFIG.SYS file configures your system by referencing device drivers and invoking special DOS commands. In other words, the CONFIG.SYS file modifies the normal operation of the system. The CONFIG.SYS file must be in the root directory on your hard disk or floppy disk.

DOS commands often found in the CONFIG.SYS file include BREAK, BUFFERS, COUNTRY, DEVICE, FCBS, FILES, LASTDRIVE, and SHELL. Only four of these are discussed in this unit: BREAK, BUFFERS, DEVICE, and FILES.

The BREAK Command

The BREAK command simply tells DOS to respond to the [Ctrl][C] or [Ctrl][Break] key combinations as soon as possible. These key combinations terminate the execution of commands or processes prior to completion. To increase the frequency with which DOS scans for these keystrokes, the BREAK command is entered in the CONFIG.SYS file in the following form:

BREAK=ON

Normally, DOS only checks to see if [Ctrl][C] or [Ctrl][Break] have been pressed while

- Reading the keyboard

- Writing to the screen (console)

- Writing to the printer

  If you set BREAK to ON, DOS also monitors for [Ctrl][C] or [Ctrl][Break] while

- Reading from disk

- Writing to disk

The normal setting is for BREAK to be OFF. You can check for the current BREAK command status by entering the following command form at the DOS prompt.

```
BREAK
```

The BUFFERS Command

The BUFFERS command tells DOS how many memory buffers should be reserved in random access memory (RAM) when your computer system is booted. A *buffer* is a temporary storage area in RAM used by DOS to minimize the number of times DOS must read and write to your disk. Because the buffer is in internal memory (RAM), the data or code in a buffer can be accessed faster than data stored in external memory (on your disk). The use of buffers increases data access speed.

The BUFFERS command has one disadvantage—the greater the number of buffers reserved, the greater the amount of RAM used for this purpose. Each buffer uses 532 bytes of RAM, except for *look-ahead buffers* (also referred to as a *secondary buffer cache*), which use 512 bytes and are described later in this section. If RAM is used for buffers, it cannot also be used to load programs or data, such as word processing documents, worksheets, or databases. The amount of RAM, coupled with the needs of your application program, dictates the minimum and maximum number of buffers you can use. Most software programs will indicate in their documentation the minimum amount of RAM required to run the program and the number of buffers that should be set in the CONFIG.SYS file.

You can use from 1 to 99 buffers in regular memory. The default number of buffers is determined by a combination of the maximum disk drive size and available RAM. Table 11.2 indicates the default values.

TABLE 11.2
Default buffer configurations

SITUATION	NUMBER OF BUFFERS
Default (less than 128KB with 360KB disk)	2
Less than 128KB with a disk storing greater than 360KB	3
RAM equals 128KB to 255KB	5
RAM equals 256KB to 511KB	10
RAM equals 512KB to 640KB	15
Less than 40MB hard drive	20
40–79MB hard drive	30
80–119MB hard drive	40
Greater than 120MB hard drive	50

The syntax of the BUFFERS command is

```
BUFFERS=nnn[,L]
```

The number of buffers follows the equal sign. Remember, you are limited to 99 buffers.

The L following the number of buffers is replaced by the number of secondary buffer cache or look-ahead buffers. If you use this option, the number must be separated from the number of regular buffers by a comma. The secondary buffer cache can be used to speed up some disk operations on an 8088 or 8086 microprocessor. With faster microprocessors (80286, 80386, 80486, and Pentium) the SMARTDRV.SYS feature should be used instead of look-ahead buffers.

A look-ahead buffer allows DOS to read more than just the current cluster or allocation unit of data called by an application program. It is most effective when dealing with sequential files. If you choose to use look-ahead buffers, then DOS reads the data requested by the application plus the subsequent clusters assigned to the file. The assumption is made that if the application accesses record 5 (in a database) you will probably read records 6, 7, and 8 next. By asking your computer to read into memory the clusters that contain those records—in advance of the application's asking for the data—you speed up access time. When the application needs to access the data in the look-ahead buffers, it is already available in a buffer. The default number of look-ahead buffers is zero, but you can set it within the range of 1 to 8. Eight is the preferred setting.

The FILES Command

DOS makes an arbitrary decision on the number of files you will need to open at one time. DOS assumes that eight files open at the same time is a workable situation. With earlier versions of DOS, if you omit the FILES command from your CONFIG.SYS file, DOS uses the eight-file default. The eight-file limitation was not a hindrance in the past, but with more powerful applications, now it is. The install program for many applications will automatically increase the eight-file limit or give you instructions on how to do so.

The FILES command is the mechanism DOS uses to permit you to increase the number of allowable open files. The maximum allowable number ranges up to 255. The syntax of the command is

```
FILES=nnn
```

The most common setting would allow 30 open files. If you were to use that setting and allow 16 buffers, your CONFIG.SYS file would include the following text:

```
FILES=30
BUFFERS=16
```

Some application programs require more files and buffers than others. The above example is fairly typical of applications running under DOS 6.x. Once again, there is some overhead or memory consumption with the increase in the number of open files. It is not as great as the consumption caused by increasing the number of buffers. For every open file over the default value of eight, 64 bytes of RAM are required. If you set the FILES and BUFFERS commands too high, you may cut into the memory required to run your application program.

NOTE *The eight-file default may seem plentiful until you examine a common database application. It is not unusual for a DOS database manager to have several files open at the same time. For instance, a single database may include two or more data files, screen or layout files, index files for ordering the database, and one or more report definition files. If you work in the Windows environment, the problem is compounded because it is a common occurrence to have more than one application (a database, a word processor, a spreadsheet, and various utility programs) open at the same time.*

The values used for the FILES and BUFFERS commands are hardware based. Newer PCs using the 80386 or 80486 microprocessor usually need the BUFFERS and FILES values set higher. It is not unusual on these machines to set the values at 40 for most applications. If that were the case, the CONFIG.SYS file would include the following statements

```
FILES=40
BUFFERS=40
```

The DEVICE Command

The DEVICE command is entered in the CONFIG.SYS file to install specific device drivers. The syntax of the command is

```
DEVICE=[d:][path]filename[.ext]
```

Standard installable devices with MS-DOS and PC DOS include the following:

ANSI.SYS The ANSI.SYS device driver enables your system to use American National Standards Institute (ANSI) escape sequences. These sequences are used to define and modify functions for DOS. Among other functions, the ANSI escape sequences can modify screen colors (foreground and background), set screen width parameters, affect cursor movement, and redefine keyboard keys.

DISPLAY.SYS This device driver supports code page switching for the console.

DRIVER.SYS This device driver is used to give a physical drive a logical drive name. In the simplest terms, this driver is used to attach an external or additional floppy drive to your system and allow it to be referenced by a drive name such as A:, B:, C:, D:, or beyond.

PRINTER.SYS This driver supports code page switching for parallel ports.

RAMDRIVE.SYS This is the device driver that creates a RAM disk (also called a virtual drive). RAM disks are discussed in Unit 13.

SMARTDRV.SYS This device driver provides disk-caching for systems with a hard disk and expanded or extended memory.

Whenever you purchase a new peripheral like a mouse, monitor, or scanner, the manufacturer will often include a device driver that must be installed. Software that works in conjunction with emulation boards (to connect your PC to a mainframe and make it appear as a terminal) also require that a device driver be installed. For instance, the Intercom 1000+ developed by ICC Corporation uses a driver called ICC.DEV. To install this driver, you would add the following line to your CONFIG.SYS file

```
DEVICE=ICC.DEV
```

If the device driver file is not stored in the root directory of your bootable disk (hard disk or floppy), you must include in CONFIG.SYS the drive designation and the full path name to the driver file. The Microsoft mouse comes with a driver file named MOUSE.SYS. It may be stored in a MOUSE1 subdirectory on drive C:. To install this driver via the CONFIG.SYS file, you would need to enter in that file the command form

```
DEVICE=C:\MOUSE1\MOUSE.SYS
```

The most commonly installed driver is the ANSI.SYS file. If the driver is saved in the root directory of your bootable disk, the command is entered in the CONFIG.SYS file as

```
DEVICE=ANSI.SYS
```

GUIDED ACTIVITY 11.7

Viewing Your CONFIG.SYS File

In this Guided Activity, you will *view* the CONFIG.SYS file on your hard disk. *You do not want to modify it unless instructed to do so by your instructor.* You will only use the TYPE command to view the contents and check for either the FILES or BUFFERS command.

1. You should be logged on to drive C:.

2. Type CLS and press [Enter].

3. Type TYPE C:\CONFIG.SYS and press [Enter].

The contents of the CONFIG.SYS file will appear on your screen. A typical CONFIG.SYS file installed under DOS 6.x is displayed in Figure 11.14.

FIGURE 11.14
Typical CONFIG.SYS file

```
C:\>TYPE C:\CONFIG.SYS
DEVICE=C:\DOS\HIMEM.SYS
DEVICE=C:\DOS\EMM386.EXE /X=A000-C7FF NOEMS
buffers=15,0
files=30
DOS=UMB,HIGH
LASTDRIVE=Z
FCBS=16,0
DEVICEHIGH /L:2,12048 =C:\DOS\SETVER.EXE
DEVICEHIGH /L:2,22656 =\DEV\MDSCD_FD.SYS /D:MSCD000 /N:1
DEVICEHIGH /L:2,44592 =C:\DOS\DBLSPACE.SYS /MOVE
STACKS=9,256
DEVICEHIGH /L:1,9072 =C:\DOS\ANSI.SYS
DEVICE=C:\SB16\DRV\ASP.SYS /P:220

C:\>
```

Summary

In this unit, you have learned how to create batch files, such as the AUTOEXEC.BAT file, and how to interpret and modify the CONFIG.SYS file. You also discovered that any DOS command can be used in a batch file to automate repetitious tasks and that special BATCH subcommands also exist for use in batch files.

Command Review

In this unit, you learned about the BATCH subcommands and special commands used in the CONFIG.SYS file. Most have optional parameters. We have tried to cover both the common and the rarely used forms of each command. The following forms of this unit's commands are the most frequently used and should be reviewed carefully.

BREAK=ON	Causes DOS to monitor the keyboard for [Ctrl][C] or [Ctrl][Break] during disk access.
CALL	Executes a second batch file from within the current batch file.
DEVICE=ANSI.SYS	Installs the ANSI escape sequences.
FILES=30	Enables DOS to have up to 30 files open at one time. This command is used in the CONFIG.SYS file.
PAUSE	Causes a batch file to suspend execution until a key is pressed.
REM	Enables you to enter nonexecuting comments in a batch file. REM statements are used to document the workings of commands in a batch file.

Review Questions

1. Identify the extension required for all batch files.
2. If a file is named AUTOEXEC.BAT, how would you execute it?
3. Can DOS commands be used in a batch file? If so, why would they be used?
4. Name eight BATCH subcommands.
5. What is the purpose of batch processing?
6. In which directory must the AUTOEXEC.BAT file be located?
7. Can a batch file be stopped midstream? How?
8. When is the AUTOEXEC.BAT file executed?
9. What does the ECHO OFF command do?

10.   What does the ECHO: command do?

11.   What does the "ECHO Hi Joan—How are you today?" command do?

12.   Why would you use the REM command?

13.   What message appears when you execute the PAUSE command?

14.   Which BATCH command is used for decision making?

15.   Name four decision-making conditions that can be evaluated in a batch file.

16.   Which BATCH command must always be used with a label?

17.   How can you identify a label in a batch file?

18.   List three replaceable parameters.

19.   What is a variable?

20.   Which BATCH command permits you to use more than ten variables in a batch file?

21.   What would happen if you executed the following command at the DOS prompt?

```
FOR %S IN (JOAN JENNIFER JODI) DO DEL %S.DOC
```

22.   How would you execute the batch file GOODBYE.BAT from within a batch file named HELLO.BAT? Use the exact line of code.

23.   How many bytes of memory do three look-ahead buffers use?

24.   With DOS 6.*x*, what is the default number of buffers if you have 320KB of RAM?

25.   If you fail to use the FILES command, how many files can be open at one time?

26.   Where do you use the BUFFERS and FILES commands?

Exercises

Whenever instructed to format a disk, use your last name (first) and then your first name (such as BACON JON) as the volume label. If instructed to print data from the screen, be sure to write your full name, course number and section, course title, instructor's name, unit and exercise number, and today's date on the paper. Your instructor will indicate if the disk(s) created or printouts should be submitted for grading.

1.   Create a batch file to change the archive bit so that the file selected (use a replaceable switch) will be backed up the next time you create a differential or incremental backup using the MSBACKUP command—even if the file has not been modified. Call the batch file ARCIT.BAT.

2.   Create two batch files. One, called READONLY.BAT, marks a file as read-only. The second batch file, called READWRIT.BAT, should remove the read-only status from a specified file. In both cases use a replaceable switch.

3. Create a batch file that first copies all modified files from the C:\WESTDATA.DS6 directory to drive A: and then copies all files that exist in the C:\WESTDATA.DS6 directory to drive A:, but only if the files do not already exist on the disk in drive A:.

4. Assume that you are using WordPerfect 5.1 and the program files are stored in the directory C:\WP51. In that directory, you have your WordPerfect documents stored in a C:\WP51\WORDS directory. WordPerfect is invoked by typing WP at the DOS prompt. Create a batch file that changes to the WP51 directory, starts WordPerfect, and then (after exiting from WordPerfect back to DOS) displays the following message on your screen:

   ```
   If you do not want to back up your files
   press Ctrl-Break, otherwise insert a
   backup floppy in drive A:
   ```

   The batch file should end with three commands. First, use a DOS command to cause the batch file to pause until a key is struck. Second, use the XCOPY command to copy only modified files from the correct subdirectory to the disk in drive A:. Finally, use the appropriate DOS command to set the archive bits off on all files in the C:\WP51\WORDS subdirectory.

5. Copy the FORMAT command to a floppy disk. Rename the command XFORMAT.EXE. Create a batch file that causes only the disk in drive A: to be formatted when you type FORMAT.

6. Use EDIT to create a batch file named FORMAT.BAT that can be used to format a 3.5-inch low-density 720KB disk in a high-density A: drive. If your computer has only a high-density 5.25-inch drive, change the batch file to accommodate formatting a low-density 360KB disk in your high-density A: drive.

7. Create a batch file that creates a backup of a file (using COPY) only if that file does not exist on the backup disk in drive A:. Call the file NOT_ON_A.BAT.

8. Create a batch file that erases all backup files created by your word processor. Assume that the backup file has a .BAK extension. Call the file DELBAKUP.BAT.

9. Create a CONFIG.SYS file that establishes 25 buffers and 30 files.

10. Create a batch file that uses a single replaceable parameter in combination with the appropriate DOS commands to first create a new directory and then change to that new directory. The batch file should be named NEWDIR.BAT. At the DOS prompt, you should be able to create and then change to a new directory by typing, for example, NEWDIR \WP51.

11. Create a batch file that uses a single replaceable parameter in combination with the appropriate DOS commands to first delete all files in a directory and then remove the directory. The batch file should be named REMOVE.BAT. At the DOS prompt, you should be able to delete all the files and remove the directory by typing, for example, REMOVE \WP51\WORDS\LETTERS.

Key Terms

Batch file	Decision-making	Secondary buffer cache
BATCH mode	structure	Set
Batch processing	Immediate mode	Subroutine
Buffer	Iteration	Variable
Condition	Look-ahead buffer	
Continuous loop	Programming structure	

Documentation Research

Documentation Research questions are included at the end of most units to encourage you to explore and discover the additional features available with DOS 6.*x*. All Documentation Research questions within the text can be answered by using the on-line reference (accessed by using the HELP command). Review Guided Activity 2.8 if you are unsure how to use the HELP command.

1. List the DEFRAG command exit codes.

2. The SET command was not discussed in the text. What does it do?

3. Where is the SET command often used?

4. Name the separators that may not be used in the LABEL command parameter.

5. Which character, when placed at the beginning of a line in a batch file, causes DOS to ignore any commands on that line?

6. How would you display comments (incorporated using the REM command in a batch file) on the monitor screen?

Creating Batch Files

Creating the CONFIG.SYS and AUTOEXEC.BAT Files, Using the DOS Editor

In Unit 9, you learned to use the DOS Editor (EDIT) to create text files. In Unit 11, you discovered the uses of the CONFIG.SYS and AUTOEXEC.BAT files. In this application, you will build these two special text files, save them to disk, and turn the disk in to your instructor.

1. Create an AUTOEXEC.BAT file to accomplish the following tasks:

   - Prompt the operator to set the time.

   - Prompt the operator to set the date.

   - Change the system prompt to display *only* current drive, path, and a greater-than sign.

   - Cause the AUTOEXEC.BAT file *not* to display the DOS commands as executed.

   - Clear the screen at the beginning of the AUTOEXEC.BAT file.

   - Have AUTOEXEC.BAT invoke another batch file named MENU.BAT.

2. Create a CONFIG.SYS file to accomplish the following tasks:

   - Allow DOS to open 75 files at one time.

   - Allow DOS to use 25 regular buffers and 5 look-ahead buffers.

3. Submit the files to your instructor on a single disk. Be sure to write your name, course and section number, instructor's name, and today's date on the disk label.

Using the BATCH Subcommands to Display Text

In this application, you create a batch file to display the following text to the monitor screen, a page at a time.

1. Create a batch file with the file specification of UNTOLD.

2. Each of the messages given below must be displayed to the monitor screen when the UNTOLD batch file is executed.

3. The operator must be instructed to press a key after one message is displayed and before the next message appears on the screen.

4. After each message is displayed, the screen should be cleared.

5. The prompt to press a key (for the next message) must be eight lines below the end of the text of the message.

6. The message must begin three lines below the top of the monitor screen.

7. Remember, the following 11 messages must each appear on the monitor screen alone. The messages are:

```
There are some facts about life that most every adult knows.
Unfortunately, they never appear in textbooks so the young,
inexperienced life traveler often disbelieves them. Here, for
the first time, are the uncensored "Facts of Life."
```

```
Believe your Dad, life really isn't fair.
```

```
Despite your good table manners, excellent upbringing,
charming personality, sparkling intellectual brilliance, and
loveable style, not everyone you meet will love you, approve
of you, or even like you.
```

```
Occasionally during your life—despite advanced planning,
strategic action plans, and prayer—it will rain on your
parade.
```

```
When you least expect it, no matter how cautious and careful
you are, you will do something unbelievably stupid—and you
will remember it with a clarity that exceeds 20/20 vision.
```

```
Of course, there is hope. And believe it or not, charity.
Despite these "Facts of Life," only half the story has been
told.
```

```
As the survivors can attest, virtually all the bad stuff in
life can be endured and overcome. Many of the traumas and
tragedies are even useful—eventually.
```

```
Though you will find you are not as wonderful and marvelous as
you imagined, you're not nearly as terrible as you feared.
```

Unless you choose to hang around with terribly mean and
vicious people, no one will remember the dumb things you've
done.

Throughout your growing years, you may have felt duty bound to
render an opinion on everything from environmental protection
to the proper coordination of lipstick and blush hues. Please
be advised—you are not required to have an opinion on
everything.

One final interesting fact: I've yet to meet an adult who,
when given a choice, determined to go back to being a kid
again.

8. Submit the file to your instructor on a disk. Be sure to write your name, course
and section number, instructor's name, and today's date on the disk label.

Creating Multiple Subdirectories

In this application, you create a self-booting floppy disk with several subdirectories. The disk will also contain an AUTOEXEC.BAT file and several small batch files. Once your disk meets all the requirements listed below, submit it to your instructor.

1. Format a blank disk with the DOS system files. The disk must be bootable.

2. Create the following directories on the disk:

```
\BATCH              \1-2-3\DATA
\WORD\BOOK1         \DOS
\VENTURA            \UTIL\NU
```

3. Create an AUTOEXEC.BAT file that changes the current directory to \BATCH
each time the system is booted.

4. Be sure that the AUTOEXEC.BAT file also includes commands to prompt for current time and date and that it changes the system prompt to display the current
drive and directory followed by a greater-than sign.

5. Create four batch files and save them in the \BATCH subdirectory. The batch files
should be named 1-2-3, WORD, VENTURA, and NU. They should change the current directory to the directory named, execute the program (respectively, 1-2-3,
WORD, VENTURA, and NU), and then transfer back to the \BATCH directory.

You will not have the program files on your disk, so no program will be started.
However, your batch file should invoke the program as if it were on the disk.

6. Test the AUTOEXEC.BAT file by booting your system with the project disk in
drive A:. When done, remove the disk and reboot your personal computer.

7. Submit the disk to your instructor. Be sure to write your name, course and section number, instructor's name, and today's date on the disk label.

DOS Redirection, Pipes, and Filters 12

Learning Objectives

At the completion of this unit, you should be able to

1. list and define standard MS-DOS devices,

2. list and define the default DOS standard devices,

3. explain the difference between a serial port and a parallel port,

4. explain one use of the NUL: device,

5. define DOS redirection and give an example, using DOS commands,

6. redirect output to a new disk file,

7. append output to an existing disk file by using redirection,

8. explain the difference between pipes and filters,

9. list and use the DOS filters,

10. explain the switches that may be used with the SORT filter,

11. explain the switches that may be used with the FIND filter,

12. explain how the MORE filter is used,

13. discuss the ASCII collating sequence and how it affects the SORT filter.

Important Commands

FIND

MORE

SORT

Understanding Standard Devices on your Personal Computer

Despite covering a great deal of territory relative to DOS commands, we have yet to explore the area of **standard devices**. DOS permits us that luxury because it assumes that all activities use the two default devices, one input and the other output—until we instruct the machine otherwise.

The default device for normal input operations is referred to as the console, specifically the console keyboard. The default output device is also the console, specifically the monitor screen (terminal or workstation). Thus, the operating system looks to the console for both input and output unless instructed otherwise. As already implied, the keyboard and the display monitor compose the console. In DOS shorthand, the form of the parameter is simply "CON:". This parameter should look familiar because you used it in the COPY CON: command exercise.

As we consider additional standard devices, we must return to the basics of computing. What are standard input devices? What are standard output devices? The answer would include, in addition to the console, such items as a light pen, printer, modem, and disk drives. DOS is less concerned with the specific peripheral than it is with the method of interface. For DOS to accept input and send output to a peripheral, it makes available several standard devices known as **serial ports** or **parallel ports**. Serial ports are used to connect peripherals to your computer or to connect one PC to another. Parallel ports are most commonly used to connect a printer to your PC.

A parallel communications port on a PC is used to transmit eight bits over eight pins on the parallel cable simultaneously (that is, one byte at a time). Keep in mind that one byte equals one character, such as a number, letter, or special character. The transferral of the eight bits must be handled concurrently so that the eight bits represent the same character on the receiving end as they did on the transmitting end. Transmitted signals weaken over time and space and can get out of synchronization. For this reason, parallel printers are placed close to the computers they serve. Parallel cabling is usually no more than six to ten feet in length, otherwise you run the risk of distorting the data transmitted.

A serial port has the capability of transferring data one bit at a time over a cable. Thus, it requires eight transmissions to equal a single character (byte). Though the rate of data transmission is cut by one-eighth over short-range parallel transmissions, serial cabling can be run greater distances without encountering the problems faced by parallel communications.

With serial transmissions, the **baud rate** (speed of transmission) must be specified and the **parity** set as none, even, or odd. Serial printers must by synchronized to the same baud rate that the serial port is transmitting. Serial printers will include a table in their documentation, indicating the proper attributes required for communications with your PC. Serial ports are also commonly used for data communications from one PC to another using a modem. The most common form of serial transmission is RS-232.

FIGURE 12.1
Serial and parallel ports on a desktop personal computer

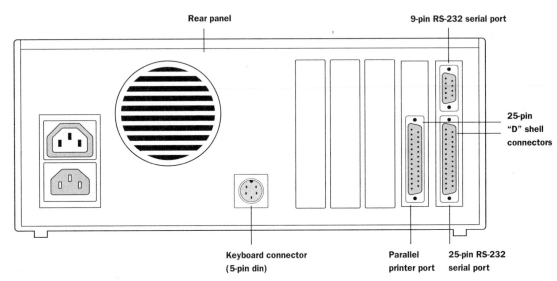

Rear panel

9-pin RS-232 serial port

25-pin "D" shell connectors

Keyboard connector
(5-pin din)

Parallel printer port

25-pin RS-232 serial port

The discussion of serial versus parallel communications is really a discussion of cabling requirements. Figure 12.1 shows the back of an IBM PC.

The figure shows five types of cable connections used to connect your PC to its peripherals. The 25-pin parallel connector and 25-pin serial (RS-232) connector are identified in the lower-right corner of the illustration. The newer PS/2 models and some PC AT compatibles now use a nine-pin serial port adapter similar to the nine-pin port identified in the upper-right corner of the figure (though that port is used for connection to the computer's monitor).

Returning to the discussion of standard devices, Table 12.1 indicates which type of port the listed peripherals use.

TABLE 12.1
Standard devices and peripherals

DEVICE	PORT
Light pen	Serial
Modem	Serial
Mouse	Serial or parallel
Network printer	Serial or parallel
Printer	Serial or parallel
Tape backup unit	Serial

Until the introduction of DOS 4.*x*, the IBM PC family of personal computers could only handle two serial and three parallel ports. DOS 4.*x* increased the number of available serial ports to four. To use these devices, the operating system must know how to address each.

The following list includes the DOS reserved words for each standard device. These terms may not be used as file names. They are specifically "reserved" as names for the devices indicated.

Keyboard	CON:
Monitor screen	CON:
Null device	NUL:
Parallel port #1	LPT1:
Parallel port #2	LPT2:
Parallel port #3	LPT3:
Serial port #1	COM1:
Serial port #2	COM2:
Serial port #3	COM3:
Serial port #4	COM4:

Two of the above standard devices have aliases. The following two standard devices may be referred to, using the reserved words listed below:

Parallel port #1	PRN:
Serial port #1	AUX:

It may be easier to remember the reserved words for standard devices if you know the root words from which they are derived:

AUX:	Auxiliary device
COM:	Communications port
CON:	Console
LPT:	Line printer
PRN:	Printer

Even though we have referred to each device name as ending with a colon, the colon is optional. For example, the line printer #1 may be called PRN or PRN: or LPT1 or LPT1:.

Each of the reserved words representing a device may substitute for a parameter in a DOS command (where a file name might otherwise be used). We'll explore several examples in which this is the case.

A note on the NUL: standard device may be helpful. Null means "amounting to nothing." Under DOS, the NUL: device is a nonexistent device. It does not exist, yet DOS does not return an error message because DOS recognizes it as an appropriate nonexistent device. Without using NUL:, DOS would return an error message indicating that the source or target device "does not exist."

NUL: is useful as a programmer's tool and can be used to substitute temporarily for an input or output device in the early stages of creating software. Further, NUL: can assist in the diagnosis of hardware and software problems. When a problem is encountered, the first step is to determine if the error is hardware- or software-related. By substituting NUL: for the input or output device stipulated in the software, a determination can be made on where the "bug" or problem is located. After substituting NUL:, if the program runs with the same errors, the problem is most likely software-related. If the program runs without errors after the NUL: substitution, the problem is with the input or output device that was replaced by NUL:.

Redirection of Standard Input and Output

The ability to redirect standard input and output (I/O) is built into DOS, enabling a program to accept input from a device or file other than the standard default device or file. The same principle applies to output. Earlier, we indicated that the console (CON:) is the default I/O device for DOS. If the default devices were always used, then all input for any program would be restricted to the keyboard. Further, only the monitor screen could receive output. Such a situation would limit the value of the computer because output could not be directed to a modem or printer. Further, input could not be accepted from a light pen, modem, graphic tablet, or any other peripheral. *Redirection* of standard input and output devices eliminates this restriction.

A specific example might help. The DIR command lists to the screen a directory of all files on a specified disk. For example, assume that a disk in drive A: holds the following files:

```
FORMLTR.DOC      ADDRESS.DBS
HMBUDGET.WS      FORMLTR.BDC
ADDRESS.DBF      HMBUDGET.BWS
ADDRESS.NDX
```

If the command DIR A: is entered via the keyboard, where does the standard input for the command come from? Where does the standard output go? The input for the command obviously comes from the disk in drive A:. DIR reads the directory table and displays the output (the list of files) to the console. In a literal sense, the command is

```
DIR A: CON
```

where A: indicates the standard input and CON: indicates the standard output. This syntax is inaccurate; it is shown only to explain that the output device is "understood" to be the console (specifically, the monitor screen).

Suppose it was important to obtain a complete listing of all files on a disk in printed form. With a short listing, like the example above, the [PrtSc] (print screen) key can be used. Suppose the disk includes 70–80 files. The solution is to redirect output from the DIR command to the printer. The symbol for DOS redirection is the greater-than or less-than sign (> or <).

To redirect the output from the DIR command to the printer, we would enter the following command:

```
DIR A:>PRN
```

Remember that PRN is an alias for LPT1:, so it is assumed that a printer is attached to parallel port #1. *With the exception of NUL:, it is important to always have a device (printer, modem, or the like) attached to the standard device indicated.* If output is redirected to a nonexistent device, the computer will freeze—at best. The results can be even more unpredictable.

Notice that the greater-than or less-than signs used to stipulate redirection serve as pointers indicating the flow of data. Consider the symbols as the head of an arrow. In the above example, the directory listing (input) is redirected from the A: drive to PRN (output destination), the parallel printer.

If the objective is to create a file in which the directory data can be stored, a slightly different version of the DIR command can be used:

```
DIR A:>B:FILELIST.DOC
```

NOTE *The redirection symbol (>) can be preceded and followed by an optional space. The redirection works either way.*

This command creates a new file on the disk in drive B: that stores all the directory data for files on the disk in the A: drive. In both of the examples, the console screen will not display the directory listing. The output has been redirected away from the monitor screen to another device (PRN) or to a file (B:FILELIST.DOC).

There may be occasions when you need to append data by redirection to an existing file. To understand how to accomplish the addition of new data to an old file, you must first understand how output redirection works. If a file is to be created via redirection, DOS first determines if a file with the same file name exists on the target drive. If it does not, DOS creates the file. However, if the file already exists, DOS sets the write pointer to the beginning of the existing file and, in effect, the old file is overwritten by the redirected data.

For example, if drive B: includes a file named FILELIST.DOC and you entered the command

```
DIR A:>B:FILELIST.DOC
```

then the data from the DIR command listing will be written to the FILELIST.DOC file and the previous data is overwritten without warning.

By using a double greater-than or less-than sign (>> or <<), the redirected data is appended to the file rather than overwriting it. The important point to remember is that simple redirection to a file (using > or <) will destroy an old file with the same file name. However, the append redirection symbol (using >> or <<) will add the new data to the end of the old file.

NOTE *When building batch files, you can use redirection with the NUL: standard device to avoid displaying DOS messages to the screen. For instance, if you were to copy three files during an installation program (INSTALL.BAT), the screen would display the three file names (as they were copied) and then the message "3 file(s) copied." To suppress any display to the screen, you could enter the command as*

```
COPY A:FILE?.TXT C: >NUL:
```

This assumes the three files are FILE1.TXT, FILE2.TXT, and FILE3.TXT.

GUIDED ACTIVITY 12.1

Redirecting DOS Input and Output

In this Guided Activity, you will first create West Student Data Disk #8 and then use it for the Guided Activities in this unit. You will then use the DOS redirection capability to redirect output from a DOS command (DIR) to a file, then will redirect that output to your printer.

1. Insert a blank formatted disk in drive A:.

NOTE *If the next step is unsuccessful, ask your instructor where the West Student Data Disk files are stored.*

2. Label the disk as West Student Data Disk #8 and then reinsert it in drive A:.

3. Type XCOPY C:\WESTDATA.DS6*.TXT A:/V and press Enter.

4. Log on to drive A:.

5. Type CLS and press Enter.

6. Type DIR and press Enter.

Nine files with the .TXT extension should now be on the disk. We have limited the number of files so that the text from the DIR command will be limited to a single screen. Your screen listing should appear similar to Figure 12.2.

FIGURE 12.2
DIR listing after copying .TXT files to data disk

```
A:\>DIR

 Volume in drive A has no label
 Volume Serial Number is 2232-1AD4
 Directory of A:\

BECOMING TXT          53 10-04-88    7:22p
MYSTERY  TXT          91 10-06-88    7:03p
SAYING   TXT         193 10-04-88    7:51p
PUBLISH  TXT         265 10-04-88    7:59p
TRUCKIN  TXT         719 07-13-89    8:11a
STRATS1  TXT        2056 10-19-91    3:15p
STRATS2  TXT        1908 10-19-91    3:15p
PAPER    TXT        1043 05-08-93   11:29a
WAR      TXT         121 01-18-94   11:19a
         9 file(s)         6449 bytes
                        1447936 bytes free

A:\>
```

7. Type CLS and press Enter.

8. Type DIR > A:FILELIST and press Enter.

The previous step generates a directory listing but then redirects it to a file called FILELIST on the disk in the A: drive.

9. Type DIR and press Enter.

FIGURE 12.3
*DIR listing with
the FILELIST file*

```
A:\>DIR > A:FILELIST

A:\>DIR

 Volume in drive A has no label
 Volume Serial Number is 2232-1AD4
 Directory of A:\

BECOMING TXT         53 10-04-88    7:22p
MYSTERY  TXT         91 10-06-88    7:03p
SAYING   TXT        193 10-04-88    7:51p
PUBLISH  TXT        265 10-04-88    7:59p
TRUCKIN  TXT        719 07-13-89    8:11a
STRATS1  TXT       2056 10-19-91    3:15p
STRATS2  TXT       1908 10-19-91    3:15p
PAPER    TXT       1043 05-08-93   11:29a
WAR      TXT        121 01-18-94   11:19a
FILELIST            579 07-24-93    7:22p
       10 file(s)       7028 bytes
                     1445888 bytes free

A:\>
```

Figure 12.3 displays the screen response. Notice that a new file resides on your West Student Data Disk #8. The date and time portion of the directory listing will correspond to the date and time maintained by your computer when the file was created. If using DOS 6.0, the file is 579 bytes in size. If using DOS 6.2, the FILELIST file is 627 bytes because of the addition of commas in numbers.

10. Type TYPE A:FILELIST and press [Enter].

Your screen will display the complete directory listing (created by the DIR command) stored earlier in FILELIST.

FILELIST was created by the redirection of input from the default standard device—that is, the console—to a file created to store the directory listing. When DOS initially creates FILELIST, it is an empty file (0 bytes long) as shown in Figure 12.4. The DOS DIR command, if invoked prior to completion of the redirection, would list the 0 byte size. After the redirection is complete, the file is closed and DOS records (in the disk directory) the true size of the newly created file as shown in Figure 12.3.

The output redirected to FILELIST can now be redirected to the printer, using the TYPE command and DOS redirection.

11. Be sure your printer is turned on, the paper is loaded, and the first sheet is set to the top of the page.

12. Type TYPE A:FILELIST > PRN and press [Enter].

✓ CHECKPOINT 12A Indicate where the output of the TYPE command is redirected in the last step.

13. Redirect the DIR command listing for the C:\WESTDATA.DS6 directory to a file named A:FILES.TXT.

14. Type DIR A: and press [Enter] to check that the file was created.

FIGURE 12.4

*File list
generated by
redirection of
FILELIST*

```
WAR      TXT       121 01-18-94   11:19a
FILELIST           579 07-24-93    7:22p
         10 file(s)         7028 bytes
                         1445888 bytes free


A:\>TYPE A:FILELIST

 Volume in drive A has no label
 Volume Serial Number is 2232-1AD4
 Directory of A:\

BECOMING TXT        53 10-04-88    7:22p
MYSTERY  TXT        91 10-06-88    7:03p
SAYING   TXT       193 10-04-88    7:51p
PUBLISH  TXT       265 10-04-88    7:59p
TRUCKIN  TXT       719 07-13-89    8:11a
STRATS1  TXT      2056 10-19-91    3:15p
STRATS2  TXT      1908 10-19-91    3:15p
PAPER    TXT      1043 05-08-93   11:29a
WAR      TXT       121 01-18-94   11:19a
FILELIST             0 07-24-93    7:22p
         10 file(s)         6449 bytes
                         1445888 bytes free

A:\>
```

GUIDED ACTIVITY 12.2

Redirecting Input for a DOS Command

In this Guided Activity, you create two files. The first, INPUTS, contains only two carriage returns (created by pressing the Enter key). It will be redirected to help execute two DOS commands (DATE and TIME). The second file, STATUS.BAT, redirects the output from three commands (DATE, TIME, and CHKDSK) to a text file (STATUS.TXT) and then types the results to the screen. Each time the STATUS.BAT file is executed, the results are appended to STATUS.TXT.

1. Be sure that West Student Data Disk #8 is in drive A: and log on to that drive.

2. Type CLS and press Enter.

3. Type EDIT A:INPUTS and press Enter.

4. Press Enter twice.

   These are the only keystrokes in this file and they will be used to accept the default date and time displayed by the DATE and TIME commands in the STATUS.BAT file.

5. Save the file and close it.

6. Use EDIT to create the following batch file (on the disk in drive A:), using the name STATUS.BAT. Double-check to be sure the file is entered correctly before exiting from EDIT.

```
DATE<INPUTS>>STATUS.TXT
TIME<INPUTS>>STATUS.TXT
CHKDSK>>STATUS.TXT
TYPE STATUS.TXT
```

7. When done, save the file and exit the DOS Editor.

8. Type STATUS and press [Enter].

Notice the display from using the TYPE command. Your screen should appear similar to Figure 12.5.

FIGURE 12.5
Screen response after executing the STATUS.BAT batch file

```
A:\>TIME<INPUTS>>STATUS.TXT

A:\>CHKDSK>>STATUS.TXT

A:\>TYPE STATUS.TXT
Current date is Sat 07-24-1993
Enter new date (mm-dd-yy):
Current time is  7:24:44.01p
Enter new time:
Volume Serial Number is 1B6B-1904

   1457664 bytes total disk space
     14848 bytes in 14 user files
   1442816 bytes available on disk

       512 bytes in each allocation unit
      2847 total allocation units on disk
      2818 available allocation units on disk

    655360 total bytes memory
    603440 bytes free

A:\>
A:\>
```

NOTE *If your screen displays a directory, it means you probably have Delete Sentry loaded and the directory is C:\SENTRY. You may also have more files listed.*

In the next step, you reexecute the STATUS.BAT file. The text file (STATUS.TXT) is twice as long and stores data regarding the disk in drive A: that reflects both executions of the batch file.

9. Type STATUS and press [Enter].

Pipes and Filters—DOS Building Blocks

In home construction, pipes are used to convey material (gas, air, water) from one location to another. Filters, on the other hand, are used to alter material passing through the home. A furnace filter eliminates dust from the forced-air system; thus, it alters the material (air) being piped throughout the house.

DOS pipes and filters function in parallel ways. Piping allows the output from one program or command to be used as the input for another program or command. In a sense, it directs the standard output to become the input for another operation. The programs or commands become chained together. A pipe is indicated using the | character. For clarification, there is a difference between piping and redirection. Piping can serve as a connection between DOS commands, that is, output from the first command becomes the input for the second command. It can also connect programs or subroutines. Redirection only deals with devices. The output of data may be redirected to the printer, a modem, or the console. You cannot redirect data to another DOS command.

The DOS piping operation creates one or more temporary files in the root directory of the default drive. DOS 2.0 names these files %PIPEx.$$$, where x is an integer. DOS versions 3.0 and higher create files using an eight-digit hexadecimal number based on output from the PC's internal clock. It is important that these files not be erased until the piping operation is complete.

DOS filters accept data from standard input sources and then modify the data. The three standard DOS filters are SORT, MORE, and FIND.

The SORT Filter

The most commonly used and easily understood filter is the SORT command. SORT is an external DOS command that manipulates text data that it receives as input and then outputs the data in sorted form. With DOS 2.x and earlier versions, the sort is performed using the ASCII collating sequence. Beginning with DOS 3.x, a modified ASCII collating sequence is used.

In the ASCII collating sequence, each alphabetical and numerical character is assigned a binary value. There are significant differences between the ASCII text sort and a regular alphabetic or numeric sort. The left column below lists selected characters in random order, while the right column lists the same characters after an ASCII text sort such as would be generated by DOS 2.x or earlier:

Random Elements	DOS 2.x Sort
junk5mail	#
20	%
z	1
Apple	10
710	101
APPLE	20
Zoo	710
10	99
junkmail	APPLE
1	Apple
junk mail	Zoo
101	apple
99	junk mail
%	junk5mail
apple	junkmail
#	z

By examining the above example, you will see that the ASCII text sort more closely approximates an alphabetic rather than numeric sort. However, the results are still puzzling until you recognize that uppercase alphabetic characters are considered completely different characters than lowercase characters. Thus the letter "a" follows the letter "Z" in this type of sort. Characters are evaluated beginning with the left-most character unless directed otherwise. Numbers are not necessarily put in numeric order. Remember, each character place is assigned an ASCII value and then sorted based on that value. The range of values is outlined in Table 12.2.

TABLE 12.2
ASCII character groupings used in sorts

CHARACTER(S) (IN ASCII COLLATING SEQUENCE)
space (considered as a character)
special characters (@, #, $, %, ^, &, etc.)
numbers (in ascending order: 0, 1, 2, 3, 4, 5, 6, 7, 8, 9, etc.)
uppercase letters (A, B, C, D, E, F, G, H, etc.)
lowercase letters (a, b, c, d, e, f, g, h, etc.)

Each special character and each nonprinting character (Shift, Ctrl, Alt) is assigned an ASCII value. If the ASCII text sort is not understood, then the DOS 2.*x* SORT filter will generate some unexpected results.

Effective with DOS 3.1, a modification was made to the sort based on binary values. The ASCII collating sequence is still used, with one exception. Lowercase letters a–z were given equal value to uppercase letters A–Z. Table 12.3 demonstrates the effect of the different sorts.

TABLE 12.3
Examples of DOS sorts

RANDOM ELEMENTS	DOS 2.*x* SORT	DOS 3.*x* SORT
APPLE	APPL	APPL
APPL	APPLE	APPLE
apple	LIME	apple
orange	apple	LIME
LIME	orange	orange

For the duration of our discussion of the SORT filter, you should assume use of modified ASCII collating sequence used by DOS 3.1 or higher.

In a previous example, we wrote directory information from a disk directly to the printer. That command form was

```
DIR A:>PRN
```

NOTE *When using the redirection character, a space before and after the greater-than sign is optional.*

For the next few examples, we'll expand the file listing from an earlier example to include the following directory listing:

```
FORMLTR    DOC    14496    10-22-86    8:12p
HMBUDGET   WS     11717    9-14-85     12:47a
ADDRESS    DBF    98373    8-15-86     10:30p
ADDRESS    NDX    963      8-15-86     10:30p
ADDRESS    DBS    1123     8-15-86     10:30p
FORMLTR    BDC    13888    10-09-86    7:22p
HMBUDGET   BWS    9124     8-13-85     1:05p
```

The command used to generate a random listing of files could be modified to print an ASCII text sorted directory. Assuming that the A: drive is the default drive, the command would be entered as

```
DIR|SORT>PRN
```

This command takes the output from the DIR command and "pipes" it with the | character to the SORT filter. The filter in turn modifies the directory listing into an alphabetical sort. The results are then redirected (>) to the printer (PRN), which (if turned on) would produce a paper copy of the directory listing. If the default drive were not A:, then the command would be entered as

```
DIR A:|SORT>PRN
```

Either command would generate a printed report like the following:

```
ADDRESS    DBF    98373    8-15-86     10:30p
ADDRESS    DBS    1123     8-15-86     10:30p
ADDRESS    NDX    963      8-15-86     10:30p
FORMLTR    BDC    13888    10-09-86    7:22p
FORMLTR    DOC    14496    10-22-86    8:12p
HMBUDGET   BWS    9124     8-13-85     1:05p
HMBUDGET   WS     11717    9-14-85     12:47a
```

The SORT Switches

The SORT filter includes two optional switches. First, the sort can be created in reverse ASCII text sort order, that is, 9 is sorted before 1 and Z before A. The syntax of the command would be

```
SORT/R
```

The second SORT switch stipulates the column on which the sort will begin. Without this switch, DOS assumes the sort to begin in column 1. The syntax of the second switch is

```
SORT/+n
```

where n represents an integer.

The directory listing generated by the DIR command lists bits of data beginning in specific columns. Beginning column numbers for each bit of data are listed in Table 12.4.

DATA	COLUMN NUMBER
File name	1
Extension	10
File size	14
Date created	24
Time created	34

By knowing the beginning column locations, you may specify the output of the DIR command to be sorted by file name, extension, file size, date created, or time created. Though it may not be very helpful, a directory of files by creation date in reverse ASCII text sort order may be generated by using the command form

```
DIR A:|SORT/R/+24>PRN
```

A slightly more useful form would be to sort by file size, using

```
DIR A:|SORT/+14>PRN
```

It should be noted that if you sort by column 24 (Date created) or 34 (Time created), the sort is not in chronological order. Rather, the sort treats the data as a text string and sorts according to the ASCII collating sequence. For example, the following dates are in ASCII order but not chronological order.

```
01-01-89
01-02-88
01-05-88
01-06-88
03-24-87
```

Likewise, the following times are in ASCII collating sequence order, but not in chronological order. Remember that the ASCII sort starts with the left-most character and works to the right while ordering them. Therefore, in the above list, the 01 (first two columns) is evaluated before the 87 or 88 (last two columns) is ever reached. In the following list, the hour is evaluated and sorted before the a.m. (a) or p.m. (p) is ever reached:

```
1:00a
1:29a
2:16p
2:19a
3:18p
6:39a
```

The MORE Filter

Included in the discussion of the DIR command (in Unit 2) was the /P switch. Remember that it displays a directory listing one screen at a time. After displaying a page of text, the command pauses until you strike a key. The MORE filter provides the same functionality for a variety of DOS commands. MORE displays data from the standard input device in blocks of one page (one screen). After displaying a full page of output, the message "—More—" appears at the bottom of the screen. Pressing any key causes the next page of text to scroll onto the screen. The process continues until all subsequent pages of data have been displayed.

In Unit 9, the TYPE command, which displays the contents of an ASCII text file, was also discussed. A common problem encountered with the TYPE command is that text from long text files scrolls off the screen before it can be read. A practical solution is to use the TYPE command in combination with the MORE filter. The following command displays one full screen of the text file LETTER.TXT at a time:

```
TYPE LETTER.TXT|MORE
```

Another useful situation for the MORE filter is in combination with the CHKDSK command when using the /V switch. The CHKDSK/V command checks each file and displays the file name and its path. When this command is executed on a hard disk or a floppy disk with numerous files, the data scrolls off the screen before you can read it. When you combine CHKDSK/V with the MORE filter, you can view one full screen of data at a time. To execute the command on drive C:, the command would be

```
CHKDSK C:/V|MORE
```

GUIDED ACTIVITY 12.3

Using the SORT and MORE Filters

In the last Guided Activity, you created a file called FILELIST. Since the DOS files are typically installed on your hard disk in alphabetical order, this activity will use the SORT filter coupled with the FILELIST file to list DOS external commands in reverse alphabetical order.

1. Be sure West Student Data Disk #8 is in drive A:, then log on to that drive.

2. Type TYPE FILELIST and press [Enter].

   The files are not in alphabetical order.

3. Type CLS and press [Enter].

4. Type TYPE FILELIST|SORT and press [Enter].

CHECKPOINT 12B What is the | symbol called?

You should see a list of files like that shown in Figure 12.6.

TIP *For the next step, you can quickly reenter the last command stored in the keyboard buffer by pressing [F3]. Then you can type / R and press [Enter], which saves several keystrokes.*

FIGURE 12.6

Screen display using alphabetical sort on FILELIST file

```
A:\>TYPE FILELIST!SORT


                           1445888 bytes free
              10 file(s)        6449 bytes
      Directory of A:\
      Volume in drive A has no label
      Volume Serial Number is 2232-1AD4
      BECOMING TXT        53 10-04-88   7:22p
      FILELIST             0 07-24-93   7:22p
      MYSTERY  TXT        91 10-06-88   7:03p
      PAPER    TXT      1043 05-08-93  11:29a
      PUBLISH  TXT       265 10-04-88   7:59p
      SAYING   TXT       193 10-04-88   7:51p
      STRATS1  TXT      2056 10-19-91   3:15p
      STRATS2  TXT      1908 10-19-91   3:15p
      TRUCKIN  TXT       719 07-13-89   8:11a
      WAR      TXT       121 01-18-94  11:19a

      A:\>
      A:\>
```

5. Type TYPE FILELIST|SORT/R and press [Enter].

   You should see a reverse-sorted list, as in Figure 12.7.

NOTE *We used the TYPE command rather than actually using a DIR command. Almost the same result would be generated by the next few steps. Be sure that you understand the difference.*

6. Type CLS and press [Enter].

7. Type DIR|SORT and press [Enter].

FIGURE 12.7

Screen display using reverse alphabetical sort on FILELIST file

```
      TRUCKIN  TXT       719 07-13-89   8:11a
      WAR      TXT       121 01-18-94  11:19a

      A:\>
      A:\>TYPE FILELIST!SORT/R
      WAR      TXT       121 01-18-94  11:19a
      TRUCKIN  TXT       719 07-13-89   8:11a
      STRATS2  TXT      1908 10-19-91   3:15p
      STRATS1  TXT      2056 10-19-91   3:15p
      SAYING   TXT       193 10-04-88   7:51p
      PUBLISH  TXT       265 10-04-88   7:59p
      PAPER    TXT      1043 05-08-93  11:29a
      MYSTERY  TXT        91 10-06-88   7:03p
      FILELIST             0 07-24-93   7:22p
      BECOMING TXT        53 10-04-88   7:22p
      Volume Serial Number is 2232-1AD4
      Volume in drive A has no label
      Directory of A:\
              10 file(s)        6449 bytes
                           1445888 bytes free


      A:\>
      A:\>
```

8. Type DIR|SORT/R and press Enter.

9. Type DIR C:\WESTDATA.DS6|SORT and press Enter to list and sort the files in the C:\WESTDATA.DS6 directory.

   In the preceding step, the directory listing scrolls off the screen. The MORE filter can be used to generate one page of screen display at a time. You must then press any key to proceed to the next page of screen display.

10. Type DIR C:\WESTDATA.DS6|SORT|MORE and press Enter.

11. Each time the "—More—" prompt appears at the bottom of the screen, press any key—until the DOS prompt returns.

12. Type DIR C:\WESTDATA.DS6|SORT/R|MORE and press Enter.

13. Again, each time the "—More—" prompt appears at the bottom of the screen, press any key—until the DOS prompt returns.

    Next, you will sort using the column switch in the next two steps. Column 14 is the beginning of the file size data (in bytes) from the directory.

14. Type CLS and press Enter.

15. Type TYPE A:FILELIST|SORT/+14 and press Enter.

    In the following steps, you will redirect the output from the SORT filter to a printer.

16. Be sure your printer is turned on, the paper loaded, and the first sheet set to the top of the page.

17. Type TYPE A:FILELIST|SORT/+14>PRN and press Enter.

    The printed report will list the same files as shown in the Figure 12.8 screen dump.

FIGURE 12.8
Report generated by sorting FILELIST based on file size

```
A:\>TYPE A:FILELIST|SORT/+14


FILELIST                 0 07-24-93    7:22p
                      1445888 bytes free
BECOMING TXT            53 10-04-88    7:22p
MYSTERY  TXT            91 10-06-88    7:03p
WAR      TXT           121 01-18-94   11:19a
SAYING   TXT           193 10-04-88    7:51p
PUBLISH  TXT           265 10-04-88    7:59p
TRUCKIN  TXT           719 07-13-89    8:11a
PAPER    TXT          1043 05-08-93   11:29a
STRATS2  TXT          1908 10-19-91    3:15p
STRATS1  TXT          2056 10-19-91    3:15p
  Directory of A:\
        10 file(s)        6449 bytes
  Volume in drive A has no label
  Volume Serial Number is 2232-1AD4

A:\>
A:\>
```

During the remainder of this Guided Activity, you will experiment with the SORT option by using a different directory listing of the DOS commands on your hard disk and observing the results. The text assumes the files are stored in C:\DOS. If they are located elsewhere, change the commands appropriately.

18. Type `DIR C:\DOS|SORT` and press Enter.

19. Type `DIR C:\DOS|SORT/R` and press Enter.

20. Type `DIR C:\DOS|SORT/+14` and press Enter.

21. Type `DIR C:\DOS|SORT/R/+14` and press Enter.

The FIND Filter

The third and final DOS filter is the FIND command. The FIND filter seeks occurrences of a specific text string in one or more specified files. The syntax of this external DOS command follows.

```
FIND "textstring" [d:][path][filename.ext]
```

If we sought to locate all occurrences of the phrase "Strategic Defense Initiative" in a file called EINSTEIN.DOC on the A: drive, then the command would be executed as

```
FIND "Strategic Defense Initiative" A:EINSTEIN.DOC
```

Without adding one of three possible switches, the results would duplicate each line in which the text string appears. The results would appear as shown in Figure 12.9.

FIGURE 12.9
Results of FIND filter

```
C:\>FIND "Strategic Defense Initiative" A:EINSTEIN.DOC

---------- A:EINSTEIN.DOC
writing to you regarding a program called "Strategic Defense Initiative."
Yes, "Strategic Defense Initiative" is the same as what has affectionately
cannot support "Strategic Defense Initiative" as it is currently defined.

C:\>
```

It is important to note that the FIND filter is case-sensitive. The text string used as a parameter for the filter must be identical to the text sought. In other words, "Strategic Defense Initiative" will not match with "strategic defense initiative" or even "Strategic defense Initiative"—unless you use the /I switch to ignore case. The text string in the command form must be enclosed in quotation marks.

Examine the following two text phrases. Assume this text is part of a document named A:EINSTEIN.DOC.

```
1:    I was initially opposed to the Strategic Defense Initiative.
2:    However, Warthog's fine expose of SDI in the article
3:    "Strategic Defense Initiative" changed my mind.
```

When you use the command form

```
FIND "Strategic Defense Initiative" A:EINSTEIN.DOC
```

DOS locates both occurrences of Strategic Defense Initiative (lines 1 and 3). You cannot use the FIND filter to locate text within the document that is enclosed in quotation marks. The following command form is incorrect and would return the error message "Parameter format not correct."

```
FIND ""Strategic Defense Initiative"" A:EINSTEIN.DOC
```

Multiple files may be searched using a single FIND command. If you seek all occurrences of "Strategic Defense Initiative" in files named EINSTEIN.DOC, STARWARS.TXT, and SDI.DOC, the command would take the form of

```
FIND "Strategic Defense Initiative" A:EINSTEIN.DOC A:SDI.DOC A:STARWARS.TXT
```

The resulting screen display might appear as shown in Figure 12.10, assuming that the text string appears in EINSTEIN.DOC and STARWARS.TXT but not in the SDI.DOC file.

FIGURE 12.10
Results of FIND filter search through multiple files

```
C:\>FIND "Strategic Defense Initiative" A:EINSTEIN.DOC A:SDI.DOC A:STARWARS.TXT

---------- A:EINSTEIN.DOC
writing to you regarding a program called "Strategic Defense Initiative."
Yes, "Strategic Defense Initiative" is the same as what has affectionately
cannot support "Strategic Defense Initiative" as it is currently defined.

---------- A:SDI.DOC

---------- A:STARWARS.TXT
The technical title is "Strategic Defense Initiative."
More often the "Strategic Defense Initiative" is referred to as "STARWARS" by

C:\>
```

Unfortunately, global file name characters such as the asterisk and question mark cannot be used in file names or extensions with the FIND filter. This is a severe limitation, particularly when you are searching through numerous files that might include the sought-after text string. Utility programs from third-party vendors enable you to perform such global searches.

The FIND Filter Switches

The FIND command has four switches. They are as follows:

/N Lists the relative line number of each line containing the text string.

/C Counts the number of lines containing the text string.

/V Lists the lines in the file that do not contain the text string.

/I Ignores case when searching for the text string.

Without adding one of these switches, FIND lists each line of text that contains the desired text string. If no occurrences of the text string have been found, the display will list the file name but nothing else. At times, knowing the relative line number is helpful. The /N switch lists the relative line number at the beginning of the line in which the text string appears. When determining the relative line number, DOS begins counting at the first line in the file. Blank lines are also counted. Figure 12.11 is an example of the listing created using the /N switch.

```
C:\>FIND/N "Strategic Defense Initiative" A:EINSTEIN.DOC

---------- A:EINSTEIN.DOC
[17]writing to you regarding a program called "Strategic Defense Initiative."
[24]Yes, "Strategic Defense Initiative" is the same as what has affectionately
[35]cannot support "Strategic Defense Initiative" as it is currently defined.

C:\>
```

The basic FIND command without any switches searches the named file(s) for lines of text that include the specified text string. The process is reversed when you use the /V switch. The command

```
FIND/V "bombardment" LETTER.TXT LETTER3.DOC
```

lists to the monitor screen lines in the files LETTER.TXT and LETTER3.DOC that do not include the word "bombardment."

If you seek to find "bombardment" whether it is in upper- or lowercase, you would use the /I switch to ignore case. The command would appear as shown below:

```
FIND/I "bombardment" LETTER.TXT LETTER3.DOC
```

The final switch is the /C or "count" switch. Rather than displaying the lines containing the text string, the /C switch displays the number of lines that include the text string. If we modify the command used to find occurrences of "Strategic Defense Initiative" to generate only a line count, the command would be

```
FIND/C "Strategic Defense Initiative" A:EINSTEIN.DOC A:SDI.DOC A:STARWARS.TXT
```

The screen display would appear as shown in Figure 12.12.

```
C:\>FIND/C "Strategic Defense Initiative" A:EINSTEIN.DOC A:SDI.DOC A:STARWARS.TX
T

---------- A:EINSTEIN.DOC: 3

---------- A:SDI.DOC: 0

---------- A:STARWARS.TXT: 2

C:\>
```

While the /V, /I, and /N switches may be combined, the count (/C) switch cannot be combined with any other switch on a single execution of the FIND command. If /C is used, the other switches are ignored.

NOTE *The switches used with the FIND command can immediately follow the command on the command line, or can be placed at the end of the command line. For example, the following two commands are equal:*

```
FIND/C "good news" NEWSRPT.TXT
FIND "good news" NEWSRPT.TXT/C
```

GUIDED ACTIVITY 12.4

Using the FIND Filter

In this Guided Activity, you will examine the STRATS1.TXT text file (already on West Student Data Disk #8), using the FIND filter to locate occurrences of specific words within the file.

1. Be sure that West Student Data Disk #8 is in drive A: and you are logged on to that drive.

2. Type CLS and press [Enter].

3. Type EDIT STRATS1.TXT and press [Enter].

4. Read the file so that you are familiar with its contents.

5. Exit the DOS Editor without saving the file.

6. At the DOS prompt, type FIND "successful" STRATS1.TXT and press [Enter].

   The search conducted by the FIND filter will display the messages shown in Figure 12.13. Only one occurrence was found.

FIGURE 12.13
Results of FIND search for "successful"

```
A:\>FIND "successful" STRATS1.TXT

---------- STRATS1.TXT
8.   The most successful students may well end up at the

A:\>
```

7. Type FIND "Successful" STRATS1.TXT and press [Enter].

CHECKPOINT 12C Must the text string in the FIND command be surrounded by double quotation marks?

The FIND filter is case-sensitive, so different occurrences of "Successful" are found in the file. To combine all occurrences without regard for capitalization, complete the following steps.

8. Type CLS and press [Enter].

9. Type FIND "successful" STRATS1.TXT/I and press [Enter].

This displays all occurrences of "successful" regardless of case, as shown in Figure 12.14.

FIGURE 12.14
All occurrences of "successful"

```
A:\>FIND "successful" STRATS1.TXT/I

---------- STRATS1.TXT
What Are the Characteristics of Successful Students?
3.   Successful students speak in class, even if their
5.   Successful students turn in assignments that look neat
every one of them is not brilliant. Successful students seem
8.   The most successful students may well end up at the

A:\>
```

In the next two steps be sure to use the case specified.

10. Type FIND "class" STRATS1.TXT and press [Enter].

The results of searching for "class" are shown in Figure 12.15.

FIGURE 12.15
Screen display of lines found that include the text string "class"

```
A:\>FIND "successful" STRATS1.TXT/I

---------- STRATS1.TXT
What Are the Characteristics of Successful Students?
3.   Successful students speak in class, even if their
5.   Successful students turn in assignments that look neat
every one of them is not brilliant. Successful students seem
8.   The most successful students may well end up at the

A:\>FIND "class" STRATS1.TXT

---------- STRATS1.TXT
1.   Not surprisingly, they attends classes- -regularly.
what was covered in class.
3.   Successful students speak in class, even if their
questions that the instructor knows many in the class are
4.   They see the instructor before or after class about
relative to the class discussion.
6.   They are attentive in class. They don't chat, read, or

A:\>
```

11. Type FIND "Class" STRATS1.TXT and press [Enter].

No occurrences of "Class" are located because the FIND filter is case-sensitive. The screen responds with

```
---------- STRATS1.TXT
```

meaning that the specified text was not found.

FIGURE 12.16

Result of the FIND search for lines without the text "class"

```
Sometimes they just want to ask a question or make a comment

5.    Successful students turn in assignments that look neat
and sharp. They take the time to produce a final product
that looks good, a reflection of a caring attitude and pride
in their work.

stare out windows. In other words, they are polite and
graceful, even if they get a little bored.

7.    Almost all work and assignments are turned in, even if
every one of them is not brilliant. Successful students seem
driven to complete all work.

8.    The most successful students may well end up at the
instructor's office door at least once during the semester.
They'll go out of their way to find the instructor and
engage him/her in meaningful conversation.

Information by David Shults, Mohave Community College,
Riviera, AZ 86442 from INNOVATION ABSTRACTS, Vol. X No. 17,
1988.


A:\>
```

12. Type FIND "class" STRATS1.TXT/V and press [Enter].

    This command form displays the lines that do not contain the "class" text. The end of the screen response to this search appears in Figure 12.16.

    Notice that numbered item 6 is missing the first line because it does include the text "class." Check Figure 12.15 to verify this.

13. Type FIND/C "time" STRATS1.TXT and press [Enter].

    The monitor screen will display the results of the search as

    `---------- STRATS1.TXT: 3`

    There are three lines in the STRATS1.TXT file that include at least one occurrence of the specified text "time."

14. Type CLS and press [Enter].

    The next step will indicate the relative line numbers where the text "time" is found in the file regardless of case.

15. Type FIND/N/I "time" STRATS1.TXT and press [Enter].

    The results of the command form are displayed in Figure 12.17.

16. Type CLS and press [Enter].

FIGURE 12.17

*Result of FIND
search using /N
and /I switches*

```
A:\>FIND/N/I "time" STRATS1.TXT

---------- STRATS1.TXT
[6]Moreover, they are on time. If they miss a session, they
[26]Sometimes they just want to ask a question or make a comment
[30]and sharp. They take the time to produce a final product

A:\>
```

Finally, the next step will look for occurrences of "time" in two different files and display the results.

17. Type `FIND/N/I "time" STRATS1.TXT STRATS2.TXT` and press Enter.

The results are shown in Figure 12.18.

FIGURE 12.18

*Results of
searching for
"time" in two
files*

```
A:\>FIND/N/I "time" STRATS1.TXT STRATS2.TXT

---------- STRATS1.TXT
[6]Moreover, they are on time. If they miss a session, they
[26]Sometimes they just want to ask a question or make a comment
[30]and sharp. They take the time to produce a final product

---------- STRATS2.TXT
[1]TEN TIMELY TEST TAKING TIPS
[8]2.    ARRIVE ON TIME
[9]You will be able to use the entire time allotted for the
[28]that will take longer to answer. Adjust time accordingly.
[31]If you are having a difficult time understanding a
[48]10.  USE ALL THE TIME ALLOTTED
[50]that they know more than you do. Use as much time as you
[51]need. Take your time! You can do well!

A:\>
```

Notice that both embedded and whole word occurrences of the text string are listed, plus all occurrences in both upper- and lowercase (because of the /I switch). Further, DOS indicates which file the text string occurred in and the line number (because of the /N switch).

Summary

In this unit, you discovered the value of pipes and filters in DOS and learned how you can redirect the output from a DOS command to the printer or to another DOS command.

Command Review

In this unit, you learned several DOS commands. Most have optional parameters or switches. We have tried to cover both the common and the rarely used forms of each command. The following forms of this unit's commands are the most frequently used and should be reviewed carefully.

DIR A: >B:LIST.TXT	Creates an ASCII text file on drive B: called LIST.TXT by redirection of the output from the DIR command.
DIR >PRN	Redirects the output from the DIR command to a printer connected to parallel port #1.
DIR ǀ MORE	Generates a listing of all files on the default drive, one full screen at a time.
DIR ǀ SORT	Generates an alphabetical listing of all files on the default drive.
DIR ǀ SORT/R	Generates a listing of all files on the default drive in reverse alphabetical order.
FIND "Germany" A:COUNTRY.DOC	Locates all occurrences of the word "Germany" in the file COUNTRY.DOC on the disk in drive A:.
FIND/N "Germany" A:COUNTRY.DOC	Locates all occurrences of the word "Germany" in the file COUNTRY.DOC on the disk in drive A: and indicates the relative line number on which each occurrence appears.
TYPE FILEONE.TXT >PRN	Redirects the listing created by the TYPE command to a printer connected to parallel port #1.

Review Questions

1. Define the difference between a serial and a parallel port. Why is this a concern when discussing DOS standard devices?

2. How many DOS standard devices are there? List them.

3. Which standard device(s) is/are considered the default device(s)?

4. Which standard device is typically used for debugging? How would a programmer use this device?

5. If standard devices did not exist, other than the default device, how would computing be limited?

6. What does redirection of standard input and output mean? Give an example.

7. When redirecting output to a disk file, how can the output be appended to an existing file?

8. Define DOS pipes and filters. What is the difference?

9. What is the difference between a pipe and redirection?

10. What is the ASCII collating sequence?

11. What is the difference between the DOS 2.*x* and 3.*x* SORT filters?

12. In what order would the following file names be sorted by DOS 2.*x*? By DOS 4.*x*?

    Zebra
    cat
    Antelope
    939
    ANTELOPE
    CATwalk
    129
    93

13. Name the switches that are used with the SORT filter.

14. Name the switches that are used with the MORE filter.

15. Name the switches that are used with the FIND filter.

Exercises

Whenever instructed to format a disk, use your last name (first) and then your first name (such as BACON JON) as the volume label. If instructed to print data from the screen, be sure to write your full name, course number and section, course title, instructor's name, unit and exercise number, and today's date on the paper. Your instructor will indicate if the disk(s) created or printouts should be submitted for grading.

1. Create a batch file called ALPHA.BAT that displays a directory listing of all files in alphabetical order by the file name without using a switch with the DIR command.

2. Create a batch file called BYDATE.BAT that displays a directory listing of all files in order of creation date without using a switch with the DIR command.

3. Use the appropriate DOS filter to determine if the word in the first column below is in the file listed in the second column. If it appears, indicate the number of times it occurs in the file. All files are stored in the C:\WESTDATA.DS6 directory or on West Student Data Disk #1.

    ```
    battle        WAR.TXT
    college       TRUCKIN.TXT
    newspaper     PAPER.TXT
    students      STRATS2.TXT
    ```

Key Terms

Baud rate	Parity	Serial port
Parallel port	Redirection	Standard device

Documentation Research

Documentation Research questions are included at the end of most units to encourage you to explore and discover the additional features available with DOS 6.x. All Documentation Research questions within the text can be answered by using the on-line reference (accessed by using the HELP command). Review Guided Activity 2.8 if you are unsure how to use the HELP command.

1. Does the SORT command differentiate between upper- and lowercase characters?

2. Will the FIND filter accept global wild card characters in the file name or extension to be searched?

3. Can the FIND filter locate the phrase "Tax file" if a carriage return separates the two words in the file?

4. When using the redirection character with the MORE command, what must be the source?

5. What is the maximum file size that can be ordered with the SORT filter?

6. If the /+n switch is not used with the SORT filter, what default value does n assume?

7. List the FIND command exit codes.

Using DOS Pipes and Filters

Searching for Text Phrases in a File

In Unit 12, we discussed redirection and DOS filters. In this application, you search a text file for all occurrences of a specific phrase, and redirect the results to a printer.

1. Obtain a copy of the file SEARCH.TXT from your instructor. This file is an ASCII text file.

2. Use a DOS filter to locate all occurrences of the phrase "He should have known better." The period should be included in the search.

3. Redirect the results of the search to a printer.

4. Repeat the above search for the phrase "He should have known better." However, this time you should redirect (to a printer) a listing of relative line numbers where the phrase occurs in the file.

5. Submit a printed copy of the results to your instructor. Be sure to write your name, course and section number, instructor's name, and today's date on the printout.

Using DOS Pipes, Filters, and Redirection

In this application, you use the pipes, filters, and redirection learned in Unit 12. All files for this application are in the C:\WESTDATA.DS6 directory.

1. Find all occurrences of the word "like" in the file MYSTERY.TXT. Redirect the results displayed on the screen to your printer. The printed report should be submitted to your instructor. Be sure to write your name, course and section number, instructor's name, and today's date on the printout.

2. Find all occurrences of the word "products" in the file FLAGS.DOC. Redirect the results displayed on the screen to your printer. The printed report should be submitted to your instructor. Be sure to write your name, course and section number, instructor's name, and today's date on the printout.

3. Display one page at a time of the DIET.DOC file on your monitor screen. Demonstrate to your instructor that you can accomplish this task.

4. Redirect the contents of the SAYING.TXT file to your printer. The printed report should be handed in to your instructor. Be sure to write your name, course and section number, instructor's name, and today's date on the printout.

Miscellaneous DOS Commands

13

Learning Objectives

At the completion of this unit, you should be able to

1. list the seven types of uses of the MODE command,

2. list the MODE command forms used to control the screen and keyboard,

3. explain the MODE command parameters associated with the communications protocol, including baud rate, parity, data bits, and stopbits,

4. explain the uses of the ANSI.SYS device driver,

5. discuss the use of escape sequences,

6. describe how the PROMPT command accesses ANSI.SYS functions,

7. list and explain the forms of the MODE command that provide printer control,

8. define a virtual or RAM drive,

9. rate the speed differences among a floppy disk drive, a fixed disk drive, and a virtual drive.

Important Commands

ANSI.SYS

CHCP

MODE

PROMPT

RAMDRIVE

Seven Modes of Operation

The MODE command is used to accomplish seven seemingly unrelated functions, though each does affect the mode of operation of the microcomputer system. The MODE command has seven options or formats that enable you to:

- Switch the monitor display mode.

- Prepare a device (*console* or printer) for *code page switching* (also called character set switching).

- Set protocol for a serial port.

- Set the characteristics of printer output to an IBM compatible or Epson printer connected to a parallel port.

- Redirect parallel port output to a serial port or cancel the redirection.

- Display the status of one or more devices attached to your system.

- Set the typematic repeat rate when a key is pressed down.

Several of the MODE command functions will be discussed briefly in this unit.

NOTE *The results and actions of the MODE command vary greatly with the hardware in use. In fact, the primary use of the command is to adapt the operating system to the equipment on hand. For that reason, it is difficult to demonstrate or guide you through specific projects with most of the MODE command functions. Out of necessity, sections on the MODE command concentrate more on an explanation of the function and less on step-by-step exercises.*

The MODE Command—Changing Display Adapters

The first MODE command option is to set the kind of display monitor adapter expected by the system and indicate the number of characters displayed vertically across the screen. The syntax of this option is

```
MODE [mode][,s][,t]
```

where *mode* represents the display adapter type and characters across the screen (see Table 13.1). The s is replaced with either an R or an L to shift the screen image, respectively, to the right or left. The t parameter generates a test pattern.

The display adapter/width options are listed in Table 13.1.

TABLE 13.1
*MODE
command
switches*

BW40	Disables color after switching to the color/graphics display adapter and generates 40 characters per line across the screen in monochrome.
BW80	Disables color after switching to the color/graphics display adapter and generates 80 characters per line across the screen in monochrome.
40	Displays 40 characters per line on the color/graphics display adapter.
80	Displays 80 characters per line on the color/graphics display adapter.
CO40	Enables color after switching to the color/graphics display adapter and generates 40 characters per line across the screen.
CO80	Enables color after switching to the color/graphics display adapter and generates 80 characters per line across the screen.
MONO	Causes the monochrome display adapter to be the active display adapter and generates 80 characters per line across the screen. There is no 40-character option with the monochrome display adapter.

If you omit the last two parameters, you can simply switch display modes. For instance, you can switch to 40-column color display by entering at the system prompt

```
MODE CO40
```

To switch back to 80-column color display, simply enter

```
MODE CO80
```

The following option of the MODE command does shift the screen display slightly to the right or left. To switch right, the R parameter is used, while L switches the display to the left. The type of display adapter must be stipulated in the command.

If you are using a monochrome display adapter and monitor, the form of the command is

```
MODE MONO,R
```

or

```
MODE MONO,L
```

In the 40-column mode, the R or L shifts the screen one character in the specified direction. In 80-column mode, the shift is two characters to the right or left, as indicated. If you cannot shift to the right or left, an error message will be displayed on the screen. For instance, if the screen text could not be adjusted to the right, you will see the message

```
Unable to shift screen right
```

If you try to use the MONO mode on a color display (or vice versa), DOS will issue the error message

```
Function not supported on this computer - mode
```

The *mode* is replaced, in the error message, with the nonsupported mode (such as MONO). To generate a test pattern for a color/graphics display and shift the screen right, the following command form may be used:

```
MODE CO80,R,T
```

When you combine the T parameter with a right or left shift, a screen message will ask if the monitor image is properly aligned. If you respond with no, the screen will shift again in the direction originally indicated. A yes response ends the command and the test pattern disappears. The test pattern is not supported by all hardware. If you do not get a test pattern, your equipment may not be fully supported by the DOS 6.*x* MODE command.

Code Page Switching

The word "International" in International Business Machines (IBM) Corporation indicates that DOS is not just a North American product. MS-DOS provides national language support through the use of *code pages*. If you are familiar with any foreign language, such as Spanish, French, Portuguese, German, or the like, you know that those languages use characters and accent marks not found in English. Through the use of various code pages, DOS enables your system hardware to display and print non-English language characters.

The computer assigns a numeric value to each keyboard character. When data is stored, those numeric values—not the alphabetical characters—are used. To display or print readable text, those numeric values are then translated into characters. The translation process uses a code page or table that equates a numeric value to a specific character. A code page may contain a maximum of 16 rows and 16 columns of values; that is, 256 numbers representing both printing and nonprinting characters.

The code page works in conjunction with a keyboard designation. Obviously, there must be a correlation between the code page and the keyboard used to generate the characters of a given language.

Default Code Pages

Once DOS is installed, a default country code is loaded and a default keyboard code is used. If you format a hard disk or floppy disk, you have accepted the default United States country code 001. Further, unless you specify differently, MS-DOS assumes the use of the United State keyboard (code US).

The MODE Command and Code Page Switching

The MODE command can be used to specify which code page should be loaded into RAM and used. The process includes several steps because you may need to change not only the code page, but the keyboard code too.

Switching code pages is not really a concern unless you need to create documents in a non-English language. Keep in mind the following—if you create a document after loading code page 863 (Canadian-French), and then try to read that document after loading a different code page, some of the text will be indecipherable. You must view, print, and edit a document using the same code page.

This is just a brief introduction to code page switching. Fortunately for United States and other English language users, the selection of a code page, keyboard code, and country code is automatic—just use the default system choices.

The MODE Command—Changing Printer Output

Printer output can be affected by using the following MODE command syntax:

```
MODE LPTn[:][c][,l][,r]
```

where n represents the printer port number (that is, LPT1, LPT2, or LPT3), c represents the characters per line, and l is the lines per vertical inch. The r switch indicates the retry setting. Five retry settings are available:

e	Returns a time-out error if the port is busy.
b	Returns a busy signal if the port is busy.
p	Continuously retries the port until it accepts output.
r	Returns a ready signal if the port is busy.
n	Takes no retry action (the default setting).

A time-out (setting e) occurs if the printer is off-line, turned off, in an error situation (ribbon out or paper jammed), or busy. The latter situation might occur if the printer is connected to a network system or if it is shared by two or more printers via an electronic autoscan switch.

The power-on default value for this MODE command option is

```
MODE LPT1:80,6
```

The options are limited. For vertical lines per inch, only two values may be used: 6 or 8. Similarly, only the values 80 or 132 may be used for characters per line. It should be noted that these commands do not work with all printers. A prime example is the Hewlett-Packard LaserJet Series II and Series III printers. You cannot adjust the lines per vertical inch or the characters per line using the DOS MODE command. This is true of any printer with an 8-inch platen that does not support 132 columns of printable characters.

The MODE Command—Switching from Parallel to Serial

Another optional use of the MODE command is to switch output from a parallel port (LPT1:, LPT2:, or LPT3:) to a serial port (COM1:, COM2:, COM3:, or COM4:). The command syntax is

```
MODE LPTn[:]=COMm[:]
```

where n is the number of the parallel port and m represents the serial port number. Remember, the parallel port options are only 1, 2, or 3, while the serial port options are 1, 2, 3, or 4.

To send data output to serial port #1 instead of parallel port #1, the command form would be

```
MODE LPT1:=COM1:
```

DOS normally sends data to your printer through a parallel port. However, many printers are designed to attach to either a parallel or a serial port. In fact, because of the distance from your workstation to the printer, if it exceeds 10 feet, you may want to use serial rather than parallel cabling. Serial cabling can travel a greater distance without loss of characters or data.

If you have a serial printer connected to your system, you would use the above command to redirect output from parallel port #1 (LPT1:) to serial port #1 (COM1:). Of course, you could also redirect the output to a different serial port. The following MODE command form redirects output from LPT1: to COM3:.

```
MODE LPT1:=COM3:
```

To cancel the redirection, you would simply enter

```
MODE LPT1:
```

GUIDED ACTIVITY 13.1

Using the Print MODE Option

All the MODE command forms are hardware-dependent, so, given the multiplicity of systems in use, it is impossible to present Guided Activities to demonstrate each option. This activity assumes that a dot-matrix printer is attached to your personal computer. First, you set the printer output to condensed print (132 characters per line, 8 lines per vertical inch) and print a directory listing. Then the activity will guide you in resetting the printer output to 80 characters per line with 6 lines per vertical inch.

1. Log on to the hard disk directory containing your DOS files, probably C:\DOS.

    If you do not have a printer attached to parallel port #1 (LPT1:), do not proceed. Rather, substitute a port designation to which a printer is attached. If no printer is available, do not complete this activity.

2. Be sure the printer is turned on and the paper is set to the top of the page.

3. Type MODE LPT1:132,8 and press Enter.

The screen will return the following message:

```
LPT1: not rerouted
LPT1: set for 132
Printer lines per inch set
No retry on parallel printer time-out
```

4. Type DIR > LPT1: and press Enter.

CHECKPOINT 13A What is redirected to the printer attached to LPT1:?

Check your printer and notice the condensed print size.

5. Type MODE LPT1:80,6 and press Enter.

The monitor screen will respond with the message

```
LPT1: not rerouted
LPT1: set for 80
Printer lines per inch set
No retry on parallel printer time-out
```

6. Type DIR > LPT1: and press Enter.

CHECKPOINT 13B What is LPT1:?

Check your printer and notice that the print size has returned to normal; that is, 10 characters per inch.

The MODE Command—Setting the Serial Protocol

One function of the MODE command is to set or initialize the parameters used by the serial port. These parameters are referred to as *protocol* for data communications. The term "protocol" refers to a set of defined rules governing the exchange of data between two computer systems (micro to micro, micro to mainframe, or mainframe to micro).

Computers that communicate using data communications must speak the same language. They must speak at the same speed (baud rate), speak in uniform word sizes (*data bits*), and know when each word or packet of data ends (*stopbits*). The two computers must also know how error checking occurs so that signals scrambled over telecommunication lines (often telephone lines) may be repeated and corrected. Parity is a device used for error checking.

The baud rate indicates the number of changes in an analog signal per second. At or below 600 baud, the baud rate is roughly the same as the number of bits per second (bps) transmitted to the receiving computer. At higher speeds, the baud rate and the bps may differ. A more accurate measure of transmission speeds is bps, which represents the number of *binary digits* (1s or 0s) transmitted each second. Remember that serial communications transfer one bit at a time. Baud rates are established by the hardware (modem) in use. To designate the baud rate, you can use just the first two digits of the rate; thus, 12 means 1200 baud and 19 means 19,200 baud. Most PCs use modems operating at 300, 1200, or 2400 baud. The higher speeds are becoming more popular as the cost drops.

There are three common parity-check options. There may be no error checking, or parity may be set as either even or odd. Data is communicated in blocks. Each block includes bits of data represented by binary digits, whose value is either zero (0) or one (1). If even parity checking is used, the parity bit is set to either 0 or 1 in order to make the value of the entire transmitted block "even." If parity is odd, the reverse happens. The receiving computer then checks the parity of each block of data received. If it does not match the expected parity, a message is sent to retransmit the last block of data. Versions of DOS subsequent to DOS 4.*x* also support two new parity options: MARK and SPACE.

Word length is set by the data bit's size. The range of options is 5–8 data bits, though the most common settings are either 7 or 8 bits. Those 7 or 8 bits represent a character. The receiving computer must know how long each "word" is. For a computer to not know word length can be compared to a reader's trying to read a book without spaces between words. Youwouldfinditfrustrating,confusing,anddifficultto interpret.

The syntax of this form of the MODE command is

```
MODE COMn[:] b[,p][,d][,s][,r]
```

You must substitute values for the letters listed in the above syntax diagram, as follows:

n = serial port number
b = baud rate
p = parity
d = data bit value
s = stopbits
r = printer retry parameter

You must specify the baud rate, but other settings are optional. Remember, with DOS 4.*x* or higher you can have up to four serial ports numbered COM1:, COM2:, COM3:, and COM4:. The baud rates include the following options. The actual rate is in the first column followed by the acceptable two-digit code in the second column.

```
110      11
150      15
300      30
600      60
1200     12
2400     24
4800     48
9600     96
19,200   19
```

Your parity options include EVEN, NONE, MARK, SPACE, and ODD. Word length or data bit size typically is set to 7 or 8. Stopbits are set to 1, 1.5, or 2.

The retry parameter tells DOS what to do when the output is directed to a busy serial port. The retry options are:

E	Returns "error" code if the port is busy.
B	Returns "busy" code if the port is busy.
P	Continuously retries the port until it is no longer busy.
R	Returns "ready" code if port is busy.
N	No action taken (the default setting).

If the MODE command were used to set the baud rate as 1200, parity at EVEN, data bits at 7, stopbits at 1, and with continuous retries if timeout errors occur, the following command form would be appropriate:

```
MODE COM1: BAUD=1200 PARITY=E DATA=7 STOP=1 RETRY=P
```

or

```
MODE COM1: BAUD=12 PARITY=E DATA=7 STOP=1 RETRY=P
```

The command can also be entered as

```
MODE COM1: 12,E,7,1,P
```

When using the latter form, you can omit a parameter, *if* you leave in the comma as a placeholder. For instance, if the parity did not need to be set (or was set earlier and did not need to be changed), the command can be entered as

```
MODE COM1: 12,,7,1,P
```

If you fail to stipulate a parameter, such as parity, either the last parity setting invoked by the MODE command in the current work session remains in effect or the default parity setting is used (if you have not stipulated a parity option in the current work session).

Most computer users involved in telecommunications use **terminal software**, which makes it easy to set the communications protocol without using the MODE command. You may never have to do more than select options from a terminal program menu, and the software then invokes the MODE command for you. That is why this section is presented as background information and no Guided Activity is provided. It should be noted that some print-sharing devices require you to issue the MODE command because they use the serial port on your PC to communicate with a printer. It is helpful at least to understand generally how and why the MODE command is used.

The CONFIG.SYS File Revisited

In Unit 11, the CONFIG.SYS file was discussed. Remember that it loads certain information into memory when your computer system is booted. CONFIG.SYS is a special file that configures your system. Some of the options it provides include

- Control over the number of files open at one time

- Control over the number of buffers used to transfer data to and from disk

- The ability to specify the last drive

- The ability to load device drivers

DOS allows you to install drivers for RAM drives (RAMDRIVE.SYS, discussed later in this unit), extended memory, a mouse, clock/calendar cards, print spoolers, and other memory-resident software. Each of these devices requires that a device driver be installed via the CONFIG.SYS file. The form of the command is

```
DEVICE=[d:][path]DRIVERNAME.EXT
```

A device driver (stored in the C:\DRIVERS directory) for an internal clock might look like the following:

```
DEVICE=C:\DRIVERS\PCCLOCK.SYS
```

One useful device driver, shipped as a separate file with MS-DOS, is ANSI.SYS.

Screen and Keyboard Control with ANSI.SYS

The ANSI.SYS driver gets its name from the American National Standards Institute (*ANSI*). The ANSI.SYS device driver provides extended screen and keyboard support. The extended display and keyboard features provided by ANSI.SYS enable you to

- Set screen colors on a color monitor

- Set *display attributes* (flashing text, high-intensity text, and inverse video) on a color or monochrome display

- Position the cursor when at the DOS level and display messages on screen at specified locations

- Redefine keys on the keyboard

To access these features, you must include the following command line in your CONFIG.SYS file.

```
DEVICE=ANSI.SYS
```

If this file is not in the root directory of your hard disk, you must specify the path to the device driver. If it resides in your \DOS subdirectory on drive C:, the command in CONFIG.SYS will read

```
DEVICE=C:\DOS\ANSI.SYS
```

Once the ANSI.SYS device driver is installed, you can communicate with the file and use its built-in features via the PROMPT command. In an earlier unit, you used the PROMPT command and a meta-string to change the DOS or system prompt. Now, with ANSI.SYS loaded, you can use the PROMPT command to change screen colors, display attributes, or change the cursor location.

All ANSI.SYS sequences must begin with the ⟦Esc⟧ key code. However, at the DOS prompt, pressing the ⟦Esc⟧ key voids all keystrokes entered prior to pressing the key and displays a slash on the screen. Figure 13.1 displays the result of typing FORMAT A:, pressing the ⟦Esc⟧ key, and then typing DIR A: before pressing the ⟦Enter⟧ key.

FIGURE 13.1
Using ⟦Esc⟧ to cancel the preceding portion of a command line

```
C:\>FORMAT A:\
    DIR A:

Volume in drive A is BACON JONAT
Volume Serial Number is 16F2-256A
Directory of A:\

DOCFILES     <DIR>      06-04-93   10:01a
TXTFILES     <DIR>      06-04-93   10:01a
ZIPFILES     <DIR>      06-04-93   10:01a
        3 file(s)            0 bytes
                      1379328 bytes free

C:\>
```

Notice that the DIR command is executed, but not the FORMAT command. The point is, simply pressing ⟦Esc⟧ can never communicate with the ANSI.SYS driver—since ⟦Esc⟧ serves another function at the DOS prompt.

The PROMPT command overcomes this obstacle. The $e meta-string equates with the ⟦Esc⟧ key. By following the PROMPT command with the $e meta-string, you can communicate with ANSI.SYS. These sequences are referred to as "escape sequences" because they all begin with a representation of the ⟦Esc⟧ key.

NOTE *You can also send the escape character to activate ANSI.SYS by using some editing programs. However, the scope of this book is on DOS and its uses. Therefore we will only discuss accessing ANSI.SYS with the PROMPT command.*

Many texts display escape sequences using the following type of notation:

    ESC[10;15H

Because the PROMPT command uses the $e meta-string to represent the ⟦Esc⟧ key, we are using the following type of notation:

    $e[10;15H

The two notations mean the same. In both cases an ESC or ⟦Esc⟧ or $e character must signal the beginning of an escape sequence.

The complete form of an escape sequence varies, depending on whether you are controlling the display color, display attributes, or cursor location. In all cases, to communicate with ANSI.SYS from the DOS prompt, the syntax includes the following:

- PROMPT command

- The $e meta-string

- The left square bracket ([)

- An appropriate numeric code or text string
- A *terminating code* that indicates the specific ANSI.SYS function being executed

The syntax would look like the following:

```
PROMPT $e[99,99z
```

In the syntax diagram 99 would be replaced by a numeric code or series of numbers (99,99) and z would be replaced by one of the following terminating codes:

A	moves the cursor up the number of rows indicated
B	moves the cursor down the number of rows indicated
C	moves the cursor forward the number of columns indicated
D	moves the cursor backward the number of columns indicated
f	moves the cursor to a specified row, column
H	moves the cursor to a specified row, column
m	modifies screen colors or display attributes
2J	clears the screen and moves cursor to the upper-left corner of the screen
K	deletes text from the cursor location to the end of the line
s	saves the current cursor location
u	restores the cursor to the last saved ([s) cursor location

NOTE *These terminating codes are case-sensitive. For instance, saving the current cursor location with the PROMPT command would require the following entry at the DOS prompt or in a batch file: PROMPT $e[s. If you capitalize either the e or s, the results will not be what you expect.*

Cursor Movement and Message Displays with ANSI.SYS

The PROMPT command can also be used to move the cursor to specific screen locations and display messages. The terminating codes used for cursor movement were listed earlier. The exact syntax of each of the escape sequences is shown below.

PROMPT $e[row;columnH Moves the cursor to the row and column indicated.

PROMPT $e[row;columnf Moves the cursor to the row and column indicated.

PROMPT $e[rowA Moves the cursor up the number of rows indicated.

PROMPT $e[rowB Moves the cursor down the number of rows indicated.

PROMPT $e[columnC Moves the cursor forward the number of columns indicated.

PROMPT $e[columnD Moves the cursor backward the number of columns indicated.

PROMPT $e[s Saves the current cursor location.

PROMPT $e[u Restores the cursor to the location last saved using the ESC[[e sequence.

PROMPT $e[2J Moves the cursor to the upper-left corner—the *home position*. Same function as performed by the CLS command.

PROMPT $e[K Deletes text from the current cursor location to the end of the current line.

A typical screen displays 80 characters horizontally across each line and 25 lines vertically on the screen. Some screens can display more or fewer characters across (40 or 132) and more lines per screen (43 or 50). Each of the 25 or more vertical lines is considered a row and numbered 1 to 25. Each character position (beginning at the left edge of the screen) is considered a column and numbered 1 to 80. Therefore, to move to the dead center of a typical 80 column by 25 line screen, you would enter

```
PROMPT $e[13;40f
```

or

```
PROMPT $e[13;40H
```

To move the cursor down five rows after the last cursor location, you would use the command form

```
PROMPT $e[5B
```

NOTE *If you use the PROMPT command to access ANSI.SYS, and wish it to also display the default drive and path, you must include the PROMPT pg command in your batch file or reexecute it at the DOS prompt. Using PROMPT to access ANSI.SYS negates any other previous use of PROMPT.*

GUIDED ACTIVITY 13.2

Using the PROMPT Command and ANSI.SYS to Move the Cursor

In this Guided Activity, you will use the PROMPT command to communicate with the ANSI.SYS driver and modify the location and display of your system prompt.

1. Turn on your computer system and go to the C:\DOS directory or the directory containing your DOS command files.

2. At the DOS prompt type CLS and press [Enter].

NOTE *In the PROMPT command Guided Activities that follow, be sure to carefully type the command indicated and double-check it before you press [Enter]. If you change capitalization or mistype one or more characters, the results will not be what you expect.*

3. Type PROMPT $e[5B and press [Enter].

Notice that the DOS prompt disappears and the cursor drops down five rows (lines).

NOTE *If you do not get the desired results, the ANSI.SYS driver may not be loaded in your CONFIG.SYS file. Check the file or ask your instructor for assistance.*

4. Type CLS and press [Enter]. Because the PROMPT command is set to drop five rows, the cursor cannot go to the home position—as it normally would when invoking the CLS command.

5. Type TEST1 and press [Enter].

6. Type TEST2 and press [Enter]. Each time, the cursor drops another five lines.

Because the PROMPT command (accessing ANSI.SYS) cannot move the cursor off the screen, in one of the next two steps (depending on the number of lines displayed on your screen) the cursor only drops a couple lines—even though five was indicated.

7. Type TEST3 and press Enter.

8. Type TEST4 and press Enter.

Figure 13.2 shows the results of the past few steps.

FIGURE 13.2
*Using PROMPT
to drop five lines*

```
TEST1
Bad command or file name




TEST2
Bad command or file name




TEST3
Bad command or file name
TEST4
Bad command or file name
```

9. Type CLS and press Enter. Only the cursor remains on the sixth line down. CLS moved the cursor to row one and the PROMPT command moved it down five more lines.

The next step will cause the DOS prompt to reappear, displaying the current drive and path.

10. Type PROMPT pg and press Enter.

11. Type CLS and press Enter. Because the prompt was reset in the previous step, the cursor can once again move to the home position on the screen.

In the next step, you combine three meta-strings in order to move the cursor (while still displaying the DOS prompt indicating the default drive and path).

12. Type PROMPT $e[5B pg and press Enter.

The results of the previous step are displayed in Figure 13.3.

FIGURE 13.3
*Combining three
PROMPT
command
meta-strings*

```
C:\DOS>PROMPT $e[5B $p$g



    C:\DOS>
```

The next meta-string will cause the DOS prompt to erase the entire screen, move to the home position, and then display the DOS prompt with the default drive and path.

13. Type PROMPT $e[2J pg and press [Enter].

14. Press [Enter] several times. Notice how the prompt behaves. It continues to clear the screen and stay in the upper-left corner of the screen.

15. Type DIR and press [Enter].

CHECKPOINT 13C What happens at the end of the DIR listing? Do you understand why?

In the next PROMPT command form, you will store the current cursor location, place the current time at the top of the screen (home position), return to the stored cursor location, and then display the DOS prompt with the default drive and path.

16. Type PROMPT $e[s $e[1;1H $t $e[u pg and press [Enter].

Before proceeding, let's dissect this command form:

$e[s	Saves the current cursor location.
$e[1;1H	Moves cursor to row 1, column 1.
$t	Displays the current system time.
$e[u	Moves the cursor to the saved cursor location.
pg	Displays the DOS prompt with the default drive and path.

17. Type DIR and press [Enter].

Notice the left-over detail on the top line along with the system time. The next command form includes the $e[K meta-string. It clears text from the cursor location to the end of the current line and will cause the time to appear on the top line by itself.

18. Type PROMPT $e[s $e[1;1H $t $e[K $e[u pg and press [Enter].

The line with the system time is now cleared.

19. Press [Enter] 2 or 3 times. The cursor remains at the bottom of the screen, and the time (which continues to increment) remains by itself on the top line.

20. Type DIR and press [Enter].

21. Type CLS and press [Enter]. The time continues to change as the system time changes.

In the next step, two more meta-strings are invoked.

$e[25C	Moves the cursor 25 columns (characters) forward on the line.
$d	Displays the system date.

22. Type PROMPT $e[s $e[1;1H $t $e[K $e[25C $d $e[u pg and press [Enter].

CHECKPOINT 13D If you knew you would execute the command in step 22 whenever you booted your computer, how could you automate the process?

23. Press [Enter] several times and notice the date and time displayed at the top of the screen.

In Figure 13.4, the PROMPT command displays the system date and time at the top of the monitor screen.

FIGURE 13.4
Date and time displayed using the DOS PROMPT command

```
15:55:39.52                          Sun 07-25-1993
C:\DOS>PROMPT $e[s $e[1;1H $t $e[K $e[25C $d $e[u $p$g

C:\DOS>
C:\DOS>
C:\DOS>
C:\DOS>
C:\DOS>
C:\DOS>
```

To return your system to normal, complete the next step.

24. Type PROMPT pg and press [Enter]

CHECKPOINT 13E What does the last step accomplish?

25. Type CLS and press [Enter].

NOTE *It can get very tedious typing these long PROMPT commands with meta-strings. To save time and effort, you can enter these commands from either an AUTOEXEC.BAT file or any batch file.*

Setting Screen Colors and Display Attributes with ANSI.SYS

The following codes are used in escape sequences to establish the colors and display attributes listed. Note that some numbers are specifically used for *background colors* while others are used for *foreground* (text) *colors*. Still other codes are used to generate display attributes.

0	All attributes are turned off
1	High-intensity or bold text
4	Underscored or underlined text (only on a monochrome display)
5	Blinking or flashing text
7	Inverse video

8	Hidden or concealed text
30	Foreground Black
31	Foreground Red
32	Foreground Green
33	Foreground Yellow
34	Foreground Blue
35	Foreground Magenta
36	Foreground Cyan
37	Foreground White
40	Background Black
41	Background Red
42	Background Green
43	Background Yellow
44	Background Blue
45	Background Magenta
46	Background Cyan
47	Background White

Remember that when setting screen colors or display attributes, you must use the m terminating code for your escape sequence. Keeping these guidelines and codes in mind, you could change your color monitor's background screen color to blue with this command form:

```
PROMPT $e[44m
```

To change the background color to green, you would use the command form

```
PROMPT $e[42m
```

The foreground or text color can be altered by inserting a number corresponding to the foreground color desired. Magenta (purplish-red) text can be generated by the command form

```
PROMPT $e[35m
```

NOTE *If you set the background and foreground to the same color, you will not be able to read the screen text.*

Both the foreground and background colors may be set with a single command line. To establish white text on a green background, you would use this command form:

```
PROMPT $e[42;37m
```

or

```
PROMPT $e[37;42m
```

Finally, you could establish a text display attribute in the same command line by adding the appropriate code. The following command form would cause flashing white text on a blue background.

```
PROMPT $e[5;37;44m
```

Using PROMPT to Alter Screen Colors and Attributes

The first portion of this Guided Activity can be accomplished on any system with ANSI.SYS loaded. The last portion requires a color monitor.

1. Turn on your computer system and go to the C:\DOS directory or the directory containing your DOS command files.

2. At the DOS prompt type CLS and press [Enter].

3. Type PROMPT $e[5m and press [Enter].

   The system prompt disappears. You invoked a display attribute meta-string that will cause the text on the screen to blink. Nothing is blinking or flashing until you type some characters.

4. Type DIR and press [Enter]. As the listing scrolls down the screen, it will be flashing.

5. Before the display drives you crazy, type PROMPT $e[0m pg and press [Enter].

   This command form turns off the blinking for any new text and displays the DOS prompt with the default drive and path. Notice that the prompt is not blinking but the residual text is.

6. Type CLS and press [Enter].

   In the next step you will add a screen heading in bold or high-intensity type. The bold will be turned on, then off, and the cursor moved to row 3, column 1, before the DOS prompt is displayed.

7. Type PROMPT $e[H $e[1m MY COMPUTER SYSTEM $e[0m $e[3;1H$p$g and press [Enter].

   Before proceeding, let's examine the several meta-strings composing this command.

$e[H	Moves cursor to home position. When row and column numbers are omitted, DOS assumes the home position as the target.
$e[1m	Turns on bold text.
MY COMPUTER SYSTEM	Text string to appear in bold text.
$e[0m	Turns off all display attributes; that is, returns display to normal.
$e[3;1H$p$g	Moves cursor to row 3, column 1, and displays system prompt—without displaying a space first.

   See the results of the bold prompt in Figure 13.5.

FIGURE 13.5
Bold attribute screen text generated by PROMPT and ANSI.SYS.

```
MY COMPUTER SYSTEM
C:\DOS>PROMPT $e[H $e[1m MY COMPUTER SYSTEM $e[0m $e[3;1H$p$g
C:\DOS>
```

8. Type CLS and press [Enter].

9. Type DIR and press [Enter].

The prompt got buried in the directory listing. This would not happen if we cleared the line of all text after the DOS prompt. In the next step you will clear the first line, center the MY COMPUTER SYSTEM text string, and display the default drive and path through the DOS prompt.

10. Type CLS and press [Enter]. This clears the screen to help you see what to enter next.

11. Type PROMPT $e[H $e[K $e[1m $e[31C MY COMPUTER SYSTEM $e[0m $e[2;1H $e[K $e[3;1H $e[K$p$g and press [Enter].

There are a few new meta-strings in this command. They include:

$e[31C	Moves the cursor over 31 columns before displaying the text string MY COMPUTER SYSTEM.
$e[2;1H	Moves cursor to row 2, column 1.
$e[K	Clears text from the cursor location to the end of the current line.
$e[Kp$g	Clears the line and then displays the system prompt.

The screen still looks a bit messy but can be cured by invoking the CLS command.

12. Type CLS and press [Enter].

NOTE *The following steps require use of a color monitor.*

13. Type PROMPT $e[44;33m pg and press [Enter].

By adding the pg meta-string, we preserve the DOS prompt. The only change appears to be the color change of the block behind the DOS prompt. Though the codes indicate a blue background and yellow foreground color, the yellow may look more brown or tan depending on how you have adjusted your monitor's brightness control.

14. Press [Enter] 3 or 4 times. Notice the spreading of the new background and foreground colors.

15. Type DIR and watch the screen as you press [Enter]. The new colors continue to spread.

16. Type PROMPT $e[34;43m pg and press [Enter] to reverse the colors.

17. Type DIR and watch the screen as you press [Enter].

In the next step you will change only the foreground (text) color to white.

18. Type PROMPT $e[37m pg and press [Enter].

19. Type CLS and press [Enter].

20. Type DIR and press [Enter].

The following step will change only the background color from yellow (brown) to blue.

21. Type PROMPT $e[44m pg and press [Enter].

22. Type TREE C:\ and watch your screen as you press [Enter].

CHECKPOINT 13F What does the TREE command display?

The following command restores your display attributes and colors to normal.

23. Type PROMPT $e[40;37m pg and press [Enter].

24. Type CLS and press [Enter].

Keyboard Reassignment with ANSI.SYS

The final use of the PROMPT command is to communicate with ANSI.SYS in order to redefine keyboard keys. This may not seem very functional. After all, why would you ever want to redefine a J to generate an O, or a D to generate an I? From time to time you may need DOS to access the extended *ASCII character set*, which includes characters not available on the typical computer keyboard such as the ¼ and ½ characters.

To reassign a key, you would use the following PROMPT command syntax.

    PROMPT $e[oldkey;newkeyp

You can also redefine a key to generate a text string, by replacing the newkey parameter with a text string.

Unfortunately, it is not as simple as entering the old and new key names. You must use the scan codes (numbers) for the old and new keys. The p is the required termination code for this function. If you want the key redefinition to conclude with a carriage return, the termination code must be 13p rather than just 13.

Table 13.2 lists the scan codes for the IBM PC. Notice that codes are given for the key by itself and in combination with the [Shift], [Ctrl], and [Alt] keys.

TABLE 13.2 Scan codes in the ASCII character set	**KEY**	**KEY CODE**	**WITH SHIFT**	**WITH CTRL**	**WITH ALT**
	a	97	65	1	0;30
	b	98	66	2	0;48
	c	99	67	3	0;46
	d	100	68	4	0;32
	e	101	69	5	0;18
	f	102	70	6	0;33
	g	103	71	7	0;34
	h	104	72	8	0;35
	i	105	73	9	0;23
	j	106	74	10	0;36
	k	107	75	11	0;37

TABLE 13.2
(Continued)

KEY	KEY CODE	WITH SHIFT	WITH CTRL	WITH ALT
l	108	76	12	0;38
m	109	77	13	0;50
n	110	78	14	0;49
o	111	79	15	0;24
p	112	80	16	0;25
q	113	81	17	0;16
r	114	82	18	0;19
s	115	83	19	0;31
t	116	84	20	0;20
u	117	85	21	0;22
v	118	86	22	0;47
w	119	87	23	0;17
x	120	88	24	0;45
y	121	89	25	0;21
z	122	90	26	0;44
1	49	63		0;120
2	50	64		0;121
3	51	35		0;122
4	52	36		0;123
5	53	37		0;124
6	54	94		0;125
7	55	38		0;126
8	56	42		0;127
9	57	40		0;128
0	48	41		0;129
-	45	95		0;130
=	61	43		0;131
TAB	9			0;15
SPACE	32			

Table 13.3 shows the scan codes for characters not on the standard IBM keyboard.

	SCAN CODES	CHARACTERS		SCAN CODES	CHARACTERS
TABLE 13.3 Scan codes for additional nonkeyboard characters*	¢	155		gamma	226
	¿	168		pi	227
	½	171		sigma	228
	¼	172		tau	231
	¡	173		theta	233
	alpha	224		omega	234
	beta	225		phi	237

* These codes are identical to the ASCII codes that are numeric representations of the characters, numbers, and symbols generated by pressing keys on the keyboard. The entire list has not been included, just the most commonly used character values.

To reassign the Alt 2 key combination to generate a ½ symbol, you would use the following form of the PROMPT command.

```
PROMPT $e[0;121;171p
```

Additionally, if you wanted Alt 4 to generate a ¼ symbol, the command form would be

```
PROMPT $e[0;123;172p
```

If you want to cause the Ctrl D key combination to generate a DIR listing of drive A:, you can use the following command form.

```
PROMPT $e[4;"DIR A:";13p
```

Notice that the multiple keystrokes are enclosed in quotation marks, and the 13p ends the string with a carriage return. After redefining this key, you can simply press Ctrl D to generate a DIR listing from drive A:.

NOTE *To reset a key to its original definition, use the following syntax:* PROMPT $e[oldkey;oldkeyp. *If you had redefined the letter A (capital A), you can reset the key to its original use by entering* PROMPT $e[65;65p.

GUIDED ACTIVITY 13.4

Redefining Keyboard Keys with ANSI.SYS and PROMPT

In this Guided Activity, you redefine keys using the PROMPT command to access the redefinition features of ANSI.SYS.

1. Turn on your computer system and go to the C:\DOS directory or the directory containing your DOS command files.

2. At the DOS prompt type CLS and press [Enter].

3. Type PROMPT $e[32;49p pg and press [Enter].

   The first meta-string redefines the [Spacebar] (code 32) to be a number one (code 49). The p is the terminating code. Now when you press the [Spacebar], you will generate a "1".

4. Press [Spacebar] 3 times and press [Enter].

   Figure 13.6 shows the results of the key redefinition.

FIGURE 13.6
The redefined [Spacebar] key

```
C:\DOS>PROMPT $e[32;49p $p$g

 C:\DOS>111
Bad command or file name

 C:\DOS>
```

5. Press [Spacebar] and then press [Enter]. You'll notice that the [Spacebar] is still redefined.

   In the next step you will attempt to redefine the [Spacebar] back to its original use.

6. Type PROMPT $e[32;32p pg and press [Enter].

   Notice the "Bad command or file name" error message. If you look at your screen and Figure 13.7 carefully, you will see that when you attempted to type the space after PROMPT, it came out PROMPT1. You have redefined the [Spacebar] and actually have no way to change it back. Whenever redefining keys, be sure you do not "paint yourself into a corner."

FIGURE 13.7
Screen showing the redefined [Spacebar] character as a "1"

```
C:\DOS>PROMPT $e[32;49p $p$g

 C:\DOS>111
Bad command or file name

 C:\DOS>1
Bad command or file name

 C:\DOS>PROMPT1$e[32;32p1$p$g
Bad command or file name

 C:\DOS>
```

   The only way to regain the space character is to reboot your system.

7. Press [Ctrl], [Alt], and [Del] simultaneously to reboot your system.

8. If prompted, enter date and time.

9. Type CLS and press [Enter].

In the next step, you will redefine the `Ctrl``D` key combination to generate a text string to invoke the DIR A: command.

10.   Type `PROMPT $e[4;"DIR A:";13p $p$g` and press `Enter`.

Notice that the `13p` terminating code means that `Ctrl``D` will generate the text string (DIR A:) and follow it with a carriage return (the character generated by pressing `Enter`).

11.   Place West Student Data Disk #8, created in Unit 12, in drive A:.

12.   Press `Ctrl``D`. You do *not* need to follow this by pressing the `Enter` key.

Figure 13.8 displays the results of pressing `Ctrl``D`. Notice that the results were the same as if you had typed `DIR A:` and pressed `Enter` at the DOS prompt.

FIGURE 13.8

Keystrokes generated by pressing `Ctrl` `D`

```
A:\>
A:\>dir

 Volume in drive A has no label
 Volume Serial Number is 1B6B-1904
 Directory of A:\

BECOMING TXT        53 10-04-88    7:22p
MYSTERY  TXT        91 10-06-88    7:03p
SAYING   TXT       193 10-04-88    7:51p
PUBLISH  TXT       265 10-04-88    7:59p
TRUCKIN  TXT       719 07-13-89    8:11a
STRATS1  TXT      2056 10-19-91    3:15p
STRATS2  TXT      1908 10-19-91    3:15p
PAPER    TXT      1043 05-08-93   11:29a
WAR      TXT       121 01-18-94   11:19a
FILELIST           579 07-24-93    6:01p
FILES    TXT      2069 07-24-93    7:22p
INPUTS               6 07-24-93    7:23p
STATUS   BAT        87 07-24-93    7:24p
STATUS   TXT       888 07-24-93    7:33p
       14 file(s)      10078 bytes
                     1442304 bytes free

A:\>
```

The final step is to redefine the `Ctrl``D` key combination so that it no longer generates the text and carriage return.

13.   Type `PROMPT $e[4;4p $p$g` and press `Enter`.

By listing the code (4) for `Ctrl``D` twice, you in effect tell DOS and ANSI.SYS to let those keystrokes represent their normal function.

14.   Press `Ctrl``D` and press `Enter`.

This time the screen simply shows the ^D characters as displayed in Figure 13.9.

FIGURE 13.9
Normal screen display generated by pressing [Ctrl] [P]

```
Directory of A:\

BECOMING TXT          53 10-04-88    7:22p
MYSTERY  TXT          91 10-06-88    7:03p
SAYING   TXT         193 10-04-88    7:51p
PUBLISH  TXT         265 10-04-88    7:59p
TRUCKIN  TXT         719 07-13-89    8:11a
STRATS1  TXT        2056 10-19-91    3:15p
STRATS2  TXT        1908 10-19-91    3:15p
PAPER    TXT        1043 05-08-93   11:29a
WAR      TXT         121 01-18-94   11:19a
FILELIST             579 07-24-93    6:01p
FILES    TXT        2069 07-24-93    7:22p
INPUTS                 6 07-24-93    7:23p
STATUS   BAT          87 07-24-93    7:24p
STATUS   TXT         888 07-24-93    7:33p
        14 file(s)       10078 bytes
                       1442304 bytes free


C:\>PROMPT $e[4;4p $p$g

 C:\>^D
Bad command or file name

 C:\>
```

The DOS RAM Drive

Three types of disk drives are used with PCs. The two most obvious ones are floppy disk drives and hard disks (sometimes referred to as fixed disks). Both of these types must be formatted first, and subsequently may be used as secondary storage. On both types of media, stored data can include application program code, operating system code (DOS), and user-created files (data files, text files, database files, and so on).

The third type of disk is less tangible and less easily understood. It is the *virtual disk* or *RAM drive*, which is invoked using the RAMDRIVE.SYS device driver. Under earlier versions of DOS, PC DOS called this device driver VDISK.SYS while MS-DOS used the file name RAMDRIVE.SYS. The RAM drive (also called a *virtual drive*) is invoked and configured from the configuration file (CONFIG.SYS). Once created, a virtual drive can be treated as any other disk drive or hard disk, with two exceptions:

- Virtual drives never need to be formatted before use,

- Virtual drives are volatile (transitory) memory or storage.

A virtual drive is created from a portion of memory. Files may be copied to it or from it. However, when you reboot the computer or if the system loses power, any data stored on the virtual drive is lost.

Why are virtual drives used? A floppy drive is a slow method of transferring data to and from the CPU. It must get "up to speed" before data can be read. That takes milliseconds, which ultimately slows down the process time. A hard disk is faster, but is still a mechanical device. It operates faster than the floppy drive, but slower than a virtual drive. By contrast, there are no mechanical parts to a virtual drive. It does not have to get up to speed, operating at the speed of electrons. Any electronic device is faster than a mechanical device. Speed is what makes the virtual drive attractive.

The virtual drive is created in conjunction with the DEVICE command and placed in the CONFIG.SYS file.

NOTE *This command is not generated via the keyboard, but from the CONFIG.SYS file, which is read immediately after the resident portion of DOS is loaded and before the AUTOEXEC.BAT file is read.*

To install the virtual drive, the following syntax is used:

```
DEVICE=RAMDRIVE.SYS [d] [s] [n][/m]
```

where d is the disk size of the virtual drive in kilobytes and s represents the sector size (bytes per sector on the virtual disk). The n parameter indicates the maximum number of files or directories the virtual drive can contain. Each file or directory equates to one entry. If you intend to have 12 files on the virtual drive, the directory parameter must be set to 12 or a larger number.

The default settings for the RAMDRIVE command are represented by issuing the command

```
DEVICE=RAMDRIVE.SYS 64 512 64
```

This would create a RAM disk 64KB in size, with 512 bytes per sector, and capable of holding 64 directory entries (files).

The disk size in kilobytes can range from 4 to 31,744 (PC DOS) or 16 to 4,096 (MS-DOS). Sector sizes include 128, 256, and 512 bytes. File entries can range from 2 to 1,024.

The /m parameter tells DOS the type of memory to use in the creation of the virtual drive. If you use extended or expanded memory, more conventional memory (below the 640KB barrier) will be available for your application program. To place the virtual drive in *extended memory* (memory above the 1MB level) you use the /E switch. To use *expanded memory* (memory swapping using the Lotus-Intel-Microsoft specification) you would use the /A switch. If you fail to stipulate either the /E or /A switch, DOS uses conventional memory for the virtual drive.

To create a virtual disk composed of 64KB, 128-byte sectors, and 32 directory entries in extended memory, the command form would be

```
DEVICE=RAMDRIVE.SYS 64 128 32/E
```

When the virtual drive is installed, the screen displays the following message:

```
RAMDRIVE Version 6.0 virtual disk x:
```

where x is the drive designation of the virtual drive. The first virtual drive is always given a drive designation one higher (in the alphabet) than the highest drive name. If your computer has two floppy disk drives (A: and B:) and a hard disk(C:), then DOS assigns the virtual drive the name D:. On the other hand, the virtual drive would become B: if your system only had a single floppy drive. If you had two hard disks (C: and D:), the first virtual drive becomes drive E:.

GUIDED ACTIVITY 13.5

Using the RAM Drive

In this Guided Activity, you will create a small (64KB) virtual drive and then copy files to the drive. You will also graphically see that any data stored on a virtual drive is lost when the computer system loses power or is rebooted. Drive D: is used for the virtual drive in this Guided Activity, which assumes that your personal computer has only one hard disk drive.

CAUTION   *If you are working on a PC connected to a network, DO NOT CONTINUE with this activity unless given specific directions by your instructor. Depending on the network software and configuration, you may not be able to complete this Guided Activity.*

1. Be sure you are logged on to the root directory of your hard disk.

2. The assumption is made that your AUTOEXEC.BAT file opened a path (using the PATH command) to the directory containing your DOS files.

    The next few steps will protect your existing CONFIG.SYS file. You will return the file to its original condition by the time this activity is completed.

NOTE   *You could simply edit the CONFIG.SYS file with EDIT, and a backup file (CONFIG.BAK) would be automatically created. CONFIG.BAK would save the CONFIG.SYS file in its original form—unless you edited it again. For that reason, we are instructing you to take an extra precaution and make a backup copy of CONFIG.SYS under the file name CONFIG.OLD.*

3. Type `COPY CONFIG.SYS CONFIG.OLD` and press `Enter`.

4. Type `DIR CONFIG.*` and press `Enter`.

    You should see at least two files, CONFIG.SYS and CONFIG.OLD. There may be a third file called CONFIG.BAK.

    In this Guided Activity, you will need to reboot your computer and not have it execute the AUTOEXEC.BAT file. The next step renames it so that it is not executed. You will return it to its original name by the end of the activity.

5. Type `REN AUTOEXEC.BAT AUTOEXEC.OLD` and press `Enter`.

6. Type `CLS` and press `Enter`.

7. Type `EDIT CONFIG.SYS` and press `Enter`.

NOTE   *The CONFIG.SYS file displayed on your screen was created during the DOS installation process. It may have been subsequently modified to "fine-tune" your computer system. It is important that you do not arbitrarily modify a CONFIG.SYS or an AUTOEXEC.BAT file without understanding what you are doing. That is why you made backup copies of these files in the first steps of this Guided Activity.*

8. Press `Ctrl` `End` to move to the end of the text file and press `Enter` to leave a blank line between the last line of the old CONFIG.SYS file and the new line of text.

9. Type `DEVICE=C:\DOS\RAMDRIVE.SYS 64 512 12` and press `Enter`.

FIGURE 13.10

*Screen display
when creating
the CONFIG.SYS
file*

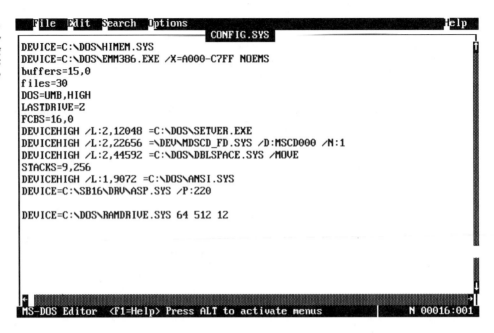

```
 File  Edit  Search  Options                                    Help
                           CONFIG.SYS
DEVICE=C:\DOS\HIMEM.SYS
DEVICE=C:\DOS\EMM386.EXE /X=A000-C7FF NOEMS
buffers=15,0
files=30
DOS=UMB,HIGH
LASTDRIVE=Z
FCBS=16,0
DEVICEHIGH /L:2,12048 =C:\DOS\SETVER.EXE
DEVICEHIGH /L:2,22656 =\DEV\MDSCD_FD.SYS /D:MSCD000 /N:1
DEVICEHIGH /L:2,44592 =C:\DOS\DBLSPACE.SYS /MOVE
STACKS=9,256
DEVICEHIGH /L:1,9072 =C:\DOS\ANSI.SYS
DEVICE=C:\SB16\DRV\ASP.SYS /P:220

DEVICE=C:\DOS\RAMDRIVE.SYS 64 512 12




MS-DOS Editor  <F1=Help> Press ALT to activate menus         N 00016:001
```

The monitor display should appear similar to Figure 13.10.

10. Save the CONFIG.SYS file and exit the DOS Editor.

11. To reboot your system, simultaneously press the [Ctrl], [Alt], and [Del] keys.

   Assuming that you have a personal computer system with one or two floppy disk drives and a single hard disk, the message displayed below will appear.

```
Microsoft RAMDrive version 3.07 virtual disk D:
     Disk size:           64 k
     Sector size:         512 bytes
     Allocation unit:     1 sectors
     Directory entries:   16
```

NOTE *Make a note of the drive letter used by the RAM drive. It may be a letter greater than D: such as E:, H:, or any letter up to Z:. Whatever that drive letter is, you must substitute it in the following steps every time the directions tell you to use drive D:.*

12. Enter the date and time.

13. Type CLS and press [Enter].

14. Type DIR D: and press [Enter].

   Figure 13.11 shows the screen response you should receive.

NOTE *In the next step, you can use any disk that has all the student files that are available in the C:\WESTDATA.DS6 directory. West Student Data Disk #6 has the original 44 files plus 7 new files. The 7 files are not required. If you do not have West Student Data Disk #6 handy, simply create one by copying the original 44 files to the disk in drive A:.*

15. Place West Student Data Disk #6 in drive A:.

FIGURE 13.11
*Empty directory
listing on
drive D:*

```
C:\>DIR D:

 Volume in drive D is MS-RAMDRIVE
 Directory of D:\

File not found

C:\>
```

16. Type `DIR A:/W` and press [Enter].

As shown in Figure 13.12, 51 files are listed on the screen.

FIGURE 13.12
*Files on the disk
in drive A:*

```
 Directory of D:\

File not found

C:\>DIR A:/W

 Volume in drive A has no label
 Volume Serial Number is 0A65-16FB
 Directory of A:\

ALIGN.DOC        BECOMING.TXT     CLASSES.DB       CLASSES.DBS      MISC.ZIP
DIDYUNO.PM4      MOM1.DOC         DASHIT-1.DOC     WAR.DOC          DIET.BAK
DINOSAUR.DOC     FAMOUS.DB        FAMOUS.DBS       FLAGS.BAK        FLAGS.DOC
INDEFENS.DOC     JUNK.DB          JUNK.DBS         MOM2.BAK         CHANGING.PM4
MOM3.BAK         DIET.DOC         MONSTERS         MYSTERY.TXT      MOM2.DOC
PUBLISH.BAK      MOM3.DOC         SAYING.TXT       HUMOROUS.PM4     WIN_MODE.DOC
ALIGN.WP         PUBLISH.TXT      TODOLIST.DOC     WINNEWS1.DOC     TRUCKIN.TXT
DINOSAUR.WP      STRATS2.DOC      STRATS1.DOC      STRATS1.TXT      WAR.WP
PAPER.WP         STRATS2.TXT      PAPER.TXT        WAR.TXT          DIALECTS.TXT
SYMPHONY.TXT     HAYDN.TXT        HAYDN2.TXT       SPEECH.TXT       SPEECH2.TXT
SPEECH3.TXT
        51 file(s)       68644 bytes
                       1373696 bytes free

C:\>
```

17. Type `COPY A:*.* D:` and press [Enter].

After 15 files are copied, the process stops and an error message appears that reads

```
Cannot make directory entry - D:INDEFENS.DOC
15 file(s) copied
```

The 15 files (plus the volume label) use all 16 directory entries allotted when you executed the RAMDRIVER.SYS to create the RAM drive.

18. Type `CLS` and press [Enter].

19. Type `D:` and press [Enter].

✓ **CHECKPOINT 13G** Which drive is drive D:?

20. Type DIR and press Enter.

The screen should resemble that shown in Figure 13.13 and display 15 files now on your virtual drive.

FIGURE 13.13

Directory listing of virtual drive D:

```
D:\>DIR

 Volume in drive D is MS-RAMDRIVE
 Directory of D:\

ALIGN    DOC     1792 09-19-87    9:15p
BECOMING TXT       53 10-04-88    7:22p
CLASSES  DB       566 10-04-88    8:08p
CLASSES  DBS      485 01-01-80   12:30p
MISC     ZIP    24327 10-13-91    8:17p
DIDYUNO  PM4       63 05-08-93    7:19p
MOM1     DOC      419 10-04-88    7:28p
DASHIT-1 DOC       18 05-12-93    8:12a
WAR      DOC     1946 10-13-91    8:24p
DIET     BAK     2560 11-10-87   11:54a
DINOSAUR DOC       26 05-08-93    7:51p
FAMOUS   DB        26 05-08-93    7:45p
FAMOUS   DBS       24 05-08-93    7:46p
FLAGS    BAK      909 05-08-93    7:44p
FLAGS    DOC     2048 01-09-88    5:17p
       15 file(s)      35262 bytes
                       24576 bytes free

D:\>
```

Notice that the number of bytes free (24,576) when added to the bytes used by the files (35,262) approximately equals 64KB. That is the size of the drive you set up when using the RAMDRIVE command.

21. Type DEL *.* and press Enter.

22. When prompted, type Y and press Enter.

23. Type DIR and press Enter.

No files are on the RAM drive now.

24. Type COPY A:*.TXT D:/V and press Enter.

This copy process will abort after 15 files are copied—that is OK. You have reached the memory limit on the virtual drive. Your screen should list the text files shown in Figure 13.14 as they are copied to the RAM drive.

At this point you could go in and edit one of the files using EDIT.

25. Type EDIT SAYING.TXT and press Enter.

The monitor display will appear as shown in Figure 13.15.

26. You could edit this file, but instead just exit the DOS Editor.

27. Open the door to disk drive A: or remove the disk from the drive.

FIGURE 13.14
*Files copied to
RAM drive*

```
   Directory of D:\

   File not found

   D:\>COPY A:*.TXT D:/V
   A:BECOMING.TXT
   A:MYSTERY.TXT
   A:SAYING.TXT
   A:PUBLISH.TXT
   A:TRUCKIN.TXT
   A:STRATS1.TXT
   A:STRATS2.TXT
   A:PAPER.TXT
   A:WAR.TXT
   A:DIALECTS.TXT
   A:SYMPHONY.TXT
   A:HAYDN1.TXT
   A:HAYDN2.TXT
   A:SPEECH.TXT
   A:SPEECH2.TXT
   A:SPEECH3.TXT
   Cannot make directory entry - D:SPEECH3.TXT
           15 file(s) copied

   D:\>
```

In the next few steps, you will check to see if the virtual drive data is volatile (evanescent)!

28. To reboot your system, simultaneously press the Ctrl, Alt, and Del keys.

29. After the power-on self-test concludes, the screen will indicate that the virtual drive is installed. Enter the time and date when prompted.

30. Type DIR D: and press Enter.

FIGURE 13.15
*Listing
SAYING.TXT file
on virtual
drive D:*

```
 File  Edit  Search  Options                              Help
                        SAYING.TXT
 I DON'T CARE HOW                                              ↑
 TALENTED, SKILLED,
 OR TECHNICAL
 YOU ARE.

 IF YOU AREN'T A
 PEOPLE PERSON, YOU
 WON'T MAKE IT.

 THAT'S WHAT
 MAKES OR BREAKS A
 SUCCESSFUL PERSON
 IN ALL PROFESSIONS.




 MS-DOS Editor  <F1=Help> Press ALT to activate menus    N 00001:001
```

The files are gone. They disappeared when the warm boot turned the system off.

The final steps will reset the AUTOEXEC.BAT and CONFIG.SYS files to their original condition.

31. Type `REN AUTOEXEC.OLD AUTOEXEC.BAT` and press ⏎Enter.

32. Type `DEL CONFIG.SYS` and press ⏎Enter.

33. Type `REN CONFIG.OLD CONFIG.SYS` and press ⏎Enter.

34. Reboot your system.

Summary

In this unit, you learned that the MODE command serves a variety of uses, including setting the serial port protocol, redirecting output from the parallel to the serial port, and switching parallel printer output between 6 or 8 lines per inch and 80 or 132 characters in width. You also used the PROMPT command to change the background and foreground colors displayed on your monitor, to change your monitor's character attributes (hidden, flashing, bold) and to change the cursor location. Finally, you also experimented with a virtual drive and discovered its benefits and shortcomings.

Command Review

In this unit you learned several DOS commands. Most commands have optional parameters. We have tried to cover both the common and the rarely used forms of each command. The following forms of this unit's commands are the most frequently used and should be reviewed carefully.

DEVICE=ANSI.SYS	Installs the ANSI.SYS device driver when included in the CONFIG.SYS file.
DEVICE=RAMDRIVE.SYS 64 512 64	Creates an MS-DOS virtual drive when this command is added to the CONFIG.SYS file.
PROMPT $e[40;37m$p$g	Resets the monitor's display to a black background color and a white foreground (text) color. Also displays the default drive and path.

MODE COM1:12,E,7,1,P	Sets the serial port protocol to accept and transmit data at 1200 baud with even parity, 7 data bits as the word length, and 1 stopbit. If the serial port is busy, DOS continuously tries to send output until it is accepted.
MODE COM1:BAUD=12 PARITY=E DATA=7 STOP=1 RETRY=P	Sets the serial port protocol to accept and transmit data at 1200 baud with even parity, 7 data bits as the word length, and 1 stopbit. If the serial port is busy, DOS continuously tries to send output until it is accepted.
MODE LPT1:	Resets the redirected output back to parallel port #1.
MODE LPT1:80,6	Causes output to a parallel printer to be printed 80 characters wide with 6 lines per vertical inch.
MODE LPT1:132,8	Causes output to a parallel printer to be printed 132 characters wide with 8 lines per vertical inch.
MODE LPT1:=COM1:	Redirects output from parallel port #1 to serial port #1.

Review Questions

1. What are the seven uses of the MODE command?

2. What action does the MODE CO80 command invoke?

3. What action does the MODE MONO command invoke?

4. What action does the MODE BW40 command invoke?

5. What action does the MODE MONO,L,T command invoke?

6. Why are code pages used?

7. What are the five parameters used with the MODE command to set the communications protocol?

8. What is baud rate, and which rates are most common for PC users?

9. What is parity? What does it do?

10. Why is data bit size important to telecommunications?

11. How do you load the ANSI.SYS driver?

12. What are the four uses of the CONFIG.SYS file?

13. What does ANSI stand for?

14. Which DOS command is used to communicate with the ANSI.SYS device drive?

15. What does the $e meta-string represent?

16. What always ends an escape sequence?

17. What action occurs when PROMPT $e[s is executed?

18. Which version of the PROMPT command deletes text from the cursor location to the end of the current line?

19. Which version of the PROMPT command displays the default drive and path as part of the DOS prompt?

20. How are the results of the following two commands different?

    PROMPT $e[42;37m
    PROMPT $e[37;42m

21. Can the PROMPT command be used to redefine the letter A to display a letter Z on the monitor screen?

22. What would happen if you redefined the [Spacebar] to print the letter G?

23. What is a virtual drive? How is it created?

24. What is the advantage of a virtual drive?

25. What disadvantages exist for a virtual drive?

26. Which has the slowest access time—a hard disk, a virtual disk, or a floppy disk drive? Which has the fastest access time? Why?

27. When setting the characters per line (to be printed by your printer) with the MODE command, what values may be used?

28. When setting the number of lines per vertical inch (to be printed by your printer) with the MODE command, what values may be used?

29. What command form would be used to redirect output from LPT3: to COM3:?

30. After using the command form in question 29, how would you reset your computer system so that output to the printer was again directed to LPT3:?

Exercises

Whenever instructed to format a disk, use your last name (first) and then your first name (such as BACON JON) as the volume label. If instructed to print data from the screen, be sure to write your full name, course number and section, course title, instructor's name, unit and exercise number, and today's date on the paper. Your instructor will indicate if the disk(s) created or printouts should be submitted for grading.

1. Create a flashing, colorful, birthday message using a batch file and the PROMPT command. Save as BIRTHDAY.BAT.

2. Create a batch file that will clear your monitor screen, change the background color to green, display a directory listing (one page at a time), and then return the background color to normal and clear the screen. Save as GREENDIR.BAT.

3. Create three files (two are batch files) on a formatted floppy disk that accomplish the following tasks. Use the batch file names indicated.

   CONFIG.SYS: include the command(s) to create a RAM drive 220KB in size that will store at least 50 files.

   AUTOEXEC.BAT: include the command(s) to copy all files in the C:\WESTDATA.DS6 directory to the new RAM drive.

   COPYIT.BAT: include the command(s) that creates a A:\WESTDATA.DOS directory and then copies all files from the RAM drive to the new directory.

Key Terms

ANSI	Data bit	RAM drive
ASCII character set	Display attributes	Stopbit
Background color	Expanded memory	Terminal software
Binary digit	Extended memory	Terminating code
Code page	Foreground color	Virtual drive
Code page switching	Home position	Virtual disk
Console	Protocol	Word length

Documentation Research

Documentation Research questions are included at the end of most units to encourage you to explore and discover the additional features available with DOS 6.x. All Documentation Research questions within the text can be answered by using the on-line reference (accessed by using the HELP command). Review Guided Activity 2.8 if you are unsure how to use the HELP command.

1. Can you create more than one virtual drive in memory?

2. Can the MODE command be used in the AUTOEXEC.BAT file?

3. Is it better to create a virtual drive in conventional or extended memory?

4. Name the two commands that are used to load the ANSI.SYS device driver for use with the PROMPT command.

5. If there is insufficient memory for the RAM drive specified, to how many directory entries will the RAM drive default?

I

Creating a Screen Change Batch File and Virtual Drive

Creating an ANSI.SYS Screen Change Batch File

In Unit 13, you learned about the ANSI.SYS device driver and how the PROMPT command can communicate with it to modify your screen and keyboard. In this application, you will create some batch files to make it easier to change your screen colors and move the cursor.

1. Create a batch file named COLORS.BAT that cycles through five different foreground and background color combinations. Be sure that the entire screen is displayed in the new text and background colors, that the batch file stops until a key is pressed, and that the file then moves to the next color combination. The final color combination should be a black background with a white foreground color.

2. Modify the above file to include a saying centered in the middle of your screen (one saying for each color combination). The sayings may be poems, jokes, or statements of fact—you choose. Save this file as COLORS2.BAT.

3. Modify COLORS2.BAT to display the current date and time on the top line of your screen. Save this file as COLORS3.BAT.

4. Submit the disk with all three files (COLORS.BAT, COLORS2.BAT, and COLORS3.BAT) to your instructor. Be sure to write your name, course and section number, instructor's name, and today's date on the disk label.

Creating Multiple Virtual Drives

In Unit 13, you modified a CONFIG.SYS file to create a single virtual disk. In this application, you will modify a CONFIG.SYS file so that it creates two virtual drives.

1. Copy the CONFIG.SYS file from your hard disk to a formatted disk.

2. Use the DOS Editor to modify the copy of CONFIG.SYS. Be sure to make the changes on your floppy disk—not on the hard disk drive.

3. Modify the CONFIG.SYS file in order to create two virtual drives. The first virtual drive should use the DOS default values. The second virtual drive should be 6KB in size, use 512-byte sectors, and have the capability of storing a maximum of 10 files.

4. Save the modified CONFIG.SYS file to disk. Submit the disk to your instructor. Be sure to write your name, course and section number, instructor's name, and today's date on the disk label.

DOS Shells and the DOSSHELL Command

14

Important Commands

DOSSHELL

What Is a DOS Shell—and Why Do I Need One?

Microcomputer users are not uniform in their needs and levels of computing skills. Secretaries, managers, engineers, and other end users often do not have time to learn the intricacies of DOS, even though doing so will enable them to complete their computing tasks more efficiently. To many, learning DOS is simply an inconvenience. At the other end of the spectrum are users who can point out the gaps in Microsoft's operating system. They point to the lack of the MOVE command (prior to DOS 6.*x*), the UNDELETE command (prior to DOS 5.*x*), and disk compression (prior to DOS 6.*x*). In between are a host of people who lose files in subdirectories and find it hard to routinely back up their files.

While previous versions of DOS addressed *hardware* needs (the introduction of two-sided disks, hard disks, and networks), version 4.*x* first addressed the *human* needs. With it, IBM and Microsoft finally moved toward a friendlier, easier, human interface for DOS. This ease of use was previously available only through utility programs called DOS shells.

A *DOS shell* is meant to address the human interface needs with menus, new commands, and visual (graphic) displays. A DOS shell allows the user access to the power of DOS with less typing and considerably less knowledge of PC DOS or MS-DOS commands.

Prior to DOS 4.*x*, if you wanted the capabilities of a DOS shell, you had to purchase it from a third-party vendor. Programs such as XTree, Q-DOS III, and Norton Commander gained wide acceptance. Other software packages (such as BackIt, AutoMenu, and Norton Utilities) provided complementary functions. Between the release of DOS 4.*x* and DOS 6.*x*, Microsoft has enhanced DOS to include many of these functions and features. It is no longer seen as necessary to buy a freestanding DOS shell or a variety of other utility programs—because those enhancements have been added to the operating system itself. In this unit, we will first discuss DOS shells in a generic sense and then concentrate on those features provided by the DOS 6.*x* version of the DOSSHELL command, DOS Shell itself.

Features Provided by a DOS Shell

Let's consider the characteristics typically available with a DOS shell. Four general functional areas are served by DOS shells:

- Menu generation
- File/disk backup utilities
- Path utilities
- Extended DOS features or commands

Menu Generators

The most popular DOS and Windows application programs today are menu-driven. You can scan a list of menu options and highlight or select one menu choice without typing more than one or two keystrokes. Prior to the release of DOS 4.*x*, raw DOS did not provide a menu-driven interface. *Menu generators* fill that need by providing a one- or two-keystroke access to application programs, such as your word processor, spreadsheet, or database programs.

With menu generators, the user does not need to be concerned with where files are stored; that is, in which subdirectory. Menu generators often require extensive setup time. The software must be configured to your exact system and directory structure. The real time savings occurs after the initial work is complete when the menu generated by the utility guides you through selecting files and programs. The Windows operating environment addresses this need. In it, all applications are menu-driven and you can open, close, or exit a file or application with one or two mouse clicks or keystrokes.

Backup Utilities

File/disk *backup utilities* simply replace the old (pre-DOS 6.*x*) BACKUP and RE-STORE commands. Such utilities may be used to back up files to disk as DOS does, or they may be used in conjunction with tape backup systems. Contrasted to earlier versions of DOS, they included a feature that DOS did not—far greater speed. File/disk backup utilities used to run faster and more efficiently than the DOS commands. The efficiency was due to their saving the files using a nonstandard file format. The weakness of this approach was that backed up files cannot be accessed or manipulated until they are restored (to a standard DOS file format), using the backup utility program.

This situation changed drastically with the introduction of the MSBACKUP command in DOS 6.*x*. MSBACKUP is menu-driven, it can save files in a compressed format (which conserves disk space and increases backup speed), and, for many users, it is the only backup utility they will need.

Path Utilities

The third category of DOS shell utilities is the *path utility*. Prior to DOS 4.*x*, trying to visualize paths, directories, and subdirectories on a DOS-formatted hard-disk truly stretched the imagination. Doing so was especially confusing for the novice user or operator, who was more concerned with getting the job done than with understanding the intricacies of DOS. The TREE command, enhanced with version 4.*x*, provides a visual image of the disk's directory and subdirectory structure, but without using the DOSSHELL command a user still could not navigate the tree structure easily—and that's where a path utility came in handy. The most common use of path utilities was to provide a visual display of the directory tree with the current or default directory highlighted. Now, the DOS Shell provides this type of visual display plus easy navigation from one directory to another. The Windows operating environment also provides this capability.

Extended DOS Features

The fourth and final functional area provided by DOS shells is their *extended DOS features*. In short, the DOS shell helps the user do things not easily accessible with "raw" DOS. Traditionally, the more noteworthy of these features are the following (several of these features are now available with the DOS operating system):

- An attribute setting feature (enhanced with DOS 5.*x* and 6.*x*)

- File protection

- A FIND file command

- Key redefinition

- Macro creation

- A MOVE command (available with DOS 6.*x* or in the DOS 5.*x* DOS Shell)

- A tag capability (introduced in the DOS 4.*x* DOS Shell)

- An UNDELETE command (available since DOS 5.*x*)

- A view file feature

Each of these capabilities is covered in the following paragraphs.

Setting Attributes

In Unit 10, we discussed using the ATTRIB command to change bits in the attribute byte of each file. A single bit in the attribute byte determines whether a file is restricted to read-only access or can be modified (marked to provide both read-and-write access). A second attribute bit may be altered by the ATTRIB command under DOS 3.1 and higher. The second bit is the archival bit. It is used by the MSBACKUP command to determine if the file has been modified since the last backup. By altering the archive bit, DOS may be tricked into backing up a file even if the file has not been changed since the last backup.

The attribute byte has eight bits. Depending on the value of these bits, the file is assigned a special property. These settings can attach one or more of the following properties to the file.

- An archived file (not modified since last backup)

- A hidden file (not visible using DIR command)

- A read-only file (can read but not modify the file)

- A system file (a DOS system file)

- A volume label (the file stores the label and really isn't a data or program file)

- A subdirectory (stores directory name)

As you have probably noticed, only six of the eight attribute bits are currently in use. The other two are reserved for future developments. Prior to DOS 6.*x*, you could only set two of these attribute bits, the archive bit and the read-only bit, using DOS. Some DOS shells allowed the user to reset the additional attribute bits. Using a DOS shell or utility program for this purpose is no longer necessary—since you can do it all from the operating system.

File Protection, the FIND Command, Keyboard Enhancers, and Macros

File protection includes the ability to assign a password to a file, directory, subdirectory, or disk. Some DOS shells go as far as providing the ability to encrypt data.

The DOS FIND command locates a specific phrase or text string in a specified file. However, it will not assist in finding that string in multiple files (without a lot of typing), nor will it help find a specific file buried within the maze of directories on a hard disk. The FIND file command provided by some DOS shells meets the second need.

Keyboard enhancers enable you to redefine certain keys to perform nonstandard functions. A few of the DOS shells have picked up one aspect of the *keyboard enhancer* feature: they allow you to redefine the function keys. Within an application program, this can cause some problems, but, operating at the DOS Shell level, it can eliminate multiple keystrokes by the operator.

Macro creation is closely related. A *macro* is simply a collection of keystrokes. If your company has a long name, for example, a key can be redefined to type out the entire name. Thus, one or two keystrokes invoke a macro capable of entering 20, 30, or more keystrokes. Macros may also be used to accomplish, with one or two keystrokes, a series of DOS or program commands.

Moving Files in Fewer Steps

Using earlier versions of DOS, moving a file included

- Copying the file to its new location
- Comparing the two files to be sure that the copy was identical with the original
- Deleting the original file

One of the most common extended DOS features, provided by third-party DOS shells or utilities, was the availability of a MOVE command. Beginning with the DOS 4.*x* DOSSHELL command, DOS users could move one or more files from one location to another on the same hard drive or disk. As discussed earlier in Unit 6, DOS now includes a MOVE command (introduced in DOS 6.*x*).

Tagging Files and the UNDELETE Command

The DOS shell tag or selection capability lets you highlight multiple files and then execute one command on all the tagged or marked files. It is no longer necessary to try ingenious uses of the wild card characters to delete or copy a group of files with dissimilar names. A complementary feature of some DOS utilities is the ability to untag files once marked and to undo a specific action just executed on a tagged group of files. This capability is available in the DOS Shell shipped with DOS and when using Windows. In the DOS 6.*x* Shell, tagging files is commonly referred to as "selecting files."

The UNDELETE command can be a lifesaver for users who inadvertently wipe out a file or group of files. Its operation is based on the premise that the sectors and clusters used by the accidentally deleted file have not been subsequently reused by saving other files. Hence, UNDELETE is most successful if invoked immediately after the accidental erasure. The undelete feature used to be available only from third-party utility packages, but is now an integral part of DOS.

Viewing File Contents

Although DOS provides the TYPE command, it is not a convenient tool for viewing a long file. TYPE scrolls through the entire file rather than giving you the ability to view one page of a file at a time. Further, you cannot scroll from the end of a file, using TYPE, to the beginning. Some DOS shells provide a view feature whereby you can quickly select a file and view its contents. Figure 14.1 displays the Q-DOS III screen when viewing a file named GANDHI.DOC.

FIGURE 14.1
Viewing a file with Q-DOS III

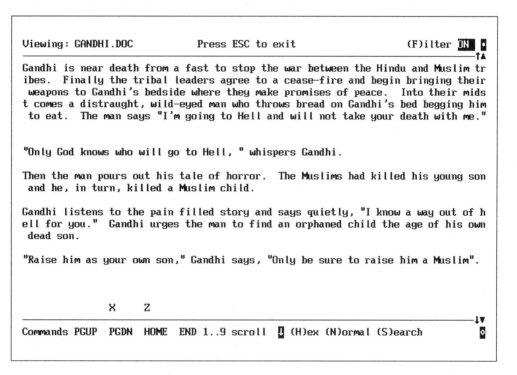

Notice in Figure 14.1 that the view is an unformatted one (words break at odd points), but is adequate to let you determine the contents of the file. By using the keys listed at the bottom of the screen, you can scroll through the file, pause and read, and then move to any portion of the file. Even with the Q-DOS III filter on (see upper-right of screen), some extraneous characters are displayed at the end of the file.

This feature is now becoming more common in word processors. For instance, WordPerfect for Windows enables you to view the contents of a file without first opening the file. It is very effective when viewing word processing documents and graphic files. It is less effective when trying to view other types of files.

What Does the DOSSHELL Command Provide?

All four functions of the DOS shell fall under the general heading of file management utilities. The essential aim of any DOS shell is to make the operating system easier to use. As users demanded more features and as third-party software provided more enhancements to DOS, the operating system was modified to provide the same functionality. DOS 4.*x* was the initial response from IBM and Microsoft to complaints about the stark, unfriendly DOS prompt. Subsequent versions of the DOS shell have been greatly improved.

The DOSSHELL command offered with DOS 6.*x* now provides the features listed in Table 14.1.

TABLE 14.1
Features of the DOS 6.x DOSSHELL command

Menu generation	N
Backup utilities	Y (using the old BACKUP and RESTORE commands)
Path utilities	Y
Extended DOS Features	
Attribute setting	N
File protection	N
FIND file command	N
Key redefinition	N
Macro creation	N
MOVE command	Y
Tag capability	Y
UNDELETE command	Y

Although DOSSHELL does not provide all the features listed, it is a great improvement over the DOS prompt that used to confront novice users. In the remainder of the text, the term "DOS Shell" will be used to refer specifically to the shell provided by invoking the DOS 6.*x* DOSSHELL command.

Welcome to the MS-DOS/PC DOS Shell

When DOS 6.*x* is installed, the INSTALL command can be directed to automatically create an AUTOEXEC.BAT file that includes the DOSSHELL command. Each time your system is booted, the DOSSHELL command (which is itself a batch file) is executed.

Components of the DOS Shell Screen

Upon executing the DOSSHELL command, the DOS Shell window (shown in Figure 14.2) is displayed. The screen is divided into several parts. You can move between the different areas (top to bottom) of the screen by pressing the ⏹Tab key, or you can move in reverse order by pressing ⏹Shift⏹Tab. You can also use a mouse to move the mouse pointer around the screen and select files or commands using a single click. A double-click selects and executes a command.

FIGURE 14.2
The DOS Shell window screen

Menu bar

Area title

Directory
Tree area

Program
List area

Status bar

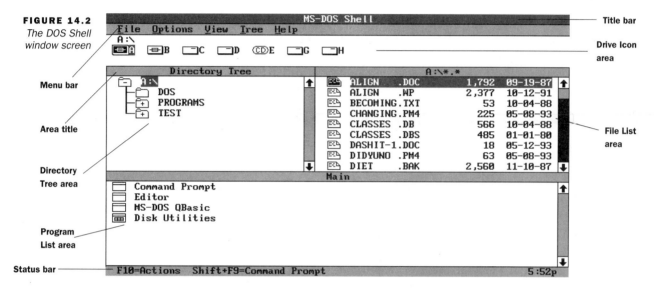

Title bar

Drive Icon
area

File List
area

DRIVE ICON AREA Includes the drive icons that appear under the menu bar and that indicate which drives are available. By selecting one of the *drive icons* (clicking on it), you make that drive the current drive.

DIRECTORY TREE AREA Displays the structure of the current drive.

FILE LIST AREA Displays the files in the current drive and directory.

PROGRAM LIST AREA Displays a list of commands or actions that can be executed, including exiting the DOS Shell to go to the DOS prompt (Command Prompt), running the Editor program (Editor), running QBasic (MS-DOS QBasic), and using selected DOS commands (Disk Utilities group).

ACTIVE TASK LIST AREA This area (not shown in Figure 14.2) displays a list of all tasks (applications or executable programs) that are currently running on your system. The task list enables you to switch from one program or task to another without unloading the first program and then loading the new task.

In addition to the five areas of the screen, you need to become familiar with several screen components:

TITLE BAR Displays the title MS-DOS Shell across the top of the screen.

MENU BAR Initially displays five options: File, Options, View, Tree, and Help. You can access the menu bar by pressing either the [Alt] or [F10] key.

AREA TITLE The bar across the top of each area is a title bar. On most screens it appears with a dark background color.

STATUS BAR Displays options and information on the currently executing process.

Starting and Exiting the DOS Shell

If the DOSSHELL command is not listed in your AUTOEXEC.BAT file, the shell may be invoked by typing the following command at the system prompt and then pressing [Enter].

    DOSSHELL

NOTE *When you install or upgrade to DOS 6.x, you can install the DOSSHELL to automatically load whenever you start your computer. This is accomplished by putting the DOSSHELL command in your AUTOEXEC.BAT file.*

To quit the DOS Shell, you have three options:

Press the [F3] key
or
Press [Alt][F4]
or
Select the File Exit command by pressing [Alt][F], [X].

Each of these options exits the DOS Shell and unloads it from memory. If you want to exit the DOS Shell and temporarily suspend it in the background, use the following steps. This manner of exiting allows you to resume or return to the shell more quickly. The steps are:

- Press [Shift][F9].

  The shell is suspended and the system prompt appears. To reenter the shell, simply

- Type EXIT and press [Enter].

Another method of temporarily suspending the DOS Shell is accomplished by selecting the Command Prompt option under the Main group in the Program List area of the screen. The DOS Shell typically gives you a menu-driven method to accomplish certain tasks—coupled with a quick-key method of accomplishing the same task. The [Shift][F9] keystrokes comprise the quick-key method.

Important Keystrokes in the DOS Shell

The DOS Shell is designed to work with keyboard input, input from a mouse, or both. Using the keyboard to access and use the DOS Shell is far less intuitive than using the mouse and requires you to memorize several keystrokes. Whereas most actions can be executed using a mouse, there are some keystrokes you *must* learn—

they will become obvious as we proceed through this unit. For now, we'll list the more common keystrokes used by the DOS Shell.

When you use the shell, many keys have specific functions. Navigating the shell is easier if you understand the effects of these keystrokes. Table 14.2 provides a list of the primary DOS Shell key assignments as a reference. The more you use the DOS Shell, the more these keys will become "second nature."

TABLE 14.2 *DOS Shell key actions*	[Alt]	Switches the ***selection cursor*** between the menu bar and the other areas on the DOS Shell window. Once you move the selection cursor to the menu bar, you can type the underscored (or highlighted) letter in the command or option name to select it, or use the arrow keys to highlight a command or option and then press [Enter] to select it.
	[Alt][F4]	Exits or quits the DOS Shell from the DOS Shell window.
	[↑] [↓] [←] [→]	Move the cursor to the next selection or choice on the screen.
	[Enter]	Carries out a command, option, or other choice.
	[Esc]	Cancels the action and allows you to back out of a previous choice.
	[F1]	Invokes the Help feature.
	[F3]	Exits or quits the DOS Shell from the DOS Shell window.
	[F10]	Switches the selection cursor between the menu bar and the other panels on the DOS Shell window. Operates the same as a.
	[PgDn]	Scrolls down through the listings of files in the File List area.
	[PgUp]	Scrolls up through the listings of files in the File List area.
	[Shift][F5]	Redraws the screen.
	[Shift][F9]	Switches to the system prompt from within the DOS Shell.
	[Tab]	Switches the cursor from one area to another in the DOS Shell window.

Important Mouse Actions

When using a mouse, a single click or double-click on the selector button (left mouse button) can substitute for some of the keystrokes listed above. The shortcuts available when using a mouse are given below.

POINT-AND-CLICK   To select an item (such as a group or file), move the mouse pointer to the item to be selected and click once. The ***mouse pointer*** looks like an arrow in graphics mode or a shaded rectangle in text mode.

DOUBLE-CLICK   To start a program or execute a command, move the mouse pointer to the name of the program and double-click. A double-click means that you press the left mouse button twice in rapid succession.

CLICK-AND-DRAG This term means that you click the left mouse button on an item (icon or text) and hold it down while moving the mouse pointer across the screen to a new location. Only when the pointer is at the new location do you release the mouse button, dropping the item there.

Generally a single click selects an item in the DOS Shell while a double-click executes a command, option, or program. You will use the click-and-drag action when you copy or move files in the DOS Shell.

Options for Starting the DOS Shell

You can start the DOS Shell in either text or graphics mode. In text mode, the mouse pointer is a rectangle and no graphic icons appear. The screens are composed of all text or block graphics. In graphics mode, the drive designations appear as icons and the mouse pointer appears as an arrow. You can also invoke the DOS Shell and cause it to be displayed in black-and-white only. The syntax of the command is

```
DOSSHELL [/m[:res[n]]]
```

where m is the display mode you desire. The options for the display mode are the following:

/B Displays the DOS Shell in black-and-white.

/T Displays the DOS Shell in text mode.

/G Displays the DOS Shell in graphics mode.

In other words, to display the DOS Shell in graphics mode, you would enter the following command form at the DOS prompt.

```
DOSSHELL/G
```

Most of the screens displayed in the remainder of this unit show the DOS Shell in graphics mode.

The res or resolution parameter may be added if the display mode supports more than one screen resolution category. Valid values for the screen resolution category are the following:

L   Low resolution
M   Medium resolution
H   High resolution

In those cases where the resolution category has more than one "lines per screen" setting, you can stipulate it also. For example, Table 14.3 lists the common resolutions for the DOS Shell in both text and graphics mode.

TABLE 14.3	TEXT MODE	
DOSSHELL command screen display modes	Low resolution, 25 lines per screen	L
	High resolution, 43 lines per screen	H1
	High resolution, 50 lines per screen	H2
	GRAPHICS MODE	
	Low resolution, 25 lines per screen	L
	Medium resolution, 30 lines per screen	M1
	Medium resolution, 34 lines per screen	M2
	High resolution, 43 lines per screen	H1
	High resolution, 60 lines per screen	H2

If you want to run the DOS Shell in high resolution at 60 lines per screen (in graphics mode), you would enter the command as

```
DOSSHELL /G:H60
```

However, you can also select the display mode by using the code in the second column of Table 14.3. For example, to select the high-resolution graphics mode with 60 lines per screen, use the following command form:

```
DOSSHELL /G:H2
```

Finally, if you want to run the DOS Shell in graphics mode (as shown above) but display it in black-and-white only, you can use the following command form:

```
DOSSHELL /G:H2/B
```

GUIDED ACTIVITY 14.1

Beginning a Hands-On Tour of the DOS Shell

In this Guided Activity, you will explore the major features of the DOS 6.*x* DOS Shell.

NOTE *In this Guided Activity, you will create and use West Student Data Disk #9. The first few steps will create the disk so that you can fully explore the capabilities of the DOSSHELL command.*

1. Insert a blank formatted disk in drive A:.

2. Copy all files from the C:\WESTDATA.DS6 directory to the root directory on drive A:.

3. Switch to the root directory of drive A:.

4. Make an A:\PROGRAMS directory.

5. Make an A:\PROGRAMS\WORDS directory.

6.   Make an A:\PROGRAMS\DATA directory.

7.   Make an A:\DOS directory.

8.   Make an A:\TEST directory.

9.   Make an A:\TEST\PM directory.

10.   Copy all files with the .DOC extension from the root directory on drive A: to the A:\PROGRAMS\WORDS directory. Fifteen files will be copied.

11.   Copy all files with the .PM4 extension from the root directory on drive A: to the A:\TEST\PM directory. Three files will be copied.

Your West Student Data Disk #9 is now ready to use.

12.   Type DOSSHELL/G at the C: prompt and press the [Enter] key.

CHECKPOINT 14A Why would you use the /G switch with the DOSSHELL command?

After a couple of seconds, the DOS 6.0 DOS Shell screen appears as shown in Figure 14.3.

FIGURE 14.3
DOS Shell reading disk information

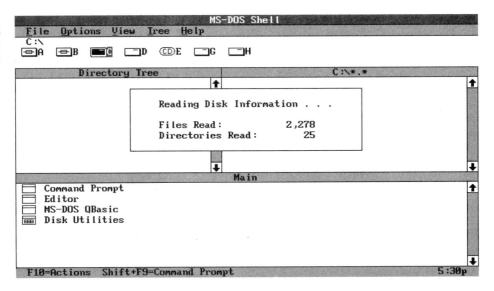

When you first load the DOS Shell, DOS scans the current drive for files and directory structure. Figure 14.3 shows that DOS is "Reading Disk Information…" and 2,278 files have been read in 25 directories (see the box in the middle of the screen).

Once the disk scan is complete, your screen should appear similar to Figure 14.4.

Notice that the screen is divided into several areas as defined earlier. The areas include the Drive Icon area, the Directory Tree area, the File List area, and the Program List area. The Active Task List area is not displayed.

NOTE   *You will know that an area of the DOS Shell screen is selected if the area title bar is highlighted (darkened).*

FIGURE 14.4
Opening DOS Shell window

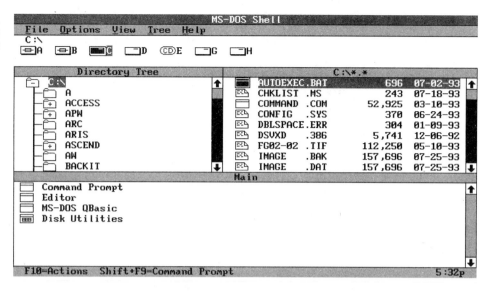

13. Double-click on the Disk Utilities option *or* press [Tab] until the Program List area is selected and then use the [↑] or [↓] keys to highlight the Disk Utilities option and press [Enter].

   The options under the Disk Utilities option include Disk Copy (uses DISKCOPY command), Backup Fixed Disk and Restore Fixed Disk (use the old BACKUP and RESTORE commands), Quick Format and Format (use FORMAT/Q and FORMAT command forms), and Undelete (uses the UNDELETE command) as shown in Figure 14.5.

FIGURE 14.5
Options under the Main group

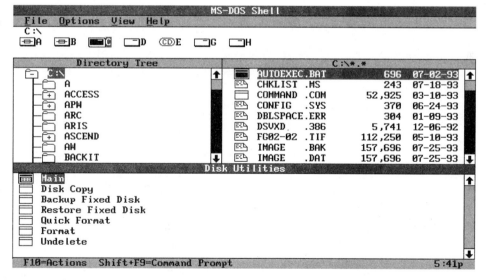

14. Double-click on the Main option icon or, with the Main group option highlighted, simply press [Enter].

   The second level (group) options disappear and your screen once again appears similar to Figure 14.4.

To view the directory tree structure for West Student Data Disk #9 and move around the directories on the disk, complete the following steps.

15. Be sure that West Student Data Disk #9 is in drive A:.

16. Click once on the A: icon in the Drive Icons area *or* press [Tab] until the Drive Icon area is selected, press [←] until the drive A: icon is highlighted, and then press [Enter].

    Your screen should appear similar to Figure 14.6. Notice the three directories (DOS, PROGRAMS, and TEST) in the Directory Tree area.

NOTE *If you are using the Delete Sentry program, there will be a fourth subdirectory on the disk named A:\SENTRY.*

The File List area displays (in alphabetical order) several files in the selected path (in this case in the A:\ directory).

FIGURE 14.6

Drive A: with three directories

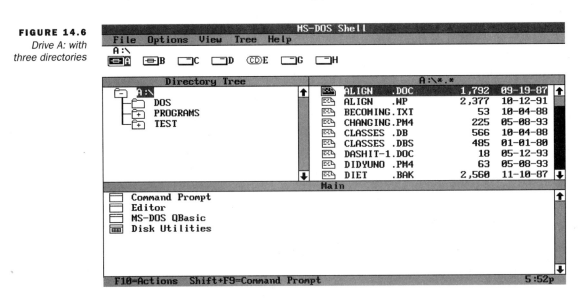

The ALIGN.DOC file is highlighted by the selection cursor. If you chose to execute an action (copy, delete, and so on), it would be effected on the file(s) highlighted by the selection cursor.

Folding and Unfolding Directories in the Directory Tree Area

Notice that in the Directory Tree area in Figure 14.6, some of the graphic file folder icons include either a plus sign (+) or minus sign (−). The symbols mean:

+   Additional subdirectories exist under the directory—but they are not currently displayed in the tree structure area.

−   Additional subdirectories exist under the directory—and they are currently displayed in the tree structure area.

If the folder is blank (empty—without either a plus or minus), that directory does not have any subdirectories.

When using a *mouse*, you can display the subdirectories under a directory by clicking once on a folder icon with a plus sign on it. To hide the subdirectories, you click once on a folder with a minus sign on it.

When using the *keyboard*, you would highlight or select the directory and then use the following keystrokes:

+	Displays one level of subdirectories under the current directory
−	Hides all the subdirectories under the current directory
*	Displays all subdirectories under the current directory
Ctrl*	Displays all directories in the tree

GUIDED ACTIVITY 14.2

Hiding and Displaying Directories in the DOS Shell

In this Guided Activity, you open and close directories to display the subdirectories under them.

1. Click once on the PROGRAMS folder icon, *or* if using the *keyboard* press Tab to move from the Drive Icons area to the Directory Tree area, press ↓ twice to highlight the PROGRAMS folder icon, and then type + to display the subdirectories under A:\PROGRAMS.

   Your screen should appear similar to Figure 14.7.

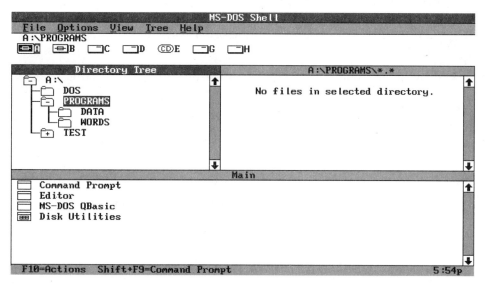

FIGURE 14.7
The
A:\PROGRAMS
directory

Notice that on the bar above the File List area, the path (A:\PROGRAMS*.*) is displayed. In the area itself is displayed the message "No files in selected directory." There are no files in the PROGRAMS directory (which you created earlier in this unit).

The folder icon for PROGRAMS now displays a minus sign (all subdirectories are visible). Before you clicked on that icon, it had a plus sign in the folder. Neither a plus nor minus appears in the folder icons for PROGRAMS\DATA or PROGRAMS\WORDS. Neither of those directories have subdirectories.

2. Click once on the WORDS folder icon, *or* if using the *keyboard* press ⬇ twice to highlight the A:\PROGRAMS\WORDS directory.

Now the files in the A:\PROGRAMS\WORDS directory appear in the File List area as shown in Figure 14.8.

FIGURE 14.8
The
A:\PROGRAMS
\WORDS
directory

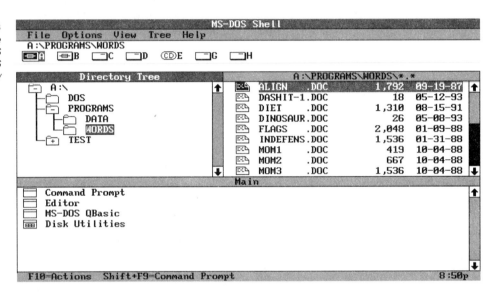

Several .DOC files appear in the list. To move to another directory, you simply click on its folder icon.

In the following step, you will close the subdirectories under PROGRAMS (that is, cease displaying them in the Directory Tree area).

3. Click once on the PROGRAMS folder icon (which has a minus sign on it), *or* if using the *keyboard* press ⬆ twice and type ‐ (a minus sign).

4. Click on the root directory folder (which has a minus sign in it), *or* if using the *keyboard* press ⬆ twice to select the root directory folder and type ‐.

All the subdirectories under the root directory fold into it (that is, they become hidden).

5. Click on the root directory (A:\) folder again to display the first level of subdirectories under it *or* if using the *keyboard* type +.

Your screen should once again appear similar to Figure 14.6 with the File List area displaying files in the A:*.* directory. The selection cursor is highlighting the ALIGN.DOC file.

6. Click on any folder icons that include a plus sign (this is in preparation for the next Guided Activity), *or* if using the *keyboard* use the arrow keys to move to any directory folder icon that has a plus sign on it and, when it is selected, type +.

GUIDED ACTIVITY 14.3

Displaying Lists of Files Within the DOS Shell

In this Guided Activity, you display files in different subdirectories without expanding or contracting the directory tree display of directories and subdirectories.

1. To display the files in the A:\PROGRAMS\WORDS directory, click on the text following the folder icon (do not click on the folder itself), *or* if using the *keyboard* press ⬆ or ⬇ to select the A:\PROGRAMS\WORDS directory.

    Watch the results in the File List area.

2. To display the files in the root directory (A:\), click on the text following the folder icon (do not click on the folder itself), *or* if using the *keyboard* press ⬆ to select the A:\ directory.

    Watch the results in the File List area.

3. To display the files in the A:\TEST directory, click on the text following the folder icon (do not click on the folder itself), *or* if using the *keyboard* press ⬇ until the directory is selected.

    Watch the results in the File List area.

CHECKPOINT 14B How many files are in this directory?

4. To display the files in the A:\TEST\PM directory, click on the text following the folder icon (do not click on the folder itself), *or* if using the *keyboard* press ⬇ until the directory is selected.

    Watch the results in the File List area.

Selecting (Tagging) Files Using a Mouse

Selecting one or more files using a mouse is easier than using the keyboard and is the preferred method, unless your system does not have a mouse attached.

You can select a single file by clicking on the file name in the File List area.

If you want to select multiple files where the file names are all in a row (in sequence), use these steps:

▪ Click on the first file name in the group.

▪ Hold down **Shift**, and then click on the last file name in the group.

The selection cursor will highlight all file names between the first and last file name indicated.

If you want to select multiple files that are not all listed adjacent to each other in the File List area, use these steps:

- Click on the first file name.

- Hold down `Ctrl` and click on the second file name.

- Continue holding down `Ctrl` and clicking on additional file names until all desired files have been highlighted.

After selecting files in this manner, you can then execute whatever action is desired on all of the selected files.

Selecting (Tagging) Files Using the Keyboard

If your system does not have a mouse attached, you must use the keyboard method of selecting files.

To select a single file, you can press `Tab` to move the selection cursor to the File List area and then press `↑` or `↓` to move the selection cursor to the file name. Once highlighted, the file is selected. Two other keys are also helpful when selecting a file:

| `Home` | Selects the first file in the list. |
| `End` | Selects the last file in the list. |

You can also type the first letter of a file name, whereupon the first file beginning with that letter is selected.

If you want to select multiple files where the file names are all in a row (in sequence), use these steps:

- Press `Tab` until the selection cursor is in the File List area.

- Use `↑` or `↓` to move to the first file name you want to select.

- Press and hold down `Shift` while you use the arrow keys to select additional adjacent file names to be included in the group.

If you want to select multiple files that are not all listed adjacent to each other in the File List area, use these steps:

- Press `Tab` until the selection cursor is in the File List area.

- Use `↑` or `↓` to move to the first file name you want to select.

- Press `Shift`|`F8`, and the word "ADD" appears on the status bar (lower-right corner).

- Use the arrow keys to move the selection cursor to the second file you want included in the group.

- Press `Spacebar` to select the file.

- Repeat the last two steps until you have selected all files for the group.

- Press [Shift][F8] to indicate that you are finished adding files to the group.

After selecting files in this manner, you can then execute whatever action is desired on all of the selected files.

Copying and Moving Files Within the DOS Shell Using a Mouse

Moving a single file in the DOS Shell is as easy as clicking on the file name and dragging it to the target location. When you initially click-and-drag, the mouse pointer changes into a bullet in the File List area (see Figure 14.9) and then into a dog-eared single document icon (as shown in Figure 14.10) when the mouse pointer moves into the Directory Tree area of the DOS Shell window.

FIGURE 14.9

The mouse pointer in the File List area, once you select a file to copy or move

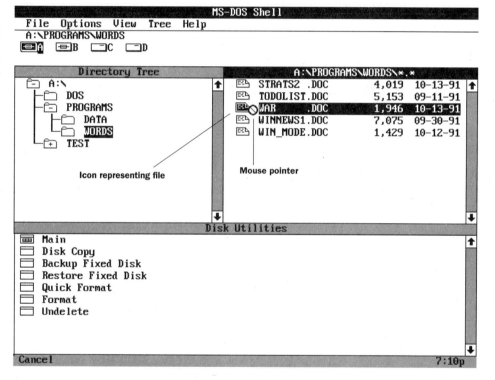

To copy files, you use the same procedure—except that you must hold down the [Ctrl] key. Remember:

Click-and-Drag	Moves the file(s) to the target directory
[Ctrl] Click-and-Drag	Copies the file(s) to the target directory

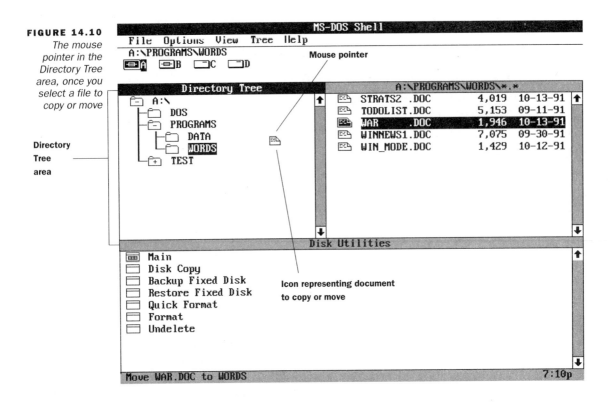

FIGURE 14.10
The mouse pointer in the Directory Tree area, once you select a file to copy or move

Directory Tree area

Copying and Moving Files Within the DOS Shell Using the Keyboard

Copying a single file using the keyboard requires you to complete the following steps:

- Select the file (in the File List area) to copy.

- Select the File Copy command from the menu bar or press F8.

  A Copy File dialog box appears, with the selected file name after the From option and the current directory after the To option. The text in the To option field is highlighted, so you can begin typing to overwrite it.

- Type the target drive and path where you want the file copied to.

- Once the options are correctly set, you can press Enter or can Tab to the OK button and press Enter.

  A message appears indicating that DOS is copying the file to the target drive and path.

  Moving a single file requires you to complete the following steps:

- Select the file (in the File List area) to copy.

- Select the File Move command from the menu bar or press F7.

A Move File dialog box appears, with the selected file name after the From option and the current directory after the To option. The text in the To option field is highlighted, so you can begin typing to overwrite it.

TIP *If the entry in a dialog box field is highlighted when you begin typing, you will overwrite the entire entry. However, you can change just part of the entry (such as just a portion of the path). To do this, press* [←] *and the cursor moves to the first character in the field, or press* [→] *and the cursor moves to the last character in the field. You can then use* [←] *or* [→] *to move the cursor to the location where you want to add or delete text. The* [Del] *key deletes the character above the cursor, and any text entered at the keyboard is inserted at the current cursor location.*

- Type the target drive and path where you want the file moved.

- Once the options are correctly set, you can press [Enter] or can [Tab] to the OK button and press [Enter].

  A message appears indicating that DOS is moving the file to the target drive and path.

GUIDED ACTIVITY 14.4

Moving and Copying Files in the DOS Shell

In this Guided Activity, you copy and move files using the DOS Shell.

1. Select the root directory folder to display file names for all files in the root directory on drive A:.

2. Click-and-drag the file named DASHIT-1.DOC from the A:\ directory to the A:\TEST\PM directory. Once the document icon is over the text or the folder icon for A:\TEST\PM, release the mouse button.

   Or, if using the *keyboard*, select the DASHIT-1.DOC file from the A:\ directory. Select the File Move command (press [Alt][F], [M]). Type A:\TEST\PM in the To option field and press [Enter].

3. If using a *mouse*, when prompted with "Are you sure you want to move the selected files?" click on Yes or press [Enter].

   You have moved the DASHIT-1.DOC file out of A:\ and placed it in the A:\TEST\PM directory.

4. Display the files in the A:\TEST\PM directory. Do you see DASHIT-1.DOC in the directory?

5. Click on DASHIT-1.DOC, hold down [Ctrl], and drag the selected file to the root directory on A:, and then release the mouse button. If using the *keyboard*, select the DASHIT-1.DOC file. Select the File Copy command. Type A:\ in the To option field and press [Enter].

6. If using a *mouse*, when prompted "Are you sure you want to copy the selected files?" click on Yes or press [Enter].

When using a *mouse*, by holding down the key when you click-and-drag, you have copied the DASHIT-1.DOC file. When using the *keyboard*, you used the menu bar to indicate that the file should be copied. It now appears in both the root directory and A:\TEST\PM.

7. Check both A:\ and A:\TEST\PM to be sure that DASHIT-1.DOC appears in both locations.

In the following steps, you will get some practice moving and copying files.

8. Copy (do not move) the following files (one at time) from the root directory to the A:\TEST\PM directory. For the last file on the list, you may need to use the scroll bars to locate the file in the File List area.

```
ALIGN.DOC
DIET.BAK
DINOSAUR.WP
```

9. Display the files in the A:\TEST\PM directory.

Your screen should appear similar to Figure 14.11 and include the four files copied to this directory (in this Guided Activity) plus three files that were originally in the directory.

FIGURE 14.11
Files in the A:\TEST\PM directory

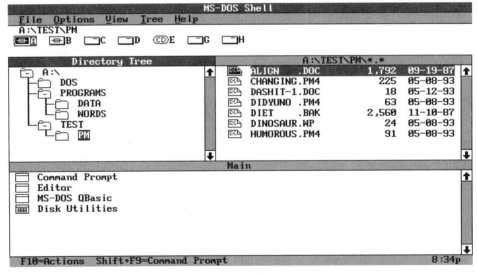

10. Display the files in the A:\PROGRAMS\WORDS directory.

11. Move the following files (one at a time) to the A:\TEST directory.

```
ALIGN.DOC
DASHIT-1.DOC
DIET.DOC
DINOSAUR.DOC
FLAGS.DOC
INDEFENS.DOC
STRATS1.DOC
```

12. Display the files stored in the A:\TEST directory.

There should be seven files in the TEST directory at this time.

Copying and Moving Multiple Files

You can copy or move several files at one time in the DOS Shell. The first step is to select the files. This process was discussed earlier in the unit. You can use either the keyboard or mouse method, though the mouse method is easier. Once the files are selected, you can copy or move the files just as you do a single file by clicking-and-dragging (with a mouse) or by using the File Copy (F8) or File Move (F7) keyboard commands.

GUIDED ACTIVITY 14.5

Copying and Moving Multiple Files in the DOS Shell

In this Guided Activity, you copy multiple files as a group to the A:\TEST directory.

1. Display all files in the A:\PROGRAMS\WORDS directory.

2. Select the STRATS2.DOC file.

3. Hold down Shift and click on the WINNEWS1.DOC file, *or* if using the *keyboard* hold down Shift and press ↓ until the WINNEWS1.DOC file is selected.

Four files should be highlighted (selected) as shown in Figure 14.12.

FIGURE 14.12
Four selected files

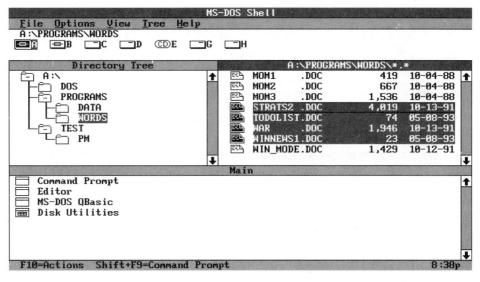

4. Hold down Shift and Ctrl, then click-and-drag the selected files to the A:\TEST directory. *Or* if using the *keyboard* select the File Copy command and, when the Copy File dialog box appears, type A:\TEST and press Enter.

5. If using a *mouse*, when prompted "Are you sure you want to copy the selected files?" click on Yes or press Enter.

6. Check the files in the A:\TEST directory. There should be 11 files in the directory now.

Deleting Files in the DOS Shell

Files can be deleted easily in the DOS Shell by first selecting them and then pressing the Del key. You can delete one or several files at the same time, using this method. The shell's default setting causes DOS to prompt you before it actually deletes each file. You can use the Options Confirmation option on the menu bar to eliminate this repetitive prompt—but be careful. The extra prompt gives you one last chance to save a file before it is deleted.

GUIDED ACTIVITY 14.6

Deleting Files in the DOS Shell

In this Guided Activity, you first copy a group of files to the A:\PROGRAMS directory and then delete them one at a time. Next, you delete a group of files from the A:\TEST directory, first with the "confirm on delete" setting turned off and then on.

1. Copy the group of five files (STRATS1.DOC through WINNEWS1.DOC) from the A:\TEST directory to the A:\PROGRAMS directory. Copy as a group, not one file at a time.

   In the following steps, you delete files from the A:\PROGRAMS directory.

2. Display all the files in the A:\PROGRAMS directory (there should be five files).

3. Select the WAR.DOC file.

CHECKPOINT 14C How do you select a single file using the mouse?

4. Press Del.

   Your screen will display the message "Delete A:\PROGRAMS\WAR.DOC?" as shown in Figure 14.13.

5. Click on Yes or press Enter to delete the file.

CHECKPOINT 14D What is the difference between clicking on Yes and pressing the Enter key in the Delete File Confirmation dialog box?

6. Use the same process to delete each of the following files (one file at a time).

```
STRATS1.DOC
STRATS2.DOC
TODOLIST.DOC
WINNEWS1.DOC
```

FIGURE 14.13
The Delete File Confirmation dialog box

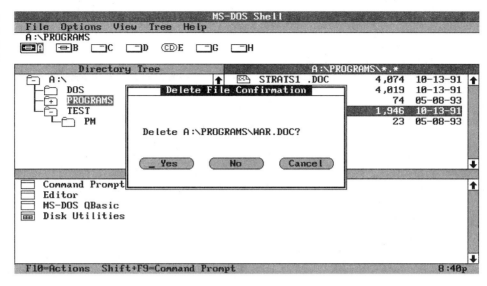

The PROGRAMS directory should be empty when you finish with the last step.

7. Display the files in the A:\TEST directory.

   In the following steps, you will delete a group of files after first setting the confirmation (upon deletion) option.

8. Select the Options choice on the menu bar. Your screen appears as shown in Figure 14.14.

FIGURE 14.14
The Options menu

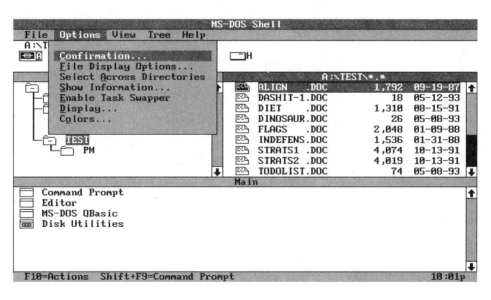

9. Select Confirmation by typing C or pressing the ⏎Enter key.

   When the dialog box appears, all three options are checked (selected).

FIGURE 14.15

*Confirmation
options box*

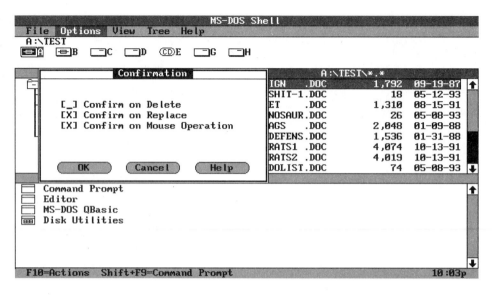

10. Click on the Confirm on Delete box and it should then be deselected. Or if using the *keyboard*, press [Tab] 3 times to move the cursor to the Confirm on Delete box and press [Spacebar]. The option should then be deselected. You want your settings to match Figure 14.15.

11. Click on the OK button or press [Enter].

12. Go to the File List area and select the DINOSAUR.DOC file name.

13. Hold down the [Shift] key and click on the INDEFENS.DOC file name, *or* if using the *keyboard* hold down the [Shift] key and press [↓] until the INDEFENS.DOC file name is selected.

14. Press [Del] and the Delete File dialog box opens.

15. Click on the OK button or press [Enter] to begin the deletion of the three files.

    You are given no warning, when the Confirm on Delete option is turned off.

    In the following steps, you turn the Confirm on Delete option back on.

16. Select the Options choice on the menu bar.

17. Select Confirmation by typing C or pressing the [Enter] key.

18. When the dialog box appears, click on the Confirm on Delete box and it will be selected, *or* if using the *keyboard* press [Tab] 3 times to move the cursor to the Confirm on Delete box and press [Spacebar]. The option should then be selected.

19. Click the OK button or press [Enter].

20. Select the remaining files in the A:\TEST directory.

21. Press [Del].

22. Click on the OK button or press [Enter].

23. When prompted to confirm the deletion of each file, click on Yes or press [Enter].

GUIDED ACTIVITY 14.7

Exiting the DOS Shell

In this Guided Activity, you exit from the DOS Shell after first changing the default drive back to C:.

1. Click on the drive C: icon or tab to the Drive Icon area and use the arrow keys to select the drive C: icon and press Enter.

2. Press F3 to exit the DOS Shell.

Summary

In this unit, you learned several uses of a DOS shell and discovered that many of these features have been added to the operating system since the introduction of DOS versions 4.*x*, 5.*x*, and 6.*x*. You then learned how to use the DOSSHELL command, including how to change directories, copy and move files, and exit DOS Shell.

Command Review

In this unit, you learned one new DOS command. The following form of this unit's command is the most frequently used.

DOSSHELL   Invokes the MS-DOS Shell from the DOS prompt.

Review Questions

1. Why is a DOS shell helpful to users with varying skill levels?

2. What are the four functional areas served by DOS shells?

3. Why is a menu generator a boon to end users?

4. What is the most common feature of a path utility?

5. List nine extended DOS features. Describe what each does.

6. What do the attribute setting and file protection features have to do with security of files and data?

7. Define a keyboard macro.

8. What is the benefit of a tag feature in a DOS shell?

9. Why might an UNDELETE command be ineffective?

10. Which function key exits the DOSSHELL command without keeping the DOS Shell in memory?

11. When using the DOS Shell with a mouse, what is the difference between the results of a single click and double-click?

12. List at least three DOS actions that may be executed from the Disk Utilities option of the DOS Shell.

13. What kind of a file is the DOSSHELL command?

14. Name the areas of the DOS Shell window.

15. Which key is held down to select multiple adjacent files in the DOS Shell?

16. Which key is held down to select multiple nonadjacent files in the DOS Shell?

17. After selecting files in DOS Shell, which key causes the selected files to be deleted?

18. What is the result of turning off the Confirm on Delete option under the Options Confirmation command?

Key Terms

Backup utility	Keyboard enhancer	Path utility
DOS shell	Macro	Selection cursor
Drive icon	Menu generator	
Extended DOS feature	Mouse pointer	

Documentation Research

Documentation Research questions are included at the end of most units to encourage you to explore and discover the additional features available with DOS 6.x. All Documentation Research questions within the text can be answered by using the on-line reference (accessed by using the HELP command). Review Guided Activity 2.8 if you are unsure how to use the HELP command.

1. Should you start Windows from within the DOS Shell or start the DOS Shell from within Windows?

2. Where do you set the DOSSHELL environment variable?

3. How would you indicate where the DOSSHELL.INI file was located (if located on drive C: in the \DOS directory)?

4. How much conventional memory is required to run the DOS Shell?

Answers

Answers to Checkpoints

2A. It displays a wide listing of files, showing files listed on each screen but providing less information about each file.

2B. It causes the file listing to pause after displaying a sceenful of data. Pressing any key displays the next screenful of data.

2C. To clear the monitor screen.

2D. Four.

2E. There is no difference. The colon is optional.

2F. There is no difference. The DIR command assumes a *.* file specification unless you stipulate otherwise.

2G. If you do not reset the date to the actual current date, new files created and old files modified will be date stamped with the wrong date.

2H. If you do not reset the time to the actual current time, new files created and old files modified will be time stamped with the wrong time.

3A. FORMAT B:

3B. You would be prompted to insert another disk to be formatted.

3C. Yes.

3D. Yes.

3E. You created another copy of West Student Data Disk #1.

3F. To prevent you from accidentally damaging it—in case you got the two disks mixed up when swapping in drive A:.

3G. DISKCOMP A: B:

3H. To format a previously formatted disk, wipe off its contents, and save time.

4A. To determine if a disk has any files stored on it.

4B. Because C: is the default drive.

4C. No. It assumes that the file name has only a single character after the "MOM" part of the file name.

4D. Yes, if a file by that name is on the default drive.

4E. DIR A:/OE or DIR A:/O:E

4F. COPY *.* A:

4G. The names of files on the disk are displayed in a wide listing in alphabetical order by file name.

5A. The root directory on drive A:.

5B. CD PROGRAMS

5C. No.

5D. A:

5E. To cause the DOS prompt to indicate the current drive and path.

6A. MOVE FLAGS.DOC \TEST\PM

6B. No. They were moved in an earlier step.

6C. DELTREE

7A. CHKDSK C:

7B. To ensure that the disk does not have files you want to save.

9A. There is no difference; the colon is optional.

9B. DIALECTS.TXT.

9C. To clear the error message from the screen.

9D. To save a file using a different file name.

9E. Yes. It will be .TXT.

10A. C:\WEST.

11A. It generates less wear and tear on your computer's mechanical parts.

11B. It stops executing of a batch file until a key is pressed.

11C. To display a blank line on screen when the batch file is executed.

11D. It turns off any messages that would be echoed to the screen when the batch file is executing, beginning with the ECHO OFF command.

11E. You do not need to type a batch file's extension to execute the batch file.

11F. A label.

11G. A replaceable parameter.

11H. Yes. All batch files must end with the .BAT extension.

12A. To the printer.

12B. A pipe.

12C. Yes.

13A. A directory listing.

13B. Parallel port #1, a printer port.

13C. The cursor moves to the home position and clears the screen after execution of each command.

13D. Place the command in your AUTOEXEC.BAT file.

13E. Changes the prompt to display the default drive and path.

13F. The directory structure for the default drive.

13G. The RAM drive.

14A. To display the DOS Shell in graphics mode.

14B. None.

14C. Click on it.

14D. There is no difference.

Answers to Even-Numbered Review Questions

1-2. It is the disk operating system that includes coded instructions for controlling the computer's internal communication, error checking, memory usage, data retrieval/storage/deletion, and device configuration.

1-4. Part of DOS is stored in ROM and takes over when the system is booted. The remaining portions of DOS are stored on disk and loaded into memory (RAM) as needed.

1-6. Correct syntax indicates the acceptable form of a DOS command, showing whether parameters and file names are optional or required. The computer understands only a specific form of each command. If the order of file names, parameters, and drive designators is mixed up, the computer will return an error message and fail to execute the command.

1-8. A file name can be up to eight characters in length. The extension may be up to three characters in length.

1-10. LETTER\TO\MOTHER.TXT—Illegal
FINAL.LTR—Legal
CALLHOME.DOC—Legal
$%&9441!.BAK—Legal but not very descriptive
1.BAT—Legal
COMMAND.COMM—Illegal, four-character extension
12345678.*90—Illegal, asterisk in extension

1-12. There is no difference. The terms are synonymous.

1-14. The NEWSNOTE.DOC file name is more descriptive and would assist the user in recalling the contents of the file.

1-16. There is no difference. Both terms are synonymous.

2-2. The Shift, Ctrl, and Alt keys.

2-4. A warm boot restarts your computer electronically without turning it off and then on. A warm boot saves time by avoiding the execution of POST (on most personal computers) and avoids mechanical wear on the system.

2-6. DIR

2-8. The /P switch.

2-10. The CLS command.

2-12. To help determine the most recent version of a file and to accurately tell when a file was created.

2-14. Yes. Type HELP at the DOS prompt and press the Enter key.

2-16. Fast help.

3-2. The /S switch.

3-4. The /U switch.

3-6. The DISKCOMP command.

3-8. Clarify or modify the command being executed.

3-10. The FORMAT command is used in both instances.

3-12. 360KB, 720KB, 1.2MB, 1.44MB, and 2.88MB.

3-14. No.

3-16. No.

3-18. Immediately after using the DISKCOPY command.

3-20. Yes.

3-22. To quickly reformat a previously formatted disk.

3-24. To create a compressed drive, to mount or unmount a compressed drive, to check or delete a compressed drive, to list all compressed drives, to display information on a compressed drive, or to change the size or ratio of a compressed drive.

3-26. DBLSPACE /COMPRESS B:

3-28. The disk drive has not been mounted, so DOS cannot access the disk.

4-2. COPY A:THISONE.TXT C:THATONE.DOC

4-4. The asterisk and the question mark.

4-6. Enter the following command at the DOS prompt: COPY C:SCREEN.MSG CON:

4-8. PRN and CON:

4-10. It compares two files to see if they are identical.

4-12. COMP compares two files byte by byte, DISKCOMP compares two disks track by track.

4-14. DEL is the second most destructive command and FORMAT is the first. FORMAT can destroy (erase) all files on a disk. DEL can erase one or more files from a disk.

4-16. DEL *.* This assumes that the default drive contains a disk with a single subdirectory.

4-18. DOS 5.0.

4-20. Delete Sentry, Delete Tracker, and the standard method.

4-22. Enter the UNDELETE/LIST command form.

4-24. The UNDELETE /ALL command.

5-2. As the number of files increases, the sheer volume of files requires some form of organization in order to find a file to print, modify, or delete.

5-4. 512.

5-6. The terms "directory" and "subdirectory" refer to the relationship between areas where data is stored on a disk. A directory can also be a subdirectory to another directory. A directory can have subdirectories or areas beneath it on the directory tree where data is stored. A subdirectory has a parent directory that is above it in the hierarchical structure, that is, closer to the root directory.

5-8. Enter the MD GAMES or MKDIR GAMES command at the DOS prompt.

5-10. Assuming that the current directory is the root directory on drive B:, type CD\WPWIN\DATA and press [Enter].

5-12. Type RD A:\LOTUS\DATA. This only works if the directory is empty (contains no files).

5-14. PROMPT PG

5-16. PATH ;

5-18. The TREE /A command displays the structure of a disk using the universal graphics characters while the TREE >PRN command displays the structure of a disk to the printer (LPT1:).

5-20. To alter the form of the DOS prompt or system prompt.

5-22. All of the DOS meta-strings are listed (with their results) in Table 5.2 of the text.

6-2. The MOVE command.

6-4. No. The command attempts to rename the directory to another position in the directory tree structure.

6-6. MOVE MEMO.WP,LETTER.WP \WPWIN\WPDOCS

6-8. To remove a directory, its subdirectories, and their files from a disk.

6-10. System and hidden files.

6-12. Yes, but it is not advisable.

6-14. Use the DELTREE \JUNK command.

7-2. (1) Header information such as volume name and serial number, (2) count of files and directories on the disk, (3) number of allocation units free and in use on the disk, and (4) internal working memory (RAM) free and available.

7-4. Data on internal working memory (RAM).

7-6. Yes.

7-8. A terminate-and-stay-resident program is one that is loaded and remains in memory—even when you run another program.

7-10. DOS 5.0.

7-12. The MIRROR and FORMAT commands.

8-2. It slows down disk access and makes your computer run slower.

8-4. The DEFRAG command.

8-6. The hard disk (drive C:) is optimized, including all files and directories, and the files are sorted in alphabetical order within each directory.

8-8. A boot sector virus, a file infector virus, and a Trojan horse virus.

8-10. The checksum values for all files scanned by MSAV.

8-12. The MSAV menu interface is displayed and you can select the actions desired by making choices from the menu.

8-14. VSAFE is a memory-resident program that continuously monitors your computer system for activity that might represent the presence of a virus.

8-16. Enter the VSAFE /3- command at the DOS prompt.

8-18. Version of WordPerfect installed on the system, and viruses located on the computer's disk.

8-20. All four of these commands were introduced with DOS 6.0.

9-2. With the EDIT command you can return to the text file and edit it. Further, you have numerous commands on the menu bar that enable you to print, find text, search and replace text, and otherwise edit the text file.

9-4. Type EDIT and press ⏎Enter.

9-6. Scroll bars.

9-8. Backspace.

9-10. Ctrl Home

9-12. To save an existing document under a new file name.

9-14. The Edit Cut and Edit Paste commands.

10-2. Considerations include: the kind of medium, the type of backup, and the frequency of the backup.

10-4. ASSIGN, SUBST, or JOIN.

10-6. The ATTRIB command sets the eleventh byte of the directory entry to mark a file as read-only or read-and-write enabled, establishes a file as a hidden or system file, and sets the archive bit to indicate whether the file has been modified since the last backup.

10-8. Write-protection would be useful if the file were a boilerplate document file or a master worksheet. Write-protecting .COM and .EXE files would also provide a partial defense against hackers and viruses.

10-10. Enter the ATTRIB command followed by the complete file name and press ⏎Enter.

10-12. You cannot copy hidden or system files.

10-14. It copies all files from the source to the target disk—if they do not already exist on the target disk.

11-2. Type AUTOEXEC at the DOS prompt and press ⏎Enter or reboot your computer system.

11-4. CALL, ECHO, FOR, GOTO, IF, PAUSE, REM, and SHIFT.

11-6. The root directory.

11-8. Whenever you boot or reboot your computer system.

11-10. Displays a blank line on the screen.

11-12. To include documentation within a batch file.

11-14. The IF command.

11-16. The GOTO command.

11-18. Any of the following is a replaceable parameter: %0, %1, %2, %3, %4, %5, %6, %7, %8, and %9.

11-20. The SHIFT command.

11-22. `CALL GOODBYE`

11-24. 10

11-26. In the CONFIG.SYS file.

12-2. There are ten standard devices, two of which have aliases. They are:

Keyboard	CON:
Monitor screen	CON:
Null device	NUL:
Parallel port #1	LPT1:
Parallel port #2	LPT2:
Parallel port #3	LPT3:
Serial port #1	COM1:
Serial port #2	COM2:
Serial port #3	COM3:
Serial port #4	COM4:

The two standard devices with aliases are:

Parallel port #1	PRN
Serial port #1	AUX:

12-4. NUL: is used for debugging. It is typically substituted for another device (such as LPT1: or COM1:) in the programmer's code. If the program runs correctly, the programmer will look further for an error in the device. If the program does not run correctly, the error is in the code—not the attached device.

12-6. Redirection enables the computer to receive input from a device other than the console (CON:) and send output to a device other than the console (CON:). The most common example would be the redirection of a directory listing to the printer (LPT1:) rather than the monitor screen (CON:). The command form would be DIR >PRN.

12-8. Piping allows output from one program or command to serve as input for another command or program. Filters accept data from standard input sources and modify that data.

12-10. A system where each character is assigned a binary code and then sorted, based upon the value of that code.

12-12 DOS 2.0 sort:

129
93
939
ANTELOPE
Antelope
CATwalk
Zebra
cat

DOS 4.0 sort:

    129
    93
    939
    ANTELOPE
    Antelope
    cat
    CATwalk
    Zebra

12-14. None.

13-2. It enables color after switching to the color/graphics display adapter and generates 80 characters per line across the monitor screen.

13-4. It disables color and displays 40 characters across the screen.

13-6. To enable the computer to use, display, and print characters that are found in foreign languages.

13-8. Baud is the number of changes in an analog signal per second. At or below 600 baud, the baud rate is roughly equivalent to bits per second transmitted to the receiving computer. At higher speeds, baud rates and bits per second may differ. Common baud rates are 110, 300, 600, 1200, 2400, 4800, and 9600. The most common rates for personal computer users are 300, 1200, and 2400 baud.

13-10. Data bit or word size tells the receiving computer the size of each block of data. Word size is typically set to 7 or 8 bits. The 7 or 8 bits represent a single character.

13-12. To establish the maximum number of files open at one time, to establish the maximum number of buffers in effect at one time, to specify the last drive that can be used, and to load device drivers.

13-14. The PROMPT command.

13-16. A terminating code.

13-18. PROMPT $e[K

13-20. Both forms of the command change the text to white on a green background.

13-22. Everytime you pressed the [Spacebar], the letter G would appear on the screen. You could not enter a space character on the screen.

13-24. A virtual drive may be accessed faster than a physical disk such as a floppy disk or hard disk. Speed is the justification for creating a virtual drive.

13-26. The floppy disk drive has the slowest access time and the virtual drive has the fastest. The floppy drive and hard disk are mechanical and must get up to speed before data can be read. The virtual drive is totally electronic. Electronic devices operate faster than mechanical devices.

13-28. 6 or 8.

13-30. MODE LPT3:

14-2. Different categories of DOS shells provide menu generation, file/disk backup utilities, PATH utilities, and extended DOS features.

14-4. A visual display of the hard disk directory tree structure with the current or default directory highlighted.

14-6. The attribute setting feature allows a file to be marked read-only. File protection includes the ability to encrypt data and assign passwords.

14-8. It allows dissimilar files to be marked and then a single command (COPY, MOVE, DEL) to be executed on all tagged files.

14-10. F3

14-12. You can copy a disk, undelete files, back up or restore files to a fixed disk, or format a disk.

14-14. Drive Icon area, Directory Tree area, File List area, Program List area, Active Task List area, title bar, menu bar, Area Title, and status bar.

14-16. The Ctrl key.

14-18. You are not prompted to confirm the deletion of files.

Index

Status bar, 237, 419–420
Stopbits, 381
Subdirectories, 142, 144–146, 415
Subroutines, 320
Supplemental disk, 235
Switch, 8
Syntax, 8
SYS command, 66, 83–84
System disk, 78–79
System files, 79, 106, 283, 415
System prompt, 15, 143

T

Target file, 9
Terminal software, 383
Terminate and stay-resident programs, 194, 225
Terminating codes, 386
Text file, 232, 235
Text selection, 246
Text string, 252
TIME command, 54–57
Title bar, 419
Toggle keys, 28–29
Tracks, 63–64
TREE command, 154–155, 161
    switches, 161–162
TSR Programs. *See* terminate-and-stay-resident programs
TYPE command, 235–236, 360

U

UNDELETE command, 126, 129–132, 202–203, 413, 415–417
UNFORMAT command, 69, 74, 202
UNFORMAT information, 74, 202
Universal set of graphics (text) characters, 162

V

Variables, 320
Virtual disk, 399–400
Virtual drive, 399–400
Virus, 215–217
    boot sector, 216
    file infector, 216
    Trojan horse, 216
Volume label, 75, 82, 415
VSAFE command, 216, 220–222

W

Warm boot, 36–37
Wild card characters, 17, 108–109, 121, 126–127, 183
Write-protect, 18, 284

X

XCOPY command, 290–292, 321
    parameters and switches, 291

Notes

Notes

Notes

Quick Reference

Command	Purpose
ATTRIB +A *Filename*	Turns on the specified file's archive bit.
ATTRIB +R *Filename*	Marks the specified file as read-only.
CD\DOS	Switches the directory path to the \DOS subdirectory.
CHKDSK A:	Provides a status report on the internal working memory and disk storage contained on the disk in drive A:.
CLS	Clears the monitor screen and moves the DOS prompt and cursor to the home position (upper-left corner).
COMP A:*.* C:	Compares all files on the disk in drive A: with like-named files on drive C:.
COPY A:FILE.DOC B:	Copies the file FILE.DOC from the disk in drive A: to the disk in drive B:.
DATE	Prompts you to set or change the system date.
DEFRAG	Optimizes your hard drive or disk by eliminating disk fragmentation.
DEL A:*.*	Deletes all files from the disk in drive A:.
DELTREE \DATA	Removes the \DATA directory together with all of its files and subdirectories.
DIR	Lists files on the current drive, including file names, date and time created or last modified, size in bytes, total number of files, total bytes free on the disk, and total bytes used.
DIR/P	Displays a vertical directory of files on the current drive, with a pause. The screen stops scrolling after 23 lines of text are displayed.
DIR/W	Displays a horizontal directory of files on the current drive. Lists only file names, total number of files, bytes free on the disk, and bytes used.
DIR/O:N	Generates an alphabetical listing of all files on the current drive.
DISKCOMP A: B:	Compares the disk in drive A: to the disk in drive B:. The comparison is made track by track and sector by sector.
DISKCOPY A: B:	Makes an exact duplicate on a target disk in drive B: of the original (source) disk in drive A:. The copy is made track by track and sector by sector.
DOSSHELL	Invokes the MS-DOS Shell from the DOS prompt.
EDIT	Invokes the DOS Editor from the DOS prompt.
EDIT NEWFILE.BAT	Creates or edits a batch file named NEWFILE.BAT.
FORMAT A:	Prepares a disk in drive A: to store data or programs. System files are not copied to the disk.

Command	Purpose
FORMAT A:/S	Prepares a self-booting system disk to store data or programs.
MD DOS	Makes a new subdirectory named DOS under the current directory.
MOVE TEXT.ONE,TEXT.TWO, TEXT.DOC \WPDOCS	Moves three files (TEXT.ONE, TEXT.TWO, and TEXT.DOC) to the \WPDOCS directory.
MSAV	Runs the Microsoft Anti-Virus program, which will seek out potential viruses on your disk.
MSBACKUP	Runs the Microsoft Backup 6.0 program, a menu-driven utility used to back up and restore files.
MSD	Runs the Microsoft Diagnostics program, which provides technical information on your system, including the computer type, operating system in use, plus details on TSR programs, mouse, LPT and COM ports, and more.
PATH C:\DOS	Opens a path to executable files in the C:\DOS subdirectory.
PROMPT PG	Changes the DOS prompt to display the current path and drive, and concludes the DOS prompt with the greater-than sign.
RD TRASH	Removes an empty subdirectory named TRASH that is under the current directory.
RD\TRASH	Removes an empty subdirectory named TRASH that is under the root directory.
REN A:ONE.TXT TWO.TXT	Renames the file ONE.TXT (on the disk in drive A:) as TWO.TXT.
REPLACE *.* A:/U	Replaces any files on drive A: that are older than the corresponding files on the default drive. In essence, it updates files when the source disk files are newer than the files on the target disk.
SYS A:	Copies three hidden system files as well as the COMMAND.COM file to a disk in drive A:, thus making the disk bootable.
TIME	Prompts you to set or change the current time.
TREE	Lists the current directory and all its subdirectories.
TREE/F	Lists the current directory, all its associated files, plus all subdirectories under the current directory and their associated files.
UNDELETE A:LOSTFILE.DOC	Restores the accidentally erased file named LOSTFILE.DOC on drive A:.
UNFORMAT A:	Restores the directory structure and files on an accidentally formatted disk in drive A:.
VSAFE	Loads a memory-resident virus protection utility that warns you of possible system activity caused by a computer virus.
XCOPY A: B:	Copies all files from drive A: to drive B:.
XCOPY A:*.DOC B:	Copies all document files (with the .DOC extension) from drive A: to drive B:.